Paul Barry is an award-winning journalist and a best-selling author with a formidable reputation for uncovering scandal, investigating crime, exposing corporate cheats and revealing failures in government departments. Barry was born in England and studied politics, philosophy and economics at Oxford University where he graduated with first-class honours in 1973. Between 1978 and 1986 he worked for the BBC, latterly on the *Newsnight* and *Panorama* programmes, before moving to Australia where he has become a headline-making print and television journalist. He is the author of other controversial books including *The Rise and Fall of Alan Bond*, *The Rise and Rise of Kerry Packer* and *Rich Kids*.

D1363149

Also by Paul Barry

THE RISE AND FALL OF ALAN BOND
THE RISE AND RISE OF KERRY PACKER
GOING FOR BROKE
RICH KIDS

SPUN OUT

THE SHANE WARNE STORY

PAUL BARRY

CORGI BOOKS

TRANSWORLD PUBLISHERS
61-63 Uxbridge Road, London W5 5SA
a division of The Random House Group Ltd
www.booksattransworld.co.uk

SPUN OUT
A CORGI BOOK: 9780552154895

First published in Great Britain
in 2006 by Bantam Press
a division of Transworld Publishers
Corgi edition published 2007

Addresses for Random House Group Ltd companies outside the UK
can be found at: www.randomhouse.co.uk
The Random House Group Ltd Reg. No. 954009

The Random House Group Ltd makes every effort to ensure that the papers used in its books are made from trees that have been legally sourced from well-managed and credibly certified forests. Our paper procurement policy can be found at: www.randomhouse.co.uk/paper.htm

Typeset in 11/14pt Sabon by
Falcon Oast Graphic Art Ltd.

Printed and bound in Great Britain by
Cox & Wyman Ltd, Reading, Berkshire.

2 4 6 8 10 9 7 5 3 1

To Lisa

Contents

Author's Note

When the subject of a book asks his friends not to talk to the author it seems a bit odd to compile a list of all those who ignored his advice. Consequently, I do not intend to identify the people whose stories and guidance have made this book possible.

Suffice to say I have been assisted by a large number of cricketers – past and present – and by an army of team officials, sports psychologists and cricket writers who have helped me understand Test cricket in general and Shane Warne in particular. Some of those who refused to talk have also been useful in helping me appreciate the hostility that elite cricketers feel towards the media.

I am indebted to Shane's schoolmates and teachers at Mentone Grammar, who have given me such a clear picture of him as a boy, and to all his ex-team-mates down the years – in Australia and England – who have shared their memories and insights. I am also indebted to those who knew him at the AIS Cricket Academy and to his many friends and acquaintances in Bristol and Accrington.

It is always a risky prospect writing about a national icon, even one as controversial as Shane Warne. But it is also rewarding. To the 100-or-more people who have helped make this book happen . . . please accept my thanks for your time, generosity and trust. I hope that the finished product lives up to your expectations and that it is as much fun to read as it was to write.

Prologue

It's Not Over Till the Fat Boy Spins

I don't care what you think and I don't care
what you write.

It's Day One of the final Test match at London's famous
Oval cricket ground. The crowd's singing 'Jerusalem'
and the Australians are already on the ropes, though
barely an hour has passed. After 16 years of being
whipped by the Old Enemy, the Poms are on the brink of
a historic victory that would see them win back the Ashes.

But the fat boy has yet to spin.

The match is a sell-out and has been for months. There
have been queues at the turnstiles since eight in the morning, and thousands of ticket holders are still lined up
outside the ground. Hundreds more are watching from
apartments and office blocks nearby. The balconies are
crammed. They're perched on the rooftops. Schoolboys in
uniform are crowding at a window for a view. Building
workers in a tower block overlooking the pitch have
downed tools and are sitting on the scaffolding. Further
afield, just about everyone in England is either tuned in to
the game on the radio or watching it on TV.

Back in Australia, where it's half past eight in the evening, two million people are also glued to their television sets, gritting their teeth as the Ashes slip away. The Poms have won the toss on a hard, flat track that's made for batting, and their two openers, Strauss and Trescothick, are smacking the Aussie fast bowlers to all parts of the ground. The first hundred is almost in sight. No wickets have fallen. English supporters are counting their cash. The Australians, who started the match as hot favourites, have blown out to 4 to 1. In another hour the Ashes will be out of reach.

But the fat boy has yet to spin.

Shane Warne has been a marvel in this epic series and not just with his mobile phone. Even the Barmy Army has grudgingly paid him respect. He's taken almost as many wickets as all the other Australian bowlers put together, and he's starred with the bat as well. He slogged his team within an inch of victory at Edgbaston, saved their bacon at Old Trafford and nearly stole the game at Trent Bridge. And always with a grin on his face and a sparkle in his eye.

You would never guess that this is a man whose personal life has just imploded, whose wife has just left him, who has trashed a $300,000-a-year TV career, and who has been shamed and ridiculed on the front page of every newspaper in the cricketing world. He has stripped naked and begged one woman for sex, the tabloids have told us, bombarded another with text messages saying 'I can't wait to f*** you', and urged a third to seduce his wife into a threesome, which he said might save his marriage. We have all read that he likes spanking, and is selfish in bed and is somewhat quick on the draw.

His resilience in the face of such disgrace is a marvel. Back home in Australia, a few days earlier, far tamer revelations have driven the former New South Wales Opposition Leader John Brogden to attempt suicide. Shane, on the other hand, seems to be thriving on the attention. He is playing better then ever. Maybe he likes the limelight, whatever its source. Or maybe he just doesn't care.

He's been standing in the slips throughout the first hour, getting into the ear of Australian captain Ricky Ponting and looking like the lair that he is. He's sporting an earring, blond spikes and zinc cream on his lips. He's wearing a sweater, too, despite the heat, prompting Pommie-captain-turned-commentator Mike Atherton to wonder if he might be injured. And now we will all find out.

Australia needs Warne to weave his magic. There's no one else who can.

He looks better once he's into it, relieved to be into the action. His second ball catches the edge of Strauss's bat and scoots away for four, but the next bites hard and spins at least a foot. He could turn it on glass, this bloke. Already you can sense the tension rise, feel the heart heading for the mouth. And then he strikes. The left-handed Trescothick fails to spot the slider – the one that looks like a leg break but keeps going straight. He plays for the turn and edges sharply to Matthew Hayden at first slip. Hayden reaches low to his left, plucks the ball off his bootlaces and hangs on tight. It's 1 for 82. Here we go, here we go, here we go.

Michael Vaughan is next man in – Captain Courageous the tabloids call him. He hammered Australia in the last

Ashes series Down Under in 2002–3 and cracked 166 in the recent Old Trafford Test. And soon he's making it look easy. He hits two boundaries to calm his nerves and those of everyone watching. Then Warne bowls one that sits up. Vaughan steps back, opens his shoulders and tries to pull it through the leg side for four. But all he does is spoon it down the throat of Clarke at short mid wicket. It's 2 for 102.

The Barmy Army's now gone quiet. They've stopped singing about Warne and his pies, and can sense the match may be turning. Next in is Ian Bell, who started the series with a Test-match average better than Bradman's but has looked terrified every time he comes to the crease. He lasts six balls before Warne strikes him on the pad with another slider. It's plumb l.b.w., leg before wicket. Three for 104. Suddenly Australia is the favourite again.

England's batsmen now have lunch to stew over. Forty minutes to steady the resolve, steel the nerves and pray that normal service will be resumed. The next man on the block is Kevin Pietersen, himself a budding superhero, with his hair striped blond like an outsize badger. Last match it was blue. He's a close friend of Warne's, a play-mate on and off the field, as readers of the *Sunday Mirror* have discovered. He's already rescued England in the one-day series in spectacular fashion, muscling Warne for six after six after six. But today he looks nervous. He prods a few, cracks a couple of boundaries, then has an almighty swish and misses completely. Hearts jump but he's still there. He prods a few more, then tries to tonk another through midwicket and is bowled all ends up. It's 4 for 131. In 15 minutes either side of lunch, Warne has all but won the match.

Okay, so we all know that there's a twist in the tail of this fairy tale. It is Kevin Pietersen who ends up the hero and England which has the happy ending. But for half an hour on that first morning, and several more times in the course of the match, it looked like Shane would slay the English dragon.

It would not have been the first time in his career, had he done so. Heroic deeds on the cricket field are two a penny in Warne's remarkable, rollercoaster life. And so, alas, is scandal. Indeed, they often seem to march together, as if there is a connection. Perhaps he needs the sting of shame to goad him to greater heights.

'My life is a soap opera', Warne often laments. It is also a puzzle. He's one of the best bowlers – or the best – the world has ever seen. A freak. A sportsman with a God-given talent. A magician who can mesmerise his opponents.

But he is also a man whose personal life teeters between tragedy and farce. A man who just can't help himself. A kid who won't grow up. A genius locked in the body of a fool.

The closest parallel that comes to mind is the young Mozart as portrayed in the famous 1980s film *Amadeus* – a giggling childish buffoon who writes magical music that could make a statue weep. Warne is almost as extreme in the heights and depths he can reach, almost as frustrating to his many admirers. It's what makes him such an intriguing subject for study.

He wants no part in this book of course or in any search for the 'Rosebud' in his life. I write to him and his brother, Jason, who is also his manager, and follow up with phone calls, but he won't even meet me for a chat. He wants to keep everything for his own (third) Shane Warne book, which he hopes will swell his fortune when he retires. After weeks of trying, I eventually speak to him face to face in November 2005 at a Test match in Brisbane, where Australia is playing the West Indies. And the conversation goes something like this.

'Hi Shane, I'm Paul Barry, I'm writing the book on you.'

'I know who you are.'

'Could we have a quick word do you think?'

'I don't want to talk to you.'

'Just 30 seconds?'

'I've got nothing to say.'

'Twenty seconds?'

'What for?'

'I just want to say this. If you don't want to talk to me that's your choice, but please don't stop your friends talking to me if they want to. It's going to be very hard to write a fair book if I can't talk to anyone who likes you.'

'Then don't write it.'

We are facing off in the bowels of the grandstand at the Gabba, near the players' dressing-room, and he is wearing his full green Cricket Australia uniform, looking like he has just had a spray tan and a new hairdo. His skin is orangey-brown and so uniform in colour that it looks unreal; it's almost like wax. He is a remarkable physical presence, nevertheless. He is taller than expected and certainly not fat, despite the endless stories about his weight. His hands and arms are huge, his shoulders strong, and he looks every inch an athlete. There's something animal about him. But it's more than that. He has charisma, the X-factor, call it what you will.

I've just watched him perform in a press conference. And perform is the only word that describes it. When the first salvo was fired he almost jumped in his seat, locking on to the questioner with his eyes, raising his eyebrows, sighing and exhaling as if to say, 'Gee, that's a hard one'. And then he talked nonstop, in an enthusiastic flood for minutes on end, with ideas spurting out so fast that it was impossible to take notes. He waved his hands, moved around, ducked and weaved. Like a boxer looking for an opening.

But now we're out in the corridor and an audience has gathered. Two large security men are stationed between us, a minder from Cricket Australia is lurking on the sidelines, and a small crowd of journalists is hovering behind. The newspapers next day call the conversation 'animated'. More bluntly, Shane is angry. Angry because he believes he should have a monopoly on the bookstands. Angry because this book will earn money that should be his.

'There should be a law against this', he tells me, 'writing a book about a person without his consent.'

I tell him that there isn't. That it's a free country. That he is a public figure who uses his fame to sell things. That journalists write about him every day and that he talks to them constantly, happily, openly, just as he did a few moments earlier.

'I've had seven books written about me and they're all bullshit', Warne replies. 'They get it all wrong.'

'Well, that's why you should talk to me', I offer. 'Surely you care what it says. Surely you care what people think about you?'

'I don't care what you write', he says. 'You'll just write lies anyway. All I care about are my friends and my family and what they think of me. I don't care what you think and I don't care what you write. And that's why I've told everyone in there [pointing to the Australian dressing-rooms] that if you phone they're not to talk to you.'

But he does care – passionately – what people think of him. He desperately wants the world to like him, to love him, to fête him, and he cannot comprehend why some do not. And of course they talk – some of them – along with scores of other people, who grew up with Warne, went to school with him, played cricket with him, drank with him, partied with him, shared his confidences, counselled him, or tried to be his friend. They talk freely and openly.

He is a walking paradox, they say. He is supremely confident, yet profoundly insecure. He is brilliant but also a buffoon. He is generous and thoughtful, but utterly self-obsessed. This book is the search for why.

1

Suck on This

Shane didn't grow up his whole life wanting to be a role model.

To his mates at the Australian Institute of Sport in Adelaide in 1990, Shane Warne was the life and soul of the party, a champion bloke, a lovable larrikin who lived life to the full.

Those who ran the Cricket Academy there were not so taken. Some of them found the 21-year-old leg spinner a pain and problem. He was overweight, he gambled, he partied too late, he drank too much beer, he smoked like a chimney, he didn't train hard enough, and he had an attitude problem.

When he finally packed his bags and headed home to Melbourne in his hotted-up six-cylinder Cortina, with its loud stereo, huge extractors and fat chrome wheels, very few of the AIS top brass were sad to see him go.

The final bust-up that led to his departure involved a training run where one of the coaches felt he wasn't trying hard enough. Warne told him to 'Fuck off' and was disciplined by being dumped from the academy's tour of Sri Lanka.

But there was an earlier, more serious incident, a fracas in Darwin where an official complaint was made and criminal charges narrowly avoided. No one has ever revealed exactly what happened. And Shane has been in no hurry to fess up. One close friend told a newspaper that the young spin bowler took off all his clothes and jumped into a swimming pool in front of two girls.

Years later, David Boon wrote in his autobiography that Warne's crime was to stick his buttocks out of a window at the team hotel and moon a couple of young women who were sitting by the pool. In sporting circles they call it a 'brown eye'.

But the truth is a little bit grubbier than that, and it provides an early pointer to the troubles that have plagued the world's most remarkable cricketer in recent years. According to one of those involved, Warne came down to the swimming pool at the university college where the team was staying, wearing only a dressing gown, and went up to three Asian girls who were sunbathing. He opened his robe in front of them, to give them a good look, and then said: 'Hey girls, how'd ya like to suck on this?'

It's not the greatest of pick-up lines, and these young women certainly weren't impressed. One threatened to go to the police if Warne was not punished. But it's the sort of gesture a 15-year-old schoolboy would no doubt find hilarious.

Looking back on his time at the academy a few years later in *Shane Warne, My Own Story*, Warne said he walked out because the coaches were too stiff to appreciate his laid-back approach. He complained about being forced to swim without goggles and having to stick a thermometer up his backside to measure heat loss and being fined for farting on the team bus, but he finally admitted: 'Okay, I stuffed up once and did the wrong thing.'

He did not mention either of the more serious incidents that got him into trouble. Nor did he show much sign of shame or remorse. In his view, the pool incident was a harmless prank, which any normal person would have forgiven and forgotten. In other words, 'Just get over it.'

It's a cry Warne has uttered many times, after many mishaps, down the years: 'Don't hang me just because I've stuffed up once.' And throughout his life people have generally obeyed. He has been regularly forgiven by his coaches, by his teachers and by his team-mates, as talented sportsmen so often are. No one has ever taken him aside and told him what he cannot do. Or no one close to him. All have been in awe of his extraordinary talent.

And extraordinary it certainly is. Warne is the best bowler the world has ever seen, and he may well be the best captain Australia never had. He has broken every record in the book and will doubtless break more. He has given pleasure and excitement to millions of people. He has entertained and electrified the game. Love him or hate him – and few people are lukewarm – you cannot deny that the man is a genius.

One of his old school friends says, 'Shane didn't grow up his whole life wanting to be a role model.' And he certainly hasn't managed to become one – or not a good one. Sometimes he tries hard: he works for charity, he looks after his mates, he shares his skills with any cricketer who wants to learn, he spends hours signing autographs while others can't be bothered.

But at times he throws it all to the wind. His attitude is, 'I am who I am, you can take me or leave me'. No one holds him back. No one tells him what to do. He is too important, too famous, too talented, too charismatic. So Shane Warne does exactly what Shane Warne wants to do. And damn the consequences.

It's almost certainly why he's so brilliant on the field. And why he is such an idiot off it.

Had he not become a sporting superstar Shane Warne might still be down at the beach in Beaumaris, sinking stubbies with his mates and sitting on the bonnet of his SS ute, clad in blue singlet, shorts and boots, and talking chicks and footy. And instead of hogging the headlines and dancing with the stars, he might be hefting beds for Forty Winks, delivering pizzas for Pizza Hut or driving a truck round Melbourne's bayside suburbs, which is what he did in the 18 months before he shot to fame.

When asked not long ago what he would be doing with his life if he couldn't spin a ball better than anyone else in the world, Warne shook his head and said: 'Mate, I honestly don't know – a bum on the beach – I don't know, I honestly don't know what I would do.'

Shane is happy to admit he is a simple bloke with simple tastes, who takes little or no interest in the outside world. He likes beer, pies and pizzas, loves Abba and Boney M, and counts *Dumb and Dumber* and *Meet the Fockers* as his favourite films. He confesses he has never read a book in his life, or never finished one, because he gets bored and forgets what has happened. And he swears that the thing that matters most to him is his family – even as he does his best to lose them.

But fame, more than anything, is what Shane Warne always craved. And fame, with all its pitfalls, is what he got. Among the many nicknames he was known by in his youth, Hollywood is the one that best sums up the man. With his earrings and his peroxide-blond hair, he always longed to be the centre of attention. Even at school, he was the clown, the joker, the one who pushed it a little too far. It was never his boyhood dream to play cricket for Australia. He just wanted to be someone. To be noticed. To be loved. To be a star.

That desire is still what drives him. It is also what continues to get him into trouble, just as it did all those years ago in Darwin.

2

Look at Me, Look at Me

He was an absolute joyful larrikin.

If you drive south from Melbourne along the edge of Port Phillip Bay, past Brighton's Golden Mile with its multi-million-dollar mock regency mansions and modern glass castles, you cross the railway line at Hampton and eventually roll into Black Rock, the tiny bayside suburb where Shane Warne spent his childhood. Here, the tide of money surging down the coast has only begun to lap at the shores, and there are reminders of what it would have been like 20 years ago when Shane was in his teens. The houses are mostly red brick, the rooves are tiled and there's a slight air of untidiness.

Black Rock is only 20 kilometres from Melbourne's city centre, but in culture and feel it is a world away. The main street has echoes of a rundown Australian country town. There's a milk bar, a chemist, a shoe shop, a restaurant, a local grocer and a solicitor's office, and not a single chain store in sight. No McDonald's, no Woolies, no 7-Eleven. It's too quiet for them to bother.

Not far from the hub – if that's how you can describe it

– is where Shane and his younger brother, Jason, grew up. It's a modest, brick bungalow on the highway south, just across the road from the sandy beach at Half Moon Bay. Despite the position, it has no million-dollar views, because traffic, bushes and the cliff top stand between the house and the water. And we're not talking blue Pacific anyway.

Warne's childhood home is a solid, comfortable, middle-class affair on a block that would have been way too small for budding cricketers. The backyard has cheap brick pavers and a couple of ferns around a small swimming pool, with a few metal chairs from the local hardware store. Or it did in December 1991 when Shane was picked to make his Test debut for Australia. And despite all his fame and fortune, nothing much has changed since then. Shane's parents still live here, for a start.

You can see them at any Test he plays in, and you can bet they haven't missed a game since he was a nipper. His mates from primary school remember his mother always coming to watch, as do the lads who played club cricket with him in his teens. But Brigitte is a woman you would hardly forget. Small, feisty and bright-eyed, with spiky, dyed-blonde hair, she is a pocket version of her son, with the same smile, the same directness and the same facial expressions. Over the years even their hairstyles have moved in step. One journalist who knows her well says, 'She's brash, loud, and full of life. She drinks with the boys and she is determined to have fun.' She also tells people who write about Shane exactly what she thinks of them: 'You write shit, you write shit, you're okay.'

If there is one obvious difference between Brigitte and her son, it would be that she always says these things, while Shane only thinks them. He has never been big on confrontation. And neither, it seems, was she with him. One of Warne's teenage friends says Brigitte was not like a mum. She never put her foot down with him or told him off. In her eyes, Shane could do no wrong.

Shane's father, Keith, is in many ways her opposite. He is tall, grey, thin and reserved, and stands quietly in the background while his wife does the talking. By common consent, he is a fine man: 'conservative, upright, straight-forward, a really decent human being, the sort of bloke you'd want for a father', as one of Shane's old friends puts it. Keith is a man with impeccable manners, and you may be surprised to know that he has passed them on to his son.

Shane's parents must now be pushing 60, but they still look fit and young. Brigitte was a runner in her youth and Keith a decent tennis player, and apart from giving Shane their genes, they did all they could to help him get a sport-ing start. Sport is king in suburbs such as Black Rock, as it is all over Australia, and both were happy to sacrifice their weekends and evenings ferrying him to athletics, swimming or cricket matches, and in Keith's case, manag-ing the junior footy team. Shane's mates liked going with him because he always had flash cars. 'We thought he looked like Clint Eastwood', one recalls, 'so we called him Dirty Harry. He just laughed.'

Shane's schoolmates reckoned his parents were great. They were friendly and welcoming, and if Shane liked you they did too. So the house in Beach Road, with its pool out the back and pool table inside, was a popular place to hang. The Warnes were more liberal than most, so the boys could play cards – blackjack, pontoon, poker – and drink, in return for which they never took liberties or drank too much, as they might have done at other houses. The Warnes were good people, says one, you wanted them to respect you.

If it all sounds like an idyllic childhood, then perhaps it was. But there must have been something in those early years that made Shane the person he is today, because for all his talent and fame and self-confidence on the field, he is said to still be chronically insecure. Despite an army of adoring fans, he is clearly convinced the world is against him. Was his father disappointed in the boy? Did his mother smother him with love? Or is this just the way he's always been?

You can never really know what goes on in a family or a marriage, or what truly forms a child, even if you live close up. But if it all was as happy as it seemed, it is even more of a mystery that he has spent his life needing so much reassurance and so much love.

Years later, staff at Sandringham Primary have a vivid picture of Brigitte Warne, dropping her two boys at school in a yellow Jaguar. But little Shane jogs fewer memories. His form teacher remembers him as one of the blond boys who sat at the back of the class, but she can't recall which one. Another believes he was nice and polite. A third sees him waiting outside the headmaster's office, and suggests he was often in trouble, then wonders if it was his brother, Jason. And an old classmate is sure he had lots of girl-friends in Year 5, which made him a bit special.

That's about all anyone can dredge up, despite years of trying since Warne put Black Rock on the map. The truth is that three decades on he doesn't really stand out. At that tender age it's only those who are really remarkable – very brilliant or very bad – who are memorable. And he was neither. His headmaster at Sandringham, Geoff Brown, says that at primary school, 'He was never in as much bother as he likes to remember. He likes to think of himself as a bit of a character. All I can say is he didn't have his gold earring in those days or his mobile phone and he just didn't stand out.'

He would in time, of course. And it was already obvious that he was good at sport: football, swimming, tennis and cricket, which is what most bayside boys played in summertime when they weren't at the beach. By the age of 12 he was playing for the East Sandringham Boys Club U14s and scoring a stack of runs. He was also getting his face in the paper for the first time, winning $20 and a sports bag as Puma's junior player of the month.

Shortly afterwards, he got his first big break. Who knows what might have happened without it? While playing for a local representative side, Nepean U16s, in a match against Mentone Grammar, he was spotted by the school's South African-born cricket coach, John Mason, and offered a sports scholarship. 'He was enormously talented even at that age', says Mason, 'and we immediately wanted him to come to the school.' He bowled leg breaks, which was rare for one so young. Better still, he bowled them well.

Mentone is a couple of suburbs down the coast from Black Rock, and a couple of notches up the social scale.

Its founders in the late 19th Century named it after Menton on the French-Italian border in the hope that it might become Melbourne's version of the Riviera. Its streets are named after Italian cities, such as Como, Naples and Florence. The boys' school, in Venice Street, is set back half a kilometre from the beach and is so modest in its shopfront that you could easily pass it by. The driveway to the original bungalow, where Mentone Grammar began in 1923, looks like the entrance to any private house in any suburban street, except for a discreet blue notice bearing the school's name. But once you are inside, the vista opens up to a huge green cricket oval, a large redbrick chapel and a mass of modern glass buildings, including a spanking new sports hall and a library.

Today Mentone has around 800 boys and a dream that has never quite come off: to be in the top rank of Melbourne's private schools. In its time, it has produced just one Rhodes Scholar and one Shane Warne, and it has become famous as a school for jocks, who win all the prizes, grab the attention and garner the glory. The secret of its sporting success is to target talented kids who can swim, bowl, bat or kick a football better than their peers, and lure them to the school. But two decades after Brigitte and Keith Warne were given free schooling for their 15-year-old prodigy, in the hope that he would win cricket matches, Mentone still treats it as a rather delicate matter. And back then, while their rivals were also scouring sports fields, chequebooks in hand, Mentone felt it had to pretend it was giving Warne a scholarship for academic merit.

It was pretty obvious, of course, that he hadn't been poached from the nearby secondary school for his brains.

He sat at the back of the class with the other scholars – bowlers, batters, kickers and swimmers – and showed no interest at all in learning. It was also obvious that he was a bit of a character. Within weeks of his arrival he had made such an impact that almost everyone knew who he was.

John Mason, his enthusiastic cricket coach, who is clearly proud to have played a role in his development, thought him 'a terrific boy: friendly, jovial, respectful'. And almost all of his Mentone colleagues agreed – except the chaplain, who remains discreetly silent about his views. He was 'a charming larrikin', 'a lovable rogue', or 'polite, but an absolute scallywag', and it was extremely hard not to like him. His schoolmates were also dazzled. Sven Samild, who was in his class in fourth grade and played in cricket and football teams with him for years, reckoned he was the tops. 'He was full of life, just one of those champion blokes', he says. 'He was great fun to be around, I could not say anything negative about him.' But like Shane's other mates from Mentone, they no longer keep in touch.

Tim Appel, who played cricket with Warne in the First XI, and was another good mate, until fame forced them apart, was also charmed. 'He was an absolute joyful larrikin', he says, recalling times when they travelled to school together on the bus from Black Rock, sitting up the back (where else?), with Shane cracking jokes and generally showing off. Warne was always the centre of attention wherever he went. Mentone's stocky opening batsman, David Guazzarotto, says, 'He just loved it. And he always had a flock of people around him.'

Warne wasn't long at Mentone before he had earned himself the nickname Twisty, although no one is quite sure how. If you ask where it came from you'll get six different answers, but his hair in those days had not yet seen a peroxide bottle and was somewhere between mousy orange and strawberry blond – in fact, the colour of a Twisty – so that's a frontrunner. He also brought packets of Twisties to school, which he would load into a buttered roll and submerge in a sea of sauce, before eating them for lunch – so that's another hot favourite. Or maybe it was because they were all discovering beer at the time, and VB bottles had those new twist tops.

Whatever the true origin, there's no doubt that Shane was noticed. Years later, most of his Mentone schoolmates tell colourful tales of his exploits on the cricket field, at the pub, with girls, or outside the headmaster's study, which suggest that knowing him has been the highlight of their lives. One is now a plumber, one a landscape gardener, one runs a fish shop, one lays carpets. Others have become pilots, financial planners and computer experts. And even if their stories are fanned by fame or embroidered in the telling, there's no denying that the teenage Warne made a big impression on them and is, generally, fondly remembered.

Even today, they still marvel at what he ate. He loved pizzas and tinned spaghetti, had little time for meat and even less for vegetables, and would happily consume baked beans and Coke till they were coming out his ears. When cricket teas of cold meat and salad were served, he would ignore them completely and manufacture a cold chip butty. Or, if he was lucky, his mum would arrive with a hot chip sandwich. Teachers who went with him on footy tours were appalled. One fellow cricketer, Raj Krishnan, who came from a family of Hindu vegetarians, says his mother would go crazy trying to figure out what to feed him. 'But what *does* he eat?' she would ask. Not surprisingly, they never had anything suitable.

One of the best stories of Shane and his diet comes from the mates at Mentone who lined him up one Friday night with a girl from the grammar school next door. On the way back from the pub after a few beers, they drove through the local McDonald's to pick up a burger. Shane, crammed in the back with his pretty date, grabbed his bun, pulled out the meat and trimmings, replaced the cheese slice and tipped in a cupful of chips, before smothering the lot in tomato sauce. The poor girl couldn't believe her eyes. He seemed like quite a nice boy, but how could she ever take him home to meet her parents if he was going to embarrass her like this?

Warne's fame on the cricket field spread just as quickly. The school's yearbook for 1986 celebrated his first full season in the First XI by describing him as 'the outstanding spinner in the competition, who bowled his leg breaks and googlies with great control and, once established, obliterated a number of opposition attacks with an array of orthodox and improvised strokes'. The team coach, John Mason, had never seen anything like him. Unlike many leg spinners, who are 'unfit, uncoordinated, and can't catch', Warne was an athlete who could bowl. Indeed, he seemed to have been built for the job, with arms like a blacksmith and fat, powerful fingers. But two things made him exceptional. One was his control and accuracy.

The other was his remarkable self-belief. There was nothing he couldn't do, or so he thought.

Few batsmen had a clue how to read him, having never seen leg spin before, and Mentone's wicket-keeper Tony Bournon was also baffled, until Shane hit on the idea of telegraphing his intentions. Rubbing the ball on the back of his trousers was Warne's signal for the googly or wrong 'un, the ball that fools the batsman by spinning the other way. Touching his ear was . . . alas, no one can remember. Luckily, the opposing team never had time to crack the code.

But good as he was, Warne's Mentone mates did not regard him as the best player in the team or anything out of the box. Stranger still, they did not even think that bowling was his best suit. In those early days, he had little variety, and Raj Krishnan, the rising star of the First XI – and Mentone's most talented cricketer – had faced him so often in the nets that he could play him with ease. Raj remembers hitting him for a massive six onto the golf course, only for Warne to return the compliment an hour or so later, by slogging him for an even bigger six over the pavilion.

Warne's batting was always exciting and sometimes a standout. In only his second match for the school, against Marcellin, he cracked a quick-fire 81 at almost a run a ball. And later in the season, he stood alone against Yarra Valley, coming in at six wickets down with just 15 runs on the board, and scoring 90 before being run out. But despite his obvious talent, he never made a century. He had a great eye and plenty of confidence, but he lacked patience and application. All he wanted to do was hit the ball as hard as he could and whack it out of the park.

Nor did he like to work. John Mason never saw him toiling in the nets, and he refused to put in the hard yards at swimming or footy, where he also had huge natural talent. Slogging up and down the pool or running round a sports field was simply not his bag.

He was far too busy being different. One picture of him from the mid-1980s speaks volumes. He is aged 16 or 17, leading the Mentone team off the field, and he is the only one with his cap on back to front, the only one with zinc cream on his nose and lips. It is a small thing, but it screams, 'Look at me. Look at me.' His brand new bat also received the standout treatment. It was a Duncan Fearnley Magnum, with black handle and black writing, all the rage in those days, and every schoolboy's dream. Graham Gooch had one, as did Allan Border. 'Warne got his and went straight down to Bat & Ball and came back with a bright orange fluorescent grip', says Raj Krishnan. 'He thought it looked fantastic. He loved it. The handle kind of matched his hair.'

'God, he was an idiot', he adds, shaking his head.

The first hint of how good Warne might be as a cricketer came in early 1986 on a summer holiday trip to Geelong, where Mentone played in an annual cricket carnival. With Mason umpiring, the school's new scholarship boy clean bowled three batsmen in a row with wrong 'uns. 'They just shouldered arms', he says, 'because they thought it was going to spin the other way.'

That night, after their victory, the boys decided to celebrate. Getting hold of some beer and Island Cooler, they smuggled it into the boarding house at Geelong

College where they were billeted, and got rip-roaring drunk. Despite one of the boys being violently sick out the window, it was two weeks before they were busted, when the Geelong boys came back to their dormitory and found all the empties stashed in drawers. Before long, word got back to Mentone. And, one by one, the team filed in to see the headmaster, Bob Hutchings, and confess.

The ringleaders were assumed to be half a dozen team members who had just been made prefects and were going into Year 12, their final year. But what was to be done with them? If all was made public, the school would have to take away their prefect badges and suspend them from the team. This was unthinkable. Mentone had won the Associated Grammar Schools (AGS) premiership twice in the previous three years and was desperate to do it again. So a choice was offered: publicity and disgrace, plus suspension from the cricket team, or secrecy and six of the best. They were all delighted to choose the cane.

Although Shane was in the vanguard of this escapade, he escaped punishment because he was a year behind his team-mates at school. But he made up for it at other times by being regularly in trouble. His key crime was to muck up in class, where he had little or no interest in lessons but was determined to get himself noticed. 'He was always pushing it, and he was not short on wit', says Tim Appel. 'Plenty of teachers decided they couldn't handle him and sent him to the head.'

A couple of years ago in a Channel 9 TV interview Warne confessed to Ray Martin that he had never paid attention at school and was always larking about. 'I was always seeing the headmaster every week. He was practising his golf swing on the back of my behind.' And in *Shane Warne, My Autobiography* he claims that these beatings were painful and often drew blood.

One of his best mates at Mentone, Darren Van de Loop, who was on a swimming scholarship, boasts that they often went along to get the cane together. And certainly the pair was regularly in strife. They were caught smoking behind the bike sheds and busted for chatting up the girls from the nearby girls' grammar school, which made them late for assembly. They were also 'always in detention for fighting and carrying on'. But they had competitions to go to and matches to play, which sometimes got them off the hook. Top sportsmen at Mentone could clearly get away with more than the average Joe, and Warne clearly stretched the bounds of tolerance further than any. As one top cricket official laments sourly today, 'His ability to charm people is right up there on a par with his talent for leg spin.'

Warne's version of his school days casts him as the cheeky rebel whose spirit could not be crushed by regular thrashings. But there's a fair bit of myth-making in this portrayal, as in any life story. It is more likely that his tales of retreating to the toilet to check the blood marks on his buttocks are a heroic exaggeration – which is another of Shane's exceptional talents. Indeed, his headmaster at Mentone, Bob Hutchings, claims to have rarely used the cane, and does not recall ever beating Warne. What he does remember is letting him off lightly for breaking the rules. 'He got himself into a few scrapes, and I certainly came very close to kicking him out', says Hutchings, 'but he was a great sportsman. That's why I kept him on. I had a few conversations with him and his father about his future . . . but he was a good cricketer and winning cricket matches was important to the school.'

Hutchings is considerably tougher than the average cricket administrator, and had other concerns at Mentone apart from sport. Yet even he was persuaded to treat Warne differently, to make allowances. And thus the saga of special treatment began. Some saw nothing wrong in it back then. Fewer would defend it now. But Sven Samild reckons it's fine: 'Famous sportsmen, musicians, artists, they're all a bit different . . . and so is he.' In other words, it was only right to give him some leeway.

Certainly, Mentone let him do precious little work. And if anybody did try to whip him into shape they failed. Rick Hardy, who attempted to teach Warne English without success, says that the teenage sports star had a very clear idea of his priorities and English literature wasn't one of them: 'He just didn't think it was relevant to his life.' Hardy found the boy easy to manage if he didn't try to get work out of him, so he soon opted for a quiet life and let Warne idle. Before long, most of his colleagues also gave up trying.

By the end, Warne was allowed to bypass some lessons entirely. Bob Hutchings, who took him for English in his last year, recalls, 'He liked late nights and he would often arrive in the morning and say, "Sir, can I sleep today?" And I'd say, "Okay, Shane, you just sit up the back of the class, but don't snore and disturb me." '

Frank Jenkins, who taught business maths and was his form master in final year, fared little better. 'None of his group was interested', he says. 'Monday and Tuesday they'd discuss the footy results. Thursday and Friday they'd talk about the next footy game. Wednesday we'd have a small window for teaching them some maths if we were lucky.'

Warne only made it into Year 12 at all because Mentone was prepared to change the rules for him. Since time immemorial, the school had laid down strict criteria for allowing pupils into the sixth form, demanding good passes in at least four subjects, to ensure they had some prospect of passing the Higher School Certificate (HSC). Shane and two other top sportsmen in the school, including another cricketer on a sports scholarship, Dean Jamieson, failed the test.

On past occasions when this had happened, the boys had been kicked out without ceremony, despite bitter complaints from their parents. But Warne was about to be captain of the cricket team and Jamieson was one of Mentone's best batsmen. So, for the first time in the school's history, the rules were broken and a new stream was created in Year 12 to take a simpler version of the HSC, which almost any fool could pass.

Around 10 boys were shunted into it. None was expected to go to university. They might get into a business course at TAFE if they were lucky, or they might end up as tradesmen. But in the meantime, they would be available for the cricket team, and with Shane in charge Mentone's First XI rolled on to victory, finishing undefeated in the AGS competition and winning the premiership for the third year out of four. As the 1987 yearbook records:

Shane Warne's captaincy was to be one of the major reasons for our successful season. He believed there was only one way to play the game and that was to attack. He led by example and was able to get the best out of the team. He was justly rewarded with captaincy of the AGS First XI.

Warne was a wonderful leader, says Krishnan. 'He was so single-minded, so determined, he just had this huge desire to win, and he made the team feel the same way. They were prepared to walk through walls for him.' John Mason's verdict is similar: 'He was a brilliant captain. He got everyone else to believe in themselves. They never even thought of losing'.

Neither did Warne. Mason still chuckles over a home match where it was vital to win the toss because the wicket was damp and batting was likely to be a nightmare. When Shane flipped the coin, it came to rest at a 60-degree angle in the long grass. It was quite clear that it was heads and the visiting captain had called correctly, but before anyone could react, Warne had picked it up and spun the coin again, claiming it hadn't fallen properly. This time it came down tails and the visiting side was put in to bat. 'I could have hugged him', says Mason, 'but I did have misgivings.' Mentone went on to win outright – bowling their opponents out twice – with Warne getting 10 wickets.

If Warne occasionally pushed the limits of sportsmanship like this, he could also be sour in defeat. When Mentone was beaten by Norwood in the final of the 1987 Victorian School Championships (a far bigger competition than the AGS) he was so 'gutted' that the entire team behaved ungraciously. Barrie Irons, who had taken over as First XI coach, told them they had to smile, shake hands and be good losers, and they did their best to comply. But with Warne as captain, the team had few opportunities to learn the drill.

By the time Shane left school at the end of 1987, he had already been blooded in the much harsher world of senior cricket, playing for the famous old club at Brighton, in what was effectively Melbourne's second grade. Neil Cassidy, who was then captain of the First XI, remembers him as a confident fellow and one of the politest boys he ever met. Warne arrived with five of his mates from Mentone, and a big rap about how good he was. But he did not set the world on fire, and he soon found the grown-up game to be harder than bullying 16-year-old schoolboys who had never seen a googly. He was suddenly up against former Victorian state cricketers, who talked tough, played the game hard and took great delight in teaching kids like him a lesson and showing them they were not so bloody good.

Warne did not have to wait long for a reality check. In his very first outing for the First XI, against Elsternwick, a couple of experienced lads set about whacking him all over the ground. Soon afterwards, Cassidy dropped him back to the seconds, because he didn't want him to lose confidence. He did not shine there either, and few at the club reckoned him anything special. The stats from the season show he broke no records. In seven matches he took just 12 wickets and scored 110 runs. And when summer was over, he took his bat and ball and went elsewhere. But one Brighton cricketer, Warne's rival for the leg spinner's spot, was amazed by what Shane could do.

Derek Leong, now a smart (and smartly dressed) Melbourne lawyer, could not believe that one so young could be so good, because leg spin is a devilishly difficult art to master. He was also struck by Warne's remarkable confidence. In club cricket, spinners tend to get taken off by the captain once they go for a few runs, so they bowl defensively and stop trying to spin the ball. But Warne's technique was so good that he was accurate even when spinning it a mile, and he never ceased attacking. 'That's what was really impressive about him', says Leong. 'It didn't bother him if he got hit. He kept cool, he didn't panic. He just kept on doing what he was doing. But he was 17 and I was 36. He hadn't had the shit belted out of him.'

The six Mentone boys who played for Brighton that summer caused quite a stir at the club. 'They were terrific lads, full of spunk and great cricketers', says George Voyage, who was club captain at the time. What really set feathers flying was that they brought their girlfriends. Brighton was a very conservative club, and a few of the old blokes were a bit taken aback and a bit envious. 'The Mentone lads would be waiting to go in to bat and the girls would be all over them', says Derek Leong. 'We couldn't see how the boys could concentrate on their cricket with such distractions.'

Remarkably, Warne was the only one who did not have a blonde on his arm. He brought his mother to watch instead.

Leong was struck then by how very different he was from the other Mentone boys. He was not on the same intellectual level, for a start. They could chat about what was happening in the world, but he could really only talk footy, cricket and other sports. And while they all had their futures worked out – university, law, medicine, the family business – he had nothing at all. 'I thought his parents must have lots of money, because he had no goals or prospects', says Leong. 'He had no idea what he was going to do. You asked him and he just said, "I dunno".'

But his parents did not have lots of money – or not enough for him to do nothing – and the bald truth was his future looked bleak. He had precious little education, even less motivation and no interest in anything but sport. The way he was going, he was likely to end up driving a truck or working in a factory. If this concerned him, he didn't show it. He was too busy being a boy: chasing girls, driving cars, drinking beer and having a good time.

Naturally, this was an area where he also had talent. On Fridays, when the Mentone Grammar boys flocked to the Bowie, or Beaumaris Hotel, to drink in the Schooner Bar, Shane was right in the thick of it, and always looking good. One thing his mates noted was the trouble he took over his appearance. 'He was very vain', says Darren Van de Loop. 'He'd be just like a girl when he was getting ready to go out. He'd be in front of the mirror for hours, making sure he looked good.'

Many years later, this vanity would land him in the worst strife of his career, when he popped a couple of his mum's fluid tablets to get rid of a double chin. In the meantime it obviously worked. 'He could get just about any girl he wanted, if he put his mind to it', Van de Loop recalls. 'Yup, nothing's changed there.' And everyone heard about his conquests. Even his teachers at Mentone got the mail. But people always talked about Shane, including the man himself, which was just the way he wanted it.

Two decades later, his schoolmates say he was like any other young lad whose hormones were running hot. Yet none seems surprised by the trouble he now gets himself into. Twenty years on, they say, he has not grown up. He's still a big kid. He acts first and thinks later. Or as his headmaster Bob Hutchings puts it: 'He's no different now to what he was aged 17. He was always a lover of life and a lover of women. He was fairly hedonistic then, he did what he wanted and never thought about the consequences. I don't think he's changed.'

3

Kick in the Guts

He never did weights himself, just came in for a chat.

If Shane did have dreams of a sporting future it was not as a cricketer. His not-so-secret fantasy was to be an Aussie Rules footy legend, pulling chicks, driving fast cars and making heaps of money, like his sporting idol Dermot Brereton. Which is pretty much what he does today. Brereton was the famous, flashy centre-half forward from the Hawthorn Hawks, who bleached his hair peroxide blond, wore an earring and drove a Ferrari. He was also a larrikin, who did what he wanted, said what he thought and let others decide whether they liked it. Warne has just taken it all to another level.

Shane had started wearing Brereton's yellow-and-brown jumper while still in kindergarten, and continued to sport a bigger version of the number 23 guernsey many years later, when all his mates were barracking for their local team, St Kilda. It remains his lucky number today, the one he bets on when he plays roulette, the one he wears on his green-and-gold one-day strip, and the one that gives his management company its name. But Warne was not the only kid in Melbourne to fantasise about being a footy star. Wanting to grow up to be Dermot Brereton in the 1980s was much like a kid in England wanting to be David Beckham 10 years later.

Shane was undoubtedly less deluded than most in thinking he could make it. His mates at Mentone remember him as a terrific mark and a terrific kick – which means he jumped well, caught brilliantly and could boot the ball long and straight. And as the school's full forward, he scored a stack of goals. But he was rarely mentioned in dispatches and his team-mates regarded him as a bit of a show pony, the type who camps in the goal square, never moves too far and hates getting down in the mud. One uncharitable verdict is: 'Guaranteed, he was the only one who never got dirty on the field.'

On occasions he could be brilliant. On Mentone's tour of Tasmania in 1987 he kicked a best-ever 16 goals against Launceston Grammar, and set a school record. 'The flamboyant full forward led superbly, marked strongly and kicked truly', the school's yearbook reported, 'as he booted sixteen goals in a match-winning display'. But even on that occasion Warne didn't win man of the match, because others were thought to have tried harder, and he never got picked for the Associated Grammar Schools side, whose team he captained at cricket.

Despite this relative lack of success it was still footy that took his fancy. And if the AGS did not think him good enough, the St Kilda Saints, his local AFL club, certainly did. They sent scouts to watch him while he was still at school, and signed him up after he left Mentone in 1987 as a contracted player, on the princely wage of $30 a game. He played the 1988 winter season in the U19s, scoring seven goals in one match, but never climbed any closer to the top. He played just one game for St Kilda Reserves, earning a match fee of $100, but was never picked again. His sole chance came against the Carlton Navy Blues on a muddy day at Moorabbin, the club's home ground near Black Rock, and it was a disaster. He copped a hiding from his opposing number and was taken off the field at three-quarter time. St Kilda's reserve team coach, Gary Colling, explained that he dragged him off because he was not chasing out of the backline. 'It happened two or three times and I just lost patience', said Colling, who claimed that Warne had been watching from the goal square, with his arms folded, as a Carlton player gathered the ball.

Warne's excuse for this sluggishness was that he should never have been on the field in the first place. He had been struck down with a virus the week before, had been shivering and sweating in bed, and had taken the heroic decision to play because he feared not getting another chance. And as it turned out, of course, he didn't. He speculated in *Shane Warne, My Autobiography*, his second attempt at a life story, that his career might have followed an entirely different path if the game had been played one week later. But the truth is that he had more talent at cricket, which suited him better, and it was a matter of time before the axe would fall. None of his mates in the U19s expected him to go all the way at footy, and few even realised that he wanted to. He wasn't the fittest bloke in the pack, and never devoted himself to training. As his schoolmates and teachers at Mentone had already observed: if there was hard work to be done, Shane wasn't in it.

Jason Dunkley, who played in the U19s with him, remembers Warne rolling up for weights sessions at St Kilda when everyone else was already hard at it. He had a customised six-cylinder Cortina at the time, in Classic Cream, with huge Dragways chrome wheels that were all the rage. And there was no mistaking the sound of his approach: engine roaring, music pumping, stereo going full bore. 'You'd be inside in the gym', says Dunkley, 'and you could hear him arrive. "That'll be Warney." He'd walk in, do a few arm curls then give up. He never did weights himself, just came in for a chat.'

The car was Shane's pride and joy and he loved to drive it. On Saturday nights, after the footy, he would take the boys over to a big pub called Derbys, at Caulfield, which had dancing, and stayed open till five am. And it would always be an exciting ride. 'Roundabouts were like ski jumps', says Sven Samild, his old schoolmate, who was also playing footy in the U19s. Whether he had paid for the car himself or been given it by his parents, no one could say.

But it wasn't just that he never became super fit. He was also too short and too slow to be an AFL star. To make it to the top as a full forward in Aussie Rules, you need to be 6 foot 3 or 6 foot 4, because you have to outjump everybody else, and Shane was just 6 foot. And to be in a running position out on the flank you need to be quick and agile, but Shane lacked pace. So it should have been no great surprise when a letter came through the front door at Beach Road in March 1989 to say that St Kilda would not be signing him for the winter season. He had become too old for the U19s and the Reserves did not want him. The club's selection committee reckoned he would not make the grade. His sluggish performance in the mud at Moorabbin had shown Gary Colling – whose mantra was work, work and more work – all he needed to see.

Shane was aghast at being rejected. In *Shane Warne, My Autobiography*, he confesses that the letter came as 'a bolt out of the blue', 'a major blow' and 'a real kick in the guts'. All he had wanted as a kid – he claimed – was to play senior footy, and this was the end of the dream. But his team-mates don't appear to have blinked an eye, and certainly did not agitate for the decision to be reversed. 'We all wanted to make it to the top', says Adrian McKenzie, who had played footy with Shane since his early teens. 'But if you're not good enough, you're not good enough. That's it.'

'And thank God he wasn't', says John Beveridge, St Kilda's development officer, who tracked his footy career. 'The world would have missed out on a marvellous cricketer.'

There's no doubt that the rebuff was a turning point in Warne's life, because it freed him up for cricket and left him with only one chance at sporting glory. But there's no evidence that he suddenly realised cricket was his future. Nor did he jump in his Cortina and zoom down to the nets to put in a few hundred hours on his bowling. He just felt lost.

During the previous two summers he had played for St

Kilda Cricket Club (which has no connection to the AFL team) but had woven no magic. It bored him, he later told journalists, and he would have been far happier at the beach with his mates, had they not been so keen to play. He had started in the Colts and worked his way up to the Fourth XI and then to the Third. In his second season he had taken some wickets and played a few games for the Seconds. But he still regarded himself as a batsman who could bowl, rather than the world's greatest spinner. And it didn't occur to him that he had a future in the game. Nor had anyone else marked him down as a superstar waiting to happen. Andrew Lynch, one of Mentone's many sports masters, who played for St Kilda's First XI in the 1980s and had introduced Warne to the club, says there was no way you could have picked that he was going to be a regular first-team player, let alone play for Australia. He was just a wild spirit who loved life, ate a lot of junk food and had a good time.

And that's how Shane wanted it to continue. So when a mate from the Second XI, Rick Gough, suggested he tag along to England to play club cricket for the northern summer, he jumped at the chance. He had been working in a local jewellery factory and on the checkout at Myers and had no plans to do anything better. So, a few weeks after being dumped by the footy team, and a few months before his 20th birthday, he boarded a flight to London for his first gig as a semi-professional cricketer.

At 25, his travelling companion had already played two seasons for Knowle Cricket Club on the outskirts of Bristol, and had enjoyed himself hugely. And Shane soon got a taste of what might be in store. They were met off the plane and driven straight to a country pub for a pie and a pint of beer. 'I sat them at the bar', says Steve Windaybank, then captain of Knowle's First XI, 'and told them where they would be playing. We needed a batsman and I knew Rick could bat, so I told him he was coming to Knowle and Shane was going to Imperial. It was one of the biggest mistakes of my life: telling Shane Warne "I'm not having you on my team."'

Warne's charm made him an instant hit with his West Country hosts, who found him polite, friendly and eager to please. Almost too eager, some thought. Years later, he still gets in touch with them when he comes to England, and they tell fond stories of their times with him. Like so many who have been touched by fame, they are proud to be able to say they knew him. And like everybody else who has spent time in his company, they revel in tales of his diet. Early on in his trip Shane was offered shepherd's pie by one of the locals. He shook his head and refused to touch it, telling them, 'I don't eat meat and I don't eat vegetables.' He ended up with a tin of spaghetti on white toast, with a large dollop of margarine on top. Thereafter it was pizzas, pies, burgers and chips, with the odd bit of deep-fried battered sausage thrown in.

Since the clubs weren't allowed to pay their players and Shane was short of money, Imperial found him a few odd jobs, such as painting fences and cutting the grass, which put 20 quid a week in his pocket. And the lads at Knowle passed the hat around and bought the boys a car, an ancient yellow Cortina, soon christened the Bumble Bee, which was the cooking version of Warne's dragster back home. It was a real rust bucket that burnt heaps of oil and belched clouds of blue smoke as it buzzed around. It was also illegal. According to Gough: 'It had number plates but nothing else, no registration or insurance, and we actually got picked up a lot of times by the police, but we were very lucky. We didn't get fined even once. We just talked cricket.' Thus did Warne's charmed life as a sportsman continue. His hosts even did his laundry for him, picking it up and returning it every week. Clearly, no one expected cricketers to look after themselves.

Home for the two boys was the third floor of Imperial's huge old wooden pavilion, which was built in the 1920s but had seen better days. Magnificent in conception, it had become a rickety old affair that creaked and swayed in the wind and was a target for vandals. It was miles from the nearest house and break-ins were common at night, because it was empty during the week. In fact, the Australian cricketer who stayed there the following year had all his gear stolen and moved out immediately. Warne and Gough were billeted in the attic flat, which was full of dead flies when they arrived and had only one bed. Someone went to fetch a spare mattress and brought back linen, towels and a Hoover, to give the place a good clean. The kitchen – which they probably never used – was down on the second floor and was where match teas were prepared. The toilet and shower were another flight down in the ground-floor changing rooms, which was a long way to go in the middle of the night after a few beers. And they had more than a few of those.

In fact Shane had never drunk so much alcohol in his life. 'Thursday to Sunday were just drinkathons', he boasted in *Shane Warne, My Autobiography*. And that was followed by Monday, when a bar called Busby's sold pints of beer for 20p, or about 50c. On his first night out on the town he was introduced to one of Bristol's strong ciders – Diamond White – and he awoke next day to the worst hangover of his life, which will be no surprise to those who know the local brew. Thereafter, it was back to lager, which he and Gough drank in huge quantities. They propped up the bar at Knowle Cricket Club, which was open all week, then moved to the George Inn, which was half a mile from the ground. Before long, its landlord had taken a shine to the boy and was keeping a paternal eye on him. Shane had never been away on his own before, and he was made to phone home each week to let his parents know he was okay.

'The life was rugged', Shane told one Melbourne cricket writer a few years later. 'You'd drink pint after pint every night and then eat a pile of fish and chips after the pubs closed.' Then there were milkshakes to swallow and fruit machines (pokies) to feed.

But Warne also played cricket and played it well, both for Knowle and Imperial. In the space of six months, he took 90 wickets and scored 800 runs in 35 official games (roughly two a week). He also toured the West Country with the local police team. And the longer the season went on, the better he played. At Imperial, he opened the bowling with his leg spin and 'mesmerised them' according to Gough. His opponents, who were not as good as the batsmen he encountered at St Kilda, had 'never seen the ball come off the pitch so quick'. In one midweek game he took a sensational 9 for 54. Never had he bowled so much in his life, nor so well.

The lads at Knowle were sad to see Warne and Gough go at the end of the summer and threw a huge party at the cricket club on the last night of their trip. Shane did his impersonation of MC Hammer, which was apparently hilarious, and rapped his way through the team one by one. Then the clapped-out Cortina was auctioned off for £135, which was £35 more than it had cost. Sadly, the poor guy who bought it had to scrap it soon after.

After that it was onto the plane and back to reality. There was no doubt Warne had changed on the trip, but more by growing than by growing up or getting serious. His beer and chip diet had stacked on 18 kilos, or almost 3 stone. And when his father picked him up at the airport he could hardly recognise him. At 100 kilograms, or nearly 16 stone, Shane was fatter than he had ever been in his life.

Back at St Kilda Cricket Club they could also barely believe their eyes. Laurie Harper, who was meeting Shane for the first time, told cricket writer Ken Piesse that he was 'huge, like a beached whale'. (He should perhaps have said bleached.) 'He had all this blond hair and was very very fat. I thought: "Who the hell is this bloke?"' Shaun Graf, St Kilda's First XI captain and coach, was also amazed and not much amused. He had helped arrange the trip to England, in the hope that it would be good for Warne's cricket, but the lad had come back twice the size and possibly only half as good. Graf, who was known as the Führer for his demanding training routines, ordered him to do a few laps of Albert Park Lake before presenting himself at the nets.

A couple of weeks later the teams were picked for the

coming season. Shane was naturally confident that he would be promoted to the First XI. Flushed with success from his deeds in Bristol, it hadn't occurred to him that his weight might be seen as a problem.

The team lists were read out in alphabetical order at a special club meeting on a Thursday evening in October, starting with the First XI: Evans, Gartrell, Graf, Jacoby, Mohr, Murphy and all the way down to Walker. Then Wingreen was in . . . and Warne was not.

Next came the Seconds, and down the list again. This time Womersley was in . . . and Warne was not. He couldn't believe it. He had taken wickets in the Seconds the previous season and played cricket for the entire Melbourne winter when others had not. And he knew how much better he had become. It was another kick in the guts.

He was soon telling people that he was thinking of giving up and going back to East Sandringham, where he had played as a boy – which is so often Warne's first re-action to disappointment. But it soon dawned on him that it would be great to play cricket for a living. He was shift-ing beds for Forty Winks, taking new ones to people's homes and ferrying the old ones to the tip, and it was not what he wanted to do for the rest of his life.

So he began to try harder. David Johnstone, one of St Kilda's top batsmen, told Ken Piesse he was always the first to get to the nets and the last to leave; and Jason Jacoby, the wicket-keeper, saw him always bowling, bowling, bowling. They also appreciated how much he had improved. He had come back from England a 200 per cent better bowler according to Johnstone, who walked out of the nets one night shaking his head and saying that the ball was never quite where you thought it was going to be when Warne was bowling. He had the flight, the trajectory and line just right, and could make the ball really zip around. His old sports master, Andrew Lynch, was also struck by the transformation, confessing, 'I had never seen a kid improve so much in just one year.'

As luck would have it, Shane did not have to serve his time in the Third XI after all. It rained and rained that spring, matches were washed out, and the club's frontline leg spinner, Jamie Handscomb, then injured his hand, so he found himself in the First XI after all. And in his second outing he showed them how good he could be. Waverley-Dandenong, led by the irrepressible Rodney Hogg, was cruising at 3 for 120 when, in Hogg's words, 'on came this little fat blond spinner'. Hogg, who had been a star fast bowler for Australia, turned to a team-mate who knew everyone in district cricket and asked him, 'Who the hell is this bloke?' No one had ever set eyes on him. As the fat boy began to take wickets, they scanned the team lists in the morning paper and found a name they didn't know, S. K. Warne.

As Waverley-Dandenong's top batsmen trudged back to the pavilion, Hogg marched out to show everyone how leg spin should be played, even though, with a first-class average of 10.75 he was hardly qualified to do so. He groped at Warne's first three balls, missing them altogether. 'I didn't know what the fuck was going on', he says cheerfully today, 'so I decided that if the next one showed above the horizon I'd belt it back over his head for six and see how good he was.' Hogg duly danced down the pitch, missed the ball completely and was stumped by a mile. Turning round to see his wicket askew, he saw St Kilda's captain, Shaun Graf, laughing in the slips and called out, 'I don't know what's so funny, this bloke's better than Sleepy [Peter Sleep, then Australia's frontline spinner].'

Hogg was so impressed that he immediately told readers of his column in the *Truth* newspaper, which was famous for just about anything but the truth, that he had just seen a kid who would take 500 wickets for Australia. 'It was my last story,' says Hogg. 'They sacked me on the spot. They thought it was too fanciful, even for them. As it turned out I was being too conservative. I should have said he'd take 600.'

Word of Warne's talent soon began to get around, and in early 1990 one of Australia's four national selectors was invited to watch him at training. Jim Higgs was an old leg spinner himself with 66 Test wickets under his belt, and there was a suggestion that he might give Warne a few tips. But one look told him there was not much he could teach him. 'He was only 20 and he was just totally outstanding. His technique was so good, his skills were excellent. You just thought, "How far is this guy going to go?"' Higgs had never seen anyone so young so good.

From this moment, Warne was on the fast track to success. After just four First XI games with St Kilda, he was invited to train with the Victorian state squad. On his first night in the nets in February 1990 he bowled brilliantly. No one could remember seeing a boy spin the ball so far and so accurately. At the age of 20, he had arrived in the right place at exactly the right time. The

Australian selectors were desperate to find a young leg spinner who might take on the West Indies and end its domination of international cricket. And Warne was one of a small handful who had this potential.

Two months later, when the season ended, he found himself sent to the brand new Cricket Academy in Adelaide, run by the Australian Institute of Sport. He was being given a free ride to the top. If he was good enough to get there, nothing would stand in his way.

4

Boys will be Boys

*He continued to do what he wanted, and whatever he
thought was in Shane Warne's best interests.*

The Cricket Academy's head coach, Jack Potter, did not
know what to make of Warne when they first met in
Adelaide in May 1990. There was no doubt the 20-year-
old was friendly, but he tried so hard to be liked at their
first meeting that Potter wanted to back away. He figured
he was 'either a con man or a very nice guy'. But he was
not sure which.

Potter had received a call from Jim Higgs in Victoria a
couple of weeks earlier, after the start of the season, asking him to accept an extra recruit, and he had gladly said
yes. The new arrival was a year or two older than the
other young cricketers and had not earned his place by
playing for Australia at junior level, as they had done.
According to Higgs, he was overweight and needed some
discipline, but he could really spin the ball, and the
academy might do him some good. It was the middle of
winter, so Potter took the new boy down to the indoor
nets at the Adelaide Oval to see what he could do. And
he was amazed. Standing there while Warne bowled, he

caught balls in a baseball glove as they bounced over his shoulder and listened to the fizz as they curved through the air. 'It was unbelievable', he says today. 'It always bounces high on those mats, but it was the noise as well.' Potter had seen plenty of talented kids in his time, but Warne was miles ahead of them.

The Australian Institute of Sport (AIS) Cricket Academy has produced a fantastic crop of Australian Test cricketers since it was set up in 1988 – with Ricky Ponting, Greg Blewett, Justin Langer, Damien Martyn and Shane Warne among its more illustrious names – but in those early days it had plenty of critics who thought it a waste of taxpayers' money, so its managers were anxious to avoid bad publicity of any sort. Unfortunately for them, Warne had a knack of attracting it, as they would soon find out.

The academy's mission was to take the brightest young cricketers in Australia and make them the best, by sharpening their skills and toughening them up. But at this stage there was fundamental disagreement about how the job should be done and whether the AIS should be doing it. While the Australian Cricket Board thought the boys could just be given a bit of coaching in the off season and introduced to a few ex-Test cricketers, Jack Potter and his deputy, Peter Spence, had a far more radical concept in mind. They wanted to treat the cricketers like any other professional athletes and show them what champions had to do to get to the top. And this created problems.

Spence and Potter wanted their charges to sprint, swim, run up sandhills, lift weights and do punishing circuits in the gym, so they could bowl better, run faster, hit the ball harder and have more stamina for long days in the field. But some of the young cricketers on their $20,000 government scholarships – Warne in particular – didn't work as hard as their new masters expected. They had not devoted their lives to pushing themselves through the pain barrier, as runners and swimmers do, and they weren't keen to start. They were young boys in their late teens, away from home for the first time, who were determined to have fun. They did not have far to look.

Half of the group, including Shane, was billeted in a big pub called the Alberton Hotel in Port Adelaide, which was well away from the AIS headquarters, and well away from any supervision. While they weren't actually allowed to drink in the bars, because it would look bad for young sportsmen to be getting pissed at taxpayers' expense, there was nothing to stop them going down the road for a few beers, which they did.

According to Brendan Flynn, who ran the AIS in Adelaide for 10 years from 1988, most of the cricketers drank too much. Australian Test teams of the 1970s and 1980s were legendary for their alcoholic achievements – with competitions on international flights as to who could drink the most beers – and it seemed to Flynn that his pupils had adopted these stars as their role models. 'Things were always happening', he says. 'One night it would be 16 people trying to get into a car to come home. Another night it would be a glass thrown in a bar. One time it was a door destroyed in the hostel.' The crowning glory was when an academy team went out on the town the night before an overseas tour. On arrival at Adelaide airport next morning to catch the flight, one of them vomited all over the floor in the public concourse, because he had drunk so much grog.

Naturally, the cricketers also partied, chased women and stayed out late, as lads in their late teens would be expected to do. And none went at it harder than Shane and his new best buddy, Damien Martyn. 'Women loved Warney', says one academy coach, 'and he loved them.' Soon he was a well-known face on the Adelaide nightclub circuit, with one club manager telling the local paper that Shane was 'outstanding' at pyjama parties.

The cricketers' carousing did not go down well with the hard-working, super-fit cyclists at the AIS, with whom some shared a hostel, and there was occasional friction between the two groups, because the cricketers would roll in at three am just as the cyclists were getting out of bed to go on their 60-kilometre training ride. Warne, meanwhile, who was staying at the pub in Port Adelaide, often arrived at training looking like he had not been to bed at all. And if he was late, as he often was, two or three of his mates would be late as well, because they relied on his Cortina for a ride into town.

When he did get to training, he was also not the keenest. He had shed some of the 100 kilos he was carrying on his return from Bristol six months earlier, but he was still the heaviest of all the cricketers, apart from one fast bowler, and his weight had a habit of climbing when it was meant to be heading down. The academy did monthly skinfold tests on the cricketers to measure their percentage of body fat, and the sum of eight of these tests was supposed to be 77, which indicated an average of around 10 per cent fat. Justin Langer and Greg Blewett, who were fitness fanatics, came in under the bar. Shane clocked in at 156, which was more than twice the body fat he was meant to have.

At St Kilda he had acquired the nickname Showbags, because he looked great on the outside but was always full of shit. And his new mates at the academy adopted it enthusiastically. But Peter Spence was not amused by him being so out of shape. 'He was on a $20,000 scholarship', he says, 'and you expect some commitment, and I thought Shane didn't have it. He was partying hard and he was ill-disciplined. We wanted to make these boys into high-performance athletes, and regular intensive training is a part of that. Shane wasn't into that. He would train for a bit, then go aside for a smoke. I just didn't think he had the discipline.'

Spence's boss, Brendan Flynn, felt much the same. 'Warnie was not suited to a sporting institution where regular daily activities have to be taken up', he says today. 'He didn't have the greatest diet in the world. He seemed to exist on fish and chips, pies and pasties, with a couple of dozen beers to wash it down and a couple of cigarettes afterwards.' Flynn and Spence could both see that Warne was a natural, whether he was bowling, batting or catching in the slips. But this only made them more disappointed by his attitude. 'There were lots of talented cricketers at the academy', says Spence, 'but there were plenty who wasted their talent, and I thought he was going to be one of them.'

Jack Potter was a bit more inclined to forgive, having shelved his initial doubts, and was charmed by the boy. So he came to an arrangement with him: 'I told him about cigarettes and rules, how he couldn't mix with Olympic athletes and smoke. And I said, "If I catch you, you're out." He just replied, "Don't worry, you'll never see me do it." And I never did. Of course, I knew that he ducked out the back for a fag.'

As a former leg spinner himself, Potter appreciated Warne's genius. And his pupil knew Jack had plenty to teach, so he was prepared to listen. Potter told him he had the skills to be a good bowler but lacked control. 'I said to him: "There are two blokes you've probably never heard of. One is called Richie Benaud, who had great accuracy; the other is Johnny Martin, who could spin it a mile. If you want to be great, you've got to put those two together."'

Potter then asked Warne how he was going to get batsmen out. 'I'll just bowl at 'em', came the reply.

'No', said Potter, 'that won't work. They'll just sit back and wait for your bad ball and hit you for four.'

Potter told him he needed variety, as well as the leg break and the wrong 'un that he already bowled, to keep batsmen guessing and sucker them into playing the wrong shot. He suggested the slider, the one that keeps straight when the batsman expects it to turn, and a more difficult alternative: 'You can take it or leave it. It's called the flipper. It bounces halfway down the pitch and looks like a long hop. Then it skids through and knocks your stumps over. Benaud used to bowl it and got lots of wickets.'

The flipper is almost certainly the hardest ball for any bowler to learn, let alone to master. It has the same rotation of the wrist as a leg break, but is squeezed out of the front of the hand with backspin, so it shoots through, straight and low. It's a ball that Australia's champion leg spinner from the 1930s, Clarrie Grimmett, is said to have practised for 12 years before bowling it in anger, and it is so hard on the hand that some coaches have refused to teach it. Not surprisingly, Warne had great trouble with it. 'He used to hit the side of the net, the roof, everything', Potter told cricket writer Ken Piesse in 1995.

But after weeks of trying in the nets, and threatening to give up, he suddenly cracked it. 'He came up to me and said, "I think I've got it",' says Potter. 'He had been playing cricket in the corridor of the hotel with a tennis ball and he had them both worked out.'

It was soon clear that Warne was one of the stars, and not just after dark. When a youth team went on a tour of the West Indies in August, with several academy members, he was voted the most popular player by the opposing team. Always positive, always the joker, he was fun to be around. But some thought him a bit full of himself. He was mad on gambling, golf and having fun, and he always wanted to be the centre of attention – farting on the bus, prancing round the changing rooms with no clothes on, even playing with his penis by bending it into funny shapes – no doubt a useful trick at parties. It was the sort of thing that schoolboys split their sides over, but they were no longer schoolboys and some got tired of it.

According to Greg Blewett, he also had 'an attitude problem', which meant he did what he wanted and not much else. He refused to run round the field at the end of a day's play – or so he claims in *Shane Warne, My Own Story* – preferring to have a drink and a chat about cricket. And when he was asked to stick a thermometer up his backside to test water loss and heat gain – which the scientists at the academy wanted to study – he baulked at it, hiding the contraption in his shorts when no one was looking and copying the reading from someone else. In his life story, he proudly tells the tale to show how ridiculous the rules were. But his minders at the academy did not find him so funny. Peter Spence admits today, 'I honestly didn't think he'd make it. He was a larrikin – that's why Australians love him – but I thought that would bring him under. And off the field, I suppose it has done.'

To pull him into line and save him from his own stupidity, Warne needed someone on his case, and he was lucky enough to find the perfect match in Terry Jenner. T. J., as he likes to be known, is a bit of a larrikin himself, who bowled leg spin for Australia in Ian Chappell's team of the 1970s, then became addicted to gambling. He had just come out of jail – broke and with a broken marriage – after taking money from his employer to gamble in the hope of being able to wipe out his debts. T. J. was still on parole when he first met Warne in September 1990 and he was still reeling from the humiliation of it all. He had been asked by the academy to help coach their young cricketers – as much for his welfare as for theirs, perhaps – and on his first day at the indoor cricket school, he had barely been able to walk through the door. 'I had to take a few deep breaths. I was too embarrassed to look anybody in the eye', he says today.

After a few weeks, he tried to persuade Peter Spence that the academy had no one worth teaching. 'I was really looking for an out', he says. Spence told him they had a talented lad, still touring the West Indies, who could really bowl and might be just what Jenner was looking for. 'You might like him', said Spence, 'but he's not easy to handle.' In his book, *TJ Over the Top*, Jenner describes his first meeting with Warne soon afterwards:

> I looked up and saw this chubby, cheeky bloke with blond, spiked hair . . .
> 'What do you want me to do?' he asked.
> 'Just bowl me a leg break.'
> Without any real warm-up he bowled this leg break which curved half a metre and spun just as far! It was seemingly effortless, yet a magnificent delivery.
> '&%#@ me', I said to myself. 'What have we got here?'

It was the best leg break Jenner had seen in his life, but it wasn't just Warne's talent that bowled him over. He liked the boy and saw in him a free spirit, a fellow rule breaker. 'He was totally uncomplicated. What you saw was what you got . . . he was young, inexperienced and a non-conformist.' Years later both men readily admit how important the other has been. 'T. J. has been fantastic for me my whole career', Warne told a press conference in 2005. 'Every time I spend with him is great.' Jenner goes further, describing Warne as his personal and professional salvation. And others are convinced he also saved Shane. Brendan Flynn is one of many who believe that Warne would never have become the world's greatest bowler if he had not met T. J. Indeed, he wonders whether Warne would even be alive.

Jenner was amazed by what Warne could do with the ball, just as Potter had been, and with the way he made it fizz. But he was soon reworking the newly learned flipper, getting Warne to slow it down and give it some loop, so it looked more like a leg break and was harder for batsmen to pick. Jenner was impressed by how quickly he could put the lessons into practice and by his cocky sense of humour, which leg spinners need for the many times when they get hit for six. He could see something else too, behind the bravado, that many people missed, and this was the insecurity that is so obvious in Warne today. He desperately wanted people to like him, to praise him, to say how good he was. 'Why is he like that?' asks Jenner, 'I don't know. Maybe that's the way he's made.'

Even if they don't start out that way, insecurity is the fate of almost every leg spinner, Jenner believes, because their daily experience encourages self-doubt. 'You're told not to bring your girlfriend to the game because she'll go off with the fast bowler. Then your dad and mum come down and you don't get a bowl. And if you are brought on, all the other parents go and sit in front of their windscreens. It's the same with your team-mates: you can see their shoulders start to droop. You get smashed around the park. No one believes in you. That's what every leg spinner has to endure.'

Leg spinners such as Warne, says Jenner, are blessed with a special G.I.F.T. But if the G means God-given, the F stands for Fragile. To illustrate the point, Jenner digs out a DVD, shot in Hobart in 2005, in which he asks Shane what a leg spinner needs most to succeed. In reply, Warne shoots back, without pausing for thought: 'Love is the overriding factor. What you need is love. It's the old arm round the shoulder from your captain to say you're going okay, make you feel good. Lots of love.'

But Shane's need for approval doesn't stem just from his leg-spin bowling. He was almost 21 when he first met Jenner, yet he was still so young, naïve and in need of support that he couldn't say anything without looking over to his new mentor and asking, 'Isn't that right, Terry?'

'He trusted me so much', says Jenner, 'he gave me a feeling of responsibility. I had to really think hard about what I said to him.'

Just as famous golfers have their gurus – Faldo had Leadbetter, Norman had Harmon – so Warne has had Jenner. Seven or eight times over the years he has helped Shane in times of trouble, sometimes with dramatic effect. However, on this first acquaintance their partnership was cut off in its prime, because having been fast-tracked into the academy because of his talent, Shane was soon being fast-tracked out again because he refused to behave himself.

Before Jenner's arrival, Warne had got himself into serious trouble on a team trip to Darwin by making obscene remarks and gestures to a couple of Asian women. Melbourne's *Sunday Age* reported two years later, after he became famous, that he had taken off all his clothes and jumped into a hotel swimming pool in front of two girls who were sunbathing. The version offered by Jenner is that he 'dropped his daks and browneyed them'. But as readers already know, the real story is far saltier than that, and was a harbinger of problems to come.

Warne was with a team from the academy, staying in one of Darwin's university colleges before a match against the Northern Territory. And it was here that the trouble occurred. Jack Potter, who was in charge of the team, came back from dinner at nine pm to find a note on his door from the college chaplain demanding he get down to his office immediately, and there he was told that one of his young cricketers had exposed himself to a female student. Some hours earlier, it seems, three Asian girls had been relaxing by the college pool when one of the academy boys had attracted their attention by sticking his bare buttocks out the window. Moments later, another had come up to them in his dressing gown, opened it wide and said: 'Hey girls, how'd ya like to suck on this?' A third had stood and laughed – until the shit hit the fan.

One of the girls, whose boyfriend was a fourth-year law student, had lodged an official complaint and was threatening to call the police. And the chaplain was in no doubt she would press charges if nothing was done. It hardly needs saying – given that the Cricket Academy had enemies in Canberra – that the affair threatened to blow up into a major scandal that might put the academy's future at risk. It also hardly needs saying that the boy in the dressing gown was Warne.

Realising the seriousness of the situation, Potter took Warne for a walk and asked him what he knew about sexual harassment. Warne said he had no idea what he was talking about. Potter then told him of the girl's complaint that he had exposed himself. Warne's reaction was to describe it all as a harmless joke and to offer a string of excuses, which apparently included the suggestion that one famous Australian Test cricketer did this constantly. Potter told him bluntly what was at stake: 'If this gets out in the press, I will get slayed and the AIS will get slayed.' He also warned him that if the AIS took no action, the girl would go to the police and press charges against him.

Brendan Flynn, who was down in Adelaide at the time, remembers getting a call late that night, which he believed to be coming from Darwin's Police Station. He refuses to go into great detail, but says he was told it was a 'major indiscretion' and he believed the police would bring charges – presumably for indecency or sexual assault. A three-way conversation between Flynn, Potter and Warne then ensued, after which it was decided that the three boys would be sent home on the bus to Adelaide, which would give them three days to think about what they had done.

Potter went back to the chaplain and told him what the AIS planned to do, and there the matter ended. The complainant was satisfied, the police were kept out of it and a scandal was avoided. But if Warne survived the incident, he did not change his ways. According to Flynn, 'He continued to do what he wanted, and whatever he thought was in Shane Warne's best interests.' And before long he was in trouble again.

By October 1990, Potter and Spence had both moved on from the academy, having apparently decided they couldn't work together, and a new team had taken over. The new head coach was an ex-South Australian fast bowler, Andrew Sincock, who had heard from Warne's mates that he was a great bloke and a wonderful character, and was inclined to agree. His first impression was of a chubby lad 'with blond hair and a big smile, who had real charisma, an aura about him. He was just really pleased to meet you and keen to get on with things. He wanted to live life, to do everything.'

Like so many people, Sincock was dazzled by Warne's charm and talent, and prepared to be tolerant about his laid-back approach to life at the academy. 'He was a 21-year-old who wanted to have a good time. He didn't like the hardest work in the world, but he did it. He didn't like running up sandhills or the gym sessions, but he did them. He never caused havoc for me.' Nor did Sincock try to curb his carousing. 'I just wanted to make sure they made it to training. They were all pretty good, including Shane. A couple of times they turned up late or a bit ordinary, but they weren't too bad.'

But Barry Causby, who took over the deputy's job from Peter Spence, had stricter ideas about how his boys should behave, and he was less smitten with the wise-cracking, blond-haired spinner. What is more, the dislike was mutual. He and Warne sniped at each other for a couple of months until it came to a showdown at training. Struggling up the sandhills one morning on their punishing weekly run, Warne was lagging behind his team-mates. Causby told him to try harder because he was letting his team-mates down, and Shane told him to 'Fuck off'.

According to Terry Jenner it was more, 'Oh, fuck off', as in 'I *am* trying', rather than the more direct, 'Why don't you fuck off?' But this fine distinction, if there was one, was lost on Causby. 'It was a tough training session', he says, 'but we expected our athletes to put in and he wasn't.' The bigger issue was undoubtedly the challenge to Causby's authority, and once again Warne became the subject of a formal complaint. Jenner took Causby out for a drink to try to hose him down and tell him that Warne was a genius, a bit of a rebel but not a bad lad. But this plea for clemency fell on deaf ears. Causby was a public servant and a stickler for discipline and he felt there was an important principle involved.

He was also angry. So angry that an AIS official had to fly across from Canberra to find a solution. A top-level meeting was held, in which Sincock and Flynn backed Causby, and Warne's fate was sealed. He had already been given plenty of chances and would not be given another. He was duly told that his punishment would be to miss out on the academy's tour of Sri Lanka in January 1991, which Causby was set to manage.

As so often in his life, Warne felt hard done by. As far as he was concerned, it was another tiny mistake that had been blown out of proportion. He was being picked on again, and he had had enough. He talked to Jim Higgs, the man who had introduced him to the academy, and told him he was quitting. Higgs tried to persuade him to hang in there and keep working with Jenner, but it had all gone too far. 'I think they struck a bit of an impasse', says Higgs today.

'So they agreed to part by mutual consent?' I ask.

'You could put it that way, yes', he chuckles.

Clearly the academy was happy to see him go, but they did not need to expel him. As Warne explained later: 'I was the only one left in Adelaide on my own, training. I thought there was no use training by myself. How was I going to learn things on my own? Okay, I stuffed up once but "Don't hang me for it", I thought. In the end I decided . . . I might as well be back in Victoria trying to play for the State.'

He wrote the academy a letter along those lines, dropped it off with Brendan Flynn and waved goodbye to his scholarship. Then he loaded his bags into his Classic Cream Cortina and roared back to Melbourne. In *Shane Warne, My Autobiography* he gives a sanitised version of events that blames the Sri Lanka ban on a 'pool prank' and ignores the blow-up at training. The nearest he comes to self-criticism – after deriding Causby and Spence for being second rate and humourless – is to say:

> I defy any 20-year-old to be on his best behaviour all the time. An environment of total discipline is not conducive to a bunch of lads living away from home, in my opinion anyway. I was just a bit of a lad. I was certainly a bit too direct in my criticism at times, and could also be a little disruptive. It might even be fair to say I was a bit of an idiot. But there was never any nastiness in my behaviour.

On 15 February 1991, a couple of weeks after leaving the academy, Warne made his debut for Victoria against Western Australia at the Junction Oval, St Kilda's home ground. He was overweight, with hair down to his shoulders, and so nervous he could hardly feel the ball in his hand. As Ken Piesse records in *The Complete Shane Warne*, his first two balls were hit for four, his third ball for three, and his first two overs cost 20 runs. On occasions, he bowled so wide on the popping crease that he was warned he could be no-balled. It was not the most promising baptism, but the veteran Test batsman Graeme Wood still remembers it well, because it was the only time he ever faced Warne and he whacked him around the ground on his way to 166. Warne's sole wicket from 37 overs that cost 102 runs, came after Tom Moody had hit him for a huge six into the dirt mounds. Trying it again two balls later, the Test star hit a skier to Damien Fleming at long on who took the catch.

Fleming was nervous as the ball came down. He knew how much it meant to Warne, who was a mate from the academy's tour of the West Indies six months earlier. And he still remembers the relief on Shane's face when he held it. But this single scalp was not enough to persuade Victoria's coach, Les Stillman, that his new recruit deserved another chance. 'He got belted down at the Junction that day', he recalls. 'I remember throwing a few balls back that had been hit for six. He bowled some terrible stuff.'

It was Warne's one and only appearance for Victoria that season. Then it was back to St Kilda, where his welcome home present was a game for the club's Second XI.

5

A Star is Warne

He liked to drink. And he liked the girls.
He had one or two, yeah.

After playing only one match for Victoria and being dumped, Warne took off to England for the winter to play club cricket again, which was a far better option than going back to delivering pizzas or humping beds for Forty Winks. This time he headed for the Lancashire League, where stars such as Viv Richards, Bobby Simpson and Kapil Dev have earned a quid over the years, and took up the job of cricket professional at Accrington, which is an old cotton town some 25 kilometres north of Manchester and 30 kilometres from the sea at Blackpool.

Warne was lucky to get the gig. Accrington's chairman, Peter Barratt, had already lined up Tasmanian all-rounder Shaun Young for the job, and Shane only came in as a last-minute replacement when Young pulled out through injury. Warne was keen, cheap and available, and Accrington was desperate. Normally they paid their pro £7000 for the season, but they offered Warne £4000 in hand plus accommodation and a car, and he jumped at the chance. So in mid-April 1991, only two days before the season was due to start, Barratt drove down the M6 motorway to Nuneaton service station to rendezvous with one of Shane's old mates from Bristol, who had agreed to drive him up from Heathrow. Barratt had no idea how he would recognise the lad, but it wasn't hard to spot him. He was tanned with lots of blond hair and he looked, well, Australian.

Accrington's cricket ground in Thorneyholme Road is out of town on the edge of the moors, with hills rising to the east. The setting is wonderful, but the facilities less so: the clubhouse is a concrete-rendered two-storey affair, the boundary walls are breeze block and the seating is white plastic. Although not one of the richer or more successful clubs in the league, Accrington does have a proud history. They've been playing cricket on this patch of turf for almost 130 years and in Accrington for 160. And in the long-distant past the locals took on an English XI and held them to a draw, with 7000 people cheering them on. Nowadays, you might see one-tenth of that number turn out for a weekend game, but cricket is still in the blood. The 14 teams that make up the Lancashire League all come from the local area, within a 20-minute car ride, and Accrington itself boasts four of them.

You don't have to stop long in this part of England to realise that it's one of the wettest areas in the country. And what strikes the Australian eye is how green it all is as a result. There are green trees around the cricket ground, green fields beyond, and impossibly thick green grass to play on. The summer of 1991 was apparently no wetter than usual, but half of Accrington's games in the early part of the season were rained on or abandoned, so

Warne spent long hours in the pavilion, dodging showers and drinking lager. And when he did to get to play, the pitches were damp and muddy. Such conditions are a great leveller in cricket, but it makes life hard for bowlers. 'You could have Allan Donald bowling', says Brad McNamara, the former New South Wales all-rounder, who spent the season with Warne in Lancashire, 'and the pitch would be so soft he'd be struggling to get his mother out'.

Warne struggled too. It took him three matches to get his first four wickets, and Accrington must have wondered what they had let themselves in for. But it was doubtless hard for him to adjust. He was often rugged up in three or four sweaters to ward off the cold, and conditions were hardly ideal for leg spin. The ball was wet, his hands were numb, the pitches were sodden, the boundaries were short and the catching left a lot to be desired. A couple of times he came up against a top-class batsman, such as the South Australian Joe Scuderi, and got hit for a few sixes. But generally he did not go for a stack of runs, he just couldn't get wickets. 'He was spinning it a long way but not landing it in the right place', says Barratt.

The rules of the Lancashire League allow each club to have just one professional, so the teams always have more bunnies than stars. With luck you might get one or two good young amateurs, but most of the players are local enthusiasts: the butcher, the milkman, the fish-and-chip shop owner, and a gaggle of pale-faced teenagers. 'There might be two or three who could play first grade in Australia', says McNamara, 'and two or three who could play second grade, but the rest are there to field and carry the beer. So they rely on the pro to win them matches. It's his job to smash a quick 100 then get 7-for to bring them home.'

But Warne's batting was no better than his bowling. On his debut he was run out for two, and in his first home game he was skittled first ball in front of several hundred lager-fuelled Accrington supporters. Eighteen months later, he told Australia's *Cricketer* magazine it was the most embarrassing moment of his life:

> I was feeling very confident and strutted out. I had a little bit of arrogance about me. The crowd was right behind me yelling and screaming. I take centre, look around the field and notice how far back the slips are for their professional, Rudi Bryson, a fast bowler from South Africa. But that doesn't bother me. Here we go.
>
> He runs in and lets it go. I'm half way forward before I realise it has passed me. It cannons into the stumps. I've been bowled – first nut. This time the crowd doesn't say much except for a few who declare: 'You're a buddin' pro. Go home pro', in their accents.

The crowd had been drinking for a few hours, according to Warne, and he had possibly sunk a couple too, because the man who bowled him was not Bryson, the South African Test fast bowler, but a local lad called Steve Dearden, who later played for Lancashire. Or perhaps it was the beers after the game that fogged his memory, because no one in the clubhouse would say a word to him until he threw his wages onto the bar and shouted drinks for everyone. After that, he was popular with his team-mates, who found him cheerful, likeable and a good laugh. The selectors were not so happy with him, though, because his poor form on the field continued, and it took him 10 innings before he passed 100 runs with the bat.

The cold obviously made life hard. 'He stopped with us for the first two weeks', says Barratt, 'and there were blankets and sweaters all over the place.' But he also fell sick. 'I got a call from him one time asking me, "Can you come and help?"', says Barratt, 'and when I got over there he had a boil on his bottom. I had to drive him to the local hospital to get it lanced.' Barratt also had to ferry him to the chemist a number of times, first for a bad cold, then for a chest infection.

But even when he recovered, Warne did not take his work as seriously as the club committee expected. It was the pro's job to take the team in hand, look after the coaching and provide leadership and, just as at the academy, he was more interested in having a good time. As his old friend Brendan McArdle puts it, 'He was a young boy and I don't think he understood the responsibilities of being a pro.'

McArdle had first set eyes on Warne 18 months earlier at Dandenong with Rodney Hogg, when the 'little fat blond spinner' had come on and bowled so well. And, just like Hogg, he had been mightily impressed. He had taken a liking to the boy and helped him land the job at Accrington. McArdle had played in the Lancashire League for many years, and on this occasion had brought over a dozen or so Australian cricketers in their early 20s. According to one of the locals, he was also acting as mentor and nursemaid to Warne.

Several of the other Australians were McArdle's mates from Melbourne University CC, which rendered them relatively well-educated and sophisticated, and their first impression of Warne was that he was a bit of a bogan. Bogan, for those who don't speak the lingo, means working-class lout. With his long, dyed-blond hair and gold earring, he was not like most other cricketers. But before long, most got to like him, and they could see he had talent. 'We all reckoned he was pretty good', says McArdle. 'He was the best leg spinner I'd seen for a very long time.'

He was also 'a bit of a cheeky prick', according to Brad McNamara, who had just started playing for New South Wales. At their first encounter, Warne asked him bluntly: 'How the fuck do you play first-class cricket bowling that sort of shit?'

The Lancashire clubs played two matches a weekend, or one if they got knocked out of the cup, and had two practice sessions a week. But the rest of the time was free. So Shane and the other Aussies spent their summer having fun: playing tennis and golf, and drinking, followed by more tennis, more golf and more drinking, before settling down to the serious business of going out to pubs and nightclubs, which they did three or four times a week. 'We had an absolute ball', says Shaun Daish, another youngster from Victoria.

Warne and Daish had digs together in a two-bed terrace house two minutes from Accrington's cricket ground, but they were rarely there alone. The club chairman, Peter Barratt, remembers going to check on them one Monday morning and finding bodies everywhere. 'There were eight of them – Australians – sleeping all over the house. They'd been out Sunday night for a good time after the game.'

When they weren't whooping it up at Warney's they were often round at McArdle's place in nearby Church. Jim Wilkinson, then cricket writer for the *Accrington Observer*, rented the house next door to McArdle, and could hear them through the wall late on Sunday nights when he was trying to get to sleep. 'There were all kinds of shenanigans and carryings on', says Wilkinson. 'Loud music, drunken uproarious noises late at night, women back there. I had to go to work on Monday mornings. They didn't have practice till Tuesday night.'

Wilkinson has vivid memories of meeting Warne for the first time in a pub across the road. 'Brendan came round one day, wanting to borrow an iron. It was about 4.30 pm. He asked if I could go across to the Old Queen to hold Shane's hand. He was fresh off the plane, sitting there at the bar with two girls. If you'd added their age and IQ together you wouldn't have got to 70, and their age would have been about 34 of that', says Wilkinson. 'I had a half-pint while Brendan ironed his shirt, and then left them to it. If you'd looked at the lad, fag in his mouth, pretty overweight, sat there with his blond hair and red leather zip-up bomber jacket, you wouldn't have thought he was any kind of athlete at all.'

Despite his excess pounds, Warne was a wow with the Lancashire lasses. 'There was a bit of summat even then', says one of his old Accrington drinking pals. 'He was very confident, and he wasn't shy with the girls.' Or, in the words of another mate, 'He liked to drink. And he liked the girls. He had one or two, yeah. He was single, a good-looking lad, a professional cricketer. Yeah, he had one or two.'

Years later, when he became famous, the British tabloids would go trawling through Accrington looking for scandal, unearthing one or two stories of his drinking and womanising. But Barratt says there was nothing major. 'He was a great guy with a good personality, very likeable', he says. 'We had some fun with him, though. You were always wondering what he was up to next.'

'What sort of thing?' I enquire.

'Oh, no serious trouble. He did a bit of it here and there. Just the normal things that a 21-year-old gets up to.'

If Barratt and his committee did worry about his off-field frolics, it was only because Warne was taking his eye off the cricket, for which he was paid to be there. Before long the locals got Australian coach Bobby Simpson to pull him into line. Simpson had played for Accrington back in the 1950s and knew the club well, and Barratt says he was in regular touch with Warne that summer. But as to what he means exactly by pulling him into line, Accrington's chairman is not saying: 'He's got plenty of press on things like that and I don't want to add to it. I never really felt he got out of hand. Altogether they were a lovely bunch of lads. He didn't get into any serious trouble.'

Warne's bowling got better in the second half of the season, and in the last six weeks he hit his straps, picking up five and six wickets in a couple of games. And one of his Accrington team-mates reckons he would have taken more scalps if he hadn't been so difficult to play. 'His bowling was superb', says Damian Clarke, 'but he was just too good for a lot of batters. He did too much for 'em. I faced him in the nets a couple of times and I don't think I actually hit the ball.'

Peter Barratt's son, Paul, who was a half-decent batsman, also had trouble. 'In the nets he could bowl five or six different balls on the trot. He'd give you the leg spinner, the googly, the slider, the flipper and the rest one after the other. And coming out of his hand you didn't know what it was going to do. He pretty much bamboozled most of the amateurs who faced him, that's for sure.' Barratt kept wicket to him three or four times and had to rely on Shane's old semaphore system to know what was on the way. 'He'd give you signals as to what he was going to do. He might play with his hanky if he was going to bowl the flipper, or scratch his head if it was going to be a googly.' Once again, few opposing batsmen cracked the code.

Despite all these plaudits, Accrington's cricket committee decided not to re-sign Warne for the following year. They had to tell him by mid-July, to give him (and themselves) enough time to make other arrangements, so they missed some of his better performances, but the truth was that he had a pretty disappointing season. In the previous season, another Australian bowler, Colin Miller, had knocked over 100 wickets and scored 1078 runs for Rawtenstall. And Peter Sleep, the Australian Test spinner whom Rodney Hogg had dubbed inferior to Warne, had done almost as well with 71 wickets and 1294 runs for Rishton. Shane, by comparison, ended up with 73 wickets but only 329 runs and Accrington felt his batting just was not good enough. One of his supporters got up a petition to persuade the committee to let him stay, and about 40 people signed, but it was to no avail.

The glossy official history, of course, puts a slightly more glorious spin on it all. If you go to the Lancashire League's website you can read a story of derring-do that would sit well in a Boy's Own Annual. It was the 'match of a lifetime' and a day on which Shane beat Accrington's arch rivals Ramsbottom almost single-handed.

It was May 1991, the first round of the Matthew Brown Worsley Cup, and Accrington was playing at home. It won the toss and made a modest 166 all out. Ramsbottom then raced to 2 for 107 before rain set in. When the match resumed the next evening, the Rams needed 60 runs to win off 18 overs and were cruising to victory. Then one wicket fell, and another, and another, and another and another, with Warne stemming the flow of runs as he scythed the batsmen down. Finally it came to the last over with 10 runs needed and three wickets left.

Accrington's wicket-keeper Mick Wilson – who seems to have been as baffled by Warne's bowling as the batsmen – takes up the tale. 'It was a Monday night and I had been working all day after playing on Sunday, so I was very tired. They went into the last over, which Shane was to bowl, needing 10 to win. There was a leg bye off the first ball which brought Jonathan Fielding on strike. He charged down the wicket and missed the ball completely. The ball spun right up out of my gloves at shoulder height, giving him the chance to get back. Exactly the same thing happened next ball.'

Fielding, who was just 17 years old, was not deterred. Next ball he charged down the wicket again and connected for a huge six into the cow pasture. And excited by this success, he tried again, missed for the third time and was finally stumped. There was now just one ball left, and three runs needed, and the poor wicket-keeper had a dilemma: should be drop back to ensure he stopped the ball, or should he stand up and risk it going for four? He took courage in his hands and was rewarded. The batsman missed, the keeper collected, and Accrington left the pitch with a famous victory . . . only to be knocked out in the next round. They have not beaten the Rams since then.

Accrington's lack of interest in signing Warne for another season may have left him disappointed, but he had other fish to fry. Thanks to Jim Higgs, who was still a national selector, he had been picked for an Australian XI to tour Zimbabwe, so he had to pack his bags and leave Lancashire before the end of the season. Happily, he was now in much better form, but in Melbourne there was some argument about his selection. Victorian coach Les Stillman, who wasn't wild about spinners and had watched Warne get battered on his debut in February, said it was premature and unwarranted. But Higgs felt Australia's selectors had a right to back their hunches, and the nation needed a spinner, so it was worth the risk.

Selection for Zimbabwe meant that he was now mixing with the best cricketers in Australia, including Mark Taylor, the tour captain, and Steve Waugh. He was also under the eye of one of the Test selectors, John Benaud, who was acting as team manager. It was a good time to bowl well, and in the second match against a Zimbabwe team that included a couple of decent batsmen, he took seven wickets for only 49 runs. Benaud noted that he spun the ball a long way, had good variety and a robust sense of humour. But Steve Waugh was less restrained. 'The first time I saw him', he bubbled, 'I just couldn't believe how good he was, you know. It was like watching a young genius. You could hear the ball fizzing through the air and it was just turning square, and I thought where's this bloke come from?'

Brad McNamara, a close friend of Waugh's for many years, heard the buzz as soon as Australia's future captain landed back in Sydney. 'Steve's not one to rave', he says, 'but after Zimbabwe he ranted on about how good he was. He said, "He's unbelievable, you've got to see him. He's the best bowler I've ever seen."'

Another of Waugh's New South Wales team-mates, fast bowler Mike Whitney, also remembers the excitement. 'Steve said to me, "Man, you should see this sucker from Victoria. He's tubby, he's got a mullet, he smokes a shit-load of cigarettes and he likes a drink, but fuck, he can spin a ball. He's got everything."'

It's a fair bet that Warne was in Waugh's ear in Zimbabwe a few times about how hard it would be for him to make the Victorian team, despite his touring success. And soon the suggestion was being made that Shane should move to Sydney. Waugh and Taylor reckoned it would be fantastic to have him playing for New South Wales and bowling at the SCG, which was a notoriously good spinner's track. So they set about persuading him to up sticks and move north from

Melbourne, with the promise of a spot alongside the Waugh brothers at Steve's home club, Bankstown.

There's no doubt the offer was attractive. And at one stage Shane even told Waugh he was coming. He was friendly with Steve's younger brother Dean, whom he had got to know in Lancashire, and he must have felt that his prospects would be better than in Victoria, where the odds were stacked against him. Two other good spinners, Peter McIntyre and Paul Jackson, were ahead of him in the pecking order for the state side and his debut against Western Australia had been a bit of a shambles. What's more, Victorian coach Les Stillman was inclined to think all three of them were a waste of space. Stillman made no secret of his belief that spinners were a luxury, and that the way to win matches was to have four good fast bowlers. In fact, Victoria had just won the Sheffield Shield with this policy in place.

As the countdown to the season began, there were rumours in the Melbourne papers that Shane might be shipping out. But when the Victorian squad assembled for their first practice match at the MCG, he was still there and still in a dither. So, half an hour before the game was due to start, Les Stillman and Victorian captain Simon O'Donnell decided it was time he made up his mind. The ultimatum went pretty much like this: 'If you are not going, good. If you are, piss off now, we don't want you playing today.' Warne was given half an hour to choose what his future would be. 'I suppose it was pretty daunt-ing, pretty ruthless', says Stillman today, 'but it got a decision out of him.' And that was to stay and play.

Warne was immediately rewarded for his loyalty – or

his reluctance to upset his old team-mates – because he was pencilled in for Victoria's first match of the season at the MCG. And on this, his second, outing he did himself justice, taking four wickets in an innings against Tasmania and having Australia's number three batsman, David Boon, dropped for 0. His performance was a taste of things to come, with close fielders clustered round the bat and pressure mounting. Almost one-third of his 47 overs were maidens, and he gave away only 75 runs, a remarkable feat for a leg spinner.

A couple of weeks before the game, the Melbourne *Sunday Age*'s cricket writer Mark Ray had been tipped off by Brendan McArdle about a young leggie at St Kilda who 'could be anything', which presumably meant his potential was limitless. Ray had taken a trip down to the Junction Oval to watch him in the nets. 'He was chubby, with long spiky, blond hair', he recalls. 'He wasn't cocky, but he looked you straight in the eye, which is good. And I took this picture of him in a T-shirt which had huge letters that said: "Save water, drink beer".'

Ray was an old spinner himself, had played five seasons of first-class cricket for New South Wales and Tasmania, and knew a bit about the craft. It was immediately clear to him that Warne was a freak. 'He had a phenomenal talent. He could spin the ball a mile but he was accurate too. They told me if I stood behind the bat I would hear his fingers snap, and I could, from 25 metres away.' Ray reckoned the only other bowler who had ever spun the ball like that was Chuck Fleetwood-Smith, whose genius had not brought him happiness. 'He was a phenomenal womaniser and drinker', says Ray, 'and he ended up a wino on the banks of the Yarra.' He clearly had concerns that Warne might end up in similar disarray.

Ray littered his profile – the first to be written on Warne – with descriptions of Warne as 'a bit of a lad', 'a real lad', 'a character' and 'an exuberant character who enjoys a good time', and he noted that the 22-year-old's time at the Cricket Academy had earned him 'a reputation as a conceited trouble maker'. But he also took the line that leg spinners need to be mad to succeed – because they get bashed around so much – and that Warne would fit in well, even though he added the rider: 'Recent observations at close quarters suggest he is not clinically "crazy".'

So even before his career had taken off, Warne was a man whose fame travelled before him. He was also someone who could make cricket traditionalists shake their heads in horror, as he must have done with this sales pitch to Ray about his approach to getting wickets:

> People say to be patient to work the batsman out, but I'm a bit impatient and aggressive, so I think 'Stuff you, mate, I'm going to get you out.' I'll do anything to get a wicket, even try a head high full toss.

A head-high full toss: surely that's not cricket? Yet Warne readily admitted he had used it several times on the Zimbabwe tour.

> We call it the Derryn Hinch ball – expect the un-expected – I usually give midwicket and square leg the nod to move back a bit, then zing it straight at

the batsman's head. It can often surprise him into a mishit.

Within a month, other newspapers were also getting wound up about Shane's prospects, calling him 'the most exciting spinner in the land' and spruiking him for the Test team, despite his inexperience. The national selectors were also taking him seriously. After only two more matches for Victoria – in one of which he went wicketless – he was picked to play for an Australian XI against the West Indies. It was just before Christmas and he accepted the present with thanks, bagging a seven-wicket haul at Hobart's Bellerive Oval.

A couple of days later he was back at the MCG again, but this time as a punter, watching the Boxing Day Test against India with Brendan McArdle, Dean Waugh and a few of his mates. 'We had a couple of beers before we got there, then we got to the ground and had a few more beers', he later recalled. As they stood in the Members Pavilion, pie in one hand, beer in the other, they looked up to see the Australian team coach, Bob Simpson, and team manager, Ian McDonald. It must have been a shock to both parties. As Warne told the story, 'They said, "You look like you're having a good day?" I said: "Yeah, it's pretty good so far." They said: "You know you're a chance to play in the next Test match?"'

Warne had only played four matches for Victoria and had been carrying the drinks two weeks earlier, when he had been made twelfth man against Queensland. And with a few beers inside him, it must all have seemed like a huge joke, so they went back to the Members Bar with their pies and continued having fun. Soon Dean Waugh was introducing Warne to passers-by and shouting to the crowd: 'Hey this bloke's going to play for Australia.' Two days later, Warne got a call from McDonald to tell him it was true.

Warne's reaction was to ring his family and mates and call them round to Beach Road for a celebration party. Next morning, he was too sick to drive, so his father drove him down to the MCG in his Porsche. Shane was supposed to talk to the media and be measured for his gear, but he was so hung-over that he had to head straight for the toilets for a quick vomit. He didn't quite get there, he happily confessed in *Shane Warne, My Own Story*. Then it was off to try on his sweater and baggy green cap and smile for the TV cameras, with an obliging comment on how he felt about the uniform: 'It's beautiful, mate.'

That night the new spin wizard made Channel 9's national news bulletin in a staged backyard celebration with his mum and dad, this time drinking orange juice. Not for the first time, Shane's fashion sense had apparently deserted him. He was sporting a white, purple and orange tracksuit, which would look a treat on the popular TV show *Kath and Kim*, and a huge gold earring. At 97 kilos, he was still grossly overweight. And with his chubby face and long spiky blond hair, he looked like a teenage John Daly. The beer and chips in Accrington had porked him up again.

His mother, Brigitte, was in matching blonde spikes and a white sweatshirt with a message embossed across the chest. But what was even more striking was the way in which she and her husband were standing – like soccer players being introduced to the Queen. Dad was formal, shaking hands with his son. Mum, meanwhile, looked fit to burst. Then, in a short interview, Shane told how proud and privileged he was to be asked to play, and how he had never expected it. After that, there were shots of him bowling in the nets, in very tight white shorts with long white socks pulled up to his knees. And finally it was left to another great Australian spinner, Richie Benaud, to say that he felt 'a touch of apprehension' but also 'a touch of delight' that there was a leg spinner back in the side.

Whether it was daring or desperate to pick him, who could say? But it was only two years since he had been demoted to the St Kilda Third XI and only a year since he had spun out of the Cricket Academy. And since then he had played just seven first-class matches, including four for Victoria, and taken only 26 wickets. It was almost unheard of to risk someone with so little experience and so little form. In England, where leg spinner Ian Salisbury was about to be drafted into the Test team, the selectors would be criticised for picking someone with 70 first-class games under his belt. And there was not yet much evidence on the scoresheet to show that Warne was so much better.

Back in Black Rock his mates couldn't believe it. They're still having trouble today. 'He plays a couple of matches for the Thirds and a year later he's playing Test cricket', says Tim Appel with a touch of poetic licence. 'He couldn't believe it, and neither could we. All of us have had more than a couple of beers since then, talking about how many chances he was given and saying, "That should have been me."'

Jason Dunkley, his footy mate from the St Kilda U19s, was also amazed. He was up on the Murray River in a houseboat, having a holiday with a bunch of old friends, when he picked up a paper and read the big headline: 'BE WARNED'.

'Hey, can you believe this?' he called out, 'Warney's playing for Australia.' Dunkley had watched Shane play cricket and not thought that he was anything special. Nor had his schoolmates at Mentone considered him good enough. But naturally they broke off their journey in Echuca to stop and watch him all the same.

Warne, meanwhile, was on his way to Sydney to prepare for the big day. Mark Ray, who had become one of his fans, saw him at the team hotel in the Rocks shortly after he arrived, standing in the lobby with his parents, looking lost and overawed. He did not know many of the team, and Steve Waugh, whom he knew best, had been dropped after a run of poor form, but David Boon, the team's biggest drinker, was kind enough to take him for a quiet training session. On New Year's Eve, Boon and Geoff Marsh pulled him up onto the roof of the hotel to watch the fireworks. 'We took a few beers, quite a few', Shane enthused afterwards.

Come match day, 2 January, Warne kept close to Marsh so he knew where to go, but when he arrived at the SCG he was still unsure where to dump his gear. Each of the team had their own special place in the dressing-rooms where they liked to sit, so he held back for a bit. 'I waited for a time, and then just sat at the end of a bench. I was scared I would sit in the wrong spot', he told the *Herald Sun*'s Trevor Grant. And when he did drop his bags in an empty space, he was immediately ribbed by his team-mates for stealing Steve Waugh's seat, before it had even got cold. Another sort of welcome to the team.

With Australia batting for the first day and a half, he spent the time in the pavilion, soaking up the atmosphere, but when he did finally take the field it was to a standing ovation from 14,000 fans, who had seen the message flashing on the big electronic scoreboard next to the Hill: 'Congratulations Shane Warne, Australia's 350th Test player'. He was probably too excited to notice that the ground announcer called him Steve. It took an agonising 27 minutes for him to get off the mark, with the crowd cheering optimistically at a couple of leg byes. He ended up hitting two fours and racking up a useful 20 runs before being caught behind off Kapil Dev, one of his child-hood heroes. Bruce Reid, in next at number 11, lasted just two balls.

As Warne walked out shortly afterwards with the rest of the Australian team, his captain, Allan Border, called out some helpful advice: 'Hey, Warney, make sure you don't do a Johnny Watkins on us.' It was just the sort of encouragement he did not need, because Watkins was a leg spinner who had been catapulted into his first Test at the SCG in 1973 after just five first-class matches, and had been so nervous on his debut that he had barely managed to hit the pitch. After a succession of wides and full tosses he had lasted only six overs before being taken off, and had never played Test cricket again.

Nor did Warne have much time to settle. Although Border had promised to protect him and not bring him on too early, one of Australia's opening bowlers, Bruce Reid, a tall, lanky beanpole of a man, pulled up in his fourth over with a torn muscle and was forced to leave the field. So the new kid was hauled into the attack after just 18 overs for the last over before tea. Not surprisingly, he was so nervous and his hands so sweaty that he could hardly hold the ball. All he could think of as he ran in to bowl was not letting the ball bounce twice before it reached the batsman. But it was fine. Somehow, he got the first three to land on the spot, and while the fourth was overpitched and driven for four, the next two were also on target. After tea he was brought on again at the Randwick end and wheeled away until stumps. He bowled accurately, beat the bat a few times and conceded only 39 runs in 19 overs, which was remarkably economical for a leg spinner.

All in all, it was a tremendous start to his Test career. Next day's papers trumpeted a chorus of approval, led by Richie Benaud, who predicted a long and illustrious career. 'Warne showed us enough yesterday', said the spin guru, 'to let us all see that he has the ability and potential which has caught the eye of the Australian selectors.' Australia's other leg-spinning legend, Bill O'Reilly, also gave Warne his blessing. Welcoming him to 'the important spin society' in his column for the *Sun Herald* and *Sunday Age*, he decreed that the boy had passed all tests and would do well. Wishing him 'a long, busy and highly successful career' he promised 'easy pickings' if Warne stuck to the fundamentals of line and length, and predicted he could have 'a tremendous impact on the game'. No doubt he wanted to believe it, but it was remarkably prescient, all the same.

O'Reilly's chief concerns were with Warne's appearance. He took a swipe at his weight, describing him as 'built on rather lavish lines for a 22-year-old', and suggested that a sheep shearer should get rid of the 'long mop of hair on the back of his neck'. Luckily, he had not spotted the new dangly gold earring that Shane's brother, Jason, had given him for Christmas, which might have given him apoplexy. Warne had been too shy to display it in his first match for Australia, and had assured a journalist that he just wore it in his 'free time . . . anything to do with cricket, it comes out: training, playing, anything'. A few days earlier, trying on his new Australian cap for the press, it had been there all the same, as it was for his TV interviews, but Bill obviously hadn't spotted it in the pictures.

Plaudits aside, there was still plenty of cricket to be played at the SCG and plenty of balls to be bowled. And Shane's cavalcade of fans soon started wondering whether the pundits had spoken too soon, because once India's best batsmen, Shastri and Tendulkar, got going, they began to treat Warne with disdain. Over the next two days, he bowled another 26 overs and got hit for another 111 runs, or more than four an over. 'Shastri and Tendulkar just went on a rampage and just whacked me all over the park', Warne said later, 'and I thought: "What's this all about? I just don't belong here. I'm not good enough to play."' A huge six down the ground off Warne brought up Shastri's 150, and an amazing shot, hit inside out over the cover boundary, followed from Tendulkar. Eventually, he managed to have Shastri caught in the deep by Jones for 206, trying to belt another six, to finish with figures of 1 for 150. One match, one wicket, he thought. It might well be the tally for his Test career.

More seasoned observers thought he had done okay. There was not much any spinner could do against batsmen in that sort of form, and he had neither lost his nerve nor fallen apart. He had been too scared to risk too many googlies or flippers and he clearly had a lot to learn. But it could have been worse. And in the next match it was. Selected for the Fourth Test in Adelaide three weeks later, he bowled another 23 overs and got no wickets at all, to take his Test figures to 1 for 228.

After that he did not get picked for Perth, although that was no surprise with the ground's reputation as a fast-bowling paradise. And so it was back to Victoria, where he also did badly. He took 2 for 216 in two matches against New South Wales and South Australia and was then made to carry the drinks in the last match of the season, with his fortunes as a professional cricketer apparently waning again. But luckily Jim Higgs and the other national selectors had not lost faith. Having backed a hunch in the first place, they still felt Warne could be a winner . . . if he was prepared to knuckle down.

6

Fame at Last

Ah well, that's the end of Shane as we know him.

After the season finished, the Australian Cricket Board sent Warne and others to Adelaide for a bit of extra coaching at what was termed 'Camp April'. Bob Simpson, the team coach, had vetoed the idea of him spending another season in England, where he would almost certainly stack on even more weight. And the fitness coach at the Cricket Academy, now being run by ex-Test wicket-keeper Rod Marsh, had been asked to take the boy in hand and help him get fit.

Marsh himself had also taken an interest in Warne's future and had issued a very public invitation for him to come back to the academy, to work with Jenner and get himself in shape. 'It would be better for his cricket', Marsh had told Melbourne's *Herald-Sun* during his Test debut, 'if he spent a hard winter in Adelaide rather than go to England for some soft club cricket, easy bucks and a good time.'

But in the first instance, Shane was not going to the academy. He took the opportunity, instead, to stay with his old mentor, Terry Jenner, in his small unit in Campbelltown. He soon discovered that Jenner also thought it was time he got serious about life. Jenner was shocked by how overweight he was, how much beer he was drinking and how casually he seemed to be taking his career. So he decided to give him a talking to. As he tells the tale in his book, *TJ Over the Top*:

> Shane was a natural but everything had come relatively easy to him. He hadn't been forced to make too many sacrifices. Like most kids in their early 20s he enjoyed a drink and a smoke and the company of his mates. I felt he needed to lose some weight, get leaner and meaner, which would show his detractors he was serious about cricket.

And detractors there certainly were: his Test figures were hopeless, he was fat and unfit, he had virtually no first-class experience, and spinners (some thought) were a waste of time anyway. He was also determinedly un-conventional – with his bottle-blond mullet and gold earring – in what was the most conventional of sports. In short, he stood out a mile, and he wasn't yet good enough to get away with it.

Jenner's chance to pull him into line came one evening when Shane turned up at his flat with a slab of beer under one arm and a bottle of red wine in each hand. When Terry showed no signs of opening any of them, Shane asked, 'Are we going to have a beer?'

'No, we're not going to have a beer', Jenner replied sternly.

'What's wrong?'

I said, 'I'm angry, Shane', and launched into my speech, telling him how he hadn't made the necessary sacrifices to play for Australia. I didn't want him to make the mistakes I did.

When Jenner took Warne to the airport the next day to catch his flight back home, his pupil asked permission before lighting up a cigarette in the car, which was a great leap forward, because he had never done so before. 'It's not good for you', Jenner told him, launching into another lecture about getting fit and taking his talent seriously. Shane looked uncomfortable.

'You wouldn't want me to lie to you, Terry, would you?' he asked.

'No', T. J. replied.

'Well, I'm not going to make any promises.'

'I couldn't get angry with him', Jenner says today. 'But I told him, "There's a lot of people who have put a lot of faith in you. Don't let them down."' Luckily, Jenner was the one person in the world that he was prepared to listen to.

Two weeks later Shane's mother, Brigitte, phoned from Melbourne. 'I don't know what you said', she told Jenner, 'but it's working. He is running every morning and he's given up drinking beer. He has already lost four kilograms'. Soon, he was also changing his diet to cut out the pizzas, chip rolls and cheese sandwiches and substitute pasta, cereal, fruit and salad. He also began drinking

3 litres of water a day and went on the wagon. Heaven knows what pain this must have caused.

There is no doubt that the telling off from Jenner and the months that followed it marked a crossroads in Warne's career. He had never worked hard enough at his football to get properly fit and to give himself a decent chance. Nor had he done the hard yards at school or cricket. Now, he accepted it would take more than talent to get to the top. As Richie Benaud had warned in his column on Shane's Test debut praising the boy's potential, he would only fulfil his talent through 'sheer hard work'.

Having set Warne onto the straight and narrow, Terry Jenner was determined not to give him a chance to slide back to his old ways. 'I said to Rodney [Marsh], "We've got to get him back to the academy. He's so good we can't get let him go." He needed some discipline in his daily schedule. I didn't want his talent to go to waste.' But getting Warne readmitted to the AIS after all the trouble he had caused two years earlier was far easier said than done. Rob de Castella, head of the Australian Institute of Sport, wanted nothing to do with Warne, even though he was now playing for Australia, and it took some strong lobbying by Marsh to get de Castella to change his mind. Even then, permission came with conditions attached: 'They presented Shane with a document to sign [if he wanted to come back] that meant he could never be himself', says Jenner. Eventually, a compromise was reached whereby Warne would stay in Jenner's apartment and train at the academy as a guest. Then, four or five weeks later, when he agreed to submit to the fitness programs and abide by the rules, he was allowed back in full-time, with Rod Marsh agreeing to take responsibility for any breaches.

Jenner used this second spell at the academy to rebuild Warne's flipper from scratch and work on ways of fooling batsmen. Meanwhile, Warne sought advice from as many other old spinners as he could find, including Jim Higgs, Peter Philpott and Richie Benaud. Over the next four months, he trained hard, stuck to his diet, and rapidly shrank back to the 82 kilos he had weighed as an 18-year-old when he was at his fittest for footy. Nor did he touch a drink. 'The first beer he had was when he left the academy in August', says Marsh. 'We had a celebration on his last night and I had to persuade him he could do that.'

After his second stint at the academy, the new slimline, hard-working Warne was given another chance at Test cricket with selection for the Australian team to tour Sri Lanka. Marsh, in an expansive mood – perhaps after sinking a few tinnies himself – told Shane confidently that he would take 500 wickets in a glorious Test career. And with this valedictory ringing in his ears, Warne went off to join the party.

And party it was. Mike Whitney remembers them spending a fair bit of time at a popular bar in Colombo called the Pink Elephant, whose proprietor became very fond of the team. 'Shane used to sit at the bar with Hooter [Errol Alcott, the team physio] who had this way of holding his drink and cocking his pinky, and Shane would do exactly the same.' It was when the Australian team was dividing itself into the Julios (the Latin lovers, as in Julio Iglesias) and the Nerds, and Shane was determined to be a Julio.

As in most teams he's been a part of, Shane was popular, especially in these early days, and Mike Whitney, who roomed with him, was particularly taken: 'I loved the bloke. He was just such fun to be with.' But his cricket did not go so smoothly. During the First Test in Colombo, he remained 499 wickets short of Marsh's optimistic career target, and his career appeared to be going down the gurgler again. In the first innings he was flogged for more than 100 runs and failed to take a scalp. Sri Lanka's captain, Arjuna Ranatunga – with whom he would have several run-ins over the years – was particularly harsh on him, hitting three sixes and two fours in a savage assault that took 29 runs off three overs. Not surprisingly, Warne was soon asking himself the same old questions: 'Am I good enough? What am I doing here?' And concluding, 'I don't really belong.'

He had worked his butt off to get fit that winter, had practised his skills in the nets every day, and given up beer and beans. He had even had a haircut. Yet he still could not buy a wicket. On this evidence it was hard to escape the conclusion that he just didn't have the talent to take wickets at that level.

Australia's headline writers clearly thought the same. 'Warne fails', blared *The Sydney Morning Herald*. 'Warne ploy looks grim', echoed Melbourne's *Herald Sun*, warning that the search for the next great Australian spinner had just hit a wall, and that he and his backers on the selection panel were in for a rough ride.

As he waited to bat in Australia's second innings, Warne buttonholed his captain, Allan Border, and told him his doubts: that he wasn't good enough, that he shouldn't be there, that all his hard work was wasted. Border, who did not believe in giving up or in advertising weakness, just kept on squinting at the game. But as Warne's complaints continued, he eventually turned to him and said: 'Mate, I'm a big believer in guys who keep trying, who keep putting in, keep working hard. If you keep hanging in there, one day it will click for you.'

With a huge deficit of 291 to make up from the first innings, after Sri Lanka's superb 8 for 547 declared, it was going to be all Australia could do to make Sri Lanka bat again, but they did much better in the second dig and clawed their way to 471, with Warne making 35. Mike Whitney, the last man in, remembers getting a big cheer from the Australian dressing-room as his score clicked over to 10. Raising his bat in cheerful salute, he had no idea what the fuss was about. But he didn't have to wait long to discover: it was only the tenth time in history – and the first in 15 years – that every batsman in a Test team had made it into double figures.

That evening, Warne was down in the dumps again, despite his contribution with the bat. Once again, he felt his cricketing future was at stake. 'I knew I had to do something', he later lamented, 'otherwise I was just about gone as a Test cricketer.' Come dinnertime, he ran into fellow spinner Greg Matthews in the foyer of the team hotel, and they went off to an Italian restaurant at the Hilton – the only place Warne has ever been happy to eat in Colombo – for a plate of spaghetti. Soon he was pouring out his woes, as he had done to Border, about his career being over and how he wasn't good enough to do the business. Matthews, who had bowled far better than Warne in the first innings and was a rival for his place in the side, tried to pep him up: 'They wouldn't have picked you if they didn't think you could bowl. So stop getting up yourself . . . You and I will do it tomorrow and we could be bowling for Australia for the next five years . . . Don't worry if they bounce twice. Go out there and spin them as far as you can, you'll be right.'

The next morning, the Singhalese Sports Ground was packed. The Sri Lankans needed only 181 to record their first-ever Test victory against Australia, and everyone in Colombo had come to see them get it. There were banners waving, and excited choruses every time a run was scored. There was also a thrill when Warne came on and got belted for 11 in one over before being taken off. So much for showing them how good he was.

At 2 for 127, it looked like Sri Lanka were easing to victory. Then da Silva was caught brilliantly on the boundary by Border, hooking at McDermott, Ranatunga fell to the same bowler five runs later and Matthews then got two in quick succession. Suddenly, at 6 for 137, the innings was in danger of collapse. With the match now in the balance, four wickets to get and only 36 runs needed, Border threw the ball to Warne, whose Test figures had ballooned to 1 for 346. 'I thought, "Gee, that's a brave move"', says Whitney. 'But I guess it was the last throw of the dice.'

Shane was not convinced it was a great idea either. The way he had been bowling, it was likely the match would be finished in a couple of overs. But he gritted his teeth and bowled a maiden. Matthews then picked up yet another wicket to make it 7 for 147 and Warne was left with the tailenders. Fortunately, Gurusinha, who had mastered him in the first innings (and who has never been dismissed by Warne to this day), was marooned at the other end.

With Matthews shouting encouragement, 'Come on, Suicide' (as in Suicide Blonde), Shane bagged his first Test wicket for eight months with the first ball of his second over: Wickramasinghe, caught at cover trying to slog him out of the park. Ten balls later, he snared Anurasiri in similar fashion. And two balls after that he finished off the innings by getting Madurasinghe, with Greg Matthews, suitably, taking the catch. In just 13 balls he had picked up the wickets of the last three batsmen without conceding a run.

It was an amazing finish, one of the biggest comebacks in Test-match history, a match Australia should never have won. And when the players came down for the presentation in front of the stands, several of the Sri Lankan players were crying. Somehow, they had snatched defeat from the jaws of victory.

As Warne readily admitted, he was not the one who had really turned the game. Man of the match – with seven wickets, 70 runs, and that confidence-boosting chat – went to his mate Greg Matthews, who generously saluted Warne's courage in the post-match press conference. But he had got wickets when it mattered and done it in his old style, by throwing the ball up, taking risks and attacking. If you look at news footage of the game, there is nothing remarkable about any of his deliveries. His victims – who were all bunnies with single-figure batting averages –

threw their wickets away. He did not mesmerise the batsmen, as he would so often in his later career. Yet he had got the monkey off his back. He was no longer excess baggage on the trip.

Border had shown confidence in him at a crucial moment and Warne had repaid it. 'It was a gamble and it paid off', his captain said after the match. 'You've done the whole lot on red and it's come up.'

Yet still Warne's progress did not run smooth. He was left out of the Second Test in Colombo because of worries about an ankle injury, bowled just 11 overs in the Third Test without taking a wicket and was dropped for the First Test against the West Indies, two months later, in Brisbane. Then the rollercoaster turned upwards again.

The next Test was at the MCG in Melbourne on Boxing Day in front of his home crowd, and Shane was picked to play. It was his childhood dream come true, even if it wasn't football, the sport he had hoped for. And he was now looking so much better than when he had walked onto the SCG 12 months earlier. His hair was short at the sides, with a new mop top that was much more in fashion than the old semi-mullet, and he was a good 10 kilos lighter.

Once again he was nervous. And once again, he bowled without distinction. 'His leg-break spun only slowly, his googly was telegraphed, and every time he tried his flipper it was either wide or over-pitched', cricket writer Ken Piesse later observed. His only victim was a tailender, Curtly Ambrose, caught in the deep. Nor did he bat much better.

When he woke on the last day of the game, with Australia poised to win, he told himself he had to do something or he was finished. He had played four and a half Tests and taken five wickets at an average cost of 90 runs apiece. The *Herald Sun*'s chief sports writer, Ron Reed, had also looked at the sums and come to the same conclusion: it was time to pay back those who had faith in him. There would never be a better chance. The pitch was wearing and was bound to take spin; the West Indies would be under pressure, chasing an almost impossible 359 to win; and his home crowd would be cheering him on. 'The critical question', wrote Reed, 'is whether he is confident enough, experienced enough or just plain good enough to answer such a challenge.'

Warne has never been one to keep his angst to himself. He likes to involve everyone in his drama, and he was soon telling Australian wicket-keeper Ian Healy of his fear that he was going to be thumped around the ground in front of his mates and would never play for Australia again. Healy, who had listened to a similar litany of worries from Warne the night before, told him to relax, stop being negative and enjoy himself.

Twelve months earlier, before making his Test debut, Warne had explained how he planned to take wickets: 'You've got to be patient, patient, patient. That's the key.' And he needed all that patience as the day unfolded. As lunch loomed, the West Indies was in awesome form, with Phil Simmons well on his way to a career-best 110, and captain Richie Richardson looking equally comfortable on 52. The odds on a West Indian victory had tumbled from 10 to 1 to even money. The best team in the world looked like it was about to steal the game from Australia, who had not won a series against them for 16 years.

Warne had delivered eight overs without looking dangerous, and the West Indies had added 134 runs without losing a wicket. He hadn't yet bowled his 'Derryn Hinch' ball, the head-high full toss. Nor had he risked his flipper, the devilish delivery that Clarrie Grimmett spent 12 years trying to perfect. He had tried it 20 times in the first innings, he said later, and not landed one right. But he had nothing much else in his locker. So he decided to give it one last throw.

There are plenty of top batsmen in the world even now who can't read Warne's flipper, which resembles a leg break when it leaves the hand and looks like a long hop as it comes through the air. And Richardson failed to spot this one until it was far too late. He started to come forward, tried to go back, then stabbed his bat down desperately as the ball skidded low off the pitch and hurried into the base of his stumps. It was the flipper from hell, the best Warne ever bowled. Looking at the replay, one can only marvel at how fast it comes through. It is over in a flash, and the ball stays so low it barely clears the batsman's boots. Richardson looks like a farmer trying to spear a rat as it runs over his feet. With about as much chance of success.

Looking back on this moment four years later, Warne would say it was the turning point in his career, the instant he realised he was good enough to strut the stage. More immediately, it was the start of a West Indian collapse. In the next two hours he took six more wickets for just 21 runs, as batsmen either froze in confusion or tried to belt him out of the attack. He bowled beautifully, teasing them with spin and variety. But his victims seemed bent on throwing their lives away. Arthurton charged suicidally down the pitch to a big-spinning leg break and was stumped. Hooper skied a pull he should never have attempted and Walsh was last man out trying to hit it into the clouds.

As Merv Hughes waited for the steepling catch to drop into his hands, the young bowler raced up to his captain, Allan Border, and swept him off his feet. It was the first time Australia had beaten the West Indies at the MCG for a decade and the first time since Johnny Gleeson in 1968 that an Australian leg spinner had taken five wickets or more on the ground. So it was little wonder that the 16,000-strong crowd gave him a standing ovation as he left the pitch or that Australian cricket writers now pulled out the superlatives to welcome a new hero. As he would prove so many times in his career, Warne was able to produce his best under pressure, when his team-mates needed him most. There could be no doubt on this occasion that he had won them the match.

You can imagine the scenes in the dressing-room afterwards, but a couple of images may help sum it up: Warne and Border hugging, grinning wildly, eyes closed, flinching at the flashlights and the shower of champagne; Warne and Border on the floor in a circle of players, shielding their heads from a cascade of beer being poured from above; or Warne and his father, tinnies in hand, laughing out loud at the foam-flecked lens. When it all calmed down, Shane and Keith Warne retired to a quiet corner with a bottle of champagne. As they sat there, Mike Whitney looked across at them and thought: 'Yeah, this kid really can fucking bowl.'

That night, Shane took Damien Martyn and Mark Waugh out on the town to the Saloon Bar, a trendy South Yarra night spot, with a few local journos in tow. 'Warne, with his spiky bleached hair, wore an engaging smile and an earring', the *Herald Sun*'s Trevor Grant observed, 'and a T-shirt with a motif saying: "Nobody can upset this little black duck".' As soon as he arrived a free-drinks card was slapped into his hand, the standard treatment for celebrities at this star-gazing bar. But instead of having his name on it, Shane's card was simply marked: The Champ. 'The boy had arrived.'

At six am the next day, he was woken by a call from a radio station; and his arrival in Sydney at midday was greeted by a mob of TV cameramen and news reporters. Eventually, Australia's team manager, Ian McDonald, had to step in to stem the flood of interviews. Watching the TV news that night and reading the papers the next day, one of his close friends thought sadly, 'Ah well, that's the end of Shane as we know him.' But his sudden fame was only a small taste of what was to come.

Ball of the Century

He's bowled him. Mike Gatting can't believe it.

Any kid who has grown up playing cricket in England or Australia knows that what matters is the battle for the Ashes. It's the one against the Old Enemy, the one you always play in the backyard, the one you *really* hate to lose. Shane Warne knew from childhood that beating the Poms was the best thing that could happen in cricket, and losing to them was . . . well, let's not even go there. So his first ball in a Test match in England was bound to be something special, at least for him.

But as we all know, it turned out to be so much bigger than that. It was the 'BALL OF THE CENTURY', 'THE WONDER BALL', 'THE BALL FROM HELL' or quite simply 'THAT BALL', the one that will forever be his trademark. More than anything he will ever do – text messages, bookmakers and slimming pills included – it will always define his career.

As an ex-Pom, I remember watching it on TV with a mixture of shock, astonishment and despair. One moment, England was chasing a small Australian total and coasting at 1 for 80. The next minute it was reeling, the series was as good as lost. Warne's victim, Mike Gatting, a gritty, stocky, English-yeoman sort of bloke, who normally ate spinners for breakfast, walked off looking shell-shocked, as if a bomb had gone off. And it had.

The bare facts of it are that at 3.06 pm on 4 June 1993, a leg break from Warne landed outside Gatting's leg stump at Old Trafford and spun 60 centimetres or roughly 2 feet to the left, clipping the top of his off stump and removing the bail. But that doesn't begin to describe how amazing it was. I remember thinking it was impossible for the ball to have spun past Gatting's bat *and* hit the wicket. And that's clearly what Gatting thought too. Looking back at the tapes, what immediately strikes you is how quickly the ball comes through and how slowly the batsman departs. The ball drifts, dips, spits off the pitch and wreaks its havoc in about the time it takes to blink twice. Gatting stares at his wicket, then at the umpire, clearly expecting a reprieve, and stands there for almost 10 seconds. 'Now what's happened?' the commentator asks, as he stands rooted to the spot. 'He's staying there. The bail's off. He's bowled him. Mike Gatting can't believe it.' Finally, he tucks his bat under his arm and trudges off, shaking his head in disbelief. As England's hero Ian Botham later quipped, no one had seen Gatts look so cross since the day that someone stole his lunch.

To call any delivery the Ball of the Century is pretty ridiculous when you consider how many millions have been bowled down the years. Warne himself has served up 120,000 in his cricketing career and about 40,000 in Test matches. And hundreds of other bowlers in the last 100 years, with at least 10 million balls between them, have bowled jaffas that were completely unplayable. But you would be hard-pressed to find anyone disputing this ball's right to the title, because even if there have been such brilliant deliveries, none has ever had such a dramatic effect.

As Warne says in *Shane Warne, My Autobiography*, 'In the second or so it took to leave my hand, swerve to pitch outside leg stump, fizz past the batsman's lunge forward and clip off stump, my life did change.' And so did everyone else's that day in some small way, because batsmen everywhere suddenly realised Warne had a weapon that could pierce any armour. And he could have chosen no better moment to fire his Exocet than in front of a huge TV audience, with his very first ball in his very first Test against England.

When Warne is asked about the delivery, he generally puts it down to luck, saying he could easily have bowled one just as good and missed the stumps completely: 'It was just the man upstairs saying it was meant to happen.' But the better you are the luckier you get. And just to make his point, Warne repeated the trick in the next over to another good batsman, Robin Smith, who managed to get his bat onto the ball, only to be caught at slip instead. Later in the series, he bowled Graham Gooch by landing the ball outside leg stump and spinning it behind his legs. 'That's not supposed to happen', the TV commentator piped up. And that was exactly the point. Warne could do things that no one else could, and keep on doing them.

England never got back into that Test or into the series. With Warne taking four wickets in the first innings, they were skittled for 210. Another four in the second earnt him man of the match. And in the next Test at Lord's, he did it again, taking eight more wickets as Australia marched to an even bigger victory, after which England sacked seven players, including Gatting, and had to hold a cocktail party so the new ones could get to know each other. But that was only the start of the carnage. Gooch resigned as captain after the Fourth Test at Headingley, when the Aussies went 3–0 up, and Ted Dexter, the chairman of selectors, fell on his sword at the end of the series, having used 24 different players in a desperate attempt to turn things around.

At this point, one wit suggested it was time to get a new lot of Ashes as well. The original trophy – a tiny terracotta urn containing the burnt-out remains of a couple of bails – was presented to mark England's first-ever loss to Australia on home soil in 1882. This had been so shocking at the time that a mock obituary had been inserted in London's *Sporting Times*:

In Affectionate Remembrance of
ENGLISH CRICKET
which died at the Oval
on 29th AUGUST, 1882
Deeply lamented by a large circle of
sorrowing friends and acquaintances.
R.I.P.

N.B. – The body will be cremated and the ashes taken to Australia.

One hundred and eleven years later, there was even more reason to weep, because England had won only once in its last seven matches against Australia. But the Poms are good at laughing at themselves, if nothing else, and *The Independent* had a great idea for a new trophy: 'On current form, it would be more appropriate to set fire to the Long Room [at Lord's] than a couple of bails', their cricket writer Martin Johnson suggested.

> The charred remnants could then be interred inside a silage tank, to be presented to Michael Atherton, or (given that we may have to wait until Papua New Guinea are granted full membership of the International Cricket Council) one of his great-grandchildren, on the occasion of England's next Test victory.

Warne was not solely to blame for England's crumbling morale, but he had done more damage than anyone else. By the end of the Second Test he had already taken more wickets than Richie Benaud's record haul of 15 for a leg spinner on a post-war Ashes tour. And by the end of the series his tally of 34 had comfortably eclipsed those of Bill O'Reilly and Clarrie Grimmett, the gods of Australian leg spin, who had managed 28 and 29 respectively in the 1930s on pitches far more suited to spin. Not surprisingly, Benaud was moved to say: 'I think he's terrific. He's the best young leg spinner I have ever seen.'

Some were less precise in their praise. To them he was not just the best young leg spinner but the best bowler in the world. His team-mate and spin partner Tim May told people simply, 'He's the sort of thing you see once or twice in a lifetime. He's a freak.' His former team-mate Mike Whitney, who would have been glad to rank fast bowlers such as Dennis Lillee and Richard Hadlee ahead of him, also reckoned he was the tops. 'I've never seen any other bowler put so many great players under so much pressure', he says today, 'and pressure is what it's about.'

None of the English batsmen could master him and only a few could keep him out. One who managed to frustrate him was 40-year-old veteran off spinner John Emburey, recalled by the selectors in one of several moments of panic. Standing with his bat high above his head, front-on to the bowler, pads locked together, he managed to block out all balls pitched outside his leg stump and survived to share a century stand at Edgbaston with Graham Thorpe, one of England's coming stars. Graham Gooch was about the only other Englishman who ever looked like conquering him, making 133 in the second innings of the First Test before being bizarrely dismissed for handling the ball. But eventually even he succumbed. In the second innings of the Fifth Test at Edgbaston, he was bowled round his legs without playing a shot – one of those dismissals that was not meant to happen. Warne had deliberately fired the ball into the footmarks left by the fast bowlers and spun it more than half a metre.

It demanded unbelievable precision to do this, but Warne could do such things to order. If you put a plate down on the wicket, he would hit it every time. If you moved the plate a few inches and made him bowl from round the wicket instead, he would still land it right on the spot. 'It's hard enough to do that as a seamer', says Mike Whitney, 'but try doing that out the back of your hand, spinning it like he does and getting the drift. It's fucking unbelievable, unbelievable, unbelievable.' He shakes his head in wonder. 'The position of the seam has to be exactly right – not just nearly but exactly – the revs on the ball have to be exactly right and the speed of the ball again, exactly right. Yet he does it again and again and again.'

The scientists who marvelled at the exactitude of soccer wizard David Beckham's free kicks, which could curve over a wall of players to duck inches under the bar, just out of reach of the goalie, would have shaken their heads in wonder at Warne as well. But few did not. From 1993 to 1995, he was at his peak, the best he would ever be, perhaps the best anyone would ever be. For six Test series in a row he was Australia's leading wicket taker, often by miles, taking 120 wickets in 21 matches at an average of 21.54, and at a rate of almost three an innings.

Against South Africa in January 1994 he was simply brilliant. At the SCG in Sydney he took 12 wickets with a series of balls that were quite as good as the one he bowled to Gatting: a couple of them flippers, a few of them big-turning leg breaks. And in the process, more records tumbled: it was the first time he had taken 10 wickets in a match and the best performance ever by an Australian against South Africa on home soil.

Come the next Ashes series in Australia in November 1994 he was still on fire. England's batsmen were so worried going into the contest that they studied an hour-long videotape of all the ways he had got people out, but it probably terrified them even more. His 11 wickets in the first match propelled him to number one in the world rankings while his eight scalps in the second innings sent England crashing to defeat.

Some batsmen now went out to face him, columnist Peter Roebuck observed, as if they were marching into the valley of death. And once there, they remained petrified. Eight of his first nine overs in that second innings were maidens. 'He was easily the best bowler on either side', admitted England's captain, Mike Atherton, who was so baffled by Warne that he and his vice captain, Alec Stewart, borrowed binoculars and climbed high into the grandstand behind the bowler's arm to see if they could figure out what he was doing.

Nor did Warne's progress stop there. In the Second Test against England at the MCG in December a six-wicket haul in the first innings took him to 151 Test wickets. 'I've taken 150 more wickets than I thought I would after my first Test against India', he quipped, only just tongue in cheek. 'After that experience I thought I would be sent back to playing club cricket and enjoying a few beers with my friends at the beach.' In the second innings he took a hat-trick and had fans waiting three hours for autographs, which he dutifully signed as he sat in the boot of his new BMW.

So what was it that made him so good? And why had it so suddenly come together? The best answer is probably that success breeds success and that his remarkable natural talent was at last reaping its due reward. But those who had spotted his abilities several years earlier, such as Jim Higgs, could point to a succession of things that marked him out. First was his technique, which allowed him to bowl accurately for hours on end. Next was his control over a huge variety of deliveries. Third was his intelligence: knowing which ball to bowl to whom and when. Fourth was his ability to deceive batsmen about where the ball was going to land and what it was going to do. And last was his nerve or confidence, which allowed him to try everything most of the time. He was also a risk taker. What made him so good a bowler was what made him such a handful off the field. He did not observe limits or obey rules.

Last year at the Gabba in Brisbane, when I was waiting to talk to Warne about this book, I listened to him boasting about how he could baffle batsmen with the weapons in his armoury. 'I can bowl five or six different leg breaks', he told a small group of journalists, 'and I'm not being big-headed about it. I can bowl in close to the stumps, out wide, in the middle, with a higher arm, a round arm, side spin, overspin – all for one delivery.'

He did not even mention his drift, which is what made the Ball of the Century such a belter. 'The advantage I've got over most other leg spinners is my drift', he said on another occasion. 'That's what plays on a batsman's mind as he's playing the shot, the drift . . . It floats away, and they have to second-guess the shot. They think it's there but it's not.'

Warne gets this drift because he tweaks the ball so hard. If you watch on super slo-mo you can see how much the ball spins in the air – far more than English spinner Ashley Giles achieves, for example. And the resulting drift leaves the batsman utterly confused about where the ball is going to land. As the ball comes out of the hand it looks like it is going to pitch on middle stump, so you get your feet and head in position only to find that it's swerving towards your toes. That puts you off balance because you have to twist your body forward and round to the left to reach it. Then the ball hits the deck and leaps across in front of you, which puts you even more off balance as you lunge and nick it to slip.

And remember, folks, we're still talking about the leg break, which is just one of Warne's weapons.

Shane has at least four others in his box of tricks, which are the ones that really cause the damage. Foremost of these is the flipper – the one that did for Richardson – the skidding backspinner that keeps low and stays straight. Quick ones clock in at 110 kilometres an hour compared to 75 kilometres an hour for the average leg break, which is incredibly fast for a so-called 'slow bowler'.

Then there's the zooter, which is a bit like a flipper that runs out of gas. It looks like a leg break but 'floats out the front of the fingers with some backspin on it', according to Warne, and then goes straight on. The zooter doesn't do much at all, which makes it dangerous if you've just seen a ball that looked the same and leapt sideways.

Next is the topspinner, which is bowled with overspin, not sidespin. This one loops in the air, drops far shorter than you expect and bounces high off the pitch without turning. It's the one that breaks the wicket-keeper's nose because it rears up in his face, or because the batsman has tried to cut the ball and got a top edge.

Then there's the wrong 'un, the one that spins from off to leg, or right to left as you look at it from the batsman's point of view. Also called a googly, it goes the opposite way to the standard leg break, but if it's bowled really well, it looks just like it.

Warne says good batsmen can read all these deliveries, either by picking them as they are bowled (from the action and position of the hand) or by looking at how the seam is turning in the air. But you have precious little time to make a decision – it takes about one second for the ball to reach you – and you have no idea how much the ball will turn, bounce, drift or shoot. So batting is still appallingly difficult. Australia's Test wicket-keeper in the 1990s Ian Healy watched Warne for 2000 overs from behind the stumps before facing him as a batsman and found himself under the pump, even though the ball was doing nothing off the pitch. 'Had there been any turn in the wicket I would have been rendered shotless . . . I would have been no chance', Healy admitted. Until then he had never appreciated the huge pressure that Warne puts on batsmen.

Brad McNamara, who played for New South Wales through the 1990s, has no doubt that Warne is the best bowler he has ever faced. And like Higgs he has his list of reasons. First is that Warne is really quick, so you can't use your feet against him: 'He's almost medium pace and the ball's spinning a foot. You have hardly any time to make up your mind.'

Second is that he is really accurate. 'He never gives you an easy ball, so he builds up the pressure. If you want to score runs off him you have to take risks, and that gets you out.'

Third is that he has fantastic variation. 'His flipper is a

killer. It looks like it's bouncing halfway down the pitch so you step back to wallop it over square leg, then it stays low and skids through. You're bowled. He has also got six different types of leg spinner that all look pretty much the same but spin different amounts.'

Fourth is that he is incredibly strong mentally. 'He can take being hit around, and he still comes back at you. You can have all the variation in the world, but it won't get you anywhere unless you're mentally tough, and he is.'

And fifth is that batsmen are scared of him. 'The Poms in 1993, the South Africans in 1994. He is one of those bowlers who is already three wickets ahead when he goes out on the pitch.'

You could talk for ever about what makes Warne so formidable as a bowler, but he also has the ability to size up a batsman, find his weakness and think him out. He might starve you of balls you can hit, forcing you to take risks to score runs. Or he might offer you a few tasty ones before offering you another that looks the same but does something different. For example, he might serve up a couple of leg breaks outside off stump that can be hit for four, then follow with a topspinner that bounces high, goes straight on and has you caught behind as you try to crack another boundary.

The key to it all is deception, which is why leg spinners are often compared to magicians or card sharps. The art is to make the batsman think something is happening when it isn't, or that nothing is happening when it is. It's like the old three-card trick, where any fool can spot the black queen until someone puts money on where it is. Or like trout fishing, where you lure the fish with a brightly coloured fly that conceals a deadly hook inside.

What ties the package together is that Warne is supremely, unnaturally confident, and an almost irresistible force. Sandy Morgan, who played cricket for Queensland in the 1970s, says: 'There's a lot of sportsmen out there with equal ability but the ones who rise to the top are those who genuinely believe they are the best. The best cricketers, 99 times out of 100, are the guys with the biggest egos. Every time Warne bowls he expects to take wickets. Every time he bats he expects to make runs. Every time he sees a woman he expects to get laid.'

Warne's version of this is that if you're confident you can do anything. He believes he is going to get you, and he wants you to believe it, too. Hence, all the other variety in his repertoire and the displays he puts on for batsmen and umpires: throwing his arms in the air, gasping in shock, whistling like he can't believe the last ball didn't get you, and giving you the full 'Gee, you're so lucky' stare. And he doesn't so much appeal to the umpire as *demand* that the batsman be given out because, for God's sake, he so obviously is. It's all part of the fun he has, but it's also a performance that is designed to unsettle his opponent, to get into his head. So he will talk to the captain or fiddle with the field or just pause at the top of his run to make the batsman wait between balls; or he will try to hurry him up, to deny him time to recover from the last delivery. It is about setting the tempo, taking control, getting the upper hand.

And then, of course, there is sledging. But more of that in a moment.

'Sex Test Flop'

He wasn't so hot in bed – and was
'too chubby' anyway.

While the 1993 Ashes series certainly marked the start of something special for Warne on the cricket field, he was soon protesting that it was also the point at which his private life came under intense public scrutiny and 'bad things happened'.

Sadly, that is the price of fame: suddenly everyone wants to know what you eat, where you drink, what you listen to and who you're on with. And Warne was hot property, with men and women alike. To the average Joe and Joanna, he was not just a fantastic bowler or the best leg spinner in the world or even the lad who had scared the Poms shitless. He was a celebrity, a hunk and a young Aussie icon who was right up there with ex-*Neighbours* stars Jason Donovan and Kylie Minogue. And as such he was bound to be news all over the cricketing world, but especially in England. So when the papers had finished raving about the Ball of the Century they naturally went looking for other things to write. And the scandal sheets went searching for scandal. Before long, the press pack had sniffed out the fact that he had played in the Lancashire League two years before, and soon afterwards they descended on Accrington to see what they could dig up. Warne wasn't quite as marketable as David Beckham or Paul Gascoigne (Becks and Gazza to the tabloids) but he could still sell papers. So it was no surprise – two weeks after THAT BALL – when England's tabloid, led by the *Daily Sport*, came up with a kiss-and-tell story from one of Shane's former lovers.

The *Sport* is almost a parody of a newspaper, in that it has always aimed further down market than Rupert Murdoch's *Sun* and *News of the World*, which the casual observer might have thought was as low as one could possibly get. It specialises in stories that could not possibly be true but are nevertheless hilarious, my personal favourite being the splendidly headlined 'Aliens bit my bum' or the more recent 'Aliens gave me a boob job'. Hauntings are another favourite, as is anything to do with sex and sports stars, which is where Shane came in.

Naturally, the *Sport* pays good money to get its stories, and on this occasion it had opened its chequebook to entice a 20-year-old blonde Accrington hairdresser called Lisa Ramsden to dish the dirt and pose in a swimsuit with one of her breasts half-exposed. The lovely Lisa had enjoyed a brief fling with Warne in 1991, before returning to her long-time boyfriend, with whom she had since had a child. She claimed that Shane had pestered her to go to bed with him and then begged for a return match after she had had enough. Or not enough, as it turned out. It was harmless stuff by comparison with the text-messaging sagas of later years, but it was sufficiently shocking for

Shane's tabloid baptism, because the article included one of his love letters and appeared under the unflattering headline 'Sex Test Flop', which prompted his Australian team-mates to call him Dudley for some time thereafter. As Lisa told the *Daily Mirror* in an almost identical story published the same day:

> He wasn't so hot in bed – and was 'too chubby' anyway. He was so jealous he hated her even talking to another man. His non-stop kisses and cuddles embarrassed her in public. Shane wrote Lisa a letter pleading: 'Why don't we keep trying – I know I'd be good for you' – but all in vain.

On the morning of the *Mirror* article, which was matched by yet another in the *Sun* under the banner headline 'Oz star Shane was no wizard in bed', the Australian team was staying at a London hotel, where a couple of Warne's mates kindly left the newspaper open for him at breakfast and stayed to watch his reaction. Fortunately for historians, Robert Craddock from the Brisbane *Courier-Mail* happened to witness the scene and was able to relate it to his readers several years later:

> Shane Warne walked into the breakfast room at London's Westbury Hotel and found his own private life on toast. London's *Daily Mirror* had paid one of Warne's girlfriends from his old English league cricket days to reveal private love letters penned from the hand which would later rock the cricket world. It was mildly embarrassing stuff – particularly

as Warne's girlfriend and future wife Simone had just arrived in town – and several chuckling teammates loitered at breakfast for the precious moment when their wide-eyed young teammate opened the papers and saw a saucy letter he had written two years before. Warne, on his first Ashes tour and the brightest young prospect in world cricket, saw the story, momentarily stopped chewing his breakfast and read the entire piece without any conspicuous sign of emotion. His subdued demeanour was no different to an investor seeing his stocks had dropped a point or two overnight. Then he calmly resumed his breakfast, and headed off to scalp England in the second Test with a four-wicket haul at Lord's a few hours later.

In fact, the exposé had rather more effect on Warne than he let on, because he subsequently cut all ties with his old mate Brendan McArdle, whom he apparently blamed for the story. McArdle was friendly with several journalists and had been in the press box at Old Trafford as Warne's remarkable ball to Gatting was bowled. Even worse, as far as Warne was concerned, he was named in the article as the person who had introduced Shane to Lisa in the first place. But it was unlikely that he had played any part in the story's genesis. It had appeared first in a Manchester paper, The News & Echo, and been sold to the nationals by a local news agency which specialised in such stuff, and the cricket writers had not been involved.

Nevertheless, it was 10 years or more before Warne made any attempt to patch things up with the friend who had been so good to him, and the relationship remains awkward even now. 'We talked a bit a couple of years ago, repaired some of the damage, but it will never be the same again', says McArdle ruefully.

The story set feathers flying in Lisa Ramsden's life as well. For several days after the initial article was published, rival newspapers and photographers camped outside the house in Oswaldtwistle where she lived with her new husband and one-year-old son. And by the end of the week she was so upset that she complained to the *Accrington Observer* that her life had been made a misery and that she could not leave the house because everyone was staring and pointing the finger at her. She had been branded a 'bimbo and a bitch', she said, and had fallen out with family and friends. 'If I had known how the stories would appear', she lamented, 'I would not have done it for a million pounds. I am absolutely devastated, and now I just want to start picking up the pieces of my life.'

The unhappy hairdresser then went in to bat for her former lover, telling the *Accrington Observer*:

Since Shane became famous, all the papers have said he was a womaniser and a big drinker, but he was never like that when I knew him . . . I now feel sorry for Shane . . . I felt disgusted when I read those awful headlines about Shane being a flop in bed.

Ms Ramsden was so upset with the coverage that she took her case to the UK Press Complaints Commission, charging that the *Sunday Sport*, *Daily Mirror* and Lancashire

News & Echo had distorted her story or made parts of it up. And a year later her complaint was upheld. The journalist from the press agency who sold the stories to Fleet Street had made no tape recording of their conversations and had conveniently mislaid his notebook, so he could offer no defence. Even worse, the photographer who snapped Lisa in the swimsuit had apparently convinced her it was for a modelling shoot and not for the newspaper. Welcome to the world of the UK tabloids.

Such stories, of course, were the downside of fame. And there were plenty more where they came from, such as the one that listed 'Ten things you don't know about Shane Warne', which Shane insisted he did not even know himself, or the *Daily Mirror*'s colourful (and probably accurate) account of his time in Bristol. His mates there claimed cheerfully that Shane had been out on the town five nights a week, and in the pub for the other two, and Warne himself was quoted, admitting, 'I used to drink, smoke and go out and find women. That was all I wanted to do all the time. But when I think of how I was – Jeez!' But there was an upside too: Australia's *60 Minutes* was prepared to pay him $20,000 to appear in a profile with his new blonde fiancée, a promotions model called Simone Callahan, and soon people were throwing yet more money at him in the hope that he would help sell their products.

Overnight, he had become one of the most marketable sportsmen in Australia and the hottest cricketer in the world. And a new sort of cricketer at that, who did not just wear his baggy green, brandish a bat and look tough. With his cheeky smile, street-smart attitude and back-to-front cap he was a marketer's dream. It was as if he had spent his whole life waiting to be in an ad. And in a way he had. Fame, not cricket, had been his childhood dream, and at the age of 24 it was all coming true: more money than he had ever imagined and more chicks than he had ever dreamed of. Within a year of THAT BALL he had become the richest cricketer in history (soon to be eclipsed by Sachin Tendulkar, it is true), with big brands falling over each other to sign him.

The biggest catch of all for Warne was Nike, who whisked him off to the USA to meet a far bigger sporting superstar, Michael Jordan, before signing him up to a five-year deal on $200,000 a year. By Christmas 1994 the company was producing its first-ever cricket boot, the Nike Air Flipper, which showed how much he had galvanised the sport or, more likely, that he had transcended it. Cricket was never likely to be more than a marginal sport for Nike, and they would not recoup their investment from selling Air Flippers, but he was worth the investment for what he said about the brand. Like the great tennis champion John McEnroe, Nike's favourite flag bearer, Warne was a rebel who challenged the establishment, who obeyed no rules, who did it his way and yet was brilliant enough to be the best.

By mid-1994 the deals were coming in about as fast as Shane could do the ads. In June he signed a three-year deal at $100,000 a year with the clothing chain store Just Jeans, and set about filming a bizarre campaign featuring him on top of a cliff, hurling an iron into the ocean, which was apparently a huge success for the company. 'We sold tens of thousands of pairs of non-iron pants because of it', says Just Jeans founder Craig Kimberley. Shane was also accepting $20,000 a year to wear Oakley sunglasses and

$50,000 a year from Coca-Cola to spruik its sports drink, Powerade. Then there was another $50,000 a year for putting his name to a column in Melbourne's *Sunday Age*, which journalist Mark Ray would write for him, and an undisclosed sum for occasional sports commentary on Melbourne's MMM radio station.

Before long he was off to buy himself a $300,000 Ferrari 355 convertible and looking round for a $2 million mansion in Brighton, which was several rungs up the ladder from his parents' place in Black Rock. It was not bad for a bloke who had been driving a clapped-out Cortina and sleeping in an old cricket pavilion four years earlier, or who had been hefting beds for Forty Winks as recently as 1991.

A dozen years later we take it for granted that top-flight cricketers such as Warne rake in a million dollars a year or more for their talents, but in the early 1990s this sort of earning power was phenomenal, like nothing the sport had ever seen. Test cricketers in the 1970s had earned $200 a Test match until Packer's World Series Cricket pumped money into the game, and even after that, hardly anyone had made a living out of playing. Mike Whitney, who was in and out of the Test team in the 1980s and early 1990s, didn't dare give up his day job, cutting grass and driving trucks, until 1989. And even at that stage, Test players such as Ian Healy were making less than $10,000 a year by playing for Australia. So for Warne, in his early 20s, to be raking in 50 times that amount was really quite remarkable.

Soon, Warne was also being courted by Kerry Packer's Channel 9, which was looking to cast a new generation of cricketers who might ultimately replace Ian Chappell, Bill

Lawry, Richie Benaud and Tony Greig. The idea was to blood them on a new cricket show and train the best to be commentators. Warne – who joined the network at the same time as Mark Taylor, Ian Healy and Michael Slater – shone immediately. He had a great cricket brain, told a good story and could sell himself on air. Better still, he got along well with Kerry – who told people he 'liked the boy' – and with James Packer, who wrote a foreword in Warne's first life story, *Shane Warne, My Own Story*, praising Shane as 'a good bloke' whom he was 'proud to call a friend'.

Despite all this fame and fortune, Channel 9's head of Sport, Gary Burns, thought Warne was still just a big kid. In 1996 they flew to the US Masters together, partly as a reward, and partly to see how Warne would go as a golf commentator. Burns had expected them to meet at Sydney Airport, but came home from the office to find Shane bowling leg breaks to his kids and doing magic tricks such as plucking coins from their ears.

Some hours later, as Burns and Warne settled into the big leather seats in First Class, they were presented with lunch menus for the flight. Shane took one look at his and snapped it shut, declaring, 'I'm not eating anything, mate. Plane food's shit.'

'Have the caviar. It's fantastic', Burns urged, not knowing about Warne's terror of all foods except pizza.

'Fucking caviar? That would kill a brown dog', Warne replied.

Shortly afterwards, when the hostess came to take their order, Shane asked her if she had 'any of those snacky things?'

Minutes later she was back from Economy with four Le Snak packets of processed cheese and biscuits – the stuff that five-year-olds have for play lunch. Warne grabbed them, ordered a Midori and lemonade, and all was fine. Burns, meanwhile, tucked in to caviar and French champagne.

Many hours later, Gary was walking across the grass outside the clubhouse at Augusta, a place steeped in tradition and stuffy self-importance, when he heard a loud shout from the balcony: 'Burnsy, Burnsy, come up here.' He looked up to see Shane waving a Coke and a packet of Twisties, beckoning wildly like a kid on a school outing, saying, 'It's okay, it's sweet, we're allowed.'

Others reported that fame had not spoilt the boy. George Voyage, who had known him since his Brighton days, met him on a flight to Sydney in 1994 and watched him get mobbed on arrival. Polite as ever, Shane had time to stop and sign autographs, chat to people, sign a child's plaster cast, shake hands and say 'Have a good day' to everyone.

Craig Kimberley, the owner of Just Jeans, met him several times at store openings and functions and found him 'terrific, really personable'. He could 'only say good about him'.

Damien Fleming, Warne's Australian team-mate who had known him since the academy's tour of the West Indies in 1990, thought he handled fame and adulation 'much better than most of us would have done'. Shane did not mind that everyone wanted to talk to him. Indeed, he loved it. He loved the limelight and loved to be loved.

But it was not all smiles and roses. In 2005 Warne

admitted to journalist Piers Morgan that all this attention went to his head. And some already saw the sense of entitlement growing. One of his partners in crime from Mentone Grammar, Darren Van de Loop, ran into him one night at Melbourne's Crown Casino. 'We were in the middle of a non-smoking area', Van de Loop recalls, 'and he just pulled out a Benson & Hedges and lit up. I said to him, "Hey, you can't smoke here", and he just said, "Well, who's gonna stop me?"'

Warne's good mate Merv Hughes also told people, without going into detail, that he had been moved to talk to him about his yobbo behaviour. It was not a good look for a sporting role model, said Merv; sponsors wouldn't like it. He needed to pull his head in.

Even Warne seemed to think that fame did not improve him. 'The problem with some people is that when they have success, they begin to believe their own publicity', he admitted in 1997. 'It happened to me. You get aloof. You go into your own world.' The following year, *60 Minutes*, in another profile, asked Shane what the public thought of him and he replied without pausing: 'Arrogant, rude, obnoxious, bighead . . . is what people think.' And in some ways he certainly was.

Which brings us back to sledging.

9

Fuck off, Fuck off

Warne just calls you a cunt all day.

When the young New Zealand batsman Mathew Sinclair walked out to bat against Australia at Auckland's Eden Park in March 2000 he must have been expecting a bit of a welcome. He had scored a double century on his Test debut against the West Indies and might easily have been playing for Australia himself, because he had been born at Katherine in the Northern Territory. But he was hardly prepared for the greeting he got from Shane Warne as he arrived at the crease, which was: 'Fuck off, you buck-toothed fuck'.

'I know my teeth stick out a bit', he told mates in the bar that night, 'but what was that about? I've hardly even met the guy before'.

Warne's friend and Australian opening batsman, Michael Slater, also had a tale to tell that year. He was batting for New South Wales in a game against Victoria, and Shane was fielding in the slips with one of his mates, Darren Berry, keeping wicket. It was a dreadful time for Slater, who must have been close to a nervous collapse.

141

His marriage was falling apart, he was fighting an illness that would end his career, and his place in the Australian side was under threat. There were also (absolutely false) rumours doing the rounds that he was a cocaine addict. It was just the sort of time you need your mates, like Shane, to give you some support. Instead, Warne took it in turns with Berry to sing, 'Tick, tock, tick, tock, tick, tock.'

'I knew what they were getting at', Slater told ABC TV host Andrew Denton in mid-2005. 'They just thought I was a time bomb waiting to explode.' Even though Shane was a mate, he was happy to light the fuse, which shows you can expect no mercy from anyone at this level of Australian cricket.

Warne is notorious for his sledging – defined by the Macquarie dictionary as 'the practice among bowlers and fielders of heaping abuse on a batsman' – but he is not the worst among recent Australian Test cricketers. That honour would probably go to current Australian selector Merv Hughes, who reckons he got a quarter of his wickets by provoking batsmen; or to past captain Steve Waugh, who espoused a policy of 'mental disintegration'; or to star fast bowler Glenn McGrath, whose most famous sledge among many spits and snarls was to ask West Indian batsman Ramnaresh Sarwan, 'What does Brian Lara's dick taste like?' and then to threaten 'I will fucking rip your fucking throat out' when Sarwan gave him an answer he didn't like. But Warne is no shrinking violet, even in this company. And the Australian team is the undisputed sledging champion of the world.

In *Shane Warne, My Autobiography* he happily tells the Slater story, characterising it all as a bit of fun. And his moral code clearly puts few such things off limits. When Aussie Rules superstar Wayne Carey caused a national scandal in 2002 by sleeping with his team-mate-and-best-friend's wife, Warne was asked whether Wayne's public disgrace was acceptable material for a good, sharp sledge. He had no hesitation in saying yes: 'Once you cross that white line and stay within the rules, you do whatever you can to win.'

And it seems that this has been his dictum since school days. 'When Shane was bowling he would have the opposing batsmen, just kids, on the verge of tears', says David Guazzarotto, who used to field at short leg in the Mentone team. And what's wrong with sledging your way to victory? Warne asks in his autobiography: 'If I can get a batsman out by saying something that affects his game so much, then why not? That's a chink in his mental armoury.'

Most Australian cricketers would almost certainly agree with him. It's a battle out there, not cucumber sandwiches, they say; it's a man's game and you don't give a bloke a drink and wish him good luck when he comes to the crease. But older cricketers, such as former Australian captain Brian Booth, regard sledging as a cancer on the game. And a section of the public hates it just as much. In a poll for msn.com.au in 2003, one in three of the 33,000 respondents voted to ban sledgers for life. Not for one match, mind you, but for life.

The word 'sledging' dates from the 1970s, when it was coined by Ian Chappell's Australian team, which did its utmost to make it famous. But it does not surface in the *New Shorter Oxford English Dictionary* until much later, which may say something about how slow the Poms were to catch on to the tactic. Bob Woolmer, who opened the batting for England in the 1970s and now coaches Pakistan, could easily have filled them in. Woolmer had to endure a huge barrage of abuse from fast bowler Dennis Lillee, who reportedly took him through the entire Australian alphabet, which 'started with f and ended with f'. Chappell's men were so famous for their aggressive attitude and foul language that they were dubbed the Ugly Australians – a tag that has stuck to most other Australian Test teams since then, with Steve Waugh and his boys particularly worthy of the name.

It is all such a far cry from the traditional image of the game. In England at least, cricket is still regarded as a quiet, genteel pursuit that provides an excuse for putting up a marquee and hoeing into the Pimms, or in more rural climes, putting up a tent and getting into the beer. It's the sort of game where the vicar is welcome and where the most fun you can have as a spectator is to fall asleep in a deckchair. It is also one where people play fair, where they know how to behave and where they treat each other with courtesy, or so legend would have it. It's an old-fashioned, old-worldly sort of pastime, which is why the travel writer Bill Bryson, who calls England home, once observed:

It has always seemed to me a game much too restrained for the rough-and-tumble Australian temperament. Australians prefer games in which brawny men in scanty clothing bloody each other's noses. I am quite certain that if the rest of the world

144

Two of a kind. Shane and his mum, Brigitte, December 1991.

Shane's schoolmates reckoned he was a better batsman than bowler . . .

. . . while Shane dreamed of being an AFL footy star.

The Likely Lad. Shane at 21 in Lancashire, where he played for Accrington.

Chubby meets baggy. Shane tries on his Australian cap, December 1991.

Showered with praise. Shane and his captain, Allan Border, after skittling the West Indies with 7 for 52 at the MCG in December 1992.

Howzat? It's the Ball of the Century . . . Shane's first ball in the Ashes in 1993 makes him famous. Mike Gatting can't believe it.

Blond on blonde. The perfect match. Shane and Simone in 1993.

Not quite the traditional cricketer . . .

. . . but always happy to oblige a fan.

So why am I always in trouble? Shane celebrates Australia's Ashes win in style, Trent Bridge, 1997 . . .

. . . and gets snapped with a ciggy. So who wants to be a role model, anyway?

'I was very naïve and stupid.' Shane confesses to receiving US$5000 from an Indian bookie, December 1998.

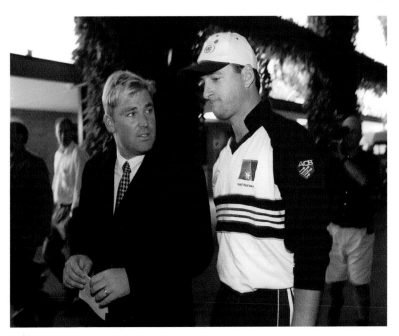

How did we go, mate? Warne and Mark Waugh after facing the press.

World Cup hero, London 1999. Another amazing comeback.

Always the centre of attention.

Never out of the headlines. In mid-2000, Warne bombarded English nurse Donna Wright with obscene phone messages . . . and was sacked as Australia's vice-captain.

Busted. Warne, after testing positive to a banned drug, February 2003. Shane told reporters his mum gave him the pill so he would look better on TV.

SHANE WARNE DRUG-TEST CRISIS

THE Daily Telegraph

Wednesday, February 12, 2003

$1*
Including GST XM

DEVASTATED

By ROBERT CRADDOCK

SHANE Warne will fly into Australia today to face an anti-doping tribunal which will decide if his career is over.

The star spinner was sent home from cricket's World Cup last night after testing positive to a banned drug.

He faces a two-year ban unless an emergency hearing before the Australian Cricket Board decides there are special circumstances in his case.

Warne said he was "shocked and devastated" to find he had tested positive to the banned diuretic last month.

He said a weight loss pill was responsible and he had no idea it was banned.

Warne's explanation: P2
The drug and how it works: P3
Paul Kent: Forgiving Shane P3
Is his career over: Sport P88

How was I to know? Warne claimed he never listened to briefings about drugs. He faced a maximum two-year ban.

Just a big kid.

Shane and his mum leave the drug hearing in Melbourne, February 2003. Warne escaped with a 12-month ban.

He's back! Warne's fans bring out the banners after his 12-month ban.

That's better news. Shane sets a new world record of 533 Test wickets.

vanished overnight and the development of cricket was left in Australian hands, within a generation the players would be wearing shorts and using the bats to hit each other.

And the thing is, it would be a much better game for it.

Bryson is clearly too young to have lived through the bodyline era, when the Poms bombarded the Australians with bouncers – in the days before helmets – and packed the leg side with close-in fielders to collect the ball as it popped into the air. But what he also failed to appreciate is that Australian cricket already comes close to his future fantasy. In interstate matches such as the Sheffield Shield (now known as the Pura Cup), games are played at war-like intensity. In Mike Whitney's description, 'Everyone sticks it up each other, everyone is sledging, everyone is playing it like it was a Test match. It is real serious shit, and there are some really tough, hard players out there.'

Playing at this level for the first time is an incredible shock: 'like being in the army reserve, then being para-chuted into the middle of a pitched battle', according to Mark Ray, who played for New South Wales and Tasmania in the 1980s. 'There is a fast bowler roaring down the pitch, sledging you, swearing at you, glaring at you, trying to knock your head off. Maybe trying to hurt you. There are three or four guys round the bat and at least one of them will be having a chat to you. It is in-credibly intimidating. There is real physical fear and you can't back away. The bowler loses all respect for you if you do, and then you're really in trouble.'

As a batsman at this level you have to stand and get hit, and that hurts, even if no one lets on. 'You think, "Oh, maybe it didn't hit him after all",' says Whitney, 'then you watch the replay and you see how much it would have hurt. That ball is travelling at 140 kilometres an hour and it's bloody hard. It has cracked into the ribs under the arm and they don't even rub the spot, they just walk down and tap the pitch.'

The scene in the dressing-room at the end of the day can resemble a war zone, especially if you are playing a team like the West Indies in the 1980s, with four ferocious fast bowlers, or even the current England team. There are batsmen everywhere, wrapped in ice, with big purple bruises on their backs, legs and bodies, knowing that they may soon have to go out there and face the barrage again.

Television ads – at least in Australia – now accentuate this element of combat. It's the battle for the Ashes, taking on the Old Enemy, the fight we've all been waiting for, the clash of the century, complete with shouted appeals, screaming catches and huge hits over the boundary. No 'After you, please' or 'More tea, vicar?' here. What gets bums on seats is conflict and aggression. And however much they may betray the game's traditions, snarling fast bowlers and stand-up fights provide great theatre. So it is not surprising that players on the pitch show little mercy. The whole ethos of the modern game in Australia – and of modern sport – encourages it.

Warne came back to Australia after his Ashes triumph in late 1993 noticeably more aggressive, more intimidating and more like a fast bowler in his attitude than he had been on departure. Success had made him cockier, no doubt, but he had also been studying at the feet of the master. Merv Hughes, Australia's star sledger, had taken almost as many wickets in England as Warne and had cracked the talented but fragile Graeme Hick with a barrage of bouncers, abuse and calls of 'arsewipe'. Taking his cue from Merv, Warne had invited Matthew Maynard, another England batter, to 'take [his] fucking shot back to Wales' after dismissing him with a googly. And on his return in the second innings he had greeted him with a cheery, 'This is your last chance, mate. You won't be on the plane to the West Indies if you fail again.' According to Maynard, the sledging worked. 'For some reason it got me thinking about failing . . . I hooked at one from Merv Hughes I should have left . . . and got caught in a trap they set for me.' Maynard, who clearly had chinks in his mental armour, claimed he had never been spoken to like that in all his years playing cricket. Welcome to Warne's world, buddy.

By the time the Test series against South Africa started in December 1993, Warne was in even more hostile mode, with a spectacular send-off to the Proteas' rising star Daryll Cullinan. Having bowled him with a brilliant flipper in the Second Test at the SCG, Warne ran down the pitch with his arms in the air, shouting at him to 'Fuck off', which was completely superfluous since he was already on his way back to the pavilion.

Warne loves to boast that Cullinan was his bunny – he dismissed the young South African 12 times in inter-national cricket – and delights in telling people that Cullinan had to seek psychiatric help because of him. But he has never suggested that he went too far in screaming

'Fuck off'. Warne's story is that he had it coming. The young prodigy had just scored an unbeaten triple century in South Africa and had long been billed as a superstar in the making. And according to Warne he was full of himself.

> He was chirping at us [i.e. sledging] all the time. He never stopped abusing our batsmen . . . Every time I came out to bat he said, 'Hey fatso, save some lunch for us will yer.' Our reaction was, 'Who does this bloke think he is? He's been in Test cricket five minutes and he's carrying on like this.'

So the 'Fuck off' was payback, according to Warne. Or in the language of the playground: 'He started it, miss. He did it to me first.' But it was not the only time that Warne or the team behaved badly against South Africa, and there had been complaints from the umpires to the International Cricket Council about 'bitter sledging' during the Ashes series a few months earlier. So in January 1994, the ACB decided reluctantly it was time to crack down, issuing a warning to Australia's cricketers that the next instance of bad sportsmanship would be punished. One of three crimes the ACB Chairman Alan Crompton highlighted in a public statement was 'send-offs' of the sort that Warne had given Cullinan. These were 'cowardly and un-Australian', said Crompton. In fact they were 'un-any other country you care to name'.

It would take Warne just five weeks and one Test match to do exactly what he and the team had just been warned not to do.

Perhaps the pressure got to him. Perhaps his inner brat prevailed. Perhaps fame just went to his head. The papers were fêting him as the Wizard of Oz and the Sultan of Spin, and singling him out as the man who held the key to the next three Tests in South Africa. After his brilliant performance in England and his demolition of South Africa in Sydney, much was expected of him. But there was also huge excitement at the prospect of battle resuming between the two old rivals on South African soil: it was the first time an official Australian team had toured there for more than 20 years, because of apartheid, and national honour was at stake.

And at last Warne appeared to have met his match. In the opening two matches of the one-day series, Hansie Cronje belted him for six after six on his way to scores of 112 and 97, with Warne picking up only one wicket. He then hit a brilliant 251 for Orange Free State on the eve of the first Test and, even worse, had the nerve to tell journalists that Warne was not really so hard to pick. The South African press loved it – here was someone who could smash the world's best spinner all over the park – and so did the crowds, chanting 'We want Warne' or 'Warne's a Wanker' whenever Cronje came to the crease. Warne, for his part, was so worried that he wrote home to his fiancée Simone, lamenting that he could not find a way to bowl at him.

Throughout the tour, the Australians complained of South African fans being rude and aggressive – which some might say is their national talent. And there was a definite frontier feel to it all: hard men with leathery sunburnt skin, huge amounts of alcohol and guns, guns,

guns. When the opening Test match got under way at the Wanderers Stadium in Johannesburg, the crowd was as hostile as any the visitors had experienced. The Bullring, as the ground is known, was more like a Bearpit. Writing in his tour diary, Steve Waugh complained that some people seemed to have come 'for the sole purpose of abusing us whenever they see fit'.

As lunch drew near on a bad-tempered third day, the Australians were under the cosh. South Africa was building a big second-innings lead and Cronje was hammering his way to yet another century. Warne had spent most of the morning out near the boundary, where he had been heckled and hit by an orange. But even if he was fired up by the time he came on to bowl, nothing could excuse his explosion at Andrew Hudson when he trapped him third ball. Warne raced down the pitch with his teeth bared, eyes ablaze, chasing after him and screaming as he walked away: 'Fuck off. Go on Hudson, fuck off outta here.' He was hysterical, and so angry that he had to be forcibly restrained from running after the batsman and physically attacking him.

The mild-mannered South African batsman looked back in astonishment as he made his way to the pavilion. He had neither provoked the attack nor deserved it. Everyone agreed he was the most decent, gentle, Christian human being one could imagine. This time Warne could not claim someone else had started it or that it was anyone else's fault but his own.

There is no sign that he felt immediate remorse for this vicious rant, even though his captain, Allan Border, instantly took him aside. And when Cronje reached his match-winning century later in the day, Warne conspicuously failed to applaud. But Australia's papers next day left him in no doubt what the public would soon be thinking, blasting his behaviour as 'boorish', 'crass', 'rude', 'vitriolic', 'outrageous', and 'an embarrassment'. Summing up the mood in *The Age*, and describing the incident as 'particularly distasteful', Peter McFarline observed: 'He is fast developing a reputation as an extremely bad-mannered young man on the field.'

Three months earlier at the MCG, Warne had thrown a ball hard to Healy and hit Hudson smack on the wrist, forcing him out for two matches. Though not deliberate it had been reckless and hot-headed. He had also mocked Chris Cairns's knee injury the month before in a Test against New Zealand by hobbling around in front of him. And there was the famous 'Fuck off' to Cullinan, which now seemed like a dress rehearsal. It was enough, said *The Sydney Morning Herald*, to justify a new term in the cricketing lexicon, 'a Warneing', which would stand for:

> . . . unacceptable behaviour on the cricket field involving vile language to batsmen, especially after they have been dismissed; unseemly theatrics when appeals have been turned down designed to unnerve umpires; intimidation of batsmen, often in the form of hurling the ball at the stumps but as close as possible to the batsman; a melodramatic defiance of the conventions of cricket.

In the *Herald*'s opinion, Warne had behaved outrageously all season and deserved to be suspended, red-carded, or even dropped for good. The paper's columnist Peter Roebuck chimed in for good measure that success had come too fast, too young and too easily for him and that 'the boyish innocence' had given way to 'a disturbing snarl'. McFarline added hopefully in *The Age* that he might be discarded from the team, commenting that 'cricket has a habit of disgorging its bad apples'.

What made all this into more than a passing storm was the limp reaction of the match referee, Donald Carr, who called Warne in for a dressing-down with his captain, Allan Border, and coach Bob Simpson, and then fined him the paltry sum of $400. This was a penalty of around one-tenth of his match fee for one of the ugliest incidents that cricket writers could remember. Merv Hughes was also fined $400 for telling South African batsman Gary Kirsten he was 'a weak little prick', which was the third time in 15 Tests that this serial offender had been penalised.

Almost everyone except the Australian team now demanded far tougher punishment, with one senior cricket writer describing Hughes's 'ferocious sledging and mouthing off at rival players' as 'nothing short of out-rageous'. The ACB also realised it was time to make a stand. Taking a lead from press criticism and its own warning five weeks earlier, it increased the fines tenfold to $4000 and issued a statement that charged the pair with bringing the game into disrepute and providing 'a totally inappropriate role model for young Australians to follow'.

But before the ink was even dry, Merv Hughes was in trouble again. As he ran off the pitch on the last day of the game, a spectator shouted abuse and spat at him. Hughes instantly retaliated by smashing his bat against the wire fence and shouting back: 'Mate, if you've got something to say, let's fucking hear it right now.' When the spectator backed off, Hughes repeated the challenge, which was soon relayed on sports bulletins around the world, then gave him a free character assessment: 'You're like every prick I've met here. You're weak as piss.' All of which earned him another $2000 fine and a good behaviour bond.

This new embarrassment brought a fresh volley of criticism from the press, who now turned their guns on the team and its management. Team culture – if one could use the word – encouraged such behaviour, one columnist argued. And even Mark Ray, a cricketer himself, joined the chorus, describing the team as 'a bunch of prima donnas who expect the high life as a matter of course, and who . . . struggle when things get tough'. A symptom of this self-importance, he suggested, was their habit of wearing designer sunglasses on planes, and their insistence that you could not be a nice bloke and a winner. Yes, it's hard out there, Ray conceded, it's a tough game. But the South African team had soaked up similar pressure without disgracing themselves, and were polite and modest to boot. It all came down to leadership, Ray suggested. And while the king of South African cricket, Ali Bacher, ruled with an iron grip, the Australian authorities did not. Border, Simpson and the ACB – as many had pointed out at the beginning of this saga – had let bad behaviour go unpunished for years. And Australia's captain had hardly set a good example himself. Border had been fined in 1992 for failing to attend a disciplinary hearing and had twice been reported by the umpires. He had also flattened his stumps in a match at Lord's in 1993. With him as captain, the Australians could be as ugly as they liked.

But far from being chastened by all the storm of public criticism, Australia's cricketers were outraged, and not at Warne or Hughes who had caused the hue and cry. Steve Waugh reserved his ire for those who had tipped off the media in advance about the referee's action, which he thought disgraceful. And the rest aimed their anger either at the press, for never having played cricket and not realising that it was a man's game, or at the ACB, for overruling the ICC and/or interfering with something that the captain, coach and tour manager were supposed to handle. They even discussed boycotting the next tour match in protest.

Warne, by contrast, did at least apologise, both to Hudson and to his army of fans. He told AAP's Patrick Keane that he was stung by the suggestion he was a bad role model and wanted to be given a second chance to win back his fans. It was his old catch cry: don't hang me just for one mistake. He then promised that the real Shane Warne was not a loud-mouthed hoon. He had had trouble coping with success, he said, and could feel his sudden rise to the top was changing him, not always for the better. 'I've got a really short fuse at the moment and I feel myself snapping', he told Keane. 'I'm letting everything get to me when I shouldn't . . . The continual ride over the last 18 months has got to me and I'm just burning up. I feel angry all the time.'

Writing in the Australian *Cricketer* magazine shortly afterwards, he also laid on the remorse and vowed, 'It was a mistake I deeply regret and one I will never repeat.' Five years later he was still busy apologising, confessing in an ACB-sanctioned Shane Warne video: 'It was probably one of the things I most regret in my life, and I've no idea why [I did it].'

But despite all his breast beating and admissions of guilt, one wondered whether it was the act he regretted or the fact that it had attracted such savage criticism. He simply hated not being loved. Certainly, he continued to brag about humiliating Cullinan and telling him to 'Fuck off'. And he did not exactly reform. Three years later he was in trouble for mocking South Africa's number 11 batsman, Paul Adams, after dismissing him, in what *The Age* called 'one of the most childish and embarrassing acts committed by an Australian Test cricketer'. Labelling his behaviour 'puerile', 'demeaning' and 'immature', the paper's Patrick Smith went on to say: 'Under pressure, he turns into a boor. The pleasant young man of television interviews is readily interchangeable with an immature hothead'.

Even today, after a dozen more years to grow up, and a decade as captain of Victoria or Hampshire, the brat is rarely far away. Warne argues that he needs to be aggressive to perform at his best. 'We play at a very high level of arousal', he once said, 'on the edge of fury, if you like.' But even when he is not furious, he can still be 'rude and crude' as his Hampshire team-mate Kevin Pietersen puts it, or downright offensive. 'Warne just calls you a cunt all day' is how South African captain Graeme Smith famously described Shane's witty sledging in 2002.

Nor has he stopped since then. In 2004, umpires had to haul him out of a stand-up row on the pitch with Essex captain Ronnie Irani, who accused Warne of calling his mother a whore (which Warne denied). And in 2005, Sussex captain Jimmy Adams complained bitterly that Warne had set out to humiliate one of his players (which Warne claimed was payback for earlier taunts to one of his batsmen). And so it goes on. But his philosophy is abundantly clear. 'There are no mates out on a cricket field', he argues in *Shane Warne, My Autobiography*. 'We all play to win.' And as long as sledging is legal, he intends to keep using it as a weapon. His book even gives advice on how to avoid being spotted by the TV cameras or picked up on the stump mikes as you slip in the knife.

But if you think that Warne is alone in this 'anything goes' attitude, think again. In the USA in 2004, Professor Sharon Stoll set the jocks a-jumping with a study on elite athletes' moral values. Conducted over 17 years by the Center for Ethics at the University of Idaho, with an extraordinary 72,000 interviews, Stoll's study concluded that sport was good for 'teamwork, loyalty, self-sacrifice, work ethic, and perseverance' but lousy for 'honesty, fairness, and responsibility'.

Among the questions she posed were:

1. If one of your mates is bad at maths because he has been training hard for the team, should you let him cheat in the exam by sitting next to you and copying your work?

According to Professor Stoll, sportspeople (and particularly men in teams) tend to say yes.

2. If one of your mates gets hit on the head by a dangerous pitch at baseball, should the team deliberately throw at the culprit's head when he comes in to bat?

Again sportsmen tend to say yes.

3. If an illegal play favours your team and the referee has not spotted it, should you point it out and stop the game?

Here, sportsmen tend to say no, arguing that it's the umpire's job, not theirs, to police the game. One can imagine a similar question being put to Australian cricketers about whether they should walk if they are out or wait for the umpire. Or indeed whether it is okay to abuse batsmen if it will pick up wickets.

Professor Stoll wraps up her study with the observation that sport today is about winning and that teams (and professional male teams in particular) will increasingly do whatever it takes to win. The ethics of sport, she says, have become how to get away with it.

It is worth putting these findings into an Australian framework, because the values of 'teamwork', 'loyalty' and 'self-sacrifice' that Stoll highlights are almost exactly the values of mateship that we are so often told to admire. They are about standing up for your mates, looking after your mates and being loyal to your mates no matter what they do. These are the very values that Australian sporting teams and young Australians are encouraged to display on and off the field. And in Stoll's experience, based on years of research, they thrive at the expense of 'honesty', 'fairness' and 'responsibility' . . . with Shane and his mates leading the charge.

10

Playing Away

Probably the one mistake he made in life was to
get married.

When Warne arrived in South Africa in 1994 he was
fêted like a rock star. 'It was like Elvis had risen
from the dead', according to Australian wicket-keeper Ian
Healy. 'Young girls would scream his name whenever he
left a venue.' He would come back to the hotel to find 20
phone messages, and would be woken up at two am by
groups of revellers banging on his door. And it was a
similar story back in Melbourne when he turned up at
store openings for Just Jeans or gave motivational
seminars to their staff. 'There were women all over him',
says founder Craig Kimberley. 'They really chased him.
They would write lipstick messages on his shirt or try to
follow him to the toilet. We had to protect him; several
times we had to drag them off.'

For a pants man like Shane the attention must have been
a thrill, but there was a problem in taking advantage of
what was on offer, because he was engaged to
be married and would soon be a family man. Shane had
met Simone Callahan at a celebrity golf day in Melbourne

in 1992, where she was working as a Foster's girl, no doubt clad in short skirt, white boots and skimpy top, handing beer to the players. And it was 'love at first sight of the legs', as one reporter laughingly described it. Legend has it that he lost her phone number and was snubbed when he met her again by chance. But they ran into each other again at another celebrity golf day and it was third time lucky.

Simone was 22 at the time and Shane 23, and fame was still a long way off. He had just made his Test debut in Sydney and was working hard to lose weight. He had certainly not yet established himself as a professional sportsman and he was not even a budding superstar. Nor was he pursued by women everywhere he went. He was a chubby cricketer with a bad haircut and a good line in chat, who was still living with his mum. Simone was a pretty blonde girl who had left school aged 15 to become a hairdresser, then graduated to modelling and pro-motions work. 'It was a fairy tale', Simone told *New Idea* nostalgically, years later, as it was all falling apart. 'Shane swept me off my feet, and we were so in love.'

Simone wasn't his first serious girlfriend, but she may well have been only his second. And he certainly seems to have wanted to get hitched to someone. After dating Accrington's lovely Lisa Ramsden – who told the papers that Shane declared his love within a week and promised 'they would be good together' – he had fetched another Lancashire lass called Jackie Coo over to Australia. And he was still seeing her in 1992 when he started dating Simone. Jackie Coo was also a pretty blonde, but it is not clear whether she had a hairdressing pedigree too.

Lisa and Simone both found Shane to be soft and incredibly romantic – or so the papers claimed – a man who wrote love letters and sent them flowers. And Simone soon succumbed to his charms. By January 1993 she was travelling with him on the Australian tour of New Zealand, and five months later she joined him for the Ashes series in England, where Shane proposed to her on a rowing boat in the Lake District, or on the Thames, or on the Serpentine in Hyde Park, depending on whose version you believe. As Maurice Chevalier would say, 'I remember it well.' Soon afterwards, she was starring as his fiancée in a *60 Minutes* profile, walking arm in arm through the park, sitting beside him on a couch during the interview, and watching him play cricket from the grandstands with some of the other cricketers' wives. She was a pretty, sunny girl with a lovely smile and a happy laugh: the sort that Shane would have been happy to bring home to his parents.

In many ways she was, and is, just like Shane. According to those who know them well, she looks like him, eats like him and talks like him. Suburban girl meets suburban boy. By common consent, she is polite, pleasant, nice, lovely, uncomplicated and sincere. But everyone agrees she is also a bit slow on the uptake. 'There's no rocket science going on', as one of Shane's mates puts it. 'He's a spin bowler, she was a promotions model. They have both got blond hair, she's got big tits. If she hadn't married she'd still be putting on a red lycra suit when the grand prix comes round.'

Journalists who toured with the pair in those early days were struck by how young and naïve they both seemed. In

New Zealand, for example, where the players and journalists hopped round the country, hugger-mugger, on small planes, one cricket writer sat behind them and heard them squabbling all the way: 'It was a teenage tiff like you wouldn't believe.' A couple of years later, another saw a fax sent to Shane at the team hotel from Simone, who had stayed back in Australia. 'It was really gushy, lovey-dovey', he says, 'the sort of thing a 16-year-old would send.' Warne later confided to him that they were both reading *Men are from Mars, Women are from Venus* and kept turning to each other to ask: 'Who does this remind you of?' They both seemed to have so little experience of the world, to be so ill-equipped for the pressures they would have to face.

By the time they finally got married in September 1995 – after twice postponing the wedding because of Shane's cricketing and sponsorship commitments – these pressures were mounting. Shane was a hundred times more famous and a hundred times richer than when they had met. His management company was telling potential sponsors he was the most recognisable man in Australia, and magazines everywhere wanted a part of him, preferably with no clothes on. A British tabloid had offered huge money for him to pose in nothing but a jockstrap, and a UK Sunday newspaper had offered a five-figure sum for pictures of him topless. Or so his agent claimed. Remarkably, Shane had turned down both invitations. Less surprisingly, he had also knocked back requests from a British lads' magazine to talk about his sexual conquests and to say what he looked for in a woman. Apart from blonde hair and big breasts.

An English TV production company was also said to be offering $200,000 for a fly-on-the-wall documentary about Shane and Simone, with the marriage as its centrepiece. Luckily, someone was smart enough to say no to this one too, or the pair might have found themselves portrayed as another couple of crass, nouveau-riche Australians, to compete with Noelene Donaher in the BBC's savage *Sylvania Waters*.

The big Australian women's magazines went to war over exclusive rights to the wedding pictures but the Warnes rejected them too, in the hope of having a private ceremony. They spent money hiring security guards to keep the media away, but the pictures ended up in Kerry Packer's *Woman's Day* regardless. One of the guests took her snaps to Rabbit Photo to get them developed, and the shop owner slipped the best ones to the magazine for money.

The wedding was a glamorous affair and a huge thrill for cricket fans, because so many Australian players, past and present, were there. The venue was fabulous: Como House in South Yarra, a white Italianate pile set in two hectares of green lawns and spreading cypress trees. In the pictures that did see the light of day, Simone looked ravishing, while Shane was dashing and handsome. For once he was eating soup not pizza, but he was drinking beer, Foster's of course. The score of blondes to brunettes (female), for those who are interested, was 8:3, with none of the darker-haired variety being above the age of 10 or below the age of 40. In other words, they were kids or mums. And the tally of pictures in which Shane was looking at Simone or touching her affectionately, for those who might think this is significant, was zero out of six.

Nevertheless, they appeared to be the perfect couple, the envy of all, even without the fame, the Ferrari and the $2 million bayside mansion with its big black wrought-iron gates. But already you could sense who might be getting most from the deal. 'Simone's been fantastic. It's great to have her support', Shane told Marjory Bennett from Sydney's *Sun-Herald*.

When you've finished your cricket, you've got to unwind. When I've had a hard day, she cops me being angry or a bit disappointed and on my good days she might be feeling a bit flat. It's a stressful life. She's learning to cope with it; it's all pretty new to her, too.

It was Shane, Shane, Shane, too, when they ventured out at night, because people would not leave them alone. 'It's hard at times, especially if we're out to dinner and some-body comes up and asks for an autograph', he said. 'Simone doesn't get much time to spend with me so we like to make it quality time when we're together.'

'We go to restaurants a lot', he told another profile writer. 'I love pasta, could eat it every night, so we eat a lot of Italian. Simone loves Mexican, especially nachos, so we compromise.' In fact, his mates wondered if they ever ate at home because neither seemed to like cooking and Shane almost certainly could not. According to Australian batsman David Boon, his fridge contained nothing more than 'a block of cheese, half a loaf of bread, butter, a carton of milk and a dessert bowl, covered in glad-wrap, full of leftover canned spaghetti'.

But Shane was never at home anyway. From the beginning, he was on tour with the Australian team for anything up to eight months a year, and even when he was back in Australia he was not necessarily in Melbourne. There were Tests and interstate games to be played in Brisbane, Sydney, Adelaide, Perth and Hobart, and a constant round of store appearances, sponsor functions and celebrity golf days. He also did stuff for charity, helping other cricketers with fundraisers and sporting nights. In 1996–7 he played in five countries on five continents, clocking up 24 Tests and more than 30 one-day internationals in just 21 months.

After going on tour with Shane to New Zealand and England in 1993, Simone rarely went overseas, so she did not see him getting the Elvis treatment in South Africa, and wasn't around to cramp his style. Taking wives on tour was frowned on by the Australians' captain and coach, Allan Border and Bob Simpson, because they were reckoned to weaken team spirit. You couldn't bond with your mates or concentrate on the job, it was thought, if you had to go back every night to a partner – or, God forbid, to a family. Consequently, wives were banned on the 1989 Ashes tour of England, and there was not much change in 1993 when partners (all of whom were female, of course: surely that goes without saying?) were banned from the team hotel until the series was won. 'That was AB's [Allan Border's] way', says Michael Slater. 'He thought it was a distraction.'

Whether or not this separation was good for cricket –

and team psychologists today don't think so – it was bad for relationships and worse for the wives, who were left to fend for themselves, make their own way to matches, cheer their partners all day and then not see them at the close of play. Steve Waugh's wife, Lynette, to whom he is still married despite years of touring, wrote a chapter in his recent autobiography, *Out of My Comfort Zone*, in which she described 'the chill' that she felt near the Australian team.

> It wasn't an environment that welcomed women. You so wanted the team to win, but a part of you didn't, because you knew that your partner would be locked away in a dressing room for hours, followed by a long celebration out on the town and then a day to recover. You would often return after cheering and sweating over your partner's success for seven hours to an empty hotel room.

In a nearby hotel, of course. Meanwhile, as Michael Slater pointed out, 'There was nothing to stop you [the players] going off and getting some slag bag.' Or as Lynette put it, 'Single players could – and did – meet girls on tour and take them into the hotel.' And not just the single players.

With this sort of welcome mat, it was hardly surprising that Simone chose to stay in Melbourne most of the time, particularly after 1996 when she became pregnant with her and Shane's first child. So Shane was left to tour the world for months at a time, staying with his mates in five-star hotels in exotic locations, with every need catered for, living an 'unreal lifestyle in an unreal world', as Test star

Michael Slater put it. 'There is no other sport that takes you away from your family like it does', says Slater, who split with his childhood sweetheart, Stephanie, in 2001 after too much touring and too many temptations.

Cricketers may not be led astray quite so frequently as NBA pro-league basketballers in the USA, whose team buses often roll in from interstate to be met by 20 or 30 scantily clad, well-endowed groupies, ready to fight their way up to the players' rooms. Nor could any cricketer – Shane included – break the record of Wilt Chamberlain, the NBA's greatest star, who claimed to have screwed 20,000 women in his long career, which on my reckoning is one a day for 54 years. But cricketers certainly get women a-plenty and it has always been so.

Even in the 1960s, Australian state cricket teams partied their way round the country. In Adelaide there were a couple of women who linked up with every Sheffield Shield side when it arrived and whose phone numbers were passed on to any team that was due to hit town. In other cities, teams would swap numbers of will-ing women. One ex-Queensland fast bowler, Sandy Morgan, then barely out of his teens, recalls boarding a plane from Brisbane for his first tour and sitting beside a fellow cricketer who spent the whole trip busily scribbling on bits of paper and sealing them in envelopes. As they flew in to land, Morgan asked what he was doing. 'Letters to the wife', came the reply. 'One from Sydney, one from Melbourne, one from Adelaide, one from Perth. Now I can concentrate on the real business.' Which was having fun.

Test players in the 1980s and 1990s found it even easier

than this, because they were far more famous. Mike Whitney, who never reached the same sort of superstar status as Shane, says: 'It was like fairyland, it really was. You've got people carrying your bags, money is being thrown at you left, right and centre, you've got girls all over you like a cheap suit, and if you want to enjoy all these fruits of your labour you can.'

And wherever Shane went he received 10 times the attention, 10 times the adulation, 10 times as many women and 10 times as much interest as the rest of the team. There was little chance that anyone in his position, and least of all he, could be expected to be faithful to his wife or fiancée 100 per cent of the time. How else would he fight the boredom, night after night in his hotel room? He did not read books, had no interest in the outside world and no passion for chess or bridge. So drinking, gambling and sex were bound to figure high on his list of attractive pursuits. But the trouble with Shane was that he didn't even seem to be trying to be good. As one close cricketing mate says laconically, 'We've all got skeletons in our closet, but he is deadset Rookwood.' For those who don't get the joke, it is the name of Sydney's largest cemetery.

One of Shane's TV mates, who is also one of his greatest admirers, says he just can't help himself, that he will hit on anyone, including the tea lady, and that he has been dragged out of clubs all over the world by his Channel 9 minders. 'He just can't control himself', says another of his mates in the media. 'There's no doubt his dick does the talking. He likes women. And he knows how to collect them. He just turns his charm on them.'

'He chases women, blonde women, insatiably', says a current member of the Australian team, giving the example of a flight from Sydney to Melbourne with all the Australian players on board. 'Shane walked down the aisle, spotted this blonde girl, gave her the eye, turned on the glow and then started chatting to her. By the end of the flight he's got her mobile number and they're side by side. He does it with his eyes. He just gives you this look.'

One such woman recalls meeting Shane at an overseas reception for the Australian team in the early 1990s – after he took up with Simone – and asking him and his team-mates to a party. That evening she got a phone call from him which rapidly turned dirty. The next night he failed to come to the party but phoned at one am, where-upon she told him rudely to get lost. Then a friend discovered she had abused Australia's greatest cricket star, Shane Warne, and convinced her to apologise. It was a bad mistake, she readily admits, and she takes some of the blame for what happened next. She went to his hotel, phoned from the lobby and went up to his room, where without any preamble, Shane took off his clothes and suggested they have sex. She was so amazed she just laughed, and asked him, 'Shouldn't we at least have dinner first?'

It is hard for her to tell this story because she is concerned that any detail could identify her, but she has little to worry about as there are almost certainly hundreds more such stories, as she herself suggests: 'I'm sure he's been doing it for ages.'

Early on in the writing of this book, one of Shane's mates at Channel 9 told me that he reckoned Warne had a pretty good average, because he had probably had 1000 women and only got caught five times. I thought at the time this was a crazy exaggeration. But now I'm not so sure. I personally know two other women who have been propositioned (or more) by him, and my limited knowledge of statistics makes me think there must be a host of others with similar stories.

More of these would have been made public if Australian cricket writers had regarded it as their job to report on such infidelities. But they did not. Nor did they rat on the team official who saw it as his duty to carry a plentiful supply of condoms for the players or on journalists who occasionally took advantage of the service. Generally, what happened off the field remained off limits, and wives were left to use their imagination about what their partners got up to. Some were worldly enough to accept infidelity as inevitable and turn a blind eye, but Simone did not need to. Remarkably, she seemed to have no inkling that her husband was the biggest pants man of all. So she did not give him grief, as Shane put it, by phoning in the early morning to ask where he had been the previous night. She did not interrogate him about what he got up to. She was convinced for many years that he was completely faithful. And none of the team or their partners was going to dob Shane in.

Had she read a famous book called *Calypso Cricket* by Australian writer Roland Fishman, she might have been more worried. Billed as 'The inside story of the 1991 Windies tour', it rocked the cricketing world that year when it hit the bookstands. A dozen years later, according to the *Courier-Mail*'s Robert Craddock, the Australians on that tour could still remember the day it was published, just as children of the 1960s could recall where they were in November 1963 when they heard that John F. Kennedy had been shot.

One player arrived home from a football match with his father-in-law to find his wife in tears in the driveway.

'Was it you?' she asked before even mentioning what she was talking about.

Several other players' wives headed off for an interstate holiday, leaving their husbands behind and, for a while, refusing to take their phone calls. One player said it was the worst week of his life.

Fishman's crime was to describe in some detail what the Australian cricketers got up to after stumps were pulled. 'All the players are cunt struck', he wrote succinctly, 'and all the women are star struck.' One player boasted to him that he had had four different sexual partners in one night; another claimed to have bedded 30 women during the month-long tour.

For those who were interested – which was everyone – Fishman outlined how they did it. 'The players are already known, so all they have to do is stand or lean on something and wait for it to happen.' One guy's pick-up method, he reported, was to start off to his room, then turn over his shoulder to a woman he had met 60 seconds before and ask her, 'Are you coming?' Shane is reported to employ a similar technique.

What amazed the players was Fishman's amazement at

how much sex was on offer. 'It's just part of touring', they told him. But they were even more amazed when their men's talk ended up in print with their scorecards. By today's standards, the book was quite tame: there were no rapes, gang bangs, buns or spit roasts (to borrow from the dictionary of modern sporting slang) and no one was named. But their partners back home were suddenly alerted to the fun the boys were having, and the very lack of names meant that all of them were under suspicion.

No one accused Fishman of lying or making it up. No one seriously disputed that what he wrote was true, but there was a massive row about whether he should have told tales. There is a golden rule for all sporting teams – and almost any group of travelling males – that what happens on tour stays on tour. It is a conspiracy of silence in which you protect your mates at all costs. Journalists and players know their lives will not be worth living if they break the code. Which is why news of Shane's away games always come from the women he plays with.

In early 1996, four months after his marriage to Simone, Shane picked up a woman on Australia's most famous beach at Bondi. She was gorgeous and French, had just arrived in the country, and was lying on the hot sand wearing nothing but a thong when two guys came up to say hello. They were cricketers, they said, which meant nothing to her, but they were cute and they got talking. The blond one then suggested they catch up for a drink at the Australian team hotel in Sydney, and gave her his room number. She had no idea that he was the world's best spinner, nor that he had just got married, so she took him up on his offer and ended up staying the weekend. He was no great lover, she says, but he was attractive, good company and fun. They met again several times, and finally he confessed that he had a girlfriend. But it was okay, he told her: they had just split up. Only later did she discover that this was a complete lie and he was married.

So, even at this early stage, Shane was cheating on Simone. And his Australian team-mates certainly knew, because their affair was conducted openly. This is a regular feature of Warne's womanising: the fact that his friends, mates or TV colleagues may be watching doesn't hold him back. In fact, he brags about his conquests and his status as a sex symbol. In 1997, on the South African tour, he was proudly telling journalists about the faxes and messages he was receiving from women. He was even getting 'pairs of knickers through the post', he boasted. Later on, he would often forward the sexy text messages he got from women to his mates.

Some believe that this is precisely what such affairs are all about. Experts who study sportsmen behaving badly argue that they have sex with women to get respect from their mates, who are far more important to them than any girl could ever be. If you want to be the leader of the pack, you either have to be the most talented player on the field or you have to be the one who pulls the chicks. And if this is what motivates Shane – who scores on both counts – there would no point at all in keeping his affairs private. They would need to be advertised, so his mates could be impressed, which at some level they undoubtedly are.

As one of his old school friends says wistfully, 'Probably the one mistake Shane made in life was to get married. Apart from that he had the perfect life for an Australian male: play cricket for your country, be worshipped, and have as many women as you like.'

In 1999, a woman – let's call her Helen – ran into Warne in a Perth hotel. She was there on business for a big European bank and he was in town to play a Test against Pakistan. Around 11 pm, she and a colleague turned in for the night, and as the lift doors closed to take them up to their separate rooms, Warne hopped in with Steve Waugh. Thirty seconds later, her colleague reached his floor and bade her goodnight, and Waugh got out too, leaving her alone with the blond stranger. Not being a cricket fan, she had no idea who he was until a friend informed her the next day. As the doors closed, Warne turned to her with that look and said: 'So you are coming up for a drink with me, aren't you?' She replied that it had been a long day and she was too tired, but he didn't give up. 'Oh come on, just a drink. It won't hurt you.' For the record, she did not succumb.

One of Helen's friends, a well-known Australian cricketer, is staggered by the nerve of it. 'I reckon I was pretty good at picking up sheilas in my time', he says. 'But I would never, never have tried it on someone I met in a lift. I mean he had 50 seconds. The guy is amazing.'

It was some time before such stories would get back to Simone. But there are other strains on sporting marriages, apart from infidelity, and the Warnes did not escape them. In that first *60 Minutes* profile in 1993, she promised she would not be playing second fiddle to his cricket. But she would soon have discovered that was exactly the role she was expected to play in the Shane Warne Australian orchestra.

'Sporting wives have second-class status', says Steven Ortiz, an American sociologist who has pioneered research in this area. And they do not always rise that high in the sports star's firmament: 'His career generally comes first, perhaps his mother would come in second, and perhaps his team may come in third, and then in some marriages it's possible that the wife would come in fourth.'

They are like army marriages or corporate marriages, only more so, says Ortiz, who spent four years interviewing the wives of 50 baseball, basketball, football and hockey players in the USA. They give support and get little in return. Or as English cricketer Derek Pringle put it in his cautionary article 'Don't marry a cricketer': 'Top-level sport is accompanied by self analysis and narcissism, which do not lend themselves to the give-and-take required in long term relationships.'

Ortiz claims that most of the sportsmen he studied were doted on by their mothers, who were crucial to their sporting careers:

> They spoil them, they cater to them from a very young age, they chauffeur them to all of their games and practices, make their favourite meals . . . it becomes part of what I call the spoiled athlete syndrome, because the mother is a very important figure in that process.

This certainly chimes in with Shane's childhood. And guess who takes over from Mum when the boy leaves home. According to Ortiz, 'When he does get married, in a way he is replacing that first influential figure in his life, his mother, with a newer updated improved version.'

I am not privy to the secrets of Shane and Simone's marriage, but I would bet she became a passenger on his emotional rollercoaster: up with the elation of victory, down with the despair of defeat, and down even further when injury struck, as it did several times in his career. Every now and again – mostly in times of crisis – Shane admitted he was lucky to have her. As a modern international cricketer, he said:

> You've got to either be single, because of the travel, or you've got to have a fantastic and very understanding wife. And I don't think if you've got that support, you're always going to struggle because if you're away on tour and you ring your wife and they're giving you grief about, 'You didn't call last night', and all those sorts of things. 'What are you doing?' You know, I mean, you don't need to go to the ground under the pump saying, 'I'm in the dog kennel', shall we say, with the wife. So look, I'm very lucky to have a great wife – and she has been very, very supportive.

She had indeed, even before the English tabloids began lifting the lid on his private life.

11

Comeback Kid

*All I could think of was would I ever be able to play
for Australia again.*

There is no doubt that Shane Warne is mentally one of
the toughest cricketers the Australian game has seen.
Watch him on the field and you can tell it from his body
language. He may not have the majesty of Viv Richards,
the raw aggression of Merv Hughes, or the cold steel of
Steve Waugh, but even when he is fielding in the slips
there is something about the way he holds himself – chest
out, shoulders back, head high – that speaks confidence
and power.

But off the field, even the hardest nuts suffer doubt –
about whether they're good enough, whether they can
recover lost form, or whether they can come back from
injury. And Warne is not one of the hardest nuts in this
respect. Despite his talent, his records and his extraordinary gift, he remains strangely insecure about it all, as
if he feels he is in a dream from which he may soon
awake. His fears are loudest when he is injured or disgraced. He is ever ready to tell people he's had enough, it's
not worth the fight, he doesn't know whether he'll ever

bowl again, or even if he wants to. He said these things during the betting scandal in 1998, the drug scandal in 2003, when he was dropped from the team in mid-1999 and many other times along the way.

It all adds to the drama of his life, no doubt, and makes his eventual comeback more of a triumph. It is how the spoilt child shows how much he is needed. But if Shane spins out when his future is threatened it is also because cricket is everything to him, and the prospect of losing it shakes him to the core. Elite sportsmen are often vulnerable in this way, and he is among the most fragile of the breed. Cricket brings him mates, money, fame, fun, adulation and acclaim. And however much he may protest that he could give it all up for his family, he does not really mean it. Despite all the scandals in his private life, Shane's worst times have been when he was forced to watch from the sidelines. He knows that without cricket he would be lost.

There have been several moments when Warne has had to face the prospect that his career might be over, and the most serious have involved injury. Leg-spin bowling, day after day, month after month, year after year, puts huge stress on the body, and by early 1996 his shoulder and fingers were beginning to feel the strain. He had sent down almost 30,000 balls in the previous five years and the ring finger on his right hand, the one that imparts the spin, was in terrible shape. Unless he went under the knife, there was a good chance that he would have to give up cricket or stop bowling those big-spinning leg breaks. It would be like Betty Grable losing her legs, Jayne Mansfield losing her breasts or David Beckham hobbling on broken feet.

Shane's spinning finger had started swelling up in the West Indies in early 1995. Regular cortisone injections into the knuckle had deadened the pain and allowed him to keep bowling, and he wore a special synthetic sleeve on-field, but the damage got steadily worse. By the time he reached the World Cup in India and Pakistan in March 1996, the ligaments holding the knuckle together had loosened so much that the veins were popping through the knuckle, and the finger was so stiff and painful he could hardly spin the ball. In the final, he was belted for six runs an over as Australia crashed to a seven-wicket defeat against Sri Lanka. To add insult to injury, Sri Lanka's captain, Arjuna Ranatunga, not only hit him for six but stuck his tongue out at him after doing so.

Warne's right shoulder was almost as bad – sore and stiff from overuse – and the specialists recommended he have a reconstruction and hope that the finger healed with a few months' rest. But Shane was convinced that finger surgery was the only solution, because nothing he had tried, rest included, had eased the pain for more than a week or two. And since he could not have both operations at once, because the rehabilitation would be a nightmare, he had to fix his finger first. He could put up with a sore shoulder but he could not bowl at all if his spinning finger would not do the job.

Warne had an operation to repair the ligament damage in May 1996, at the beginning of winter, in a Melbourne sports clinic. All went smoothly, but he could not shake hands for weeks afterwards and there were doubts about whether he would ever bowl properly again. Other spinners had warned him that the finger would never go back to normal, but all he could do was wait and see. In the months that followed he sat up at night, unable to sleep for hours on end, worrying and wondering if he would ever be able to play for Australia again.

He expected the finger to heal within four months, but when the Australian team went off to India six months after the operation for a Test match and one-day tournament, he was forced to stay behind. He was so miserable about being left out that he sat at home in his cricket gear, watching the matches on cable TV, dressed in his whites for the Test and his green-and-gold for the one-dayers, spinning the ball from one hand to another. It was a tragic indication of how much it all meant to him. When the games were finished, he loaded a specially made tape of his 40 best wickets into the video player and tried to convince himself that he would soon be firing again. It helped his cause – and his mood – that Australia missed him badly and failed to win a single match without him.

While his team-mates were losing in India, Shane was starting on the comeback trail, more determined than ever to get back to what he loved. He had put on weight watching TV and had been stacking it on before that. But by the time he took the field for St Kilda on his first outing in mid-October he had trained and dieted enough to shed 8 kilos. He struggled to bowl and got hammered. He also had to go off the field to pack his hand with ice when the finger, which was already stiff, started to swell. His comeback continued with a couple of one-day games for Victoria and two four-day matches against New South Wales and South Australia, in which he bowled accurately but without much fizz.

By November, he was fit enough to play in the First Test against the West Indies in Brisbane, but his spin and swerve were still missing. It was not until he had a net session in Sydney in December with his old mentor, Terry Jenner, that he began to get it back. His problem, as Allan Border had pointed out, was that he was not giving the ball a proper rip, presumably because he still did not trust the surgeon's handiwork. 'I made him bowl from a stand-still', says Jenner, to force his hand to do more, 'and I told him it was going to feel different, but that was okay.' Even at this stage, seven months after the operation, his spinning finger was still twice the size of the others, and he could neither straighten it fully nor clench it into a fist. It was a miracle he could bowl at all, let alone bowl well. But in the Second Test at the SCG some of the old magic returned. He picked up seven wickets and dazzled the crowd with a ball to the left-handed Chanderpaul that was every bit as good as the one that had got Gatting in 1993. Bowling from around the wicket, Warne pitched it into the footmarks and spun it almost a metre to take out middle and leg. He had never spun a ball further, he reckoned, and according to wicket-keeper Ian Healy, it was 'as near unplayable as you can get'. Brisbane's *Courier-Mail* thought so, too. Under the headline, 'WIZARD WARNE BACK WITH BITE', Robert Craddock proclaimed: 'He is back. With arguably the best ball of his career, Shane Warne yesterday convinced a doubting world that he was ready to re-emerge as the most venomous strike force in Test cricket.'

Warne ended the five-match series with 22 wickets and went off to South Africa to seal his return with a brilliant performance in the First Test in Johannesburg, where he bagged six wickets and spun the ball as far as ever. Even the flipper seemed to be working again, which was a sign the finger was fine. Hansie Cronje was forced to admit that his batsmen had faced him with fear in their hearts. Warne, meanwhile, happily declared himself back to his best, after coming through 'the toughest period of my life . . . a dark and very long tunnel.'

He admitted how important Simone had been in getting him through:

> [She] was fantastic support throughout. There were plenty of days when I'd be grumpy about the slow recovery of my finger . . . there were others when I'd come home and hug her in delight because I'd managed to bowl a leg break at practice that afternoon. Simone understood what I was going through and was able to put up with my mood swings.

Two months after announcing to everyone that the dark days were over, such is the rollercoaster of Shane's emotions that he was back in the dumps again. At the end of the South African tour he confided to journalists that he was so tired he could not go on. He was just 28 years old – still five years younger than Grimmett was when he played his first Test, and not yet in a leg spinner's prime – but had decided he'd had enough. It was partly because he was now in trouble with Simone, who was six months pregnant and home alone without support: she had opened the paper to see him signing a girl's cheek, to the left of her G-string, in the middle of a Test match. But it was more that he had been passed over for the vice-captaincy, which had gone to Steve Waugh. He dearly wanted to be Australian captain and was sure he was the best man for the job.

However, once the fit of pique had passed, nothing (least of all Simone) was going to stop him going to England for the Ashes. As always, he was keen to get into the battle. 'Despite all the injuries, I am a much better bowler now than I was four years ago', he bragged to an English journalist. 'I have much more experience. I have improved in the areas where I was weak and I have sharpened my strengths. I have a few extra deliveries in my locker.'

As it turned out, the series was neither triumph nor disaster. Glenn McGrath took 36 wickets, he took 24. But it had its moments, with teasing headlines such as, 'WARNE CAN'T GRIP HIS BALLS', and the clever little spoof where a tabloid newspaper sent a young woman to the Australian team hotel, armed with a box of pies, to persuade Shane to pose as a pie thrower: the English term for a poor slow bowler. Otherwise, in the absence of fabulous deeds, the papers had to look elsewhere for their stories. As usual, they got stuck into his behaviour.

There was a huge fuss, for example, over his victory jig at Old Trafford to celebrate Australia's win in the Third Test and his own nine-wicket haul. He did no more than spray champagne over his team-mates on the players' balcony and give a one-finger salute to the crowd, who had baited him with banners and taunts of 'Bog off, fat boy'. But the English press picked on it with glee. Had he been a footballer, the *Daily Mail* moaned, he would have been fined for bringing the game into disrepute. Other papers piled in with headlines such as 'I've Gut You Beat' next to a photograph of him patting his belly, and 'Spin on This' alongside a picture of his upraised finger.

A month later, when the Australians retained the Ashes at Trent Bridge, Warne put on a repeat performance, grabbing a stump and waving it above his head on the balcony in a victory dance. This time, it was the Australian press who bagged him for gloating, with *The Age*'s Patrick Smith leading the charge. 'Shane Warne has made a goose of himself. Again', he wrote in his column. 'His provocations and immature actions have sullied a fine victory.' Remarkably, Warne was prepared to apologise this time. 'The relief I felt at winning the series and the effects of all the abuse I'd copped throughout the tour got to me and I went too far', he said. 'I reacted emotionally and went over the top a bit.' And the abuse had been relentless. At Taunton, a week earlier, Steve Waugh had taken his players off the field because the swearing was so foul. 'Shane can handle cries of "Fat boy". He's heard that a thousand times before', Waugh told reporters, 'but this was a bit more than that. It got beyond a joke today.'

By the end of the final Test at The Oval, Warne was ready to go home. The team had been on the road for 312 days out of the previous 365, and he had been out of Australia for the best part of six months. In his absence, Simone had given birth to a daughter, Brooke, their first child, who was said to look just like her Dad. Several counties had been after him to play cricket in England the following summer, with offers of up to $400,000, but he needed some time with his family. And the ACB wanted him to rest. In the absence of proper treatment, his sore shoulder was giving him trouble again and there was only a two-month break before the Australian season got under way, with Test matches against New Zealand and South Africa coming up. He had too much on his plate already without adding more.

Back in December 1995, he had passed the 200 Test wicket mark, and he raced past Benaud's tally of 248 during the Third Ashes Test at Old Trafford in July, but he was now approaching a more significant number. Only one slow bowler in history, the lanky West Indian off spinner Lance Gibbs, had taken more than 300 Test wickets, and Warne needed just 36 to reach the mark. He was keen to do it in front of a home crowd, and perhaps this spurred him on, because he broke his own trans-Tasman record against New Zealand with 19 wickets in three Tests in November 1997, and then tormented the South Africans in the First Test at the MCG in December to collect another six. His review in *The Age* was as good as any he had received: 'Warne fizzed them off the pitch, spun them out of footmarks, tortured the batsmen by bowling round the wicket into the rough. Each ball was a Test in itself, a battle for survival.'

He finished the job magnificently in the Second Test in Sydney, spearing 11 South African victims and passing 300 by bowling Jacques Kallis between bat and pad with a perfect topspinner. He went into a crouch, arms aloft, his eyes to the heavens and was engulfed by his team-mates. It was late and most of the 17,000-strong crowd had headed home because of rain. But around 2000 faithful souls had stuck it out and they gave him a standing ovation, their cheers echoing in the emptiness. 'Even by Warne's standards it was a command performance', wrote Malcolm Knox in *The Sydney Morning Herald* the next day. It was the 10th time he had taken 10 or more wickets in a match but it was easily his best performance since coming back from injury. He had mesmerised them, frightened them, reduced them to a rabble. 'Whenever Warne bowled it was sheer mayhem', wrote *The Courier-Mail*'s Robert Craddock, 'with airswings, half edges, a chanting crowd and the general feeling that a wicket could fall any ball.'

Picking up yet another man of the match award, Warne went off to celebrate his achievements with a Midori and lemonade. It had taken him six years and 63 Tests to reach the milestone, and only three bowlers in history had got there faster: Richard Hadlee, Malcolm Marshall and his childhood hero, Dennis Lillee, the bowler he had always copied in his backyard. 'To be in that company is an honour', Warne admitted, 'I am very proud.' If he maintained this rate of progress it would take him less than three years to overtake Kapil Dev's world record of 434. And if he continued bowling for five more years, as he promised, he would be well on his way to 600. Terry Jenner and Richie Benaud predicted he would get there. 'Every time I see him bowl', said the more famous spin king, 'it adds another year to my life.'

Naturally, there was debate about whether Warne was back to his best, but in truth he had changed as a bowler. He had learnt how to make up for his physical shortcomings with guile and experience. 'I don't think the flipper is as outstanding as it used to be', said Mark Taylor, 'but he bowls a lot of other deliveries now. He bowls a lot better topspinner, he bowls the wrong 'un better, he thinks batsmen out more than he used to.'

There were also comparisons with his idol, Dennis Lillee, that other Australian larrikin, who had passed 300 wickets faster than anyone. They were both irascible and erratic, Mike Coward told readers of his column in *The Australian*. And both were as much boys as men. But Warne was more of a puzzle. 'He can be thoughtful and thoughtless, curt and courteous', mused Coward, 'demanding and easy going, carefree and contrary. In essence [he is] as confusing as the world's finest batsmen find his bowling.'

But there was at least one batsman in the world who did not appear to be dazzled by his talent, and he was busy preparing for Australia's arrival in India in February 1998. Sachin Tendulkar, who was even more famous than Shane in his home country, had watched Warne paralyse the world's greatest batsmen by bowling into the foot-marks outside leg stump and had decided to mug up for the inevitable examination. He had deliberately scratched up the ground at training and had India's best leg spinners pitch the ball into the rough for hours on end so he could learn how to slog-sweep him against the spin, which was something no one had yet succeeded in doing. It remained to be seen whether his study would pay off.

In the meantime, there was actually some doubt about whether Warne would be able to make the trip, because his shoulder was rapidly getting worse. The specialists had told him almost two years earlier that it really needed surgery, and he could not now throw the ball without a sharp stabbing pain like a knife being dug into the joint. Saline and cortisone injections and daily massage had helped loosen it up and ease the soreness, but he had still been getting savage migraine headaches if he slept in the wrong position. To give it a chance to get better, he pulled out of the one-day series in New Zealand in February, but he was determined he would not miss out on India. It would be his first-ever trip there for a Test series and he was itching to play, both to take on Tendulkar and to get his own back on the batsmen who had showed him such scant respect on his debut for Australia in 1992.

In this he was soon disappointed, because his first match on Indian soil, against Mumbai, was a disaster, with Tendulkar smacking his second ball for six. Thereafter, it went from bad to worse, with Warne taking one of his worst-ever poundings, conceding 111 runs at seven an over without getting a wicket. Tendulkar, who scored an unbeaten 204 off 192 balls, won the first round hands down.

People either love or hate India. It is a colourful, crowded, confronting place you either want to dive into or run away from. On a trip to Delhi not long ago I ended up lying on my back in the middle of a dusty public park, surrounded by a group of eager onlookers, as a man cleaned wax out of my ear with long metal probes. Somehow, I had not been able to say 'No' convincingly enough, and had been almost wrestled to the ground. This is hardly what one encounters in the bayside suburbs of Melbourne. And Warne had no urge to get used to the experience. As he told one interviewer, he admired the attitude of Australian batsman Doug Walters, who refused to get out of the bus at the Great Wall of China, on the grounds that 'if you've seen one wall you've seen 'em all'. He also hated the food. So he barricaded himself in the hotel and lived on breakfast cereal, cheese and vegemite on nan bread, with a handful of vitamins thrown in. Then one morning he saw Geoff Marsh – who had succeeded Simpson as coach – tucking into a private stash of tinned spaghetti, so he asked whether some could be sent over for the rest of the team. A journalist soon got wind of the story and wrote that Warne had sent out an SOS for baked beans to stop himself wasting away. Back in Melbourne, this was seized on by the marketing men at Heinz who promptly had a pallet load of 1700 cans of spaghetti and beans shipped from their Dandenong factory, with TV cameras in attendance. It was a master stroke that gave the company half a million dollars' worth of free publicity and sorted Shane's diet for the duration of the trip. The cans were handed around to everyone in the Australian party, then lugged from hotel to hotel, but there were still too many for the boys to eat, so a lucky orphanage ended up with the leftovers.

Three years later, when the Australians toured India in 2001, Heinz's rival, SPC, leapt in with a similar deal, only this time they paid Warne to shoot a series of ads on location. 'I have loved baked beans since I was a kid and I still do', he dutifully told the press. 'They could become my secret weapon, giving me energy during the long and exhaustive season, regardless of where I am in the world.' But it was not just curries that Shane couldn't stomach.

On a previous trip to the sub-continent, he had been eating in a favourite Italian restaurant with a few team-mates and had been persuaded to depart from his usual fare of Hawaiian pizza (minus the ham) to risk the fettucine bolognese (minus the carrots, onions and mush-rooms). As David Boon tells the story, Steve Waugh managed to slip a half-eaten mushroom – Shane loathed mushrooms – into his pasta while he was looking the other way. Waugh then told him the bad news:

> 'Warney, they've done you, they've put mushrooms in the sauce, in the bottom!' Immediately, Shane went white, started sweating profusely, then left the table to throw up. When he returned we confessed to the trick, and the language in which we were described does not bear reporting.

Back on the pitch, in the First Test in Chennai, Warne's nightmare was continuing, despite getting instant revenge on Tendulkar, whom he trapped fourth ball with a big leg break. In the second innings, Navjot Sidhu laid into him in savage fashion, hitting him for 15 runs in one over on his way to a lightning half-century, whereupon Tendulkar returned to finish the job, with a match-winning 155 not out. As Warne was forced to admit, the little master was probably the best batsman in the world. Unlike anybody before him, he could hit Warne over mid wicket time after time, against the spin. But he was not the only one who had Warne's measure. Mohammad Azharuddin also took the long handle to him, belting him for 18 runs off his final over. It was a horror show for the man who had been so fêted only eight weeks earlier. 'In between overs on the fourth day', Ken Piesse records in *The Complete Shane Warne*, 'Warne was often seen bent over, hands on knees, and obviously distressed by the heat and his workload'. At the end he had managed to collect just one wicket at a cost of 122 runs.

The Second Test in Kolkata gave him a chance to fight back, but it got worse instead. In front of 80,000 fans at Eden Gardens, Warne was carted for 147 runs as India piled up more than 600 before declaring with five wickets down. As in Mumbai, he failed to take a wicket. And as in Mumbai, he set a new record for the worst pasting of his career. It was 'THE MOTHER OF ALL THRASHINGS' a headline in Melbourne's *Herald Sun* declared. Or as *The Sydney Morning Herald*'s Peter Roebuck put it, 'Seldom in its cricketing career can Australia have received the sort of lathering it was getting after lunch today'.

The Third Test was some relief, because Warne bowled far better and Australia won, but his tally of 10 wickets for the series at an average of 54.00 was hardly a vintage crop. The Indian leg spinner Anil Kumble had harvested twice as many scalps at half the cost, and even Australia's back-up off spinner, Gavin Robertson, had got more wickets, more cheaply. There is no doubt Warne was a great disappointment to Indian fans, who had expected him to love their dusty, turning pitches. He had arrived with a huge reputation as the best bowler in the world, but he never managed to put fear into their batsmen as he had done in South Africa and England. It remains a mystery to this day why he has never performed like a champion against India, having taken only 43 Test wickets at an average of 47 runs apiece. Part of the answer is that their batsmen are just such brilliant players of spin, but on this occasion he also had an excuse, because he was clearly not fully fit.

His shoulder was now sorer than ever, especially after he damaged his ligaments in the one-day series, and he badly needed to go home and rest. Yet for some extra-ordinary reason, the Australian team management decided to put him on the plane to Sharjah instead, for another week of one-day games. His presence there did not greatly help Australia's cause, because Tendulkar was again in extraordinary form, blasting 357 runs in three games, while Warne took yet more punishment, taking 1 for 137 in his 27 overs. But what it did do was aggravate the shoulder even more with a heavy fall in the second game. He could now only throw underarm.

When he finally got back to Melbourne in May 1998, he checked in for exploratory surgery with the same Dr Greg Hoy who had rebuilt his finger two years earlier. Warne told the papers that he hoped to avoid a major operation but would go under the knife if he had to. 'Obviously, it's a last resort', he said. 'Hopefully, they will just need to scrape a few things out but I think it might be a bit worse. We'll just have to wait and see.' In fact, it was far worse than he or the doctors expected. He had torn the rotator cuff – the four muscles and tendons that sit at the front, back and top of the shoulder and tie into the top of the arm, stabilising and supporting the shoulder during movement – and complete reconstruction was the only option. Dr Hoy sewed the cartilage back onto the bone and inserted four screws to hold the shoulder together –

he had been warned half-jokingly by the ACB that his career would also be finished if he did not get it right.

The day after the operation, Warne paraded himself before a press conference, with his shoulder heavily strapped, and admitted it was worse than anticipated. But publicly he was positive: 'The doctors say that if the rehabilitation goes well the shoulder will eventually be better than brand new', he told reporters, 'so there's no reason why I couldn't have another five years playing for Australia.' Privately he was worried that he would never be able to bowl again, or not with the same venom. He had been told that if he had played on any longer he would certainly have killed his career. It was no secret that javelin throwers who had this operation rarely recovered completely, and Richie Benaud, who had undergone it years earlier, had never bowled at his best again. Indeed it had been a major factor in hastening his retirement.

Warne was told he would be in a sling for six weeks and need 6–12 months of rehabilitation. Not surprisingly he was soon in a slump. 'At times I was upbeat but at others I was down in the dumps', he confessed in *Shane Warne, My Autobiography*. He found it hard to sleep, sometimes because of the pain but mostly because he feared he would never produce his big-spinning leg-breaks again.

In July, he told a group of fans at a sports function that there was a chance he would never play again: 'The thing is, no other leg spinner has had the operation, and it is a major one.'

In fact, it was all going to plan, but it was a long hard road back to fitness, with daily physiotherapy and tedious exercises that had to be done again and again and again.

It was hugely frustrating because sometimes he would make progress and other times he would make none. It took four months before he was playing golf, and it was not until late September that he was allowed to start bowling with a tennis ball. Then in mid-October he was told he could try spinning a cricket ball for the first time. There was only one month to go to the First Test against England in Brisbane and he was still hopeful he could play, even though he had no earthly chance of doing so. But by then, at least, the worst was over, because it was clear he would be able to play cricket again. 'I've been through difficult times when I wondered if I would ever bowl again', he told his old friend Ian Chappell, 'but those times appear to have gone and it's now a matter of when, not if.'

The English press were so desperate to find out when that would be that the ACB flew him over to appear at a press conference in Perth where England was playing its first two warm-up games. Even when he was not in the side he was still the biggest news. He would keep them guessing about his intentions for a week or two more before finally admitting what his doctors and team-mates had long since realised: he would have to miss the first two Tests at least, and might have to sit out the entire series.

At the beginning of November he made a quiet comeback at club level for St Kilda, taking a wicket with his third ball, and then settled down to the long slog of climbing back to the top. By mid-December he had clocked up 140 overs in four games for Victoria and taken eight wickets for a total of 523 runs: hardly the stuff of which legends are made. He was bowling accurately but without flair and not spinning the ball as of old. Worse still, his understudy, Stuart MacGill, was tormenting the Poms as much as Warne had ever done. There were even suggestions that the Ashes should be cut back to a three-Test series because England was no longer capable of putting up a fight. Then Australia lost the Fourth Test in Melbourne, after collapsing to 162 all out in the second innings, and suddenly Sydney was set to decide the series. England might even win. It was the perfect moment to send for the old destroyer.

News of Warne's return was broken to a packed press conference at the ACB's offices in Melbourne, with Shane himself making a dramatic entry amid a flurry of flash-lights, 'like a film star arriving for a royal premiere', as one observer described it. He told the assembled company that he felt like he was starting his career all over again, which was nice for a guy with 300 Test wickets in his kick. And he warned the Poms that he still had the wood on them. But the quote that really stood out was: 'My life has been like a soap opera, like a drama the last six months. This year has not been one of the best.'

That was an understatement. Three weeks earlier, as Shane and everyone else knew well, the shit had really hit the fan.

Money for Nothing

I realise that I was very naïve and stupid.

Shane Warne was used to bad headlines at breakfast, but the one on the front of *The Australian* on the eve of the Third Ashes Test in Adelaide in December 1998 was probably the worst of his career: 'CRICKET'S BETTING SCANDAL. TEST STARS WERE PAID BY BOOKIE'. Beneath it was the revelation that he and Mark Waugh had been fined by the Australian Cricket Board for selling pitch and weather information to an illegal Indian bookmaker in 1994–95.

The full story was that he and Waugh had accepted US$5000 and US$4000 in cash respectively during a one-day tournament in Sri Lanka in September 1994 and given information to a bookie known only as 'John' on several occasions thereafter. The ACB had known about their sin for almost four years but done everything in its power to keep it quiet. It was 'the Australian game's darkest and best-kept secret', according to *The Australian*'s Malcolm Conn, whose award-winning investigation had brought it to light. Or, in the words of Matthew Engel, editor of the cricketers' bible, *Wisden*, 'one of the biggest scandals that cricket has ever faced'.

Conn had been given the tip-off about Mark Waugh at four am in a Brisbane nightclub and had scribbled notes on a series of drink coasters because he did not have a note-book. Even though he could not read his writing the next morning he remembered exactly what he had been told. He spent the next month chasing details and trying to get the Australian Cricket Board to confirm the story, but all he got was a constant 'No Comment'. So eventually he decided to bluff them into admission by telling ACB chairman Malcolm Speed he planned to publish the next day. Speed asked him for an hour's grace, then rang back to tell him that Waugh and Warne were both involved. Till that point Conn had not even heard Shane's name mentioned.

In Adelaide the next day, 9 December 1998, the TV cameras turned out in force to see Warne and Waugh paraded before a packed press conference. Shane arrived in a natty five-button black suit, white shirt and black-and-white tie, seemingly without a care in the world. Waugh, by contrast, was in his team tracksuit, looking sick and terrified, like a naughty boy dragged straight from the playground. Both knew there had been a hue and cry over cricket corruption and match fixing the last four years. Both also knew they had sounded the alarm by accusing Pakistan's cricket captain, Salim Malik, of trying to bribe them to throw a match. Yet Warne in particular looked like a man who had no idea why taking cash from match-fixing bookies might be unwise. Much like Alan Bond on one of his many forays into court, he arrived smiling, with his chin held high, sure that his innocence would be recognised. He even appeared to be whistling.

Both admitted their error and expressed regret – in statements that had clearly been crafted by the ACB – but Waugh made a mess of his confession, stumbling over the syntax, which was so obviously not his own. He could barely lift his face from the paper to look people in the eye. Only 24 hours earlier he had done his best to deny the charge, telling *The Australian*: 'I don't know where you got your information from. I don't know if that's right.'

Warne, by contrast, was confident and defiant. Reading from an almost identical script, he eyeballed the audience as he emphasised his denials. He was 'very disappointed', he said – the faithful formula that sportsmen fall back on – and 'sorry for his actions'. But he did not look apologetic. He repeated the mantra that he had been 'naïve and stupid' (which Waugh had already uttered) and the two of them then got up and left, without taking questions. Remarkably, the press let them go.

The editorials the next day showed no mercy: *The Australian* added 'greedy' to 'naïve and stupid', the Sydney *Daily Telegraph* accused them of pocketing 'the grubby cash of a criminal', and the Melbourne *Herald-Sun* said simply it was a 'Day of Shame'. A cavalcade of famous names then lined up to chastise them: Sir Donald Bradman said he felt 'let down'; Prime Minister John Howard admitted to 'an intense sense of disillusionment'; former Test player Neil Harvey called for both to be banned; and Richie Benaud echoed *Wisden* in saying: 'It's appalling, and one of the most appalling things is it has been covered up for so long.'

So what exactly had Waugh and Warne been busted for? According to Bob O'Regan QC, who was asked by the ACB to investigate the affair after *The Australian* broke the story, they had each been approached at the Australian team hotel in Colombo during the Singer Cup in September 1994.

> An Indian who introduced himself as John told Waugh that he was a bookmaker who wanted information about games during the current series and the Australian summer. He offered to pay Waugh $US4000 for information about . . . the state of the pitch and weather conditions . . . Waugh accepted the money . . . (and) provided the information on approximately ten occasions over a five-month period until February 1995.
>
> John asked Waugh to introduce him to Warne and Waugh did so the next evening introducing him as 'John who bets on cricket'. The following day John invited Warne to his room in the same hotel and John gave him an envelope containing money. John said it was a token of his appreciation for meeting him and that there were no strings attached. Warne accepted the money which amounted to $US5000.

Warne's version of the meeting was that 'John' (whom he met first in the casino, and whose real name remained a mystery) had said to him: 'Here's US$5000, you're a great player. Go have some fun.' Warne said he tried to refuse but did not want to offend his new Indian friend.

And since nothing was being demanded in return (or so he claimed) he took the money. When John phoned him during the Ashes Series three months later to ask about weather and pitch conditions and whether the track would suit his bowling, Warne happily obliged, not once, twice, but three times. In his view, he was telling him no more than he put in his newspaper column or gave away in pre-match interviews. 'They were the sort of conversations I might have had with my dad and brother', he wrote in *Shane Warne, My Autobiography*. 'In one case he wished me a Happy Christmas, and in another he said Happy New Year.' In other words, he was doing absolutely nothing wrong. But few people reading about it in 1998 would have agreed with that view.

By the mid-1990s, betting on cricket in India and Pakistan had become a huge illegal business, run by mafia-style organised crime, in which billions of dollars were wagered each year. Matches were broadcast on cable TV almost every day and there were huge fortunes to be made for punters or bookies who could fix the results. And since many of the games were pretty pointless one-day affairs with no national pride at stake, it was not hard to get players to play badly for a bung. Indian and Pakistani players earnt far less than their western counterparts and on occasions did not get paid at all.

Not only was Warne and Waugh's US$9000 likely to have come from the same tainted pool that was used to fix matches, but the arrangement was possibly the prelude to something more serious. A common way to corrupt players was to shower them with gifts or pay them handsomely for something they could easily deliver, such as pitch and weather reports, then promise them a great deal more for throwing a match. There was absolutely no suggestion that Waugh and Warne had succumbed to such an offer, nor that they would ever be likely to. But accepting money from John made them vulnerable to threats of blackmail. And it was remarkable that both players were enlisted by John one month before they were approached again – on two separate occasions – by Salim Malik. In other words, there was more than a possibility that the two offers were linked.

It was also naïve to assume that their pitch and weather information was worthless. In India, one could bet on just about anything: who would bowl first, which end they would bowl from, what the batting order would be, which end each umpire would stand, how many runs each side would make and so on. Even the most trivial information could be used to make money. Nor was the information all so trivial: Waugh talked to John about team morale; Warne admitted chatting about team morale, the make-up of the team and whether the pitch would suit his bowling. And the bottom line was surely this: bookies did not give anyone money for nothing.

The ACB had first heard about the lads' nice little earner in February 1995 when the Australian team manager, Ian McDonald, was asked by *The Age*'s Mark Ray if he had heard rumours about players taking cash from bookies. McDonald dismissed it as rubbish, then decided to check if it was true and, after consulting team captain Mark Taylor, they quizzed the players one by one. It was immediately obvious that Mark Waugh was a likely candidate because he was a mad punter who spent all his spare time at the track or the trots. In his book, *Year to Remember*, Waugh tells how he deliberately threw away his wicket when batting for Bankstown in 1992 so he could watch Super Impose win the Cox Plate with his money on it. Next on the list of suspects was his best mate, Shane, who also loved a bet, spent his time in the casino when he wasn't chasing women, and was famous for carrying around large wads of cash in $100 bills, which he had a habit of losing at regular intervals – usually in his shoe.

To McDonald's surprise, both players immediately owned up to meeting John and taking his money. Waugh also admitted he had agreed to provide information – although he did not reveal that he had spoken to John 10 times. Warne claimed that the money was just a gift from an admirer who wanted nothing in return. Only when McDonald explained Mark's 'business deal' did the penny drop. 'I remember getting that sinking feeling and wondering if I had let myself in for something after all', he says in his autobiography. But even then, he was absolutely adamant that he was not at fault.

It was already common knowledge in cricketing circles that a number of Australian, English and New Zealand cricketers had been smart enough to reject similar offers in the past. Dean Jones, for example, had been pro-positioned in the foyer of the same Colombo hotel in 1992 by an Indian bookmaker, who had shown him a mobile phone and a biscuit tin containing US$50,000 in used notes. Jones was told the money and phone were his if he agreed to give regular updates on things such as match conditions, team tactics, players' form and the

Australian team's likely batting order. The bookie boasted he had 'narks' in every Test and one-day team in the world doing this for him already. Jones declined to join the throng and reported it straight to the Australian team management.

Greg Matthews was another Australian offered money in 1992 to provide pitch and weather information, while Allan Border was approached in 1993 to throw the Sixth Test against England (after Australia had already retained the Ashes). All said no, and it seems likely that Warne and Waugh would have known that. After Jones was approached in 1992, Australian coach Bob Simpson had made it clear to the rest of the team (Warne and Waugh included) that they should send such people packing, and Waugh was warned again in 1994 by a player he was rooming with that he should not sell information to bookies because it would come back to bite him.

As it turned out, neither he nor Warne was bitten nearly as hard as they might have been. When the ACB learnt of their crime in February 1995, it was desperate to protect its own reputation, because it had just begun beating the drum about cricket corruption. Only weeks earlier, it had delivered a dossier on Pakistan's captain, Salim Malik, to the International Cricket Council, accusing him of attempts at match fixing. One month after pocketing John's US$5000, Warne had received a late-night call from Malik inviting him to his hotel room for a quiet chat. There he had been told there was US$200,000 for him and his fellow spinner, Tim May, if they bowled badly in the First Test in Karachi. Warne went back to his room, which he shared with May, and relayed the offer to May, who reportedly said: 'Tell the rat to get fucked.'

Undeterred by this rebuff – which seems strange if it was really so blunt – Malik repeated his offer a few weeks later to Warne and Waugh at a presidential reception in Rawalpindi, promising US$200,000 if they played badly in the next day's one-day international. Again both players refused, but this time Mark Waugh let the cat out of the bag by coming into the dressing-room after the match was lost and joking that they should have taken the bribe after all. Bob Simpson started asking questions, the ACB compiled its dossier and before long the newspapers had made the bribery allegations public.

Thus, come February 1995, Warne and Waugh were the key witnesses in a Pakistan Cricket Board inquiry into their allegations. But they now had a dirty little secret of their own. If it was revealed that they had taken money from John the bookie, they would lose all credibility as witnesses and the ACB would look ridiculous. Which is, of course, why the ACB had a duty to go public, to ensure Salim Malik got a fair go. And why it also had a strong incentive to keep very quiet indeed.

The ACB had a second reason for sweeping the affair under the carpet, which was that Australia was about to embark on a tour of the West Indies, where it had not won a series for more than 20 years. Without its star slow bowler and most talented batsman the team would almost certainly slide to another defeat. And if the ACB published Warne and Waugh's offence it would face huge pressure to leave the two players at home. So, once again, the easy road was to cover it all up.

Neither of these base motives was cited by Graham

Halbish and Alan Crompton, the CEO and chair of the ACB, when they gave evidence to the O'Regan Inquiry in early 1999. They spoke only of protecting the good name of cricket and of their duty as employers to keep such matters private. They also said they were convinced that the money from John had nothing to do with match fixing, so there was no need to disclose it. They had fined Warne and Waugh $8000 and $10,000 respectively – which they regarded as severe enough punishment – and left it at that.

In their efforts to hush it all up, Halbish and Crompton had even kept the other ACB directors in the dark for a week, waiting until the Australian team was on a plane to the West Indies with the boys on board. A couple of directors asked why they had not been informed earlier and were told it was a sensitive issue, they didn't want it to leak, all hell would have broken loose at the airport, and so on. But it was still the board's prerogative to decide if the cover-up should continue, and only two of the 14 directors believed the press should be informed. 'They thought they [Warne and Waugh] were heroes', says one today. 'They wanted to protect them.' In their defence, O'Regan says, this may have been the wrong decision, but it was one that Halbish, Crompton and the board took entirely in good faith.

Ian McDonald, who managed the team's media affairs at the time – before they hired 20 others to do the job – had already written a media release, announcing the fines and outlining the offences, but it was never released. 'As an old journo, I told 'em it would be out in 24 hours', he says today. 'I thought someone was bound to leak it.

Amazingly it stayed secret, and it was a pretty big secret. I still had that press release four years later.'

The only people outside the ACB board who did get to hear, apart from team captain Mark Taylor and coach Bob Simpson, were the two chiefs of the International Cricket Council who happened to be in Sydney at the time. One of these was an Australian, David Richards, who had previously been head of the ACB; the other was Sir Clyde Walcott. The pair was given the information in strict confidence and did not pass it on to their member countries, and especially not to the Pakistan Cricket Board inquiry being conducted by Justice Fakruddhin Ebrahim. Instead, they urged the Pakistanis to be discreet about its findings, 'always bearing in mind the damage to the image of cricket if allegations were made public in any way'.

Soon afterwards, when Warne and Waugh were summoned to Pakistan to give evidence to Ebrahim, the ACB refused the players permission to go, dismissing the request as 'unnecessary', an extraordinarily arrogant response. Instead, the two players swore the briefest of statements in a hotel in Antigua. Warne later said he 'had nothing to hide' (which would have been a good reason for going) but that it would not have been safe for him in Pakistan.

Not surprisingly, when the O'Regan report was published in February 1999 it was scathing in its criticism of how the ACB had handled the affair, and damning of its conclusion that John's payments to Warne and Waugh had nothing at all to do with match fixing or Malik's attempt to bribe them. 'Both the chronology of events and the symmetry of the contacts', said O'Regan, 'suggest that there may well have been such a connection.' Malik, incidentally, was later banned from cricket for life.

O'Regan was equally unimpressed by the ACB's wider efforts to fight match fixing. Despite a series of attempts to corrupt Australian players over the years, it had done next to nothing about them: it had not taken statements from players who were approached, had not recorded the incidents in tour reports and had not briefed its players on the dangers they would face. Few in the cricketing world had fared better. As the Indian Central Bureau of Investigation lamented in 2000, during its pursuit of Hansie Cronje (who was also banned for life), no one wanted to talk about this smelly subject. Or as the ICC's *Condon Report* put it, even more strongly, a year later: there was a 'climate of silence, apathy, ignorance and fear ... Players did not want to inform on each other and there was no system to receive or process reports of improper approaches or behaviour.'

But O'Regan's harshest words were reserved for Warne and Waugh. In the first place, he was convinced they deserved far more than a fine:

> In my opinion this punishment was inadequate. It did not reflect the seriousness of what they had done. In Warne's case the fine of $8000 did little more than deprive him of the sum of $US5000 he had received from the bookmaker.

In the second, O'Regan was not persuaded that they had simply been silly:

I do not think it is possible to explain their conduct away as the result merely of naivety or stupidity. They must have known that it is wrong to accept money from, and supply information to, a book-maker whom they also knew as someone who betted on cricket. Otherwise they would have reported the incident to team management long before they were found out in February 1995. In behaving as they did they failed lamentably to set the sort of example one might expect from senior players and role models for many young cricketers. A more appropriate penalty would, I think, have been suspension for a significant time.

But if Australia's two stars did know it was wrong, as O'Regan believed, they did not stop protesting their innocence. In *Shane Warne, My Autobiography*, published two years later, Warne devotes an entire chapter to proving that his dealings with John were absolutely lily white. He uses the phrase 'I did nothing wrong' (or variants of it) on at least three occasions and offers a version of the story that snips off vital details. For exam-ple, he denies knowing that John was a bookmaker and denies talking to him about team selection and morale, even though he admitted both these things on oath to a public hearing in Melbourne in 1999. He also denies being warned by Bob Simpson about bookies on the 1992 tour. As Malcolm Conn, who broke the betting story, remarked in reviewing the book, a more appropriate title would have been, *Whatever It Was, It Wasn't My Fault*.

It was typical of Warne to refuse to take any blame and

to tell a few fibs so he looked like the victim. A psychologist who has worked with the Australian team says this is Shane's standard response to exposure: 'He is like a spoilt child when he's caught. He always blames others. And he never learns from his mistakes, because he never admits he's at fault. It happens to professional players who are indulged, pampered and cosseted all their lives. They never develop a sense of responsibility.'

Another who is closely involved with the Australian team, and who reflects the view of many who have worked with Warne down the years, has a similar take on it all: 'As a young kid he always had a bit of the star about him. When he got into a bit of trouble, people said, "Don't worry, we'll fix it up, just concentrate on your cricket." Then it got worse, they kept on covering up for him, and now it's at the stage where he just thinks he is bulletproof. Someone always steps in and saves him, someone always finds a way.'

Since he became a superstar, Warne has always been surrounded by people who reinforce his status, and who never criticise him or tell him what to do. So it is no wonder he thinks himself beyond reproach and seems convinced that his worst excesses are just an honest mistake. It is also no wonder he cannot cope with headlines or criticism that threaten to puncture the bubble in which he lives.

During the betting scandal in 1998, he claimed that he had nearly quit cricket – again. In February 1999 he told London's *Daily Mirror*, 'I can't imagine life getting much worse than it's been for the last three months.' His loyal wife, Simone, was appalled that everyone had attacked him. Seeing headlines about match fixing next to pictures of Shane, she was horrified. 'I told Shane to give up cricket', she said. 'What he was going through wasn't worth it. I said that if the worst came to the worst, we'd go back and try to live normally again.' It was an interesting choice of word.

In the long run, pocketing John's cash undoubtedly cost Warne a lot more than the US$5000 he received. London's *Daily Mirror*, which had promised him $150,000 for an exclusive column on the Ashes, sacked him the day after the story broke, boasting: 'THE MIRROR DUMPS SHANE WARNE. WE SACK AUSSIE STAR AT CENTRE OF BETTING SCANDAL', and telling its readers that Warne had dragged the entire sport into controversy. 'It was reported that he said in conversation earlier this week: "It was only five grand, mate"', the *Mirror* commented tartly. 'That seems a small price for a genuine superstar of world sport to sell off the integrity of Test cricket.' Melbourne's *Age* also dumped him as a columnist.

Shane's friends at Nike, his biggest sponsor, also wondered whether to ditch him, but decided he was genuinely remorseful and would learn from his mistake. Or, more realistically, that the public would forgive him and that it wouldn't hurt sales. Other sponsors took a similar view, hoping there would not be too many more mistakes in the future. It would not be long before those hopes were dashed.

Mark Waugh felt the public's disapproval even more directly. Unlike Warne, who was sidelined for the Third Ashes Test because of his shoulder injury, he was forced to face the crowds. He was booed as he walked out to bat at the Adelaide Oval, past banners saying, 'I don't have to pay anyone $6000 to tell me how hot it is today', then serenaded by England's Barmy Army who had composed a new ditty in his honour. Sung to the tune of Lonnie Donegan's 1960s hit 'My Old Man's a Dustman', it went like this:

Mark Waugh is an Aussie
He wears the baggy green hat
And when he saw the bookie's cash he said I'm
   having that
He shared it out with Warney
They went and had some beers
And when the ACB found out
They covered it up for years.

Waugh wanted to be anywhere else, he later admitted, preferably asleep. But he didn't stay out in the middle for long. While his partner, Sue Porter, watched from the stand in tears, he scratched around for half an hour before being dismissed. Afterwards he started getting headaches, felt sick all the time and lost weight. Porter started losing her hair in clumps. Like Warne, Waugh felt that all the fuss and criticism were totally unfair. As far as he was concerned, it was 'just a little thing' or, as Tim May told him, an 'honest, innocent mistake'. And it was all the media's fault for beating it up. Like Warne, he refused to take responsibility for what he had done.

Just as the furore about bookies and betting began to die down, the bush telegraph signalled that Australia's captain, Mark Taylor, was likely to retire after the end of the Ashes series. For Warne, who longed to be Australian captain and was one of the leading contenders, the timing could not have been worse. His shoulder injury had kept him out of cricket for seven months, and then the betting scandal had trashed his reputation. And when he did make his Test comeback at the SCG in the final Test against England in early January 1999, he bowled poorly, taking only two wickets, while Stuart MacGill ripped through the English batting and picked up 12. All in all, his stocks had never been lower. Yet he still had plenty of supporters putting him up for the job.

Warne had been appointed captain of the Victorian team in May 1996, just as his spinning finger went under the knife, and by the time he led the lads onto the field in November several pundits had already cast him as Australia's next leader. He had healed divisions in the dressing-room, they said, matured as a person, and possessed a superb cricket brain. Allan Border had even gone into print at the time with a red-hot reference:

> The more I watch Shane Warne, the more I am con-
> vinced he will make a wonderful Australian captain.
> It must surely be long odds-on that he will follow
> Mark Taylor . . . I have been impressed with his
> tactical flair . . . but more importantly the players
> love him. When he is present there is a spark that
> lights up a dressing room.

Another former Australian captain, Ian Chappell, had continued to lobby hard for Warne to be given the job, 'sooner rather than later'. And Warne had embraced the idea enthusiastically. In *Shane Warne, My Own Story*, published in 1997, he speculated that he might be offered the Australian captaincy. He felt it would be impossible to refuse such an honour. He promised to be a risk taker on the field, always prepared to take a gamble. And in the current circumstances no one would doubt it. 'The best captains', he said, 'are those who trust their gut feelings and act on them before the moment slips away.' Unfortunately, this was the principle that ruled Warne's life off the field as well and got him into so much trouble.

Others in the cricketing hierarchy were less eager to have Shane at the helm. A few months earlier, before the betting scandal had come to light, the ACB had hosted a lunch for the media in a Melbourne restaurant, in an attempt to forge better relations. At the end of the meal, CEO Malcolm Speed, Chairman Denis Rogers and Chairman of Selectors Trevor Hohns invited questions from the floor. *The Australian*'s Malcolm Conn cheekily asked, 'How many of you gentlemen have your hearts in your mouths at the prospect of Shane Warne becoming Australian captain?' Jaws dropped. There was a long silence. Three stunned mullets. 'Thank you gentlemen', said Conn, 'you have just answered my question.'

In truth, Warne had never been the frontrunner. Back in 1997, the influential Hohns had all but anointed Steve Waugh as Australia's next captain by making him Taylor's deputy, and he was still the favourite. But some had concerns about Waugh's suitability for the job: at 33 he was only a year younger than Taylor and four years older than Warne, so he was a short-term solution. He was also battling injury and there were worries about his capacity to lead. Even *Wisden* described him as an 'egotistical' batsman, while others, such as Chappell and several senior cricket writers, regarded him as downright selfish. So he was hardly a shoo-in.

While it was all still in the balance, Warne thought there was a chance to swing things his way, assuming the ACB allowed him the opportunity. There was a one-day series against England and Sri Lanka starting in mid-January and, with Waugh injured, someone else had to captain the side. Former Test stars Dean Jones and Rodney Hogg both piped up publicly to say Warne should get the job, while the *Herald Sun*'s Mike Horan, ever a Shane supporter, gave it a push with a conveniently timed profile describing him as, 'a man destined to one day captain his country'. To the surprise of some and the anger of many, Warne was duly named captain for the one-day series, with Mark Waugh as his deputy. This prompted a flood of outraged letters to the papers, accusing the ACB of covering up the betting scandal and then rewarding the culprits. But Allan Border, who was now a selector, said the betting fiasco had never been a factor in the debate. 'As far as I'm concerned they've paid the price and quite a heavy price, too', he told the press. 'I know what they did was silly and wrong, but it's all done with now.'

From a pure cricketing point of view, the choice was brilliant. With Warne as captain, Australia romped away with the CUB Series, winning nine out of the 10 matches in which he took charge. Steve Waugh took over for two games in the middle and Australia lost both. Warne also showed he had the respect of cricket fans. In one match at the MCG, a group of drunken English supporters began pelting players with golf balls and beer bottles. Australia was coasting to victory and some of the Barmy Army clearly did not like it, so England captain Alec Stewart called for Warne's help. Arming himself with Mark Waugh's batting helmet, he walked in front of the rowdiest section and persuaded them to settle down. 'I just thought Warney's a God in Melbourne', Stewart said afterwards, 'bring him out, calm the crowd down and get on with the game.'

In late January 1999 Mike Horan wrote another piece in the *Herald Sun*, puffing Warne's prospects for the top job: 'Only a few weeks ago questions were being asked whether Shane Warne, in the wake of the great bookie scandal, had blown his chance of captaining Australia. Right now he has never been closer.' Horan rated his leadership of the one-day side as 'exciting, inspirational and successful', and it was hard to disagree. Border also heaped praise upon him, as did Warne's mate Darren Berry, who was Victoria's vice-captain. Mark Taylor was also said to be barracking for Warne to replace him. And once again Warne was moved to tell the world how much he coveted the position: 'It would be a great honour to do it, and I would love the job.'

Among the few who opposed him publicly was the redoubtable Malcolm Conn, who told his readers, 'A groundswell of opinion for Warne . . . should not prevent Steve Waugh getting the job.' He then explained:

Serious concerns linger at the highest levels of Australian cricket about Warne's emotional maturity

216

to do the job ... He is a terrific team player ...
However, he can be moody and has a great capacity
to spit the dummy, sometimes blaming others,
usually the media, for his problems.

On 12 February 1999, the ACB finally voted on the
recommendation put to them by Australia's selectors that
Steve Waugh should get the job. The 14 directors took just
half an hour to decide unanimously in his favour. Waugh
was alone in his Melbourne hotel room the next morning,
watching *Sesame Street* on TV, when the news was
phoned through. Warne's consolation prize was the vice-
captain's job, which meant he still had a chance of leading
his country in the future, if he kept out of trouble.

But his chances of doing that were close to zero.
Warne's stupidity and immaturity had cruelled his
candidacy this time. And as always with Shane, worse was
yet to come.

13

Zero to Hero

Glory, glory, Hallelujah! Hooray for Warne.

Given the state of his shoulder and his poor form against England at the SCG, Warne should probably not have been selected for the West Indies tour in March 1999. He was fat and unfit, and it was impossible to hide the fact. As he sat on the beach in the Caribbean sun he was hanging out of his shorts and so obviously out of shape that he asked photographers not to snap him with his top off. He also bowled badly. In the first two Tests he took just one wicket for 129 runs and showed none of his usual fire. The old swerve was missing, the huge turn was absent and the flipper was nowhere to be seen. Yet he refused to admit that the muse had deserted him. He blamed bad umpiring decisions and bad luck, and claimed it would all come right.

However, life for Shane Warne rarely runs smooth, and in the next six months he was going to ride up and down on the rollercoaster like never before. He was also going to face the supreme test of character: the threat of losing his place in the team.

He had not really bowled at his best for three years, apart from knocking over the South Africans in January 1998 and the Poms at Old Trafford in June 1997. He had been thrashed by Tendulkar and Co. in India before his shoulder operation, and had bowled indifferently in his comeback for Victoria and worse in his sole Test against England in January. Stuart MacGill, by contrast, had been in dazzling form, spinning the ball a mile and causing havoc. His arch rival had finished the recent Ashes series as leading wicket taker, with 27 scalps at an average of only 17.7 runs apiece, which was better than Shane had ever done on home soil. And MacGill had done it in only four Tests.

Not surprisingly, Warne was beginning to wonder if his starring role might be snatched away from him and he was unhappy as a result. He was not one to suffer in silence, and he was soon chirping away to the Australian journalists on tour, who he felt had the power to write him out of the team. Malcolm Knox, who was in the West Indies for *The Sydney Morning Herald*, recalls how keen Warne was to persuade them that everything would turn out fine: 'He was Mr Conviviality, everybody's mate, always asking if you wanted a drink. Being Warney, it was perfectly transparent what was going on. If he's struggling he's really friendly. If he's bowling really well and taking wickets he doesn't give you the time of day.'

In the Third Test in Barbados, Warne again bowled badly. Then the cavalry arrived in the shape of his mentor, Terry Jenner, who was escorting a group to Barbados and Antigua for the last two Tests. Before the third day's play, he and Shane set up a couple of stumps on the oval, watched by a crowd of journalists and fans, to see if Jenner could work his usual miracle. But, alas, he could not. 'It was obvious he was struggling', says Jenner today. 'He hadn't recovered confidence in his shoulder and he just wasn't letting go. It was the only time I couldn't help him.' T. J. was not much surprised. Watching him from Australia, Jenner had already decided Warne had come back from injury too soon.

For cricket lovers everywhere – except Australia – the Third Test turned out to be one of the greatest matches in history, with the West Indies pulling off a stupendous victory, thanks to an unbeaten 153 from their star batsman Brian Lara. Chasing 490 in the first innings, they had slumped to 6 for 98 at one stage and appeared to be facing certain defeat. But they had clawed their way back and skittled the Australians for 146, to leave themselves chasing a record target of 308 to win.

Normally, Warne and MacGill would have been able to make short work of them in such circumstances, but Warne had been carted all over the ground in the first innings and had claimed only one victim: Courtney Walsh, who held the record for the most ducks in Test history. And in the second dig Warne fared no better. He could not bowl the flipper because of his shoulder, he would not risk the googly because Lara could pick it and his big-turning leg breaks simply weren't happening. Lara pulled him for six onto the roof of the Greenidge-Haynes stand to reach his 50, then lofted him to mid-on for four to get to 100. Even with six or seven men guarding the boundary, Warne could not stop the flow.

With the crowd cheering, drums beating and reggae

blaring from big speakers in the stands, the chase went down to the wire. With nine wickets down and only Courtney Walsh standing between Australia and victory, Lara finally cracked the winning boundary. Fourteen thousand West Indian fans went crazy, flattening the metal barriers, invading the pitch, kissing the wicket, rolling on it and taking pictures of each other at the crease, while Lara sprinted across the turf and leapt into the arms of a delighted supporter. His innings had been 'brilliant', 'momentous' and 'his best-ever', according to the newspapers next day, and it had achieved, in the words of the wise West Indian commentator Tony Cozier, 'one of the most stunning turnarounds in the history of cricket'.

There was little joy for the Australians, who had seen almost certain victory snatched from them. And there was none at all for Warne, who had now performed below par in four Tests on the trot. Nor was there any comfort for him from captain Steve Waugh at the post-match press conference. 'Two years back we would have won that Test easily', Waugh admitted candidly. 'Warney would have gone through them. But he's fighting his way back from two operations. His confidence is down a bit . . . He's bowling tight without bowling dangerously.' The obvious follow-up question was whether he would make the team for the Fourth and last Test. And again, iceman Waugh pulled no punches. 'There's a possibility that Shane won't play', he said. 'I'm sure he'll be able to accept that. He'll be disappointed if it happens, but he'll understand the situation.' Whether Steve really thought his mate would take so well to being sacked is doubtful. But captains have to say such things on these occasions. And the message to Warne was spot on: you're a professional sportsman, so get used to it.

That night the Australian team went out to drown their sorrows or maybe just to party, and ended up in a popular Barbados nightclub with a horde of Australian fans. One who watched them having fun was appalled by the very public spectacle they made of themselves. It was like *Calypso Cricket* revisited, except that this correspondent was not so shy about naming names (apart from his own). In an email to crikey.com.au, Australia's raciest online news site, he described the scene:

> Michael Slater . . . so drunk he could hardly stand, he in fact fell over three times due to the copious amounts of alcohol taken.

> Ricky Ponting . . . obviously drunk, pushing and shoving an Australian cricket follower, had to be held back from fighting with him.

> Shane Warne . . . sitting at the bar with a lovely looking negro lady on his lap . . . and then later leaving together.

> Mark Waugh . . . wandering around, seemingly intent on making his acquaintance with anyone from the opposite sex.

Just as it had been in 1991, the West Indian tour was a great opportunity for Warne and almost everyone else to have fun. There were parties constantly, women everywhere and places to go almost every night. But partying had never blunted his genius before, and it was not the cause of his poor form this time.

Besides, it hardly mattered what shape he was in if he was going to be dropped. And this is what now happened. Warne pleaded his case for selection: he wasn't bowling badly, he would rise to the occasion, he had never let them down. But Steve Waugh, Geoff Marsh and Trevor Hohns (on the phone from Australia) were adamant that he was not playing well enough to be picked. With Allan Border the only one backing Warne (who was himself a selector), it was decided to rely on Stuart MacGill. He rewarded them by taking five wickets in the match, which Australia won comfortably.

Journalists who saw Warne at a function the night before he was dropped had already guessed his omission was on the cards. He was 'very animated and pretty emotional', according to one tour veteran, and apparently giving Waugh all the reasons why he shouldn't be dumped. His mentor, Terry Jenner, had also foreseen the crisis. He had brought with him from Australia the bottle of Limestone Ridge that Shane had given him in August 1992 on the eve of his first overseas tour. It was the night that Rod Marsh had told the boy he would take 500 Test wickets, which was 499 more than he had at the time. Jenner figured the time had arrived to drink the bottle of red wine together, to mark a low and herald a new beginning, just as his lecture about making sacrifices had done seven years earlier. 'I saw him at Lashings [the Antiguan nightclub owned by Richie Richardson] on the night he was dropped', says Jenner, 'and told him to meet me at the hotel pool at midnight. I sat there with the bottle and an opener and a couple of glasses, waiting for him, but he never showed.'

After his sacking, Warne retired to his room and refused to come out. Afraid to disturb him, his teammates slid messages of support under the door. When he did finally emerge, it was to tell reporters he might never play Test cricket again. This caused one writer in a small town in New Zealand to blast him in the local paper, which just showed that everyone in the cricketing world was following the saga. And from a safe distance, he could say what Australian cricket writers did not dare to. Under the banner 'SUPERSTAR OR SPOILT BRAT? . . . GROW UP SHANE', the *Waikato Times* let rip:

> Shane Warne not only spat the dummy but acted like one as well when dumped from the Australian cricket team for the crucial final test against the West Indies.
>
> The man with an ego larger than his rear end hinted at retirement after his omission, to further sully a reputation which has plummeted from hero to zero over the past year. For Warne – possessor of 317 test wickets and the greatest bowler of this generation – to even consider giving the game away after this setback points at an astounding lack of intestinal fortitude and good grace. 'It takes a lot out of you when you are dropped. You're kicked in the guts. It's up to you whether you want to bounce up and fight it', Warne said. So let's see the fight, Shane.

You can't simply take ten years at the top and then turn tail when you discover that the world's axis and Australian cricket doesn't revolve around your flipper.

Publicly, Warne was philosophical about the fact that his career might be over. 'I've got a beautiful wife, I've got another kid on the way, I've got a couple of kids, I've got a nice house and car, all those sorts of things', he said. Privately, he was angry and critical of Steve Waugh. He was also lonely, missed his family and had no one to turn to. So desperate was he for support that he even sought solace from his nemesis Malcolm Conn, who had broken the betting story, opposed him as captain and flayed him in print. Was he still 'the best leggie in Australia' Warne inquired? Conn was flabbergasted. He could not believe that Warne had turned to him of all people for re-assurance, or that he needed it so badly, after all he had achieved. It was a sign of how low his morale had sunk. 'They were very tough times for him', says Jenner. 'Getting dropped gave his confidence a battering.' To add to his woes, a photographer captured him walking along the beach looking fat and miserable. And then a far bigger storm broke over his head when another photographer caught him smoking.

Four months earlier, Warne had pocketed $200,000 from the pharmaceutical company Pharmacia & Upjohn for promoting its anti-smoking Nicorette gum. His promise to quit from 1 January 1999 was backed by a $5 million advertising campaign featuring big pictures of Warne and slogans about kicking butts with help from

Nicorette. He had tried to stop several times before, he admitted, but this time he was determined to succeed.

The deal was that he should not smoke at all for four months, which did not seem that hard, given the money involved. But the makers of Nicorette obviously did not know their man. 'I don't know what they were thinking', says one sports marketing expert. 'How could they sign up a complete numbskull and expect him to say "I'm cured" at the end? What on earth did they expect?'

Heaps of people had already criticised Warne when he agreed to take the cash, arguing that he was greedy, lazy and should have done it for free, especially with one young child to breathe his fumes and another on the way. One Melbourne radio poll had found 91 per cent of the station's listeners believed he should not have been paid. But the public's roar of disapproval was more than doubled when Warne was snapped smoking a ciggie in a Barbados night spot, just four days before the cut-off date. Typically, he had chosen to resume his habit in the most public of places, in full view of Australian journalists and sports fans.

He assured the London tabloid who published the picture that it was the only time he had weakened, but others claimed to have seen him smoking openly on the beach in previous weeks. As usual, he was being less than honest with the public. Putting the best shine on it, he told everyone how hard he had tried and how hard it had been. Using the gum had helped a lot, he said, getting him down from 40 a day to zero. If only for a bit. But even though their product had failed, the manufacturers of Nicorette must have been thrilled. Warne's woes had delivered $2 million of free newspaper and TV coverage and sales were boosted substantially. Warne, for his part, came out of it smelling staler than ever and was soon back to his customary two packs a day.

If the gum had not packed enough punch to get Warne off the weed it was hardly surprising, because his smoking was almost as legendary as his appalling diet. Back in 1994, Melbourne cricket writer Gideon Haigh had interviewed Shane in a bar and observed that he lit a cigarette as they began their conversation and 'smoked more or less continuously for the next two hours'. A decade later, the Australian leg spinner Kerry O'Keeffe would do a fundraising breakfast with him at the MCG on the first day of a Boxing Day Test and find Shane chewing on a cigarette at seven am. Warne confessed to O'Keeffe that it was his fifth of the day, that he had not yet had breakfast and would probably grab 'a cheese sanger' before taking the field. By that time, Warne reckoned he would probably have smoked 20 cigarettes.

In early 2005, a *60 Minutes* TV crew came back from Sri Lanka with another great smoking story. By their reckoning, Warne was smoking at least 50 a day, with help from Brad Grapsas, the CEO of the Shane Warne Foundation, which was raising money for victims of the 2004 tsunami. Every time Shane demanded a cigarette, Grappo would light up two and hand one over. On arrival in Bangkok, after a long plane flight, the pair had not even been able to wait until they got into the terminal. As they trundled across the tarmac on a bus, Shane and Grappo had their heads out the window, blowing smoke. Indeed, Warne was so addicted to nicotine that he apparently kept a packet open on his bedside table, with one sticking out so he could grab it easily if he woke in the middle of the night.

It seemed a miracle that he could survive long plane journeys without one. In fact, one can see how the next scandal might unfold. So look out for a story that runs something like this:

SHANE WARNE GROUNDED: Cricket ace Shane Warne has been banned from flying after one of the airline's cabin staff found him smoking in the toilet on a Sydney-bound Boeing 747. Warne had set off the smoke detector, despite trying to disable it with several paper towels. 'It's not fair', he told reporters after landing. 'I really needed a smoke. Everyone knows I've tried hard to give up. I don't think you guys in the media realise how hard it is for elite sportsmen like me.' He added: 'I really can't see what the fuss is all about, I've done this heaps of times and the plane has never crashed.'

But let's get back to reality and 1999: Warne's next stop after Barbados was London for the six-week cricket carnival that is the World Cup, in which every cricketing nation in the world, including Scotland, fights to be world one-day cricket champions. Thankfully, this brought the focus back to his form on the pitch. And after surviving the media scrum at Gatwick Airport he was soon in the middle of another packed press conference wanting to talk about it. By this time he was more upbeat. In fact he was feeling 18 again. 'I've been training my butt off for the last month', he told the *Daily Mirror*. 'I've lost a stone and I'm now only a few pounds off my best fighting weight . . . In a way, to be dropped at that stage of my career may have been exactly what I needed.'

He admitted it had hurt to be discarded: 'When selectors tell you you're not needed, you're never going to do cartwheels', he said. But he repeated his line that he had not been bowling that badly and added: 'When I'm at my best, there's no doubt who's the best leg spinner in the world.' Suddenly, the old bravado was back and all doubts were banished: 'I think it [being dropped] shook some of the guys more than it shook me.' But after it was over, it was the ball that had to do the talking. And no amount of PR spin could make that happen. Nor were local fans likely to nurse him back to his best. In the first game against Scotland, he was unsettled by banners proclaiming, 'Save the Whale', and by repeated choruses of, 'He ate all the pies', and he responded by giving the crowd the finger. Luckily for him, the umpires were looking the other way, but the press were not: next day it was headlines in all the British papers. Soon afterwards, another storm blew up with the ABC's Tim Lane reporting rumours of an ugly spilt between Warne and his captain.

Steve Waugh reacted angrily to the charge by calling a press conference after training at Headingley and snapping, 'That's crap.' With Shane at his side, he continued, 'There's no problem between me and Warney. It's just ridiculous. There is absolutely no problem between us or anyone else in the team, and I don't know where the idea comes from.' Warne had already denied the rumours to his old friend. And two years later, he was still protesting. 'We couldn't believe it', he wrote in *Shane Warne, My Autobiography*. 'I said to him it was just another bit of poor journalism and not to worry about it, but we were both very disappointed because it wasn't true.'

However, a number of people since then have confirmed the story. A couple of senior cricket writers and one Australian team official say that Warne was bagging Waugh to team-mates behind his back, suggesting he lacked the flair needed to lead the team. (Guess who had it.) He was also poking fun at the midnight curfew Waugh had introduced in an attempt to curb the team's drinking and partying. And because Australia had started the tournament badly, it was easy to spread alarm. As fast bowler Damien Fleming puts it, 'Warne was unsettled, the team was unsettled, and we were losing.'

It is also now clear that Steve Waugh knew about Shane's stirring even as he denied it to the media. As he admitted in his 2005 autobiography, *Out of My Comfort Zone*: 'Warne *was* [his emphasis] causing some friction behind the scenes over the captaincy. He was lonely, hurt, annoyed and frustrated, and quite frankly sick of the media attention.'

And Shane was certainly getting plenty of it, even by his exalted standards. First it was the smoking, then the finger to the crowd against the Scots, then some rude comments about Arjuna Ranatunga, suggesting Sri Lanka's captain would do the game and his team a favour by quitting. And as always there was speculation about whether he was over the hill. But, true to form, there was worse to come, from England's most salacious Sunday newspaper, the *News of the World,* which had been scandal hunting.

For those who live on Mars, the News of the Screws, as it is famously known in Britain, is owned by Australian press baron Rupert Murdoch, who made his billions by turning his Fleet Street newspapers into sex, sport and scandal sheets. To be fair, the *News of the World* had blazed its trail long before the Dirty Digger came on the scene. But with Rupert in charge, it had taken to putting this no-nonsense invitation on its website:

WANT TO SELL YOUR STORY?
We pay more than anyone for exclusive tips,
interviews and pictures.

Detailed instructions followed on how to flog your yarn, with a few useful questions and answers, such as: 'HOW MUCH IS MY STORY WORTH?' To which the answer was: 'A major exclusive used on the front page could be worth many thousands of pounds . . . Essentially, the bigger the name, the bigger the story, the bigger the payment.'

On this occasion, the newspaper had paid a stripper and minor porn star called Kelly Handley to dish the dirt, of which, sadly, there was plenty. The story kicked off by revealing: 'Cricket superstar Shane Warne has been bowling phone-sex bouncers at a porn star behind his wife's back'. And it got rapidly raunchier from there, continuing:

The blond hunk, who loves playing the devoted husband missing his wife, edged a lurid message onto Kelly's mobile phone last week. 'I'm just watching a dirty movie', he said. 'This girl's getting bent over, mmm, she's actually getting bent over the desk. It's very good actually. Wish I could talk to you.'

Warne had picked up Handley at a strip club two years earlier on the 1997 Ashes tour of England, and she had got back in touch with him (perhaps at the paper's suggestion) when he arrived for the World Cup. She claimed she had then seen him complaining to *The Times* about how much he missed his family, and had decided to sell her story. Whether this was really her motive, and kiss-and-tell yarns always manufacture a sound moral reason for 'going public', there was obviously no doubt about the truth of her tale. Shane did not sue the porn star or the paper. Nor did he deny that he had sent the messages. He just played a dead bat and hoped it would go away.

On the day the article appeared he was due to play against the West Indies at Old Trafford, where he arrived in his 7-Series BMW, sporting a pair of white plastic sunglasses with orange lenses, to find an Australian TV crew waiting for him. Wisely, he offered no comment and slipped into the stands via the catering entrance. Out on the pitch, he bowled better than ever, sending down 10 overs for just 11 runs and taking three wickets. Obviously he liked being back in the limelight.

His form plummeted again when all went quiet a few days later – the Australian papers did not bother to follow the story – and before long the press were back to speculating that his glory days were over. 'Shane's aura is being chipped away', Ian Chappell observed in

London's *Daily Telegraph*. 'Now, as with the old gun-fighter who shows signs of vulnerability, there are a lot more opponents queuing up to do battle.' Even his old mate seemed to be wondering if the magic show had ended. 'Warne is not the first bowler to suffer a reversal after shoulder problems', Chappell warned. 'Those players who faced Richie Benaud before and after his shoulder problem in 1961 say he was never quite the same bowler after that tour.'

Other commentators observed that Shane's dip and swerve had gone, that the seam was facing in the wrong direction, that he was no longer spinning it like he used to, or that the Indians had worked him out, and that he had split with Terry Jenner. Reading these headlines and reflecting on his form, Warne became so depressed that he told his team-mates he had had enough and was going to quit. And for once, it seemed like he meant it. He had missed the birth of his and Simone's second child, a boy, back in Melbourne, and everything was looking black. Setting aside his own feelings about Shane's part in the whispering campaign against him, Steve Waugh attempted to persuade him to stay on. During a walk in Hyde Park he told him to hang in there until the end of the tournament, then go home and talk it over with Simone and his parents before making a decision.

That night Waugh wrote in his tour diary, 'To be honest, I really don't know which way Warney's going to go.' He hoped that the prospect of tormenting his old bunny, Daryll Cullinan, in the next game against South Africa would spark Warne up again. For the next week, Waugh stayed close to him, stroked his ego and made sure he felt wanted, while the rest of the team rallied round and helped get him back on track. And by the time Australia went into the semi-final against South Africa at Edgbaston, Shane was pumped up again and ready for another remarkable return from the dead. With the South Africans chasing a modest Australian total of only 213, and the score at 0 for 43, Waugh threw his leg spinner the ball and told him what he had to do: 'If we're going to get into the World Cup final we need some wickets now.' It took Warne eight deliveries to do the trick, piercing Herschelle Gibbs's defences with a ball that was every bit as good as the one he had bowled to Gatting six years earlier. Drifting into the batsman's legs, it pitched in the rough outside leg stump and spat wickedly across the body to remove Gibbs's off bail. The batsman stayed rooted to the spot, just as Mike Gatting had done, unable to believe he had been bowled. The Australians rejoiced, while a chill went through the South African dressing-room. Next over, Warne did it again, with an almost identical ball to the left-handed Gary Kirsten, who tried to sweep from way outside off stump and was also bowled.

'Warne is one hyped-up puppy', declared *Cricinfo*'s ball-by-ball commentary, as Shane pumped his fist and screamed, 'Yeah . . . Come on', in his best Lleyton-Hewitt style. Two balls later he made it three, having Hansie Cronje caught at slip to huge roars from the large Australian contingent in the crowd. The replays showed that South Africa's captain had not actually made contact, but there was no arguing with the scoreboard, which now read 3 for 53. With just five minutes of magic, Warne had rescued Australia and given his team a chance of victory.

Later on, he added Jacques Kallis to his tally to finish with figures of 4 for 29.

Two months earlier, Warne had played in the most exciting Test match in history and lost. Now he starred in the most remarkable one-day battle ever, which ended in the first tie the World Cup had seen. Needing nine runs off the last over to guide South Africa to victory, Lance Klusener hit Damien Fleming's first two balls for four and levelled the scores. Now needing just one for victory, South Africa was surely home and hosed. But a dreadful mix-up wrecked their dreams. Klusener pushed the ball back past the bowler and set off for a run, only to find Allan Donald had turned back and headed to his crease. Finally, as they stood rooted at the bowler's end, with Donald now having dropped his bat, Mark Waugh threw the ball to the bowler, who rolled it down the wicket to the keeper, who broke the stumps. Pandemonium ensued. Australia went through to the final because it had done better in the lead-up matches and Donald trudged off broken-hearted. Cronje looked like he had been shot.

The next day, Warne was God again: 'Let's shout it from the rooftops – Glory, glory, Hallelujah!' proclaimed Michael Henderson in London's *Daily Telegraph*.

There was a performance by Shane Warne that people will talk about when they are old and grey and nodding by the fire. Combining the brilliance and bravery that is granted only to the great, he took hold of this match when it was drifting away from Australia and enabled them to win it. Hooray for

Warne, and hooray for cricket lovers everywhere. He was sensational.

Ian Chappell also slipped back into eulogy mode. 'Shane Warne proved at Edgbaston that form is temporary, but class is forever', he wrote in his column.

He produced an amazing spell when Australia appeared to be dead and buried, not only taking wickets but inspiring his team-mates to produce a superhuman effort . . . Not since the days of Dennis Lillee have I seen an Australian bowler inspire his team from a seemingly hopeless situation, the way Warne did at Edgbaston.

Needless to say, Shane was made man of the match. He picked up the award again with four more wickets in the final against Pakistan at Lord's. In the celebrations that followed Australia's crushing victory he was all over his captain – the man he had been badmouthing – and right at the centre of things. But a couple of Australian journalists, who were allowed into the dressing-room later, saw an entirely different picture: Warne sitting alone with his head in his hands. In the post-match press conference, he again warned that he might bring down the curtain on his career. And the media centre was abuzz with the rumour that he had turned to Waugh at the end of the game and said: 'This is it, Tugga, enough for me.' Next day, the headlines were as much about him as they were about Australia's remarkable victory. Some of the Australian team felt aggrieved because of it. Having worked so hard together and done so much to support their star, he had hogged the headlines and stolen their glory by talking about himself.

'I will go home and think hard about my future', he told the assembled media. 'This last week has been sensational, the best week of my life . . . But I am not at all sure where I am going from here. I need to talk to my family and think things through. A lot has happened in my life in the last six months . . . I need to consider my future.' Shortly afterwards he was saying, 'My priorities lie with my family.' But surely he didn't mean it?

Warne, Waugh and the World Cup winners returned to Melbourne to a huge ticker-tape parade, where everyone could see that the biggest cheers were for Shane, their hometown hero. It was exactly the encouragement he needed to keep going – if, after his latest Lazarus-like comeback, it had ever been in doubt that he would. Three weeks later, he told the world he would play on after all. 'In the end I'm sure I would have missed it too much', he explained.

But it was no more than cricket fans and readers of the tabloids would have missed him. His life was better than any soap opera. True, he could get a bit hysterical at times with all the ups and downs, but you could not deny he was a champion. It was a mark of his astonishing self-belief and mental toughness that he could bounce back from the depths every time to scale even greater heights. And it was a sign of how much he loved the spotlight that he chose the biggest stage on which to do it. What better moment could there have been to produce his magic than in the World Cup semi-final when all seemed lost? Cue

Shane to bowl two of the best balls of his life and turn the match. You really had to hand it to him. The guy was a genius.

14

Fame Therapy

Like most famous people, Shane is one of the loneliest
people on the planet.

In 1999, Australia's team psychologist, Sandy Gordon,
was reading an article on the team bus about the film
star Minnie Driver. It was all about how lost, lonely and
unhappy she had felt after rocketing to fame in the movie
Good Will Hunting. Seeing the headline, 'FAME THER-
APY', Shane asked what the story was about. Gordon told
him that Driver's therapist in Hollywood had made her
write a list of all the friends who would love her un-
conditionally, then vow to ring them regularly. According
to Gordon, Warne immediately said: 'I couldn't do that; I
don't have any friends; they wouldn't want to talk to me;
I don't know who I am or where I'm from.'

It is hard to shed tears for the rich and famous, but
there's little doubt that adulation rarely brings happiness.
Sometimes the worst thing that can happen in life is to get
what you want most, and Shane was learning this lesson
the hard way. He had craved fame since boyhood, yet was
finding it could bring as much misery as joy. He loved the
money, the glory and all the privileges it brought, but he

hated the intrusions, the restrictions, the loss of privacy and the lack of real friends. At times, he wanted to be plain Shane again, and he knew he never could. He liked to tell people he was still the boy from Black Rock, who enjoyed kicking a footy and could walk into the Beaumaris Hotel for a drink with the lads. But the truth was he had not kept in touch with his schoolmates since hitting the big time. And it was not just because he might have been mobbed if he had met them in public. He was so busy being famous, being fêted, doing ads and being Shane Warne that he had precious little time for the people he had once been closest to. In 1994, he had even forgotten his best friend's wedding. He had been on tour in South Africa, so had been forced to turn down the invitation to be best man, but he had then forgotten to send a present or a telegram.

Not surprisingly, Shane's old friends also saw him in a different light once the world began worshipping him. When they ran into him at footy games or at the casino he seemed to be the same old knockabout bloke they had grown up with. But they did not ring and invite him over for a backyard barbecue, because they assumed he was too important and wouldn't want to come. Nor did Shane invite them to his house. They didn't have much in common anyway after all these years: what would they be able to talk about apart from him?

Fame had changed him in other obvious ways. He was no longer delivering pizzas, driving trucks or humping beds for Forty Winks. Instead, he lived in a $2 million waterfront house, drove a Ferrari and enjoyed a lifestyle that was, frankly, unreal. He received unlimited free cigarettes from a tobacco company, free sports gear and clothes from his sponsors, free meals and free drinks at Melbourne's Crown Casino and access to the Mahogany Room for high rollers. He also got free limos, free five-star hotels and people pandering to him wherever he went. As Australia's opening batsman, Michael Slater, who received one-tenth of these privileges, described it, 'The lifestyle is very fake. It's sort of unhealthy in a lot of ways . . . everywhere you go people put you on this pedestal.' This unreality helped end Slater's marriage and nearly sent him crazy. Warne, on the other hand, lapped it up.

There is a great song from the 1970s that says all you need to know about the pitfalls of fame. Called *Life's Been Good*, it was a huge hit for Joe Walsh on his first album after leaving The Eagles. It's about a rock star who has everything that money can buy. He gets around in a stretch limo and is mobbed by fans wherever he goes, but his life just ain't right. He has a mansion he's never seen, a Maserati he can't drive, and he lives in fear of being attacked. I can't quote the words that sum up the story without adding thousands of dollars to Joe Walsh's fortune, and you may need to hear it to appreciate the irony, but the song's message is that fame makes life so weird that it changes you and it cuts you off from your friends and your roots. However much you resist, it is guaranteed to leave you isolated. And Warne did not escape. As Sandy Gordon puts it today: 'Like most famous people, Shane is one of the loneliest people on the planet.'

It is true that Warne has always had heaps of mates in

the Australian cricket team and that he is popular and well-liked. He is an easygoing bloke, he is fun to be with and he tells a good story. But his fellow cricketers have always been too busy worrying about their own form and fortunes to be much help in tough times. And even they have always felt that his fame sets him apart. His new friends were fellow superstars such as Russell Crowe and Mick Jagger or rich businessmen such as Kerry Packer and his son James. He loved the fact that Sean Connery would stop him at the Cannes Film Festival and ask him to pose for a photo. And he was thrilled when Elton John confessed that he envied Shane's talent and wanted to be him. 'When you hear someone like Elton John say that', said Warne, 'it just blows your mind. As it happens, I've got a few of his records and I wouldn't mind being him, either.'

Considering how crazy it all was, Warne made a pretty good fist of staying on the rails. He did not become an alcoholic or a drug addict, like so many rock stars. And in some ways he had no tickets on himself. Despite everything, he was genuinely humble about his gift and all that he had done, and he remains so to this day.

The guys who work on Channel 10's talk show *The Panel* have seen hundreds of stars since they started it up in 1998 and they rate Shane as one of their favourites. The program's producer, Michael Hirsch, says he is one of the top 10 guests they have had on the show, in terms of how easy he was to deal with. 'If you had just read about him in the papers, you'd think he's a maniac and he's absolutely not. He's cool, honest, funny, just a regular, genuine guy who has this great gift.' Big-time or small-time, *The Panel*'s guests always arrive at the studio with their managers, support staff, and hangers-on. For a time it was Kylie Minogue who held the record for the biggest entourage with 19 people. Then a little-known American singer trumped her with 23. But when Shane came in he was on his own. When the production assistant had rung earlier to ask whether he wanted a car, there was a pause at the other end of the phone and a single word: 'Why?' Warne couldn't understand why he wouldn't want to drive himself. And when he did arrive he shunned the green room with the other stars and guests and joined the crew out the back for a fag instead.

Sure enough, on tapes of that episode from November 1998 he looks like a regular guy. He is relaxed, funny and self-deprecating and appears to be really enjoying himself. He listens, sits still and does not interrupt. He tells funny stories but does not try to hog the stage.

One of *The Panel*'s mainstays, comedian Rob Sitch, was also surprised by how polite and well-mannered he was. 'He was like some suburban boy who had been drafted into the team to make up the numbers', he says, 'who wasn't sure he deserved all the acclaim.' Warne's account of his rise to fame – as told on the program – emphasised the element of luck. He had taken a few wickets when it mattered, he said, and had been in the right place at the right time: 'All of a sudden I was playing for Australia. It happened in about 18 months.'

But modest or not, Warne loved the fact that everyone on the show was talking about *him* and that he was the centre of attention. 'I always wondered what it would be like to be in the limelight', he told one interviewer, 'and it felt great.' Nor was he just a happy passenger. According to photographers, he knew where all the cameras were at training sessions and positioned himself accordingly. And he loved to make headlines. What bothered him was that he could not turn off the attention when he wanted to and could not set limits on people's curiosity about him. He complained about journalists invading his privacy, then invited magazines to do big photo spreads with Simone and the kids, or gave TV interviews with his young daughter, Brooke, sitting on his lap. He did not understand that intrusion was the flip side of self-promotion, that it was what the Devil demanded in return for his gifts.

Warne complained that he lived life in a fishbowl and was recognised wherever he went. Tour buses stopped outside his house on the Esplanade in Brighton to take pictures over the wall, and some were lucky enough to find him sitting on his huge, colonnaded deck overlooking Port Phillip Bay, which was close enough to the road to call out for a chat. Even when the media weren't chasing scandal, they were after him constantly. 'You'd leave your hotel room', he told the *Bulletin*'s Jana Wendt, 'and there'd be four photographers following you and jumping in a car, and you'd go down the pub or you'd do whatever, and they're waiting out the front. That's hard.' Almost anything he did, however trivial, was turned into a story. And the smallest incident could be blown up into a storm. In December 1997, for example, he held a photo call in the Shane Warne Room at Melbourne's All Star Café and posed alongside a new Madame Tussaud's waxwork of him in his cricket gear. It was impossible to miss the fact that the dummy (whose dimensions had been fixed one year earlier) was a great deal thinner than Shane, and one journalist (who was tubbier than Warne) cheekily enquired whether he wished he 'still looked like that'. Warne responded by spitting the dummy himself and stomping out, telling the crowd of reporters, 'That's why I wasn't taking questions from you blokes. Okay that's it, you've ruined it.'

He could certainly have handled it better, and could easily have had a laugh about it – he was forever boasting about his beer and pizza diet, but columnists condemned him for weeks for his lack of grace. And debate also raged over whether he really was too fat, with every passing stranger stopped in the street to be asked for an opinion. Even nutritionists were asked for their twopence worth, with one warning that he risked brain damage, heart disease, scurvy and mental and physical sluggishness because of his famous diet.

The day after his dummy spit, Shane was photographed at the MCG tucking into a plate of brightly coloured jelly snakes and ignoring the meal laid out for the Australian team. Even when he took his 300th Test wicket at the SCG against South Africa three weeks later, TV interviewers were still asking about it. He tried to dismiss them by saying: 'I've got better things to do than answer stupid questions', but still the comments flew. His fitness or lack of it was something on which every fan (and every journalist) felt qualified to have a view. It was as if he had become public property. But being a celebrity, of course, he had.

However annoying this may have been, it was a bit rich to complain, because he was hardly Greta Garbo.

Provided the publicity was on his terms, he spent most of his time encouraging it. He took money for interviews with women's magazines and for profiles on *60 Minutes*, and was paid handsomely for regular columns in a number of newspapers. He also made money from his fame by selling things to the public: sunglasses, sportswear, soft drinks, sauces and Sony Music, to name but a few. And to cap it all, the photos taken at the All Star Café, which had brought all this attention to his figure, were designed to promote a business in which he had an interest.

But Shane either could not or would not see the connection. To him it just seemed unfair. His reaction to the pork stories was to bemoan Australia's appalling journalistic standards and to threaten never to talk to the media again. It seemed to escape him that he often wanted them to know how well he was bowling or what a good father he was or what he thought of the opposition or how his new mystery ball would put the Poms in a spin. It also escaped him that the British tabloids could be far crueller about such things. The *Daily Mirror*, for example, had splashed a big picture of him and the waxwork on its back page, with a question for readers to answer: 'Who is the dummy with the fat bloke?'

There was a far bigger storm in Warne's teacup two years later, in November 1999, when he was accused of sledging one of his own team-mates in the Second Test against Pakistan. In this case he had rather more reason to be aggrieved by the media's obsession with everything he did (or didn't do). The game at Hobart marked the second appearance for Australia of a big, blond fast bowler from Queensland by the name of Scott Muller. In his own words, Muller had 'busted his ass' to play for Australia and had finally got his chance at the big time. But he had not bowled with much distinction, and when he muffed a throw from the outfield, someone muttered: 'This bloke can't bowl and he can't throw.' Muller was dropped before the Test was even over and never played for Australia again. And he was still smarting from this rebuff when news broke of what had been said.

No one in the sports department at Channel 9 had actually heard the words go to air, and no viewers had complained. But a couple of days after the game a tape was sent in to *The Panel* at Channel 10 who turned up the volume to render the comment quite clearly audible. The sound quality was appalling and it was all over in seconds, but before long there was uproar, with every man and his dog, including Muller, pointing the finger at Warne. Even Shane's team-mates assumed it must be him, because he had been bowling and was standing near the stump mike, and all the guys round the batsman knew that none of them had said it. Besides, it was the sort of thing Warne would do.

Now, clearly this was a better story than walking out on a waxwork: a recruit to the Australian Test team had been slagged off by one of his own team-mates. But it soon became 10 times bigger and it has now cemented itself into urban myth, because nothing has ever convinced the press and the public that Shane was innocent.

Back at Channel 9, the head of sport, Gary Burns, conducted a post-mortem to find out how the comment had slipped through undetected. The immediate assumption was that it had come from one of the stump mikes – either at the batsman's or the bowler's end – but a close examination of the recordings from these yielded nothing more than swearing from Warne as the ball came in. The next possibility was that it had been picked up by the effects mikes at either end of the pitch. One group of these was on a temporary platform next to the commentary box, on which three cameras were lined up, behind the bowler's arm, at least 50 metres away. And sure enough, says Burns, that's where they traced it to. But no amount of denials would convince the punters or the press that Warne was not the culprit. They wanted it to be him, to have all their prejudices confirmed.

A few days later, the papers got hold of the rumour that a Channel 9 cameraman called Joe Provitera had owned up. He had apparently been telling his mates in the bar about it and word had leaked out. Sceptics noted that Joe's confession was perfect for Channel 9, because it got their star off the hook. And before long, Shane was being hauled on to *A Current Affair* to talk about it. But by this time, the evidence was mounting that Warne was not the guilty party. ABC Radio had also checked the stump microphones and found no trace of the offending comments. Various camera angles had then established that Warne's lips weren't moving at the time the words were spoken.

On the program, Warne repeated his denial that he had made the comment, adding that he was disappointed that no one seemed to believe him. 'I've said I didn't do it. That should be good enough to start with', he said, 'but the simple fact is I didn't say it.' He added that it was 'disappointing' to be doubted on his word.

A sheepish-looking Joe Provitera was then introduced to viewers. Coincidentally or otherwise, he was manning one of the studio cameras and shooting the show. So the focus now swung onto him, while Mike Munro popped the question:

Munro: Did you say that Scott Muller can't bowl, can't throw?
Joe: Unfortunately, yes I did say it. I did say it.
Munro: You certainly caused a stir mate.
Joe: I know I have. I apologise to Scott Muller, if I've offended you in any way. I didn't actually mean it. It's one of those things that came out. I stand behind the camera for six hours during the day filming the cricket. It's just a comment to another cameraman and it's been picked up by the effects mike. I know it's upset you mate. I apologise. It shouldn't have been said. I regret saying it, and I wish I hadn't said it, but I did.

Now, you might think this should have been enough to kill the story, but we live in a world where conspiracy theories flourish and a vast number of people are still convinced that Princess Diana was murdered. Not to mention that Jesus Christ had children. So perhaps it is no surprise that some felt Joe was taking the rap for Channel 9's famous star. Certainly Scott Muller believed so and made his feelings clear.

Scott had hired his own private investigator who, by this time, was sitting on a hefty report into the affair. The essence of it was that Muller claimed to have been told by

Porky Parker, the umpire who was standing at the bowler's end, that he had heard Warne make the comment. The private investigator had not been able to confirm this, because Parker wouldn't talk to them. But nothing was going to convince Muller that he was wrong.

If you weren't in Australia at the time, and following the story, it must be hard to imagine how much heat the 'can't bowl, can't throw' row generated. It even led to a punch-up in the press box at the WACA in Perth as two prominent journalists argued the toss about whether or not Warne was guilty. Eventually, the story was laid to rest by *The Australian*, which gave the tape to a voice analyst, who concluded that it was not Warne's voice. Despite that, three weeks later Warne was loudly booed by 8000 spectators at the Gabba in Brisbane, Muller's home ground, when he played a one-day match for Victoria against Queensland. Clearly they still believed that Warne had made the comments, and blamed him for Muller's dumping from the Australian team.

Given this sort of experience, it was not surprising Shane believed he was unpopular with the public and that the pressure got to him occasionally, causing him to live up to his public image as a rude, arrogant yob. In February 2000, for example, he found himself at the centre of another mini-cyclone when he abused a couple of 15-year-old schoolboys who took a picture of him during a one-day international against New Zealand in Wellington. The incident occurred while Warne was sitting in the players' area, playing cards with some of his team-mates while rain prevented play. And the cause of the fuss was that he had a cigarette hanging out of his mouth. Not only did the Westpac Stadium have a strict no-smoking policy, but Warne had painful memories of the recent Nicorette row which had been sparked off by a picture of him smoking in Barbados. No doubt the sensible course of action would have been for him to avoid smoking – and breaking the rules – in full view of the public. But was Warne ever sensible?

According to the two boys, Shannon Nightingale and Daniel Bassett, who had come to watch the game with the rest of their school cricket team, Warne went crazy when he saw the flash go off. First, he demanded the film, then he grabbed the disposable camera and tried to open it, without success. He was extremely aggressive. 'I thought he was going to hit me', said Nightingale. Warne then agreed, generously or naïvely, to let them take more pictures and bring the camera back in the dinner break. But when the match was abandoned and they still had not returned, Warne went looking for them instead. Again, he demanded the camera, but this time more forcefully. According to Bassett: 'He said, "Either you give the camera to me or I'll get security to take it and smash it." '

When the two boys tried to persuade Warne that one of their friends had taken the camera home, he apparently went 'right off his trolley'. As Nightingale told reporters, 'He was going ballistic, swearing and screaming at us'. He was also calling them 'cockhead' and 'fuckface', or so the boys claimed.

Warne's next move was to summon a security guard and confiscate the boys' bag, telling them they could not have it back unless they gave him the camera, and that they could not leave the ground. Shannon's father, Steve

Nightingale, then arrived on the scene and called the police. Eventually, it took three policemen to deal with the fracas, because Warne was so angry and upset. The upshot was that Warne was made to give back the bag and the boys were allowed to go home. 'I think the boy was a bit shocked, he didn't know what the fuss was about', Wellington Police's Inspector Gilpin later told the press, saying that Warne had been upset about being photographed while smoking.

You may not be surprised to hear that Warne's version of the story, recounted in his 2001 autobiography, presents him in a very different light, as the innocent, injured party in this whole affair. He accuses the police of incompetence or stupidity and of trying to make a name for themselves. He says he asked for the camera politely and suggested he send them the prints. He claims that his main concern was for officials at the Westpac Stadium who had told him it would be fine to smoke in the privacy of the dressing-room. (He had in fact been smoking on part of the public concourse.) As for grabbing the boys' bag, he was just 'minding it until the camera turned up'.

Typically, Warne says he 'couldn't believe it' when the police told the boys they could go home with the camera. He could not understand why common sense had not prevailed. 'Had the police not weighed in, the kids would have given me the film and more than likely the matter would have been closed.'

According to Warne, one of the policemen then suggested in a very sarcastic and 'smart-arse way' that Shane should have another cigarette so that he could take another picture. And at this point, Warne admits, he went off. 'I couldn't believe the guy's attitude, and told him what I thought . . . As I walked away, I was still annoyed at their approach.'

It did not take long for the story to break on TVNZ's six o'clock news and for the newspapers to follow up. That weekend the New Zealand papers were full of it, with headlines such as: 'SHAME ON YOU SHANE' and 'GRUMPY SHANE FUMES AT PHOTO'.

Back home, the columnists also laid into him, with tirades like this one from sports commentator Mike Gibson:

> Australians are angry. They're angry that Shane Warne – yet again – has embarrassed us. They're angry that Shane Warne – yet again – has resurrected the image of that ugly Australian who makes us all cringe. They're angry that here we have the highest profile cricketer of his generation behaving – yet again – like an unconscionable buffoon. And they're angry that no one does anything about it.

Despite public calls to punish Warne, the ACB did not, although it easily could have for his breach of the Westpac Stadium's no-smoking rule, or for swearing at the boys (if that could be proved). Instead, it endorsed Warne's black ban on one of Australia's most respected cricket commentators, Jim Maxwell, who has covered cricket on the ABC since the early 1980s. Maxwell had suggested, quite reasonably, that it would have been wiser for Warne to smoke in the toilet, rather than light up in such a public place. He went on to say that Warne's reaction showed how immature he was and made you wonder whether he was suited to being captain or vice-captain of the Australian team. Soon afterwards, when Maxwell asked for an interview with Warne, he was told by team management that the leg spinner did not intend to talk to him again.

Shane's fellow team-mates were not all so protective. Adam Gilchrist told one Australian reporter covering the story that he should not worry about the team's reaction to anything he wrote, because they knew how Warne carried on and knew that journalists were just doing their job. 'Don't worry if Warney gets the shits with you', Gilchrist told him. 'The rest of the team won't care. We know exactly what he's like.'

On the positive side, the ACB did at least try to smooth over what was now officially described as 'a minor misunderstanding'. A month after the incident, when the Australians returned to Wellington, team manager Steve Bernard organised a public reconciliation. The two boys were ushered into the changing rooms at the Basin Reserve, to hear an apology from Warne and be given a couple of match tickets. Warne then smiled his way through a press conference, parroting the line that 'the misunderstanding' had now been cleared up. Shortly afterwards, he was out on the turf with a couple of Australian journalists, complaining loudly about 'those little fucking shits . . . those little fucking smart-arse pricks', or words to that effect.

All in all, this Australian tour proved to be a bad-tempered and unpleasant affair, not least for Warne. He complained that he was harassed by talkback radio stations who rang him early in the morning in his hotel room and put him live to air or who, on another occasion, abused him when they failed to get through. During the one-day series he also copped a fair bit of abuse, including the odd banner proclaiming 'Warne's a homo'. But there were other more serious incidents: fast bowler Brett Lee was pelted with plastic bottles, cans and oranges in Auckland, and shortly after that the Australian team bus had its tyres slashed.

Despite all these distractions, the Australian juggernaut kept rolling over the Kiwi opposition and Warne passed another significant milestone in his brilliant career. With the last ball of the First Test match in Auckland, he finally overtook Dennis Lillee's Australian record of 355 Test wickets. He had been hoping to achieve it in front of his home crowd at the MCG back in December, but had failed to do so. He had flown his family up to Sydney in the expectation of getting the five wickets he needed on the spin-friendly SCG, but he had got none at all. Going into the game at Eden Park, he had still needed five more, and it had taken him until the death to do it.

His 356th victim was New Zealand's tailender, Paul Wiseman, who was caught off the glove trying to sweep. The dismissal sealed victory for Australia and saw Warne mobbed by his team-mates. His good mate Dennis Lillee sent him a message from Perth in the form of a public statement:

I'm very honoured to have achieved the record in my time, but I'm just as pleased that a bowler and a bloke as great as Shane Warne has overtaken my record. It makes me smile that I took it from one of the greatest leg-spinners, Richie Benaud, and now possibly the greatest leg-spinner of them all has repeated the dose on me. Congratulations, Warney. Well done, keep it going, and I look forward to buying you a congratulatory ale soon.

That night Shane went out to a restaurant to celebrate his long-awaited triumph, together with his mother and father and his brother, Jason, all of whom he had flown over from Melbourne. Strangely, his wife Simone was left in their Auckland hotel room looking after the children, who had also flown over to see their dad make history. It seems bizarre that they couldn't find a babysitter.

Two weeks later, he was voted one of *Wisden*'s five Cricketers of the 20th Century. No doubt his stellar performance in the World Cup had helped him earn the accolade, but his contribution to the game was far more lasting than that. He had revived the dying art of wrist spin and given a new dimension to the game. Most of all, he had brought theatre and excitement to everything he did.

'There are three elements to Shane Warne's greatness: skill, novelty and drama', *The Age*'s Greg Baum enthused in a generous yet honest citation.

At his best he has the ruthlessness of a clinician and the flourish of a performer. It was not enough to take a hat trick; it had to be in an Ashes Test at the MCG. It was not enough for him to take 300 wickets; the 300th had to be accompanied by lightning and thunderclaps.

'Australia's finest moments', Baum continued, 'but also their worst, most controversial, most splendid, most dramatic, most sordid, have all revolved around Warne.'

It was noticeable that the other giants of the game had all been knighted for their services. He was now being ranked alongside the greats such as Sir Donald Bradman, Sir Garfield Sobers, Sir Jack Hobbs and Sir Viv Richards. But for all his undoubted brilliance with the ball, his chances of following in their footsteps and becoming Sir Shane did not look good.

And what happened next probably killed them forever.

15

Oh Donna

He was a fat ugly stranger who couldn't have been less appealing.

Having been forced to turn down several lucrative offers to play county cricket in England during the 1990s, Warne finally signed to play for Hampshire for the 2000 season at $400,000 a year. Naturally, there was huge excitement at the prospect but, initially, things did not go well for him. The rain fell constantly; he bagged five ducks in his first nine innings; and Hampshire lost its first six championship matches on the trot.

But what was happening off the field was far more damaging to his already battered reputation. Simone had come over to England for the summer with their two kids – aged 10 months and three – and had set up house in Southampton, where she sat inside looking at the rain and watching videos with the children. Even though he had his family to go home to, Warne was still playing away. On 10 June 2000, not for the first time, Simone woke up to bad news. On the front of the *Mirror* was a large photo of a young blonde woman next to a banner headline proclaiming: 'SHAME WARNE: Married cricket legend harasses a mum for sex with obscene phone calls'.

Shane had been caught red-handed with his mobile phone for the second time in a year, setting the pattern for many more scandals in years to come. The three-page story began badly and rapidly got worse. God knows what Simone must have thought as she read the opening paragraph, which went like this:

> Young Mum Donna Wright last night branded cricket hero Shane Warne a sick pervert after he bombarded her with disgusting X-rated phone calls ... To her he was a fat ugly stranger who couldn't have been less appealing.

It is hard to say why one sex scandal is forgotten and another reverberates around the world, but this one would have a lasting effect on Shane's standing with the public and with women in particular. There were three things that made it so potent. First was that it was not about two consenting adults in private: Warne was being accused of sexual harassment. Second was that his alleged victim was a pretty, mild-mannered young woman 10 years his junior. Third was that Warne handled it all with incredible stupidity once it was made public.

Three weeks before the *Mirror* story hit the newsstands, Warne had been unwinding with his Hampshire teammates at a night club called Simpkins in the Midlands town of Leicester, and had tried to pick up a 22-year-old nurse who was out for the night with her friends. He gave her his room key and (some days later) left a string of explicit voice messages on her phone. Donna Wright told the *Mirror* that she was on the dance floor when a stranger came up to say his friend wanted to meet her. At the bar, she was introduced to a blond man, 'smoking a cigarette and wearing a cream V-necked top', who stepped forward and said: 'I'm Shane Warne.'

Donna claimed she was not a cricket fan and had no idea who he was. She then gave the *Mirror* an unflattering but unmistakable description of her would-be lover. 'He was really unattractive. He was podgy and very tanned. He had dyed-blond hair and I could see the roots. He seemed permanently to have a cigarette hanging out of his mouth.'

Donna told the *Mirror* that she ignored his advances and went straight back to the dance floor, but she 'bumped into him' at the bar half an hour later. Someone then said to her, 'Don't you know he's famous?' To which she claimed to have replied sarcastically: 'In that case, do you want to sign my back?' The two of them chatted amicably for a couple of minutes until one of her favourite songs started up, whereupon she grabbed her girlfriend and headed back to the dance floor.

Sometime after midnight, she said, Shane came over to her on the dance floor and gave her his hotel keycard, with a yellow Post-it note attached, on which he had written his name, his mobile number and the number of his room at the Leicester Holiday Inn. He told her he would really like to see her that night, so why didn't she come round. She replied she wouldn't be needing his key and handed it back to him, whereupon he pushed it into the back pocket of her jeans and left. 'I should have told him to shove off and thrown the key in the bin', she told the *Mirror*, 'but I didn't want a row or a confrontation in the middle of a night out with my mates.'

The next day, Donna rang the mobile number to ask what she should do with the key. 'That was the worst mistake I ever made', she said. Warne now had her mobile number and proceeded to leave a string of messages asking her for dates and saying he wanted to hear her 'sexy voice'. 'He was very forceful, he was very direct', she said. 'He was the Mr Big and he just assumed I would jump at the mention of his name.'

In the hope that he would eventually lose interest, Donna just ignored his calls: 'I suppose it was naïve of me, but I really thought it was a bit sad, not scary.' Days later, Warne phoned her at seven pm and asked to see her that night. She said, 'No.' He suggested next week. She said, 'No' again. Then he told her he had got out of the shower and was lying on the bed. She told him he was breaking up and cut him off. And when he phoned back moments later she turned off her phone.

He then left a string of voice messages as he masturbated. 'I found it very upsetting and insulting. It made my skin crawl', she told the *Mirror*, which printed extracts of some of the messages she had stored on her phone:

7.16 pm: 'Oh Donna where are you? I'm picturing the wine all over us. Both our mouths together, our tongues together . . .' [the rest is censored]

7.18 pm: (apparently performing a sex act): 'Donna, I want to hear you. I want you to be talking to me . . .' [the rest is censored]

7.21 pm: 'Oh Donna . . . [the rest is censored] . . . Call me please when you get this message.'

7.49 pm: (more calmly): 'Hi Donna, it's Shane here, just lying back on my bed smoking a cigarette. Just wanted to ring up . . . It would be nice to speak to you. OK. Bye, Donna.'

Not surprisingly, the young woman was appalled. 'He left messages saying the most disgusting things I've ever heard', she told the *Mirror*. 'It was perverted. It made me feel sick to the pit of my stomach.'

Lucy Rock – who spent a week with Donna Wright, heard all the tapes and wrote the story for the *Mirror* – had exactly the same reaction: 'The messages were vile. They were disgusting. There were a lot of references to him coming and being about to come. We didn't print much of that because it was just unprintable, but that's what it was all about. And I think it must have been really frightening for a young girl to hear. Even had she slept with him – and she didn't – it would have been unacceptable. And I thought anyone that could do that is not just disgusting, but quite stupid as well.'

When the newspaper's reporters confronted Warne with the allegations, before Hampshire's game against Lancashire, he initially claimed, 'I don't know what you're talking about.' But when they explained they had tapes of his voice messages to Donna, he changed his mind, saying: 'I'll talk to you after the match, mate.' *The Mirror* duly tackled him at the close of play, but all he offered was, 'No, no, no.' He gave the same response to Australian TV reporters who followed up the story, telling them it was a private matter between him and Simone. But he managed to cast doubt on Donna's version of events by suggesting there were 'two sides to every story'. Which, loosely translated, meant: 'Don't believe her, mate, she's lying.'

It's an old saying that you can't believe everything you read in the papers, and we all know that journalists rank alongside used-car salesmen and politicians as the last people in the world one would trust. But it's worth making the point that the Fleet Street tabloids don't normally get such stories wildly wrong. Libel laws in Britain are among the strictest and most powerful in the world, and damages run into millions of pounds. So newspapers get their facts right when they make allegations such as these or they pay the price. As to Warne's belief that this was just a private matter, the British courts would not have agreed. They have long regarded the behaviour of public figures such as Warne – even in private – as fair game, which is why the UK tabloids can write this sort of stuff every day of the week.

Needless to say, Warne did not deny the story or sue the newspaper. Wright had obviously not made it all up, because she had the messages on her mobile phone. And the nature of these pretty much proved her claim that he had harassed her. Nor did anyone (except Warne) dispute her version of events, despite the huge exposure given to the story. No one from the nightclub, for example, called the *Mirror* to say she had led him on. 'We didn't, from memory, receive a single call to say she had shown anything but disinterest in him that night', says Lucy Rock, who was convinced that Donna was telling the truth. 'Her attitude really was that he was an unattractive, fat, quite ugly man that she had never heard of at all.' This was relevant, because Warne's defence was that she had started it all.

Wright's credibility was reinforced by an interview on Channel 9's *A Current Affair* a few days later, in which she appeared nothing like the usual tabloid gold-digger. She was petite, blonde and pretty, with a small voice and Jean Seberg looks. Dressed in a simple white high-collared jacket, she could have come straight from a hospital soap, playing a sweet, shy intern. And she remained composed and credible throughout her grilling, despite getting a good going-over from the interviewer, Mike Munro.

So why had she gone public in the first place? Her answer was she wished she hadn't.

Wright: Basically I was very silly and let a lot of people play the tapes, friends and colleagues. Word got around and the press started to harass me. Then the *Mirror* approached me, said they would deal with it sympathetically, and I was just very scared that a different story would be written about me.

Munro: People think the *Daily Mirror* paid you vast amounts of money?

Wright: No. A donation will be made to my workplace, the children's unit at Leicester Hospital.

Munro: And you're not being paid for this interview?

Wright: Definitely not. I don't want paying. I just want it all over and done with.

It was quite true that Channel 9 had not paid her for the TV interview, but the *Mirror* had signed her up for £10,000 and Donna's friend had in fact phoned the newspaper, offering her story for sale. Whether she had then passed the money on to the children's unit at Leicester Hospital was not clear. But otherwise her story held up well. She seemed young, innocent, 'a nice girl' and almost mouse-like. You could believe her when she said she had wanted to avoid a confrontation. There were also those messages. 'He was performing an act', she told Munro. 'So how disgusted were you?' he asked, in classic TV fashion. 'Quite disgusted', she replied, 'very disgusted.'

Did she have any message to Shane, Munro inquired. 'Look after your family', she replied. 'Don't do this to other women.'

And any message to Warne's family?

'Yes', she said. 'I'm sorry the tape was heard.'

While the interview was going to air in Australia, *A Current Affair*'s executive producer, David Hurley, was on the phone to London, trying to persuade Warne to tell his side of the story, as ex-Australian captain Mark Taylor had strongly suggested he do. Hurley had dealt with the champion leg spinner several times before, liked him and thought him a bit of a legend. And to this end, he offered some free PR advice. Hurley, who had been New South Wales Premier Neville Wran's press secretary in the 1980s, told Warne sagely that if he wanted to come out looking good, he needed a plan. 'The bare minimum is to make an apology', he advised. 'Say, "I got it hopelessly wrong, I fucked up, I want to say sorry to my family, to my wife and to the public." Then you can argue about the details of what happened and hose it all down.'

Warne replied: 'I'm not saying any of that.' He agreed to the interview nevertheless, and turned up 24 hours later at the London studio. Channel 9 was the obvious choice if he was going to talk to any TV channel, because it employed him as a commentator and he was good friends with its proprietor, Kerry Packer. So perhaps he expected an easy ride. In any case, he came totally unprepared. 'He rocked in with no idea what to say, no plan, nil defence', says Hurley. 'It was a disaster.'

The first question from Mike Munro, who had interviewed Warne many times in happier days, gave him every chance to grab a lifeline: 'Last night Donna Wright told us she would accept an apology from you. Do you believe you have anything to apologise for?'

It was the sort of opportunity that any spin doctor would kill for: the chance to defuse the story with a *mea culpa* and a humble admission of his (only human) frailty, before taking the sting out of it all by suggesting that the 'full facts' would show him in a far better light. But Shane seemed to have no idea that the public expected contrition. Instead, he greeted Munro with a cheery, 'Good evening, Mike' and observed that the British press had already tired of the chase, so why on earth was Australia still making such a fuss? 'It's been very disappointing', he continued, 'the exaggeration and sensationalism of it all, and the inaccuracies.'

The opportunity to say sorry had clearly gone straight through to the keeper. The best he could do was this: 'One thing I would like to say, Mike, is that as an international sportsman who gets pestered a bit, I would never ever harass somebody.' This opening salvo was delivered with a tired, wounded smirk, as if to say, 'You and I know how hard this is for someone like me'. It was smug, arrogant and really quite breathtaking. Not only did the evidence of the tapes suggest he was lying, but he actually had the gall to claim that he was the victim: of the Australian media's obsession with his private life; of exaggerations and inaccuracies; of people who pestered stars such as him; and, by implication, of Donna Wright herself, for leading him on. In these first 40 seconds, he must have put himself offside with just about every woman in Australia and a fair few men as well. It really was extraordinary that he thought it an appropriate response.

'So you believe you have nothing to apologise for?' Munro then asked. Again, Warne ducked the question, while making it clear it was everyone else's fault but his own: Donna had started it, he claimed, and she had enjoyed it just as much as he had. Again, one of the pair was obviously lying. 'I think the most disappointing thing', he continued, 'is that she was reciprocating and laughing about it with her friends, and at the end of it all she has decided to come public with it all and just crucify *me*.' Oh, poor me!

As his wife Simone would say five years later in almost identical circumstances, it was clear that he just did not get it. There was no hint of apology, no expression of regret or remorse, merely a stream of righteous anger (or 'disappointment') at those who had put him in this position.

So how had she got his room key, he was asked? 'I'm not sure. I never put that room key in her back pocket', he said, shaking his head, 'I'm just not sure what happened in that situation, I really don't know, it's disappointing.'

And how had she got his mobile number? Again, he didn't know. 'It really is just disappointing', he said for the tenth time.

> Obviously my wife, Simone, she was disappointed with what I did, having some dirty talk on the phone, but the bottom line is we're like any married couple, we've had our ups and downs. She has stood by me, she knows what happened, I know what happened, and that's the end of the story as far as we're concerned . . . we're getting along well, everything is fine on the home front.

Surely, he had to be kidding? But no. In his mind, he had just made another silly mistake which everyone should forgive. Having it all splashed across the papers was just one of the crosses he and Simone had to bear. 'Being Shane Warne, that's the way it is, you've gotta live with it.' Once again, there was no glimmer of recognition that other famous cricketers kept their names out of the paper by the simple stratagem of not harassing young women, telling batsmen to fuck off, or taking money from illegal bookies.

'She claims you actually performed a sex act while speaking to her', Munro said. Warne exhaled quickly and jerked his head as if to say: 'Oh, that.' Then he was back to his old story:

> Yeah, as I said before, there was a bit of dirty talk. She did talk dirty to me and I was reciprocating with

her. You know, it's not something you like to do but unfortunately things happen . . . but I thought it was a private matter, I didn't think it was going to become public, and now that it has become public I suppose it's a mistake. If it had stayed private it wasn't a mistake.

'So do you think you've learnt from this?' Munro inquired.

Oh yes, Warne enthused: 'Hopefully I won't be talking on the phone with any people again about this sort of stuff because just in case it becomes public.'

It was a staggering admission, the final stupidity. What must his wife at home have thought about this passionate declaration of his undying love and pledge to stay true for ever? God only knows, but it was a miracle that she did not take all his clothes out of the wardrobe and throw them onto the front lawn.

So how on earth could Shane get it so wrong, both with Simone and the public? Maybe the answer was that his life had become so unreal he had lost his bearings. He no longer knew how ordinary people lived or thought. And he had got away with so much for so long that he thought himself bulletproof.

But just close your eyes for a second and stand in his shoes, and try to get a glimpse of what it is like to be him. You're the best in the world at the one thing that matters to you. You're cheered by the crowd as you run onto the pitch, fêted by team-mates again and again. You're mobbed by women wherever you go. Is it any wonder that you think the world revolves around you?

You're incredibly vain. You love to be loved. You dye your hair blond and believe you're a spunk. You wear a gold earring and mix with the stars. You drive a Ferrari and earn millions a year. Is it any wonder that you think the world will forgive you whatever you do? And is it any wonder that you take what's on offer, whatever it is?

Psychologists call it 'entitlement', the feeling that you deserve it, you've earned it, it's your due, your reward.

As one who has worked with the Australian cricket team describes it: 'You get so famous that you think you're bigger than Ben Hur. You're *entitled* to this and *entitled* to that and no one can tell you anything. Warne is absolutely like that, he feels he is beyond criticism. He will only listen to people that he thinks can help him go somewhere. He shies away from control, authority or demands for rational behaviour.' In its extreme form this syndrome is a mental illness called narcissistic personality disorder. Warne appears to be suffering a milder version.

Shane, of course, is not the first sportsman to be caught behaving badly, nor the worst. In recent years in Australia there have been dozens of allegations of rape, sexual assault and harassment aimed at high-profile sports stars, just as there have in the UK and the USA. In 2004, Jeff Bond, head of the sports psychology program at the Australian Institute of Sport for 22 years, decided to figure out why. As he studied the cases, talked to the players and searched diagnostic manuals, he too homed in on narcissistic personality disorder and noticed that some of its characteristics were exactly the ones that coaches looked for in champions. The players who could win games with their brilliance were typically egocentric, rule-breaking, impulsive, aggressive risk takers. They also behaved manipulatively to achieve their goals and blamed others (usually women) for the trouble they got into.

Bond turned this into an unpublished paper called *The Pedestal Syndrome*, in which he described how these characteristics are magnified when such people become stars. They are admired, revered, pampered and spoilt, paid huge amounts of money and given lots of spare time, then let loose in an environment where drinking and sexual conquest are marks of manhood. Naturally, they spend their leisure time in bars, nightclubs and casinos where the opportunites to misbehave are multiplied. And before long, disaster strikes. The clubs want to keep them because they are so important to the team, so they cover up their crimes. They bring in lawyers to pay people under the table and keep complaints quiet. And it gets worse again.

Bond says that none of these wayward stars can appreciate that 99 per cent of the public hate their behaviour. Nor will they ever change because they don't see that it's wrong. On and off the field they are who they are; they do what they want. And that's why they're so good. Just like Shane.

As Warne's former headmaster at Mentone, Bob Hutchings, observes about Warne's time there and about the things that have happened since: 'He did what he wanted and he never thought about the consequences. I don't think he's changed. He's made a lot of stupid mistakes, fairly puerile mistakes, and I don't know that he's going to stop. In fact, I don't think he will.' Or, as another Mentone master puts it, 'In a lot of ways he's no different

from what he was at 17. He genuinely couldn't understand why some things were off limits. He just couldn't
see someone else's point of view. It was as if he were
morally dyslexic.'

He just did not get it.

16

Life in the Old Dog

Rumours of his demise . . . clearly have
been exaggerated.

In *Shane Warne, My Autobiography,* published one year after the Donna Wright affair, the wayward leg spinner praises Simone for standing by him and bearing it all with such dignity. 'It took time for the marriage to get back to where it was before', he concedes, 'but we eventually succeeded through talking and love.' Dedicating the book to his family, he writes: 'To Simone, Brooke and Jackson. You are my life. You mean the world to me'. Inside, he promises that he has learnt a lesson: 'It's an easy thing to say that we learn from our mistakes. But in this case I have – and become a better person for it.' We would see in due course how much that promise meant.

In the meantime, his biggest worry was not his wife and two kids, who seemed to be prepared to stick by him whatever he did. It was that the scandal might rebound on his cricketing ambitions and kill his chances of succeeding Steve Waugh as Australia's captain.

'Do you still want to captain Australia?' Mike Munro asked him at the end of his interview on *A Current Affair.*

'Yeah, I'd love to', said Warne, before urging the world to forget about the whole sorry business, as he and the British press had already done. 'Let's hope we can get on and just play some cricket', he said.

> To me the story is dead and buried now. It's over. Your private life is your private life, and to me it will be disappointing [that word again] if it does go further with the cricket side of things.

But the Australian Cricket Board was not such a soft touch as the average Australian footy club, and it knew Warne well enough to be pretty sure that the Donna Wright affair was not just a one-off. The ACB's chief executive, Malcolm Speed, was soon on the phone asking for a rendezvous with Warne in London, where he was due to attend a meeting of the International Cricket Council. When they met in mid-July, the two men talked frankly for a couple of hours, and Speed produced a huge file of cuttings from the Australian newspapers, to show Shane how seriously his 'mistake' was viewed back home. Afterwards, Speed told journalists he would report back to his board, but he had few words of encouragement: 'It's fair to say he's put himself in an embarrassing position in regards to his personal life, public perceptions of him and the aspirations of the ACB.' He then added that Warne was 'disappointed' to have put at risk his hope of captaining Australia. Privately, Speed had told Warne that the majority of the ACB's 14 directors wanted him to be sacked as vice-captain.

You really have to read Warne's account of the affair to

get a sense of how unfair he thought this was, but suffice to say that the relevant chapter in his autobiography is peppered with phrases such as, 'I couldn't believe it was happening', 'I had done a great job', 'It had nothing to do with cricket', 'It had been blown out of proportion', 'It seemed a ridiculous state of affairs' and 'They hadn't even bothered to contact me for my side of the story'. This short passage, in which he reacts to Speed's news of the ACB's displeasure, best sums up his view:

> I couldn't believe it was happening. It was a mistake, yes, but it was a private matter and had nothing to do with cricket. Explicit talk on the telephone did not mean all of a sudden I'd lost my flipper or forgotten how to set a field.

In Warne's view, the ACB should have stamped on any journalist who dared link the scandal to his role as captain, by telling them it had nothing to do with his cricket – a bizarre view, indeed.

Once again, the conclusion Warne drew from it all was that he was the victim of malice and stupidity: that the press had ganged up with Donna Wright and a bunch of incompetent amateurs at the ACB to take him down. But if he genuinely failed to grasp that Australia's captain had to behave decently off the field, he was clearly not fit for the job. Two months later, in September 2000, he was duly stripped of the vice-captaincy by the ACB, who went against the advice of Australia's selectors. Trevor Hohns, Allan Border, Geoff Marsh and Andrew Hilditch wanted him retained, presumably because they shared

Warne's view that his extramural activities could be ignored.

When Speed phoned the bad news through to Warne in England – waking him in his Derby hotel at 2.15 am – Shane was amazed and 'disappointed'. 'I thought I must still be in a dream', he wrote in his column for the *Times*. 'I always said that the matter had absolutely nothing to do with cricket.' Once again, he blamed everyone but himself, and especially his 'enemies in the media' who had 'used it as an excuse to nail him'. It puzzled him that even Channel 9 had joined the mob, and he complained to Kerry Packer that *A Current Affair* had shafted him. But Packer was unmoved. He told Warne to keep his dick in his trousers and said he had only himself to blame. Many of Shane's team-mates agreed. They were tired of the things he got up to and the trouble he caused. As one team official said, 'It was a huge drain on their patience.'

Warne's sacking opened the way for Gilchrist to take his place as vice-captain. And this made Shane even more pissed off. Almost a year after being dismissed, he used his autobiography to mount a thinly veiled attack on the upstanding wicket-keeper, writing:

> We need to be careful that the captain and vice-captain are not appointed simply because they are squeaky clean and do the right things . . . We do not want a Richie Cunningham figure in charge unless he is the best person.

Richie Cunningham, for those who missed the 1970s American TV series *Happy Days*, was a freckly nerd who was bullied at school and could not get a girlfriend, until he was rescued by the Fonz who taught him to be cool. You will not be surprised to learn that Richie resembles Adam Gilchrist, who is a polite, well-mannered, intelligent man. And guess who thinks he is the Fonz? The Fonz is super smooth but also a dope; he sports slicked-back hair and a black leather jacket, and looks like James Dean, with a touch of Freddie Mercury thrown in. He is always surrounded by girls, can make the jukebox play for free, and has charisma. In fact, he could be a dark-haired version of Warney, not least because he never admits he's wrong. Gilchrist, of course, was fully aware of the moral of the story. And there has been little love lost between him and Warne ever since.

Warne also used his book to argue that he should still be considered for the captain's job:

> I have given my heart and soul to Australian cricket and I like to think I've earned the respect of the ACB. I have helped to put a few backsides on seats and made spin bowling more interesting. I play in an aggressive, animated, emotional way which reflects the pride I take in representing my country. That should have counted for something, I would have thought.

Six months after the Donna Wright affair, Warne sat down for his annual review with his captain, Steve Waugh, Australian team coach John Buchanan and team psychologist Sandy Gordon. During the session he made it clear he was still upset that the ACB had dumped him. He still thought it unfair, said it had nothing to do with cricket and failed to see he had brought it on himself. But it was not just the ACB who thought his off-field antics were unacceptable. Even before the scandal broke, popularity polls put Warne well outside the top 10 sportsmen deemed 'appropriate' for corporate sponsorship. And after saturation media coverage of his texting habits, his rating went into free fall. Lisa Wilkinson, then editor of the young women's magazine *Cleo*, told *The Sydney Morning Herald* why she thought this was so:

> Aussie blokes will apparently forgive another Aussie bloke just about anything if he can take a few wickets. But a lot of Australian women . . . are simply not that enamoured of his performance off the field. I think there's a feeling that there are likeable larrikins, and then there's Warne. Maybe the likeable variety don't look quite that pleased with themselves.
>
> There's also the issue of just what stage of life he's up to. For many women, I think he seems trapped somewhere between puberty and a kind of perpetual midlife crisis: the gold chains, the peroxide blond hair, the open-top sports car, the pinball machines and the jukebox in the basement.

Before the Donna Wright affair, the manufacturers of Leggo pasta sauces, Simplot Australia, used Warne in their marketing campaigns. When the story broke, they promptly pulled the TV ads off air, never to be seen again. Warne's biggest and best-known sponsor, Nike, also dumped him – although not till his contract ran out in 2001. Warne told the press their parting was amicable and that Nike was sad he was leaving. But there's little doubt that the company thought his star was waning and was worried that women disliked him. After his amazing performance in the World Cup in 1999, Nike produced an ad titled 'Never Give Up' that showed Shane overcoming a host of challenges – the shoulder injury, the betting scandal, separation from his family and being dropped from the team – and then making a brilliant comeback in the finals. Reaction to it split right along gender lines, according to Michael Simon, creative director of the advertising agency Foot Cone Belding. 'Blokes punched the air and went "Come On". Women said, "I don't care how good he is, he's a nob."'

Judging by a poll in *Inside Sport*, the blokey Australian magazine with scantily clad models on the cover, there was also a vast number of men who disliked him. In March 2001, a year after the Donna Wright affair, the magazine's readers voted him 'Least Admired Sportsperson of 2000', comfortably beating crooks like Mike Tyson and Hansie Cronje and brats like Lleyton Hewitt. Back in 1993, the same poll had named him the most admired sportsperson in the world. Such was the extent of his decline.

In such a climate, it would have been a brave company that would want to pay him millions to promote their products. And Nike clearly did not. At best, it is said to have offered Shane a new contract on far less money. At worst, it is thought to have told him he could have free gear and nothing else. Industry rumour says Nike

Australia was keen to re-sign him, but Nike International wanted him out, because they were tired of all the bad publicity and drama.

Warne and his agents put their own spin on the break-up by claiming that Shane had struck a US$500,000 deal with a rival sportswear company, Mitre, in the UK. But this was moonshine. The deal was never signed, and Warne went the next five years without a shoe contract. But it was not just his off-field disasters that discouraged suitors. One big international company that tried to do business with him felt he demanded far more than he was worth. It also found his manager (and brother), Jason, a nightmare to deal with, because he kept having to go back to Shane for approval. After much haggling, the company was finally convinced it had reached a deal with Warne, only to be told it had not. 'The goalposts kept shifting', an executive complained. 'Eventually we gave up trying.'

Back on the cricket field, Shane's rollercoaster was also heading down again. One month after being removed as vice-captain, he broke his spinning finger – the one that had been rebuilt by surgeons in 1996 – while taking a high catch in a match for Victoria against New South Wales. The ball landed plumb on the tip of the finger and popped up into the air again, like a ball off a billiard cue. He managed to grab the catch safely at the second attempt, but then saw the damage. That night he was too upset to face the media, but he called a press conference next day to announce that he had a dislocation fracture of the top joint, which would need to be pinned with a couple of screws to stop it moving while it healed. He would be out of the game for six to eight weeks and miss the summer

Test series against the West Indies. 'I've got 10 fingers and it just happens to be the spinning finger, the one I've already had an operation on', he told reporters. 'Everything happens for a reason but sometimes it's pretty hard to find out what that reason is. I'm just very disappointed.'

He was fit again in time for the tour to India in February 2001, and looking to make up for his thrashing by Tendulkar in 1998. But once again he endured a torrid time there, as Australia's remarkable run of 16 consecutive Test victories came to a crashing end. In the Second Test in Kolkata, Warne was belted all over Eden Gardens by V. V. S. Laxman and Rahul Dravid – as were all the other Australian bowlers – and he chalked up even worse figures than he had suffered three years before. In the second innings alone, he finished with 1 for 152 at almost five runs an over. Worse still, team coach John Buchanan took the opportunity to tell journalists that the champion leg spinner was badly out of shape and needed to work a great deal harder to retain his place in the side. 'Warney's quite distressed when he comes off the field all the time', said Buchanan bluntly. 'It's no secret that he's not one of the fittest characters running around in world cricket.' Nor, he suggested, was his mental state much better.

Asked whether Australia might drop their talismanic spinner for the deciding Third Test in Chennai, Buchanan mused that it might be a better option to go with Miller and a third seamer. 'I'm not saying he's going to be left out, he's still in the frame', he said, 'but when we walk into this Test we've really got to have 11 blokes who can give five days of hard cricket and not be affected by any physical limitations'.

Warne and Buchanan had a testy relationship at the best of times because they were such different characters. While Warne was all emotion and gut feeling, Buchanan was renowned for his use of laptop computers to analyse games and players. He was also famous for his new-age motivational messages. A tall, owlish, academic sort of man, he had been a schoolteacher before coaching the Queensland Bulls to an impressive run of victories in the 1990s, and he was about as different as one could get from Warne, the loud 'look at me' larrikin. But this very public rebuke made relations between them far worse. One respected Australian journalist who spent an hour at the bar with Warne just after Buchanan's comments were published says he launched into the coach, telling his drinking buddies what a useless prick he was, and deriding him as 'a boy with his toys'. For good measure, he then got stuck into Malcolm Gray, who had been chairman of the ACB at the time of his sacking, sounding off about what a 'cunt' he was. 'He hates me that man', said Warne. 'That's why I'm not captain.'

Steve Waugh and his team were outraged that the coach had criticised their star player so openly, even if what he said was obviously true and was already being whispered at the bar. Waugh was quick to defend his man, saying that all the Australian bowlers had been tired after the punishment they had taken. In the second innings in Kolkata they had been on the wrong end of one of the game's most amazing comebacks, in which India had scored more than 650 runs after being forced to follow on, and had eventually won the match.

Warne was selected for the Third Test in Chennai,

despite Buchanan's doubts, and received another battering, picking up 2 for 181 as Australia lost the match and the series. Again, Waugh was quick to praise his sensitive spinner, telling Malcolm Conn, 'He gave a strong performance, he gave it everything . . . I'm not going to put anyone down. That's just the way cricket goes sometimes, they played him very well.' But the scorecard said otherwise. Warne had taken only 10 wickets in the three-match series at a cost of more than 50 runs apiece, while India's new spin wizard, Harbhajan Singh, had run riot, picking up 32 wickets at an average of 17. This was three times the damage that Warne had wrought at a third of the cost.

Not surprisingly, the critics now sharpened their pens, with Conn rounding off his tour coverage by suggesting that Shane was not the only one who might face the chop: 'Two of Australia's biggest names, Shane Warne and Mark Waugh, will be on notice that their alarming downward trend will not be allowed to continue unchecked.' Conn and others pointed out that the stats showed Warne had not been as good since coming back from shoulder surgery in January 1999.

Over in England, where another Ashes tour was due to start in June 2001, the pundits seized on these reports enthusiastically. 'His bowling has been in decline for the last three years', *The Sun*'s John Etheridge stated confidently, declaring that his shoulder had never recovered and that he now lacked the element of surprise. Simon Wilde in the *Sunday Times* went further, suggesting Warne had slipped from brilliant, to very good, to average and predicting he would no longer have a major impact on a Test series. 'The case against Warne is growing', he continued. 'It seems unthinkable, but the world's greatest spinner could be left out of the tour of England.'

In fact, the selectors were not yet prepared to think the unthinkable. Steve Waugh insisted Warne be included in the party, and the chairman of selectors, Trevor Hohns, agreed he should be given the 'benefit of the doubt', because of his fantastic record on the two previous tours. Terry Jenner assured the BBC that his boy would do the business:

> If Shane Warne is fit then he doesn't believe he has any peer . . . The gift that God gave him is special. He loves playing for his country and the one thing he will want to do is beat England. I know he's not as good as he was in 1997, but he's still good.

In praising him, even Terry Jenner was joining the chorus of those who said he was past his best.

But while Warne was picked, Buchanan was sacked – not as team coach but as tour selector – and told officially by the ACB to keep his mouth shut in future. His humiliation was a mark of where power lay in the team. It was with the captain and the players, and certainly not with the coach who had guided them to 15 of their 16 consecutive Test wins.

Looking back more than 300 wickets later, it is hard to believe that anyone could seriously have thought about leaving Warne out of an Ashes Test. And it did not take long for his detractors to get egg on their faces. Australia crushed England in the First Test at Edgbaston in July, to win by an innings and 118 runs, with Warne taking eight wickets and triggering England's collapse. This took him past Malcolm Marshall's tally of 376 and his soul mate Ian Botham's 383, and lifted him to sixth place on the all-time list of test wicket takers. He claimed to be no sharper than he had been in India, telling journalists: 'It's the same stuff, mate. Some just play it better than others.' But one way or another, it was obviously not yet time to bury him with his ball. 'Rumours of his demise . . . clearly have been exaggerated', the *Times* commented drily, in homage to the American author Mark Twain who made a similar remark after reading news of his death in the papers.

Warne bagged another eight wickets in the Third Test at Trent Bridge, and picked up the man of the match award as Australia scored another big win. And in the final Test at The Oval, he did even better, taking seven wickets in the first innings and another four in the second, to take his tally for the series to 31 scalps. This was more than he had collected in 1997 and almost as good as his haul in the glory days of 1993. In the process, he also became the first Australian bowler to take 400 Test wickets, dismissing England wicket-keeper Alec Stewart to reach this new milestone. He held the ball above his head and turned slowly to face each section of the crowd, acknowledging the applause, while poor Stewart trudged back to the pavilion. He was getting used to making his exit during Shane's celebrations: he had been his 150th Test victim in the 1994 Ashes series in Australia and his 250th victim in England in 1997.

Back home against South Africa three months later, Warne bowled even better. In the First Test in Adelaide he took another eight wickets and conceded only 2.5 runs an over. Once again, he bowled Australia to victory and once again he was man of the match. By the end of the six-Test series – home and away – he had demolished another pile of records, taking an unprecedented 37 wickets in the series as Australia was crowned undisputed world champion. In Cape Town, with his family watching, he chalked up his 100th Test, 10 years after his debut in Sydney. And he could not have written a better script. He scored 63 in the first innings to take him past 2000 Test runs, and was batting at the finish with Ponting as the winning boundary was scored. He had already broken South Africa's resistance in the second innings, by taking six wickets and bowling nearly half the overs Australia sent down. In the Third Test in Durban, he was once again in cracking form, passing 450 Test wickets with another six victims, only six months after reaching the previous milestone.

He then took a deserved break. He did not go north to play for Hampshire and the Zimbabwe tour was cancelled, so he spent the winter in Melbourne getting fit and losing weight. Buchanan's public needling in India and constant abuse from the crowds in England had obviously struck home at last. He was taking longer and longer to recover between matches and needed to take more care of his body if he wanted to stay at the top. It was a familiar joke among his team-mates that he looked like an old man when he came off the field after a day's bowling. Now, he realised he needed to get fit or his career would be over.

In August 2002, he did a photo shoot for the *Australian Women's Weekly*, clad in a tight-fitting gym singlet to show off his new slimline look, and told Patricia Flokis: 'I'm in the best shape I've been for ten years.' He had cut down from four Hawaiian pizzas a week to one a fort- night, had kicked out the toasted cheese sandwiches, and banished the beer in favour of fish, fruit, protein shakes and water. He was also going to the gym at seven am five days a week, to do weights and aerobics, and was running for 40 minutes on the sixth day. On the seventh day he rested and went to the footy. Not surprisingly, in view of this program, he had shed 12 kilograms and trimmed his frame down to a taut 84 kilograms. God only knew how long it would last.

A couple of months later, the lightweight larrikin was touting his torso at the launch of a new Shane Warne wine collection. Clad in black body-hugging shirt, black trousers and black patent-leather shoes, he boasted to reporters that he had never been fitter. The beer and pizzas had gone, he said, and wine had taken its place. Shane's team-mates joked that he still pronounced it 'woyne', and it was a brave marketing strategy to present Warne as an expert. But he had friends with a winery in Northern Victoria, Zilzie Wines, and he had been to their property and taken a course. Besides, Greg Norman had a signature label, so why shouldn't he? He then answered the question himself by adding: 'I had a nice couple of bottles the other night. Don't know what they were. I suppose I should read the label. But I wouldn't even remember if I did read it.'

Shane assured reporters, who still remembered his betting and text-messaging troubles, that he had grown up in the past 12 months and been a bit more disciplined. He had also given up some of his old vices: 'I've added a bit of lettuce in my sandwich which I used to soak with butter and cheese', he said. 'I'm 33 now, I'm no longer 25 and I have got some different interests. When I look in the mirror and I see ten chins from the beer, I don't miss the beer.'

The new improved Warne immediately celebrated by bowling even better. On Australia's series against Pakistan in October 2002 he was twice made man of the match and then crowned man of the series, finishing with 27 wickets at an average of just 12.66 runs apiece. This was the highest tally ever for an Australian in a three-Test series and was quite simply stunning. With 477 wickets in his Test career, there was now only one man ahead of him in the all-time list and that was West Indian fast bowler Courtney Walsh, who had retired 18 months earlier with 519. At the rate Shane was going, he would be past him in six months.

As he boarded the plane back from Sharjah after Australia thrashed Pakistan by an innings and 20 runs, he was looking forward to having another crack at the Poms. They were already in Perth, playing their traditional warm-up game to kick off yet another Ashes tour. In the 14 months since the previous battle against the Old Enemy, Warne had got himself back to the best form of his life. It was possible that he was even better than he had been in the golden days from 1993 to 1995. But just as the planets seemed to have aligned themselves favourably, life started to wobble again. He fell heavily while fielding in a one-day game in December and dislocated his right shoulder. He was told it would need surgery and put him out of the game for four to six weeks, which meant he would miss the last two Ashes Tests in Melbourne and Sydney.

With luck, he would be fit again and bowling well in time for the World Cup in South Africa, starting in February. This was the Olympics of cricket, as far as Shane was concerned. And after doing so fabulously well in 1999 he hoped for another gold medal or two. He intended to retire from one-day cricket once it was all over and he was absolutely determined to go out on a high.

But, alas, it was not to be.

...today and not him, and of the game, I lost to Keswick, which meant he would miss the first two Tests, Tests in Melbourne and Sydney.

Wedbusday, he would be at ease and bowling well in time for the World Cup in South Africa, starting in February. This was the Olympics of cricket, as far as Shane was concerned. And after doing so absolutely well in 1998 he was positive another good record or two. He intended to retire from one-day Tests, once it was all over and he was absolutely determined to go out on a high.

But alas, it was not to be.

17

Dumb and Dumber

I am a victim of anti-doping hysteria.

It was February 2003, on the eve of Australia's first World Cup game in South Africa, that disaster struck.

The first official warning to the media was a call to a special press conference in the team's Johannesburg hotel one hour before the game against Pakistan was due to begin. But by this time word had already leaked out that Warne was in trouble. One journalist was woken by a call from his office at seven am local time to ask if he knew what was afoot. He stepped outside his room soon afterwards to take a look and saw the ACB's media manager, Jonathan Rose, coming up in the glass-fronted lift, clasping a pile of what looked like drafts of a press statement.

A couple of hours later, as the covers came off the pitch for the game against Pakistan and the stands at the Wanderers Stadium filled up with eager spectators, reporters waited in one of the ground-floor banqueting rooms at the Sandton Sun Hotel. Warne came marching along the wide marble corridor, flanked by seven or eight minders and security guards, and entered the room in a blaze of TV lights. Without any preamble he launched into a prepared statement that he was 'shocked and absolutely devastated' to have been told by the Australian Sports Drug Agency (ASDA) that he had tested positive to a prohibited drug roughly three weeks earlier. 'I am shocked', he said, 'because I do not take performance-enhancing drugs and never have, and do not condone them in any shape or form.' He explained that he had taken a single fluid-reduction tablet before his comeback game in Sydney in late January, but 'did not know it contained a prohibited substance'.

The drug that had turned up in Shane's urine was a diuretic. Sportsmen are banned from taking diuretics because they can be used to mask steroids or any other performance-enhancing drugs. They work by getting rid of fluid from the body, so provided you keep on drinking, they can flush a drug out of your system or dilute it so much that it is difficult or impossible to detect.

Warne had actually been tested as far back as mid-December (although this was not made public at the time) when he had shown small traces of a diuretic, but not enough for a positive result. Working on the assumption that he was using the drug as a masking agent, ASDA had then targeted him for a second test, in the hope of nailing him. This had been performed at the SCG on 22 January, the day before the final of the VB one-day series, during a practice session in the nets. The agency's scientists had figured that Warne was probably taking steroids, which was the only performance-enhancing drug cricketers had ever been caught using. Their bottom line was that there was no good medical reason for him to be popping diuretics, so it was reasonable to assume he was up to no good. No one could have guessed what Warne's explanation would ultimately be. But it was so bizarre (and so typically Warne) that it almost had to be true.

John Mendoza, who was then head of ASDA, remembers coming into his office on Monday 10 February 2003, the day the results came back from the labs, to find everyone ashen faced. Warne was an Australian hero, and ASDA had never had such a high-profile sportsman in its sights. He waited till early afternoon to ring Warne in Johannesburg, waking him at six-thirty am to pass on the bad news, and advising him to tell no one, including his team-mates, until the test results on his B-sample result came through. But Warne – who seemed too shocked to say anything – was incapable of keeping such a huge secret to himself.

The first person he rang was Kerry Packer, perhaps in the hope that the Big Fella would fix it for him. But even he could not wave a magic wand. Next, he told Australia's team physio, Errol Alcott, to whom he handed a foil sheet of Moduretic with two (not one) of the tablets missing. Then he told his captain, Ricky Ponting, who had been put in charge of the one-day team 11 months earlier. And that evening, he spilled it out to his team-mates at their pre-match meeting. The next morning, as the team bus made its way to the cricket ground, the ACB paraded him at a press conference to tell the world.

Back in Australia, the media showed him little mercy. After the sledging row, the betting imbroglio, the smoking fiascos, Joe the cameraman and the text-messaging scandals, this must have seemed like the final act in

Shane's increasingly chaotic career. He filled the entire front page of Sydney's *Daily Telegraph*, with a headline, 'DEVASTATED', and a huge picture that showed him looking exactly that. The back page was also devoted to Warne, dressed in his lucky number 23, green-and-gold Australian strip. Inside, there were the highs and lows of his Test career and a scathing condemnation of his stupidity. 'When he dislocated his shoulder, Shane Warne must have damaged brain cells as well', one writer commented. 'What else will explain the numbingly dumb decision by one of the greatest cricketers in history to pop a diuretic?' Several other correspondents speculated that it could be the end of Warne's career if he was found to be guilty as charged.

By the time the morning papers popped through the letter box or landed in people's front gardens, Warne was just about arriving in Melbourne, where he held another press conference at the airport to say how shocked and devastated he was at the news. By now, word was out that the offending pill had been given to him by his mother, Brigitte, who suffered from high blood pressure and took Moduretic on prescription to combat fluid retention. An explanation of why Warne had taken one had also begun to emerge. His captain, Ricky Ponting, had told journalists in South Africa that Brigitte liked to pop one of these pills before a big night out, because they made her look thinner. So perhaps Warne had done the same.

Within 24 hours, *The Australian*'s Chip Le Grand was offering a detailed (and obviously authorised) account of how it had all happened. According to a 'family friend' who seemed to know a remarkable amount about the

Warnes' innermost secrets, Brigitte had badgered her boy to take the pill so he would look his best on TV while announcing his retirement from one-day cricket at a press conference on 22 January. 'As the family friend explained', *The Australian* reported, 'Brigitte had often nagged Warne about his weight and, in particular, his hint of a double chin.' And there was no question this family friend knew what he was talking about, because it was none other than Shane himself, who was privately briefing journalists.

No doubt, Brigitte's nagging explained her son's well-known obsession with his appearance. But according to Shane it wasn't just the elder boy she chided. 'She once called her other son Jason "an embarrassment" for carrying a few extra kilos', Le Grand revealed.

Even at the time it was pretty obvious that this story was generated by Shane Warne's PR machine, or someone close to it, since it clearly established his innocence of more sinister motives for using the drug. But its portrayal of a fussing mum and her henpecked kids had a horrible ring of truth about it even if you didn't know where it came from. The fact that it came straight from the horse's mouth made it all the more biting.

On this latest occasion, it appeared she had gone on and on at Shane to take the pill until the poor boy had cracked. According to *The Australian*: 'He said, "For Christ sake just give me the tablet", and never thought anything of it.' 'She is a lovely lady,' the friend (aka Shane) continued, 'but she is full-on. To the rest of the world it seems ludicrous but, knowing Brigitte, you can understand how it happened.'

Shane had already told a version of the tale to team-mates before leaving South Africa, and assured the press that they had been supportive in his hour of need. A more realistic assessment was that they were bewildered, confused and angry. When asked by a journalist whether he thought Warne was guilty of naïvety, Ponting snapped back: 'For sure, or stupidity, one of the two.' Naïve and stupid, of course, were the two words that Warne had used in 1998 to describe the 'mistake' he had made in accepting US$5000 from 'John' the bookie.

Glenn McGrath was scarcely more sympathetic in his newspaper column a day or so later, writing: 'Much as the whole team is 100 per cent behind him, Shane has brought this on himself'. According to McGrath, all the team were aware of the risks and penalties, because it was drummed into them by a guy from ASDA at the beginning of every cricket season. Moreover, Shane and his team-mates knew that a West Australian fast bowler had recently been banned for 18 months for using steroids, so he could hardly claim, as he did repeatedly, that he was not well-informed. What McGrath might have added was that all sportsmen and their families knew there was a telephone hotline that would tell you instantly whether a drug was okay to take or not. And in the cricketers' case, there were also any number of team officials who could have helped in an instant. The Australian Cricketers' Association, for example, lists 11 people on its website that one can check with, and gives their mobile numbers.

Not surprisingly, Dick Pound, head of the World Anti-Doping Agency, was even less forgiving than Shane's team-mates, ridiculing Warne's excuse on Channel 9.

I've got to say, 'My mum gave me the stuff' is pretty new, and I've added it to my list. 'I got it from the toilet seat', 'It's not my urine', 'I don't know how it happened', 'There must be some mix-up', 'The Devil made me do it', there's a whole range of them. The common thread is that when athletes get caught, they say, 'It wasn't my fault'.

The bottom line, according to the world anti-doping supremo, was that it was an athlete's responsibility to check what went into his or her body. 'You cannot have an IQ over room temperature and be unaware of this', he said.

Warne's case was heard by a special tribunal convened at the ACB's headquarters in Melbourne, in the shadow of the MCG, on 21 February 2003, 10 days after news had broken of his positive test. It was an informal affair, with witnesses not required to swear an oath, which was possibly a mistake in view of what the three-person panel later said about the credibility of Warne's evidence. Warne was flanked by a team of two barristers and two solicitors, including one of Melbourne's top QCs, Jeffrey Sher. He was likely to be landed with a six-figure legal bill by the end of it all.

Despite the ACB's promise of greater transparency during investigations into Warne and Waugh's bookie scandal in 1998–9, the hearing was closed to the public and press. So more than 40 media were forced to spend the day standing in the drizzle outside, trying to catch a glimpse of the participants, as they waited for news. Warne arrived late, came out briefly for a toilet break and a cigarette, then left in a hurry at the close of play. News photos show him driving away that night in a big black BMW, with Simone beside him in the passenger seat and Brigitte in the back. The panel had spent four hours listening to seven witnesses, of which only two had been called in Warne's defence, and another two hours hearing submissions from lawyers. They had then spent another couple of hours trying to reach a decision. Everyone was tight-lipped about who had been called to testify for Warne, but the betting (which was absolutely spot on) was that it was him and his mum.

The ACB had called five witnesses to prosecute its case and, potentially, to mitigate the penalty. If it could be shown there were exceptional circumstances, it was possible that Warne could escape a two-year ban, which was what he and his fellow cricketers had agreed to accept in their ACB contracts. No doubt, this was what was prolonging the panel's deliberations. As they adjourned overnight, it was rumoured that they were split on the issue of how severe the punishment should be. From Warne's perspective it was vital that he avoided the maximum penalty. The chances of him staying sane, fit and motivated while he sat on the sidelines for two years were slim. With only one year off, there was still a good chance he could come back.

Fortunately for him, the ACB doctor, Peter Harcourt, felt that exceptional circumstances did exist. He told the panel there was no trace of steroids in Warne's urine, that his recovery from injury had not been unusually rapid and that there was no good reason for him to have taken steroids because they would not have helped in any case.

He might equally have said there was no good medical evidence to suggest diuretics banished double chins, that Australian horse trainers have always used steroids to keep injured gallopers on the racetrack and that Western Australian fast bowler Duncan Spencer had been banned in Australia in 2002 for taking the steroid nandrolone, which had been prescribed by his doctor to help him recover from a chronic back injury. But he did not.

Harcourt's somewhat one-sided evidence appears to have been the key factor in persuading the panel that the penalty could be reduced. But as the tribunal's report later pointed out, the absence of steroids was not proof that Warne had not used them. The reason why diuretics were banned was precisely that they made detection of such drugs extremely difficult.

Warne was told of the outcome the following morning – a Saturday – and a press conference was held around lunchtime to inform the world's media. His penalty was to be banned for 12 months from playing cricket for Australia or anybody else. He would lose his lucrative ACB contract and his gig as captain of Hampshire, which were probably worth $1m between them. Typically, he was shocked at the severity of it, rather than grateful for the let-off. 'First of all I'd like to say that I am absolutely devastated and very upset at the committee's decision suspending me for 12 months and I will appeal', said the disappointed leg spinner. 'I feel that I am a victim of anti-doping hysteria. I also want to repeat, I have never taken any performance-enhancing drugs and I never will.' Somehow it had not penetrated his brain that the rules and penalties were there in black-and-white for all to see and he had broken them. The fact that his mum had given him the pills and he was stupid enough not to have checked was irrelevant.

As ever, he was unrepentant and aggrieved, the victim of another innocent mistake and another bunch of over-zealous officials. And there was still no admission that he had almost tested positive in December as well. 'The tablet I took on the 21st of January was a fluid tablet', he said. 'I did not know it as a diuretic, I knew it as a fluid tablet. I feel that a 12-month suspension is a very harsh penalty for not checking what I took . . . It had nothing to do with cricket or trying to mask anything. It had to do with appearance.'

Few people would doubt Warne's story that it could all be put down to vanity, and I would certainly not question that element of it even if his evidence was a bit economical with the truth. There were stories galore of him strutting around the dressing-room half naked and waiting until the last minute to get dressed to go on to the pitch. 'We all laughed about it', said Victorian coach David Hookes. He also waxed his arms and legs, and liked to have his hair newly streaked when he went out to break wicket-taking records. There was even speculation – not confirmed – that he might have liked another effect that diuretics were supposed to have. One sports drug expert in Melbourne suggested that body builders liked to use a diuretic before competitions, because it made their skin look translucent.

Soon after the verdict, Warne's 'Woe is me' stories began to pop up. Monday's Murdoch papers, the Melbourne *Herald Sun* and Sydney *Daily Telegraph*, carried front-page 'exclusive' interviews with Shane under the banner headline 'MY TORMENT'. It was pretty much word for word what he had said after being dropped as vice-captain back in 2000. 'I couldn't believe it,' Shane began. 'My heart sank – I was in shock. A 12-month ban that I and a lot of other people think is very, very harsh for taking what I thought was a fluid tablet, not a diuretic.' Then came another line he had used a few too many times before: 'The past two weeks have obviously been the toughest of my life.' But perhaps he was right. Maybe his life did get worse and worse. To outsiders, it certainly seemed that way.

The following day he was back on Channel 9's *A Current Affair*, only this time with a far more friendly host, in the form of his old mate Ray Martin, with whom the only danger was that he might be licked to death. Once again, it was the same old story about being shocked, disappointed and amazed that he could have been treated so harshly. Here's an example:

> *Warne:* Yes, I did something silly. A pretty innocent mishap, but it was silly. I should have checked. I should have listened more in the ASDA meetings. The fact of the matter is I didn't. If that's a crime . . .
> *Martin:* Didn't you listen, didn't you pay any attention?
> *Warne:* No, I didn't. The same as when I was at school, I never paid attention.

The annual ASDA lectures to the cricket team were just like those safety chats on the runway, Warne explained:

I've probably caught a thousand planes, two thousand . . . If a plane was about to crash I wouldn't have a clue what to do. That doesn't mean I haven't been told. It's the same as this. I have been told by ASDA people, but I don't remember what I was told.

There was more on these lines: that he had never read a book, that he was a simple bloke who took no interest in the outside world and just played cricket. And then Ray hit him with the big one: 'Was your biggest crime vanity? As your mates say, you're obsessed with the way you look, your hair, your earrings?' Yes, said Warne:

I do take pride in my appearance. I do like to wear nice clothes. I do like to live in a nice house. I think I've earned that, because I've given my whole life since 17, 18 years old, to cricket. If it's a crime to make sure you look nice and you like nice things, well I'm guilty of that, mate.

And with that it was time to bid everyone goodnight. 'Thanks for the pleasure you've given us, Shane', said Ray. 'Good luck and thanks for talking to me.' *A Current Affair*'s phone poll the following night showed that he had failed to convince a majority of the audience. Some 14,000 people registered a vote on the leading question, 'Is Shane Warne's 12-month ban too harsh?' Six out of 10 were of the opinion that it was not. There was no opportunity to express an opinion that it was not tough enough.

Two days after that, the tribunal published the reasons

for its decision, which put a very different gloss on the whole affair and on Shane's evidence in particular. Warne's lawyers had done their utmost to stop these being released, and they had only been made public after legal pressure from *The Age* and *The Sydney Morning Herald*. And it was not hard to see why Shane wanted them suppressed, because the tribunal's conclusion was that he was stupid, reckless and quite possibly a liar. Naturally, the tribunal baulked at using the 'L' word, which lawyers always have a problem with. But it came pretty close. On the question of how many times he had taken the drug, the tribunal found Warne's testimony to be 'vague, unsatisfactory and inconsistent'. The panel still did not know whether they had got at the truth. On the question of his knowledge of anti-doping policy (where he had persuaded Ray Martin he just hadn't listened) they were even more damning, saying: 'The committee does not accept that he was entirely truthful.'

Nor was the panel much more impressed with Brigitte, whose evidence they found 'vague and unsatisfactory as to the number of tablets she had given him'.

If it hadn't been so tragic, you would have laughed at it all. But the tribunal did not. Its conclusion was that Warne had committed 'a reckless act totally disregarding the possible consequences'. This, of course, was the story of his life, or of all the things that got him into trouble. He just didn't think.

Now even his hometown papers tore into him. The *Herald Sun*'s Ron Reed, who had written some pretty complimentary pieces about Warne in the past, told his readers that the tribunal had 'shredded his credibility' and had 'stopped only marginally short of calling him a liar'. Robert Craddock, one of the most respected cricket writers in Australia, was even more damning.

> It must be quite a chastening experience for a super-star sportsman to be taken out of their pampered world, full of backslappers, $360 an hour image makers and tummy-tickling TV interviewers, and sit down before three people who wipe all that stuff to one side and interview them as if their name is John Smith. When this happened to Warne his defence fell apart.

His team-mates picked up on the panel's revelation that Warne had almost tested positive – and shown traces of the diuretic – back in December. Some felt extremely pissed off that he had told them a different story: that it was just one moment of stupidity in which he had given in to badgering from his mum. Gilchrist even ventured into print with a comment suggesting that Shane's mates felt let down. 'I think there's no doubt people don't like being deceived', he told the *Herald Sun*.

Shane had planned to spend the northern summer play-ing cricket for Hampshire again, this time as captain, but that was now off the menu. So too were games for his old club, St Kilda. In fact, there was some doubt about whether he would even be allowed to train there. But he claimed to have lots of offers, including a cameo role in a movie – perhaps a lead part in *Dumb and Dumber* – and a position with St Kilda footy club.

But the ban was obviously not going to be good for

business. He told Ray Martin it would cost him $2 million or $3 million to be out of action for a year. And while that appeared to be a wild exaggeration, it was clearly not going to be cheap. For the moment, the sponsors who had stayed with him after the Donna Wright affair, such as Oakley sunglasses, promised to hang in there. His wine collection took a hit, though. By September 2003, Zilzie Wines was lamenting that Shane's sauvignons were proving hard to shift, despite heavy discounting. And according to his brother, Jason, one or two other deals perished on the vine. Sponsorship Solutions, a Melbourne consultancy specialising in assessing sportsmen's market value, reckoned that a year out of the game would halve the fee he could command – cutting it from $130,000 a year per product to around $60,000. Repucon, another marketing consultancy, later reported he had dropped out of the Top 40 potential earners: 'He really fell off the radar.'

But the drug scandal was not as much of a worry as 'his uncanny knack of getting himself into shit', as one sponsor put it. His liaisons outside marriage were more of a concern to them. When they added it all together, mainstream sporting-goods companies no longer wanted to invest money in him, because he was too much of a risk. Up-and-coming companies with more to gain and less to lose were more likely to take a punt. However, in Warne's case you had to be a gambler even to want to do that.

The one piece of work he did pick up was for Seek.com.au, an Australian job-search site. 'Hiccup with your first career?' Warne's advertisement asked. 'Find a better one.' Sadly, it was a short-lived campaign. According to *Business Review Weekly*, by 2004 his annual income was estimated to have fallen back to $1.45 million, almost all of which came directly from cricket. He had been overtaken by team-mates Ricky Ponting and Adam Gilchrist, aka Richie Cunningham, who were above the $2 million mark.

A few months after the ban, an old schoolmate ran into Warne at a footy game in Melbourne, talking to his childhood hero, Dermot Brereton. A crowd of 50 people had gathered round the pair who were with another well-known footy star, but Shane was eager to peel off for a chat. He seemed really keen to persuade his old friend that he wasn't guilty of drug taking. 'You know I wouldn't have done that', said Warne, 'I'm not a cheat.'

'I got the impression that he needed someone to talk to', says the friend, 'that he didn't have a lot of trust in his current mates. He seemed a bit down. He told me he didn't know if he would ever play again.'

18

As Bad as it Gets

*I'd be pretty shocked if he did go down that road
again. If he does there'll be no family and no wife at
the end of it.*

Six months after the drug ban, Shane's year went from
bad to worse, with another sex shocker – this time in
the Johannesburg *Sunday Times*, which began its story: 'A
South African mother-of-three claims disgraced
Australian cricketer Shane Warne bombarded her with
raunchy phone messages for more than a year after she
had a quick fling with him.' It was just like the Donna
Wright affair three years earlier which had stripped him of
the vice-captaincy, but more tragic, more farcical and also
more sordid. The woman in question, Helen Cohen Alon,
who claimed Warne had harassed her for sex, was 12
years older than Shane and a little bit strange. But once
again, there was not much doubt her story was true
because, as the newspaper revealed, a friend of Warne's in
South Africa had paid her 100,000 Rand (A$21,000)
in an attempt to shut her up.

Cohen Alon was not the world's most convincing
witness, but the *Sunday Times* had put its top investi-
gative reporter on the case, and there were people to back

311

up some of her claims. She said she had met Warne in February 2002 at the Versace store in Johannesburg's ritzy Sandton City – where the Australian cricketers had been shopping for clothes – and he had been interested as soon as she came on his radar. 'He said I had "a nice-looking ass" and asked me for my number. I gave it to him.' Another version of events suggested she had pestered him to get his attention, but the fact that they had hooked up was never disputed.

According to Cohen Alon, she had been on at least one date with Warne and had twice visited his hotel room, where they kissed 'lightly'. Soon afterwards, he began bombarding her with raunchy text messages such as, 'Where are you now? Waiting for you. Should I get dressed or stay naked? Room 2011'. In another message sighted by the *Sunday Times*'s Michael Schmidt, Shane claimed to be lying in bed next to his wife, thinking dirty thoughts about Cohen Alon. A third message suggested she find another woman so that Warne could watch them have sex – or so says Captain Julius Smith of Sandton police, who investigated the case.

Within hours, this new scandal was all around the cricketing world, popping up on websites in India, England, America and even Taiwan, as yarns about Warne inevitably do. And soon everyone was asking the $64,000 question: 'Could he *really* have been doing this when his wife was on hand?' From the dates, it appeared that the answer was 'quite possibly', because Simone had made a rare trip to South Africa with the family in February 2002 – some 18 months earlier – to watch her husband play in his hundredth Test.

Shane refused to deny the allegations to the *Sunday Times*, despite many invitations to do so, and met publication in Australia with a similar blank silence. And when his brother, Jason, finally issued a statement, the best he could do was to attack the story as 'a blatant attempt . . . to set up someone for personal gain'. It was noticeable that he did not say, 'Cohen Alon is telling a pack of lies, this is not true, this did not happen'; or 'Shane never sent any text messages'; or even 'Shane has never had sex with "that woman"' (in an echo of that other famous philanderer). In fact, he failed to say any of the 100 things he could have said to cast doubt on it all. Meanwhile, one of his cricketing mates, the late David Hookes, was dismissing it all out of hand on his nightly radio show: 'Some dopey, hairy-backed sheila dobbed him in on the other side of the world.' So what?

In the absence of denials from Warne, Australian radio and TV stations naturally went looking for more. And Shane's shame was soon rehashed for 1.5 million viewers of Channel 9's *A Current Affair* – which was ahead of the pack on all Warne stories – in an interview with Cohen Alon herself.

For once, Shane's accuser was not a blonde. Nor did she look at all like Simone. In fact, it was hard to believe that Shane would have wanted to chase her. With her black-rimmed dark glasses, dark red lipstick, long black hair and leopard-print coat, she looked like something out of an art-house movie or the beatnik end of London's Kings Road. But more than this, she appeared to be rather confused. I remember watching the full interview coming in live to Channel 9 from Johannesburg and being amazed by her performance. It was stream-of-consciousness stuff, full of wild allegations, non sequiturs and contradictions (which were mostly cut from the program that went to air). She was not seeking money, she said, but $250,000 would be a reasonable price. And she was only speaking out because people might try to kill her. You can get some of the flavour from this unedited extract:

> I fear that something is going to happen to me because of these terrible phone calls I've been receiving and what really shocked me into reality was when I read the newspaper one morning about Hansie Cronje [South Africa's cricket captain who died in an air crash] about maybe he could have been murdered and I believe now – I'm not saying that this case could be linked to that – but I believe if they investigate this matter, which I am going to take further, especially against the allegations made against me and my name. I'm a very important person in my country, I do special events. I'm a director in show business, and I have an artist as well, my son, who I manage as well and I just need the truth to come out and I don't need this publicity surrounding my name or my children, because I'll protect them. But I feel, I feel threatened at the moment. That's why I believe the whole truth should come out.

A crowd of us stood there watching, open-mouthed. Yet she obviously had evidence that Shane had pursued her for sex, which made his behaviour seem even more desperate than ever.

Cohen Alon claimed to have engaged a US lawyer to help sell her story, but it was unlikely he would have much work to do, because she had already given almost everything to the *Sunday Times* for free. And by spilling out the rest to Channel 9, she guaranteed no other TV station would want it. Had she been able to deliver the 40 text messages that she claimed Shane had sent to her, she might well have been killed in the rush. But she had handed these over to Warne's good-Samaritan friend in South Africa, a man called Gavin Varejes, who had paid her R100,000 in an unsuccessful attempt to keep her quiet (of which more in a moment). All she had left was two or three texts that she had copied on to her new phone from the old SIM card, and the contents of these had already been published.

But there was still plenty of life in the story if someone could persuade this South African protector to talk. Once again, *A Current Affair* did the business. Gavin Varejes came on two days after Helen and introduced himself as a Johannesburg businessman who dealt in sporting memorabilia. He had known Warne socially for a couple of years, he said, but had no business dealings with him. He was in his mid-40s, with curly light-grey hair, a pin-striped suit and a matching shirt-and-tie set. And he looked almost as unappealing as the woman Warne had pursued. Nor was his body language convincing: his eyes darted left, right and occasionally upwards, but mainly pointed down towards the ground in front of him. Some questions made him particularly uncomfortable and evasive, such as why had he paid Cohen Alon R100,000 to keep her quiet? His answer to this was a classic. 'That is the subject of a police investigation, okay? They have asked me not to comment.' Then he added exactly the sort of comment he was supposed not to make: 'But I would like to say that Helen did come to extort money from me and the allegations she made are a lie.'

To his credit, interviewer Ray Martin then asked: 'The allegations about all these phone calls with Shane Warne, are *they* a lie?' To which Varejes reponded, 'You know, I don't know, Ray.'

Shortly afterwards, Martin asked him again, 'So you don't think he made these calls?' And again Varejes replied, 'I don't know exactly, I don't know.' Thus two more opportunities went begging to claim that Cohen Alon's story was just a pack of lies. From which one was entitled to conclude that, clearly, it was not.

Varejes refused to admit that he had paid Cohen Alon money, although there was not the slightest doubt that he had. But he did agree that he had talked to her and had tried to shut her up:

Varejes: I did call her. I did have a meeting with her. I did try to resolve the issue. I didn't want this to become a public issue, because Shane is a good friend of mine.
Martin: A good enough friend to stop someone going public with the scandal about him?
Varejes: Absolutely . . . I stand by my friends, good or bad, right or wrong . . . I would be honoured to think that I would be a friend of Shane Warne's. I think he is a marvellous guy . . . an incredible ambassador for Australia.

So why had Varejes paid her? If Cohen Alon's allegations were so 'innocuous', 'pathetic', 'outrageous' and 'bizarre', as he maintained, why had he parted with R100,000 of his own money to stop her going to the newspapers – which could presumably have reached the same conclusion? And had he really failed to warn Shane that a scandal was about to break? It really was hard to accept.

A year later, when Cohen Alon was found guilty of trying to extort money from Varejes, a somewhat brighter light was shed on the whole affair. Warne's faithful friend had indeed paid R100,000 to buy her silence and to get his hands on the SIM card with the 40 messages from Shane. Sometime later, she had got greedy and demanded R50,000 more, threatening to go public, and he had refused to pay. The court files revealed a crumpled, hand-written agreement, penned by Varejes and signed by them both, in which Helen had agreed to accept R100,000 in full and final payment for keeping her mouth shut.

Perhaps the most interesting thing about this informal contract was its date: 17 February 2003, which was precisely four days before Warne was to appear in front of the drug tribunal that banned him from cricket for a year. It would not have been a good moment for a new sex scandal to emerge, given that he and his lawyers were pleading for leniency. Cohen Alon had obviously picked her moment well.

Varejes had also got full value for his R100,000 because he had acquired the only proof (if there was any) of Warne's misbehaviour. In 2004 the South African police recommended that the cricketer be charged over his pursuit of Cohen Alon with *crimen injuria* or criminal insult – which can carry a jail sentence – but the director of public prosecutions in Johannesburg advised there was no prospect of a conviction. Cohen Alon only had copies of the original messages that she claimed had been sent to her, and it was technically feasible that these had been doctored. Without hard evidence of what the original messages had said, no court of law was going to convict.

Whether Warne knew how close he came to facing criminal charges we will never know. But the fallout from the Cohen Alon affair was bad enough without him being prosecuted. Six months into his drug ban, with his future already unsettled, he was facing another crisis in his private life that threatened to blow his marriage sky high. As he admitted to the *Australian Women's Weekly* six months later, 'I couldn't get much lower. That's as bad as it gets. It looked like my cricket career was over, and my family which is the most important thing looked like it was going to fall apart.' And what is more, all this was happening under the intense gaze of millions of cricket fans around the world.

Every time he looked out of his new (larger and more expensive) house in Brighton he could see a growing contingent of reporters, TV cameramen and photographers camped on the nature strip, waiting for him to emerge. Sometimes there would be close to 50, ready to follow him and his kids to school, which was only 100 metres' walk away. Shane made a point of taking Brooke on his shoulders, amid this gaggle of reporters, to foster the image of him as a caring, family man. Occasionally, a photographer would try to scale the back fence to get a picture of the Warnes' kitchen and pool area. Others were ready to chase him and Simone when they went out by car. At one point, two TV cameras tailed them separately to Port Melbourne, where they were captured on videotape arguing fiercely, before leaving in separate vehicles. It must have been a nightmare.

It was not much fun inside the house either. Simone later admitted she yelled and screamed a lot because she was so angry with what he had got them into. Shane, she reported, was too embarrassed to say much in return. Finally, things got so tense that she took their two older children to her parents' home, leaving Shane alone with their four-year-old boy. Then the TV crews started staking out her parents' house as well.

It was not long, too, before more stories came out of the woodwork. First, a female employee from Cricket Australia claimed she had fielded complaints from women about Warne every day of the week. 'There are just too many ladies with too many stories', she told Channel 7 News (9's biggest rival) with her face hidden and voice distorted. 'He made life very difficult for the staff there', she also suggested. Next was a woman who phoned the Sydney *Daily Telegraph*, claiming that Warne had bombarded her with raunchy text messages after picking her out of the crowd at the SCG and having an official ask for her number.

Finally, it all became too much for the couple to bear. Leaving behind a press statement from Simone that she would 'stand by her husband 100 per cent, and [would] continue to [do so] through this unnecessary heartache', they drove to the airport and boarded a plane to London. 'It was the wrong environment to try and talk', Shane later explained. 'We had to get out of the country.' They ended up in Spain, trying to put their marriage back together.

Simone's parting shot was, 'Certain individuals are trying to destroy our family and I will not let that happen.' It seemed to escape her that the key destroyer was Shane himself.

Their decision to flee the country was almost certainly linked to a story that hit the newsstands the morning after they left, and which had been hot gossip for a week. It featured a 38-year-old blonde stripper from Melbourne who claimed to have had a three-month affair with Warne that had only just ended. The opportunity of an exclusive interview with Angela Gallagher had been touted around the media at an asking price of $100,000 through Australia's most famous 'celebrity agent' Harry M. Miller. There was no doubt she was paid handsomely by *New Idea*, who headlined the story 'MY WILD NIGHTS WITH SHANE', and Channel 7 to tell all. What made it possibly worth the money – and so much more damaging for Warne – was that she and Shane had been playing games on his home ground. For once, he could not use the excuse of being in a lonely hotel room, miles from his family and missing Simone. He had been out on the razzle with a local lap-dancer while his wife and three kids were tucked up in bed at home in Brighton. What is more, he had been doing it night after night for weeks on end. And a fair number of his male friends obviously knew all about it. 'We'd meet up, go out to clubs and meet up with his mates', she told *New Idea*. 'He seemed to make no secret of me.'

According to *New Idea*, Gallagher and Warne had met at an exclusive Melbourne night spot called The Motel and swapped mobile numbers. Or, perhaps, as she later maintained, he had come on to her at the lap-dancing club where she worked as a stripper. Either way, he had wasted no time in texting her his most romantic pick-up line: 'Sweetie, I want to meet you in the toilets.' And the messages had become more explicit from there. Gallagher claimed she was 'taken aback' by how forward he was and had refused to let him come round when he phoned that night. But it hadn't stopped him for a moment. Shane's instant response was: 'Well, if I can't be with you, can I have phone sex with you?'

Nor had it put her off a liaison with him. When he called the day after their first meeting, she agreed to see him, and it was all go from there, with Shane on the phone 'every spare minute he had'. He led her to believe that he and Simone 'weren't together', Gallagher told *New Idea*. 'He told me they had a very open marriage . . . and I believed him. I had no reason not to.' Seeing Shane operate, it would not have been hard to reach the same conclusion.

Viewers of Channel 7's nightly current affairs show, *Today Tonight*, were soon treated to the TV version of her story, and given the chance to judge the latest model that Shane had fallen for. She had long blonde hair and a good figure, much like Simone, and wore a long black dress, silver jewellery, lots of make-up and a suede-look jacket with white rabbit-fur trim. But the startling feature was her nails, which were square, lilac or baby pink, and stuck out a centimetre from the end of her fingers. To be kind, she looked like a model. To be unkind, she was obviously a stripper. She handled herself with dignity, though, given the sensitive subject matter. 'He was always talking about how hot, horny and hard he is, constantly', she told early evening viewers. 'Probably on five different occasions I received that message.'

Gallagher appeared alongside her husband of 16 years, Paul, from whom she had been separated at the time of the affair. A thinner, younger, hungrier version of Shane, with spiky gelled hair, he had fired off his own text message to the sex-mad cricketer in the hope of getting him to go back to his wife. 'I basically wanted to go over there and kill him', he admitted angrily.

To test the truth of Ms Gallagher's allegations – and spin the story out for another episode – *Today Tonight* persuaded Shane's moll to take a TV lie-detector test. Filmed in the style of *Who Wants to be a Millionaire*, it turned out to be a big win for Angela.

'Did you have a relationship with Shane Warne?' she was asked first up.

'Yes', came the reply.

Cut to reporter/quizmaster sitting opposite her . . .

'The first question: "Did you have a relationship with Shane Warne?" You answered "Yes". The machine says you're telling the truth.'

'I knew that', said Gallagher.

'Next question: "Did SW send you a series of explicit text messages?"'

'Yes.'

'Did you have sexual intercourse with Shane Warne?'

'Yes.'

'Did Shane tell you he was in an open marriage?'

'Yes. That's why the whole thing happened. That's what I was led to believe.'

Each time the machine backed her up enthusiastically, giving scores of up to 20 when three was enough to pass, or so viewers were told.

But one question caused her trouble: 'Have you ever tried to seek a financial benefit from Shane Warne or anyone connected with him?'

Gallagher scraped past this one – apparently because her mind was 'less clear' – and then piked out on the next, which was:

'Have you chosen to speak out because you're going to be paid?'

'Yes!'

So much for her story about solidarity with the international sisterhood. She had told *New Idea* that she was 'speaking out' because she was so upset about the treatment dished out to Helen Cohen Alon.

Six months after the hubbub died down, Simone and Shane agreed to their own exclusive interview with the *Australian Women's Weekly* (proprietor Kerry Packer) to tell the world that they were staying together despite Shane's infidelities. Those who had followed Shane's scandals over the years no doubt shook their heads and wondered how she could put up with it all, but Simone had a courageous, grown-up answer. 'Leaving him would have been the easy thing to do', she told the *Weekly*'s Tracey Curro, 'but we do have a family together. We do have a good relationship. Twelve years is a long time, three children, there is a lot at stake.' It was a remarkable interview for several reasons. It seemed frank and honest and thoughtful, and it gave some idea of the trouble they had been through. And those who read it at the time might even have believed Shane when he all but promised not to do it again. 'I think this is my last chance at everything', he admitted. 'My last chance here [with Simone]. My last chance with my life. This is it.'

His account of how these things kept happening seemed so simple: 'We've all got choices, and I've made a few too many bad ones', he confessed.

> I think in the past I didn't actually think of the consequences when I did things. Sometimes, I just did it and then suddenly thought, 'Shit, what have I done?' That's sort of my life. I'm impulsive about things. I've just got to stop being as impulsive, thinking a bit more, being more aware before I do anything and actually think, 'OK, what are the consequences? What is acceptable and what isn't?'

While this was certainly true about the way Shane lived his life, it wasn't really an explanation for his three-month affair with Angela Gallagher or for his serial pursuit of anything female and under 50. And there was also his rider that you had to remain 'true to yourself', whatever you did, which sounded suspiciously like an escape clause.

What also made you wonder was his description of the Cohen Alon allegations as 'that outrageous thing in South Africa', and his claim that he couldn't possibly have been on with Gallagher for three months because he was out of the country (on dates that did not actually match the ones she had given for their affair). On second thoughts, it did not seem to be a full and frank admission of what he had done.

And Simone, for her part, appeared to have been living on Venus these last 10 years if she thought this was so out of character. She told the *Weekly* that she had been devastated when she found out about Gallagher, as you would be. But she had also thought:

> God, this is not happening. Shane wouldn't do any-
> thing like that. I've seen girls throw himselves at him
> when I'm there, so I can imagine what it must be
> like when I'm not. But I never thought Shane was
> capable of doing something like that ... I never
> thought it would happen to me, our marriage. I guess
> I wasn't living in the real world.

Too right she wasn't. She seemed still to have no idea what he got up to behind her back.

Luckily for him, she was strong, forgiving and deter-mined to make a go of it. Despite everything he had put the family through, she was still incredibly generous. 'I saw how upset he was when he told me about it all. He was pretty much at the lowest point in his life. I think he doesn't ever want to feel that again.'

And to the relief of women everywhere, she did not give him carte blanche to do it again. 'I'd be pretty shocked if he did go down that road again', she warned him, adding, 'If he does there'll be no family and no wife at the end of it.'

She could not have made it any clearer than that. Surely, if Shane was sincere when he said that his family was everything to him, he would behave himself in the future? Wouldn't he?

19

On Top of the World

To get back to where I am today is a fairy tale.

D-day for Warne's return to cricket was 10 February 2004, but the excitement started building long before that. His hometown paper the *Herald Sun* even had a millennium-style countdown: ten, nine, eight, seven, six days to go. And by then there had been a blizzard of speculation about whether he would tour Sri Lanka in March and whether he would ever dazzle again. Former England captain Mike Atherton was pretty sure he would not. 'It is an impossibility that Warne will return to his best form', he told readers of the UK *Telegraph*, explaining that he had passed his peak by 1998, and was already on the slide before his shoulder packed up. Thereafter, said Atherton, 'The greatness had gone, and only cunning, guile and bravura kept him ahead of the pack.'

But Athers obviously hadn't read the script for the next episode in the Shane Warne soap opera, nor had he seen how much work the star was putting in at rehearsals. A year's absence from Test cricket had left Shane absolutely determined to get back to the top because taking the kids to school and spending time with Simone was no match for the roar of the crowd, the fizz of the ball through the air and the sweet, sweet sound of falling wickets.

The first thing he had done was get back to his fighting weight. By December, he had begun training at St Kilda Football Club with their star player Aaron Hamill, who was also one of his best mates. Soon after, he was doing the hard yards with Russell Crowe's personal trainer, Lourene Bevaart, better known as Glacier from the *Gladiators* TV series. For the first two months of 2004 she put him through a punishing routine of daily boxing, jogging, cycling and weights sessions, and forced him to eat veggies, fruit and lean beef, backed up with protein shakes. This lethal combination saw Shane shed 8 kilos, to take him down to 85 kilos, which made him just about as fit as he had ever been. When asked how she had achieved this amazing result, Bevaart replied: 'It's easy if someone's doing everything wrong and then they stop.' But since she was five-times world karate champion, she was obviously not someone you said 'No' to. On one famous occasion in Mexico, she had apparently rescued Big Russ from a brawl with three other men. However, she refused to talk about her heroics because of the confidentiality agreement she had signed with the star.

During his 12-month ban, Shane had not been allowed to play first-class cricket anywhere in the world or to train with any team in Australia. But as D-day approached he managed to have a few net sessions in Melbourne and a tune-up in Adelaide with his old spin doctor, Terry Jenner, who reported that he was in great shape and ready to roll. Others also predicted he would shine. 'One thing about

Warney', said his old chum Dennis Lillee, 'whatever his faults might be, he's very proud. And I can't see him letting himself down by coming back and not being right. He'll be fully aware that his reputation is on the line.'

To complete his preparation, Warne hired St Kilda's Junction Oval and got a few friends together to have a private practice. A week later he led Victoria's Second XI onto the same ground for the second day of its match against Queensland's cricket academy. Three men and a dog had turned out to watch on day one, because Shane's ban had not yet expired. But now he was clapped onto the field by a crowd of nearly 1000 spectators, including his mum, dad, wife Simone, and brother, Jason. There was also a small army of reporters and at least six TV cameras to record the occasion. It was probably a record for any Second XI game anywhere in the world, but it definitely was for Victoria. Just up the road, the First XI was playing to an empty house.

In the event, it was all a bit of a let-down. Victoria spent the morning batting, then the rain set in for the afternoon. In the gathering gloom, play was called off by teatime and everyone drifted home. Warne stayed to sign autographs for a queue of kids stretching out to the front gates and was heard to say that it felt like Christmas to be playing again.

The next day the clouds cleared and Warne got to bowl. His first over was a maiden; in his second he was hit for six. Then he settled down to another 14 accurate overs in which he conceded only 26 runs and got two wickets. In previous comebacks he had been struggling with injury. This time he spun the ball hard and mixed up his deliveries. First impressions were that he was as sharp as ever. And word soon spread that the new, slimline Shane had started the day with a yoga session in the dressing-room.

Three days later the leg spinner played at the MCG with Victoria's First XI in the Pura Cup match against Tasmania. And here he showed even more of his old verve, grabbing six wickets and conceding just three runs an over. If Australia's selectors – Trevor Hohns, David Boon, Allan Border and Andrew Hilditch – had been in any doubt about picking him for Sri Lanka, this was just what they needed. He had been back only 10 days, but he was obviously fit, bowling well and raring to go. Had they been forced to choose between him and his understudy, Stuart MacGill, it might have been a more difficult decision. In Warne's year-long absence, MacGill had been Australia's leading wicket taker, with 65 dismissals, which was almost as good as Warne's best haul in 1993. But luckily, Sri Lankan pitches were made for spin and Australia would need two frontline spinners, so the problem did not arise.

All the same, no one could possibly have predicted how quickly the comeback king would repay their confidence. In early March, in the historic port of Galle, once one of Asia's most prosperous trading posts, Australia dug itself out of a seemingly hopeless position to win the First Test, with Warne triggering a Sri Lankan collapse. Coming on shortly before lunch on the last day, he took three wickets in 15 balls, followed by two more after the break, to hustle the home side out for 154. Even more dramatically, his 10-wicket haul in the match took him past the magic

500 mark. Only one other player in cricket history, West Indian fast bowler Courtney Walsh, had done this before. His 500th victim was Sri Lanka's skipper, Hashan Tillakaratne, normally the most conservative of batsmen, who was tempted into a slog-sweep that he skied to Andrew Symonds at short mid wicket. The ball was in the air for ages, with Warne yelling 'Catch it, catch it, catch it', which was entirely unnecessary, (a) because it was a sitter and (b) because Symonds was thinking about nothing else. But he caught it all the same.

Warne pumped both fists in front of him, closed his eyes and bellowed, 'Yes.' It was a 'rush of pure joy' he later told readers of his column in the London *Times*. His team-mates wheeled in to congratulate him, ruffle his hair and slap him on the back. Then he broke away, held the ball above his head and bowed to the crowd, who were remarkably appreciative of his achievement given that he had just felled their captain and pushed them to the brink of defeat at 7 for 119, and given that he had also trumped their hometown hero, Muttiah Muralitharan, of which more in a moment.

At the end of play, with Sri Lanka beaten, Warne grabbed a stump as a souvenir and said a quick thank you to veteran English umpire David Shepherd, who seemed delighted with his small part in history. He then gave the thumbs up to photographers and blew them a kiss before walking through a double line of Sri Lankan school-children who had formed a guard of honour.

After all that had happened in the previous 12 months, it was hard to believe he was being fêted again. 'I couldn't have written the script better', the spinner told reporters after the game. 'To come back here and be able to get ten wickets and win a Test match was very special.' It was a fairy tale, he admitted, and he dedicated it to friends and family. 'I'm so happy Mum and Dad are here,' he said. 'They've got me through a tough time.' Days later in his *Times* column, he extended his Oscar-style list of thank yous, giving pride of place to Simone and the three children. 'They are my life', he gushed, 'and without their patience, love and support through all the tough times, this wouldn't be possible.'

Shane's parents were almost as excited as he was. Despite all his records and rebirths, this was the best so far. 'I just have to stop pinching myself', Keith Warne, Shane's father, confessed. 'We are a pretty close family. We stick by each other. We all make mistakes and we hope to move on and be better people for it.'

After the formalities were over and the press conference done, the Australian team had a few drinks in the dressing-room before making its way up to the battlements of the 17th-Century Dutch fort just beyond the boundary. There, overlooking the Indian Ocean, wicket-keeper Adam Gilchrist led his team-mates in a rousing chorus of the team song, 'Under the Southern Cross', to celebrate a famous fight-back, by the team as well as its star. For all the strife that he caused, it was wonderful to have Shane back. 'When the game is up for grabs', Ricky Ponting observed, 'there is probably no one in the world you would rather have with the ball in his hand.'

Warne's dream run continued into the Second Test in the holy city of Kandy, whose fall in 1815 had marked the start of British colonial rule. Again he bagged 10 victims and bowled Australia to victory. In the first innings he took five of the last six wickets to fall; in the second innings he took four of the last five. And this time, even he seemed to struggle to believe it. 'Personally, if I had written the script before I was selected, to come and take 20 wickets and two ten-fors and win the series two-zip', he told reporters, 'I think Simone would have tapped me on the shoulder and said I was dreaming.' He had bowled as well as he could, he reckoned, and was 'spinning the ball big time'. Despite all his doubts and fears, a year out of the game had actually done him good. His shoulder and finger had both had a chance to heal, so he was able to put more rip on the ball again.

Warne finished the three-match series with 26 wickets, which took him to within two of Courtney Walsh's record of 519. But even though the West Indian had now retired, Shane was not going to take his crown, because Sri Lankan off spinner Muttiah Muralitharan was only four behind him, and in six weeks he would be in Zimbabwe to collect another bagful of scalps. Warne, on the other hand, would not be going into battle again until June.

The son of a Tamil confectioner, Muralitharan was even more of a hero in Sri Lanka than Warne was back home, chiefly because he had put his little island nation on the map. Like Warne, he struck fear into batsmen's hearts, and it was not just because he ran in to bowl with his eyes bulging and his mouth open, like some mediaeval demon or gargoyle.

At the beginning of Warne's year off Murali had been more than 50 wickets adrift of his arch rival, but he had closed the gap to six while Shane was in the sin-bin. His loyal fans had been hoping he would overtake the Australian during the First Test in Galle, and had erected an official billboard – the Murali 500 – to count him up to the milestone. But Warne had disappointed them.

The Sri Lankan had a better strike rate and better bowling average than Warne, and had come to international cricket nine months later. He had also taken five wickets in an innings twice as often as his rival. Yet few would have argued that he was a better bowler, because he had taken two-thirds of his wickets in his home country, where the pitches were set up for spin, and he had got more than 100 of them against the two weakest cricketing nations, Zimbabwe and Bangladesh (while Warne had taken just six against these countries).

Today, most people are generous enough to accept that Muralitharan is a genius, and one who has achieved his triumphs with an arm that has been crooked since birth. But his career has been more controversial even than Warne's, because he has regularly been branded a thrower. To be frank, his action is bizarre. He runs in to the stumps with his arms flapping like a chicken and his wrist cocked sideways, parallel to the ground. He then releases the ball with a hand movement like an Indian dancer's. To the naked eye, it does look like he is throwing, which is illegal in cricket. And any number of observers have accused him of this. The Indian off spinner Bishan Bedi, for example, claims he has never seen Murali 'bowl', which is a roundabout way of saying he chucks. England's well-known TV host and cricket fan Michael Parkinson agrees, referring to him contemptuously as Muchichuckalot. Meanwhile, several Australian umpires simply call him 'a joke'.

Complaints about Murali's action began almost as soon as he came on the international scene in 1992, but it was not till 1995 that things came to a head. In the Boxing Day Test in Melbourne he was no-balled seven times by the Australian umpire, Darrell Hair. And a couple of weeks later another Australian umpire, Ross Emerson, did it again. It was the first time in history that a visiting bowler had been pulled up in this way, and it looked as though Murali's career was over. But his action was then investigated by three different sets of biomechanical experts – in Western Australia, Hong Kong and the UK – who all gave him a clean bill of health. Using slow-motion cameras and sensors attached to his arm, they concluded that his action was legal and that his arm merely appeared to straighten (which is how, in cricket, a throw is defined).

In spite of this, Muralitharan was no-balled again in Adelaide in 1999, by the same Ross Emerson, who made no secret of his view that the bowler was a cheat. After that, a truce was declared, and this held until 2003, when the spinner began deploying a lethal new weapon called the *doosra*. This, in effect, was an off spinner's leg break. The delivery brought him heaps of wickets but it also landed him in trouble once more, because it was easy to see that it was produced with an entirely different arm action – one that even the biomechanical experts believed was illegal. So now, as Murali homed in on Courtney Walsh's world record, experts at the University of Western Australia, led by Professor Bruce Elliott, conducted new tests to see whether he or his *doosra* ought to be banned. He was given the bad tidings about the renewed scrutiny on the last day of the Third Test in Colombo in late March 2004.

When the results came through in mid-April, there was good news and bad news for cricket's next world champion. The bad news was that Elliott and his computers had ruled the *doosra* illegal: the ICC's rules stipulated that the arm could straighten by a maximum of five degrees in the bowler's delivery stride, and Murali's straightened by double that or more. The good news was that he was not the only one: according to Elliott and his team, Australia's Brett Lee and Pakistan's Shoaib Akhtar also straightened their arms by 10 degrees at times. Better than this (from Murali's point of view), the biomechanical experts believed the rules should be relaxed to make all three bowlers legal again. The ICC planned to consider their recommendation in September 2004, by which time the results of a much broader investigation would be known. In the meantime, it insisted the *doosra* was a throw and demanded that Murali stop bowling it.

This was still the situation on the first day of the First Test against Zimbabwe in May 2004, in which Muralitharan took six wickets, overtook Shane Warne, and equalled Courtney Walsh's world record. It was also the situation on the second day, in which he took two more wickets and surpassed that record. On both days he bowled the *doosra*, yet lips stayed sealed. No one dared report him.

Understandably, his achievement caused no great celebration in the world's press next day. According to the London *Times*, the reaction was 'muted, hollow, underwhelming'. Some comments, like those of former

Australian wicket-keeper Barry Jarman, were downright hostile. As a match referee in the mid-1990s, Jarman had been one of the first to raise doubts about the legality of Murali's action. 'It makes a joke of the game', he told Sydney's *Daily Telegraph*. 'It makes me sick talking about it. Everyone knows he bowls illegally.' Even Australia's Prime Minister, John Howard, a self-confessed cricket tragic, weighed into the debate, calling the Sri Lankan a chucker.

Nor was there much praise from the 400-strong crowd watching the game in Harare, because Murali's milestone left them at 6 for 63 and their team was receiving the mother of all thrashings.

But that was an entirely different story, and one that would soon affect Warne directly. Zimbabwe had effectively been forced to field its Third XI after a disastrous row over racial bias in its selection policies. The team's white captain, Heath Streak, had protested that players were being picked on skin colour first and cricketing ability second. This had led to his sacking, whereupon his 14 white team-mates had walked out in sympathy. The upshot was that Zimbabwe had sent out a team that would have been hard-pressed to beat St Kilda's Third XI or any of the English minor counties.

The reason why Zimbabwe's problems were of more than passing interest to Warne was that the Australian team was also about to arrive in Harare, to play two Tests in June. Provided this tour went ahead, there would be wickets aplenty, and Warne would almost certainly grab Murali's world record for himself. But back in Australia, there was fierce opposition to the games going ahead, and not just because the cricket would be a farce, or because the Zimbabwe Cricket Union favoured black over white. Anyone who reads the newspapers or watches TV would know that President Robert Mugabe is one of the world's nastier second-division dictators. Under his regime, political opponents are gagged, beaten and imprisoned, the murder of white farmers is tolerated or encouraged, as is seizure of their land, and thousands of people are on the brink of starvation. Australia's other leg spinner, Stuart MacGill, had already decided not to tour, because it was morally wrong to give comfort to such a regime. Warne, on the other hand, had voiced no concerns.

Predictably, the other players also left it to the politicians to decide, claiming, like Warne, that they were 'just cricketers'. Australia's politicians then passed the hot potato back to the ACB, on the basis that it was a decision for the men who ran cricket. And the ACB tossed it on to the International Cricket Council, saying it had to honour its contracts unless it was instructed not to do so. It was in this atmosphere of buck-passing and denial that the Australian team boarded the plane and went to Harare. Still the row did not die down, and eventually the ICC told Zimbabwe to pick its First XI for the Test matches – including some of the 15 white rebels – or have them stripped of Test-match status. The Zimbabwe Cricket Union promptly decided to cancel the games instead. So, after bashing up Zimbabwe's Third XI in a series of one-day internationals, the Australians got back on the plane and went home again, and Warne got no wickets.

But the show had to go on, and there was still a chance that Warne would win the prize, because Australia's next two Tests were against Sri Lanka in July – in Darwin and Cairns – and Muralitharan was now refusing to play. No doubt he was afraid of being banned for bowling his *doosra*, but he also did not want to be heckled by Australian crowds, who had always given him a hard time. And he was furious at Prime Minister John Howard, whose unsolicited criticism had prompted him to say: 'I thought of coming to Australia but now I will think three times before I come.'

Warne needed 10 wickets to catch Muralitharan and 11 to secure the record, both of which were in reach on his latest form. For once, though, the pressure took its toll. He managed to get one hand on the crown in the Second Test in Cairns, where he drew level with Murali on 527. But he could get no further. With nine men round the bat and the light fading fast, two of Sri Lanka's tailenders kept him at bay for half an hour and saved the record for their absent friend. Warne tried everything: tossing it up, pushing it through, bowling out wide. His only break was the bone in Adam Gilchrist's nose, struck by a topspinner that reared off the pitch. Warne admitted later he had tried too hard.

Shane's faithful parents were there to watch, of course, Keith with his arms folded, Brigitte eating a packet of Snakes Alive. But only a few hundred others were in the stands to keep them company. It was the footy season; it was also North Queensland; and the Sri Lankans had never been box-office magic. Nor did the rest of Australia get to see their man tilt for the top. With Warne still one adrift of his rival, Kerry Packer's Channel 9 switched back to its cheesy old game show *The Price is Right*, and even

ABC radio tired of the match and flicked the switch to its scheduled current affairs programs.

After the game, Warne was excited to have drawn level but visibly disappointed not to have seized his chance. Barring accidents or a ban on Muralitharan, the record now seemed lost for good, because the Sri Lankan had a busy Test schedule ahead of him, while Warne had nothing until November. Under such circumstances, the Australian could not resist a swipe at his conqueror, suggesting he had an unfair advantage because Sri Lanka doctored its pitches for spin. 'He has conditions where the ball turns square from ball one, so he's obviously got a lot more chance than I have', said Warne. Naturally, he also pointed out the vast number of Murali's victims that had come from Bangladesh and Zimbabwe, and reminded people that the Sri Lankan had no other great bowlers competing for wickets. 'I've got three or four of the best bowlers in the world over the last ten years', said Warne. 'McGrath, Gillespie, these guys. He's got Chaminda Vaas.' There was no doubt it was true, but it might have been best to leave it to others.

Here, by rights, the story should have ended: the best bowler in the world who never quite made it to number one. But we all know it did not, because Muralitharan's shoulder now let him down, just as Warne's had done six years earlier. In his next Test match in Sri Lanka in August, against the South Africans, the off spinner came off the field to be packed in ice and dispatched to the doctor. He had boosted his score to 532, five ahead of the Australian, but it would now be his turn to sit on the sidelines for a year. And, barring more accidents to

Warne, it was just a matter of time before the record changed hands again. It was small consolation for Murali that, shortly afterwards, the ICC's biomechanical experts recommended changes in the law that would make his *doosra* legal again.

Ironically, Warne's coronation was in India, his least favourite country, where he had so often failed to impress. He closed the gap on his rival by taking four wickets in the First Test in Bangalore and drew level on the opening day of the Second Test in Chennai. At 10.59 am on the second morning, 15 October 2004, he trapped India's nightwatchman Irfan Pathan with a near-perfect leg break that drifted in the air, caught the edge of the bat and flew into the safe hands of Matthew Hayden at slip. It was his 533rd Test wicket, and it had taken him almost 32,000 balls to get there. The record was his.

Warne was immediately surrounded by his team-mates for the ritual mobbing. And when this was complete, he peeled off to collect the ball from umpire David Shepherd (who was once again enjoying his brush with fame), and raised it to all corners of the ground. The crowd, which included his wife Simone, gave him a standing ovation and later began chanting his name.

There was universal acclaim in the papers next day, with Ponting leading the chorus: 'As far as I am concerned he is one of the all-time greats of the game and what he has done not only for cricket in Australia but for spin bowling worldwide has been remarkable.' Others tinged their praise with realism and regret. 'Today Shane Warne is being lauded and not lambasted or lampooned', wrote Mike Coward in *The Australian*.

It makes a pleasant and welcome change. At one time or another throughout his extraordinary career he has irritated, disappointed or alienated fellow players, administrators, sponsors and the media which have largely sustained him. But on a grand day such as this nothing is to be gained by listing the lapses and indiscretions.

Even on this day, few commentators could resist the observation that he was past his best. None put it quite so crudely or finally as Mike Atherton had done, but the same old sentiments were there. Peter Roebuck in *The Sydney Morning Herald* voiced it elegantly, as always: 'His final, most glorious trick has been his last. Unable any longer to impart upon the ball the energy that made it fade and dip and bite from the pitch, he has learnt to take Test wickets with straight balls.'

In fact, the raw figures suggested Warne was as good as ever. When his wickets were finally totted up for 2004, the scorecard gave him 70 victims, which was on a par with the golden years of 1993 and 1994. He had also achieved the score in just 10 months, without two Tests in Zimbabwe. And whatever anyone else believed, he reckoned he was as good as ever. A year out of the game had put him on top of the world.

20

Good Boy at Last?

I hope we can be together forever now, I really do.

In February 2005, one year after his dramatic comeback from the drug ban, Warne went back to Sri Lanka on behalf of his new children's charity, the Shane Warne Foundation, to help raise money for victims of the December 2004 tsunami. He had been invited there by his old rival Muttiah Muralitharan, who had nearly died in the huge tidal wave that hit the island's south-eastern shores. Murali wanted Warne to appear at a big fund-raising dinner. And Shane was only too happy to oblige.

On hearing about the visit, Channel 9's *60 Minutes* hitched a ride with the touring party by agreeing to fund a large part of the trip. They spent two days filming with the Australian leg spinner, flying him to some of the most badly damaged areas so that TV viewers would be able to watch him doing his bit. Jaunts like this are largely for show, of course, but it's an excellent way for celebrities to put their fame to good use, and it offered Warne an opportunity to rebuild his image, as well as to help. Walking through the devastation, miles from his native

Melbourne, he was followed by hordes of halfnaked homeless kids who all knew exactly who he was. According to the producer, Lincoln Howes, you could see their faces light up, as if they were following the Pied Piper. And Shane was genuinely nice to them: polite, interested and concerned.

There was no hope of playing cricket at the old ground in Galle where Warne had taken his 500th Test wicket, because it was buried under rubbish and rubble, but *60 Minutes* took Murali and Warne to Colombo and filmed them holding a spin clinic there. It was stinking hot – 40 degrees or more and incredibly humid – but even when the crew packed it in, Warne did not seek shelter in the pavilion. He stayed out on the oval with 200 young Sri Lankan would-be spinners, addressing even the smallest of them as 'sir' and giving them tips or signing autographs until the last was satisfied. Not only was he patient, he was also a natural teacher. He showed the reporter, Peter Overton, a non-cricketer, how to bowl a leg spinner, telling him: 'Pretend you're opening a door.' And it worked.

During a break in the filming, when he took the producer shopping for clothes, Warne was mobbed like a rock star. Everywhere he went, even while he was trying things on for size, people thrust pen and paper in his face. Yet he never lost his temper. He simply told them nicely: 'Hang on while I do this, I'll get to you in a moment.' On only one occasion did he become a bit impatient, when an English girl who had had too much to drink approached him in a restaurant, threw a beer mat in front of him and said rudely: 'Sign that.' Even then, he did what she asked and gave it back to her without protest. He could not refuse, he told the crew, because the tabloids might make a headline out of it: 'SHANE WARNE REFUSES TO SIGN FOR FAN'.

The *60 Minutes* team liked him. He was not the yob they had expected to meet. Nor was he as dumb as they had been led to believe, except that he was clearly incapable of admitting he had done anything wrong in the past. He seemed eager to give his version of all the scandals that had dogged him, putting his own spin on each of the stories. He retold the New Zealand smoking incident, for example, but with him cast as victim. And he opened up on the sex scandals, although always in terms of, 'She was a liar', 'That was a set-up', 'She had an axe to grind'. He also told tales about the rest of the Australian cricket team, and how they did what he did, in terms of going out to bars to pick up women. He lived in a bubble, he said, with his mates, his family and his cricket, cut off from the outside world. But what struck them most was that he kept on saying how important his family was. Marriage was one of the few real things in his life, he said, and he knew it was all at risk if he screwed up again. In view of what happened immediately after this, it is an extraordinary admission.

It was only two months before he was due to go to England to captain Hampshire for another season and play in the Ashes. And he was already saying that the British papers would make him a target. He complained they would pay girls to sit next to him in bars, chat him up, sleep with him and then tell their stories – as if it was not in his power to say no to them. But perhaps his fate was sealed, as he seemed to be saying. On the trip to Sri Lanka with him was his mate Brad Grapsas, chief executive of the Shane Warne Foundation. 'Shane's hopeless', Grappo confided, 'he can't help himself.'

Despite forecasts of trouble in store in England, Shane was happy that he would be escaping from the Australian press. When the *60 Minutes* crew told him he had to be kidding, that England had the most ferocious, scandal-seeking tabloids in the world, he simply said: 'I've gotta get away.' One week later, when the promo for the program went to air – reheating recent scandals and promising confessions from Shane – he no doubt felt his distrust was justified. He rang Peter Overton on his mobile to tell him how unhappy he was, then rang again after the story went to air. He was not shouting but he was clearly very upset. 'What was all that about?' he asked. 'There was nothing on the tsunami. That was all about my private life.' He was angry, furious even. He was adamant that they had let him down.

In fact, it had been made clear to him from the start that they would ask him about the scandals, that they would have to be seen to raise this stuff. If he wanted to win back public sympathy or approval, he needed to address these questions. And it was anything but a hatchet job. The final product was a typical *60 Minutes* mixture: a bit of puff and a bit of tough, tied in a glossy package. In 13 minutes there was probably no more than one minute on his private life, which was doubtless far less than the viewers expected. And it was far from hostile, as this extract makes clear:

Overton: You had an affair. What was it like to go home to the people that you trust and love the most and say to your wife, 'I'm guilty, I've had an affair'?

Warne: Well, I mean it's not easy to talk about it, it was quite a tough time in my life and it was something that I thought was personal between my wife and I. I did the wrong thing and that's something I have to live with. And it's not easy to live with because I'm embarrassed about what I did.

Overton: How did you get through that, though? A personal crisis became a public crisis becomes a media free-for-all and you're in the middle of it, trying to save a marriage, you've got three kids, how do you do it? What did you do?

Warne: Well, I think the . . . the only thing you can be is honest, and you know you've done the wrong thing, and I spoke to my wife about that. We were sort of angry and angry about the, you know, 50 people outside our house so we couldn't get out the driveway, so it was the wrong environment to try and talk and so we couldn't really talk. We had to get out of the country and we ended up going to Spain. And without, I suppose, a loving wife and a forgiving wife and a beautiful family that we've got – we had to get through that and we managed to get through that. And, you know, everything's okay at the moment and we, we're getting along fine and the kids are great and I'm enjoying that part of my life and hopefully it stays like that.

Overton: But some would say for your wife, it's hard enough being a cricketer's wife but it's even harder being Shane Warne's wife.

Warne: It would be and she's, I think, handled herself with dignity and I think she's handled herself very, very well in a lot of tough situations. And, you know, it's an unfortunate part of our lives and hopefully it's gone.

All things considered, it was an easy ride. But shortly afterwards, Shane's brother, Jason, sent an angry email to the producer, accusing *60 Minutes* of betraying them. He copied it to their boss, David Gyngell, who was Shane's (and James Packer's) mate. When Overton rang to smooth things over, he realised that Shane had watched it at home with Simone and it had been painful for both to have old wounds reopened. He told him to watch it again and ask his mates what they thought. Three weeks later, Shane phoned back, sounding much calmer. Jason sent a second email apologising for the first. They had listened to the feedback and decided that the program had been pretty kind after all.

In the meantime, despite admitting he was on a final warning from Simone, Shane had been up to his old tricks again. Not that he had ever stopped. A couple of his mates at Channel 9 recall a wedding in Sydney in late 2004 at which Shane and Simone were guests. Twenty photographers were camped outside, waiting to get a shot of him drinking, smoking or standing on the balcony. Even in this situation, Warne was determined to hit on a girl at the reception. A couple of his mates had to drag him off and tell him not to be so stupid. They just could not believe how reckless he was.

More immediately, he was due in New Zealand for a three-match Test series starting in early March 2005. Here, less than a month after *60 Minutes* went to air, Shane picked up a waitress at the Lone Star Café in Wellington and started sending her text messages. The young woman, who was then 22 years old, sent him one back saying: 'I thought you were married.' Warne texted her again to say that he and his wife 'had an arrangement'. The girl's father saw these messages and reacted angrily. Then a friend set about trying to sell the story. A week later, the bare bones were revealed in New Zealand's national tabloid, the *Sunday News*, which had been offered an exclusive interview with the girl, plus the messages, for $30,000. The newspaper had declined to pay the money, but had realised there was a story when it was told it could have its own exclusive interview with Shane if it agreed to back off. Next, the newspaper received a letter from Warne's lawyer refusing to confirm whether the cricketer had sent the messages or not, but stating they were 'private between the two parties' and could not be published without consent. This was all the confirmation the *Sunday News* needed, and on 27 March, during the Third Test, it ran the story, although it did not name the woman or reveal what the messages said.

It is a fair guess that there would have been some tension in the Warne household at this time, and not just because Shane was straying again. Two weeks before, with the press pack at his heels, he had announced he was upping sticks and moving to England. He was due to take up a two-year contract with Hampshire in April 2005, with an option for another two years, and he had bought a house in Southampton, which he claimed was now his home. 'Down the track it will probably be home for the family as well', he said. 'I'll live over there and . . . come back and play my stuff for Australia and head back. I'm only in Australia for a couple of months each year.'

There was one big problem with this scenario, which was that he had not broken the news to Simone. Two days after Shane's announcement she said she knew nothing about it and had made no plans to go. They had just renovated their Federation home in Brighton; two of the kids were settled in schools there; and all her family and friends were in Melbourne. Shane went anyway, at the beginning of April, and Simone then agreed to follow in June. This would give her enough time to pack up the house and wait for the children to finish term. It would also allow her to say goodbyes, on the basis that Shane seemed to be setting no limit on how long they might stay away.

Crucially, it would also give Shane eight weeks on his own. But surely he could keep out of trouble for that long?

The Southampton terrace the Warnes would be going to was a far cry from their beautiful Melbourne mansion, which occupied a large block in the leafiest and quietest part of Brighton. Set behind high walls with a solid electric gate across the driveway, it looked like one of those sprawling English country houses, with domestic offices and stables behind. And it was almost as big. At the front and sides it had high, wide verandahs, which were interrupted by an arched entrance hall and capped at one end by a small tower with a chateau-style roof. The front garden boasted a lily pond, a jacaranda, a liquidambar and a huge *Magnolia grandiflora*, which had probably been planted in the days when the house stood by itself amid acres of pasture. Clearly, it had been a big estate in years gone by, until its owners sold off the land for building, and it had obviously been grand before the Warnes moved in. But their renovation had practically doubled its size, adding a pavilion out back, with a vast marble-floored kitchen and full-length glass doors that opened on to a swimming pool and tennis court.

By contrast, the new home that Simone and Shane were heading for was extremely modest. A £350,000 town-house, formerly owned by the Southampton soccer star Matt Le Tissier, it was in a dinky new estate called Ocean Village, which appeared to be full of retirees and not at all family-friendly. Kids were not allowed into the communal garden and pets were discouraged. The house also had linoleum floors, a small kitchen and was a long car ride away from the nearest shops and schools.

One reason Shane wanted to be in England – as he explained to the guys from *60 Minutes* – was to get away from the scrutiny of the Australian media. But if he thought he was going to be left in peace, he was in for a rude shock. Days after he arrived, a photographer for *The Sun* caught him with his trousers down at Hampshire's flash new cricket ground, the Rose Bowl. He was standing on the steps, with a cigarette dangling from his mouth, daks around his ankles, looking down at the area that had caused him so much trouble in his life. If he wanted to get away from a crude and intrusive media, he had come to the wrong place.

Typically, he was soon loading bullets for the tabloids to fire. Within days of landing, he was trying his charms on a 28-year-old TV accounts executive called Michele Masters, who was entertaining clients at a Southampton football match. Michele knew Shane well from his previous spells in Hampshire, so he tagged along when the party moved to a local bar-cum-restaurant called Dock 4. 'He stayed with us for the remainder of the evening and we kissed', Michele told Southampton's *Daily Echo* two months later. 'He wanted to come back to my house but there was no way he was going to do that.'

With a kiss to encourage him, Shane was soon texting Michele relentlessly. 'He was making it very obvious he was just after one thing', she told the *Daily Echo*, 'and I really wasn't interested.' Her coolness put him off for two weeks, but then the text messages and phone calls started again, telling her she was 'sexy and gorgeous'. Eventually she succumbed. 'He asked to come over and I said OK. He stayed until the early hours but then he had to go because he had a cricket match that morning.'

Before long, Warne had several others on the go. A month after he arrived – or perhaps even sooner – he was having hot sex with a 31-year-old blonde saleswoman, Kerrie Collimore, and pursuing a 20-year-old archaeology student, Rebecca Weeden, whom he also knew from his spell in Southampton the previous year. He was also out on the razzle with his new Hampshire team-mate Kevin Pietersen, who was 10 years younger than him and unmarried.

While he was rooting away like there was no tomorrow, Warne agreed to be interviewed by Piers Morgan for a cover story in *GQ*, a top UK magazine. Morgan is famously the ex-editor of the *Daily Mirror* and one of Fleet Street's more colourful characters. His blokey interviewing style persuaded the leg spinner to reveal far more of himself than usual. It has to be said that Morgan's story is not an entirely flattering portrait: Warne comes across as vain, insecure and none too smart. And also, quite frankly, lost.

In the interview, Shane accepted some degree of responsibility for his troubles over the years. But as always, he blamed the media for exaggerating. 'The public aren't dummies', he protested. 'They see through the garbage, and they know when headlines aren't backed up by facts.' He then condemned the women who had sold their stories to the papers. 'It's just another form of prostitution', he told Morgan. 'It's as low as you can possibly get and I just don't understand how they can do it.' Finally, he gushed about what a wonderful wife Simone was, telling Morgan:

> She is one of the most incredible ladies I have ever met. She has come out of this with a lot of dignity . . . She is strong and straight down the line . . . she's a very sexy and beautiful lady. I have been very lucky to marry someone so special, which is something I maybe forgot over the years.
> *Morgan:* Do you feel you owe her one?
> *Warne:* Oh, more than one, mate. You don't often get as many chances as I have had. And I would have understood if she had wanted to walk. But I hope we can be together forever now, I really do.

Anyone reading that would have been forgiven for thinking that Shane had finally seen the light and changed his ways. But even as he was saying that Simone was his everything, the only woman in his life, he was conducting two, if not three, hot affairs that were guaranteed to blow his marriage sky high.

It is hard to know how to describe the man, but 'stupid', 'hypocritical' and 'deluded' are words that spring to mind. If his family was genuinely so important to him, why on earth did he continue to put it all at risk?

Yet there is a more charitable explanation. There was a sadness and fatalism about the way he talked to Morgan about his personal life and marriage, as if he already knew it was doomed. As if the bomb was already ticking. And perhaps he had finally realised it was.

21

The Old Enemy

*Is there anyone out there who can give Australia a
decent game of cricket?*

In the 130-odd years that Australia has played Test
cricket, only 400 players have represented their country,
and only half of these are still alive today. So the members
of this small club rightly regard themselves as being part of
an elite. Nowadays, they are even received into the
brotherhood in a special ceremony. Gone are the days when
you went to the manager's hotel room to be thrown your
gear – cap, shirt and long-sleeve jumper – or got your father
to drive you to the ACB's offices to get your kit. Today, you
are escorted onto the pitch by the entire Australian team
and handed your new cap in a formal presentation. A living
legend such as Richie Benaud or Ian Chappell is there to
welcome you and make the speech. And you are left in no
doubt about what is expected of you.

In essence, to play cricket for Australia is to carry the
hopes of the nation, to shoulder the burden of 130 years
of history and to walk in the footsteps of Sir Donald
Bradman and his 'Invincibles', who played 38 matches in
England on the 1948 tour without being beaten. As an

Australian cricketer you are expected to play the game as if you were fighting for your life and more, which is why Steve Waugh took his players to visit the battlefield at Gallipoli, *en route* to England in 2001, to show them what mateship and sacrifice really mean.

There is no such fierce tradition or national pride in English cricket, where almost one-quarter of the team since 1980 has been rejects from Australia, refugees from South Africa and Zimbabwe, or people who were born in Britain's former colonies. And where the whole lot could be sacked lock, stock and barrel after a couple of bad results. It is impossible to imagine England's players being taken to Trafalgar before a football match against Spain, or Dunkirk before a World Cup qualifier against the Germans, or (indeed) to the site of Newgate Prison before a Test against Australia. Yet Australia sees absolutely no problem in telling its cricketers they're like the diggers who fought at Gallipoli, because sport defines the nation. We engage in it with warlike intensity and depend on it to carry our flag to the rest of the world.

And by God, we are good at it. Despite a population of fewer than 20 million people, which is one-third the size of Britain and one-fifteenth the size of the USA, Australia beats the world at pretty much everything it turns its hand to: rugby union, rugby league, swimming, surfing, sailing, netball, triathlon, tennis (once upon a time), clay-pigeon shooting and last but not least, cricket, in which it has to be said there is rather less competition.

Come 2005, Australia was undisputed champion of the cricketing world, having soundly beaten off all of its rivals since losing to India on foreign soil in 2001. Some were beginning to wonder if it was the best team ever – even better, perhaps, than those Invincibles. Under Taylor, Waugh and Ponting, the Australians had not lost a Test series for 13 years, except on the Indian subcontinent (where visitors always found it difficult to win and where batsmen seemed to be immune to Warne's magic spells). And since last beating England in 2002–3, they had lost only one game that mattered. The three other defeats were in dead rubbers, after the series had already been won.

So, as the 2005 Ashes series drew near, you had to be English and a super optimist or a member of the Barmy Army to believe that the next battle between the old enemies was likely to bring an English victory. The best one could realistically hope for was that the Poms would put up a decent fight for a change, which they had failed to do for almost 50 years. And even that prospect looked doubtful if you cast your eye back over recent history.

Only five years earlier, in 1999, England had sunk right to the bottom of the international cricket rankings, by losing to New Zealand at The Oval, rounding off a decade in which it had lost considerably more Test matches than it had won. But the problem with English cricket was more fundamental than a run of bad results. Unlike the Australians, the English expected to lose, especially against Australia. And I say this from personal experience. Although I have been an Australian citizen for more than a decade, I grew up in England in the 1950s and spent the first 35 years of my life suffering its sporting incompetence. Sure, we won the soccer World Cup in 1966, but no Englishman had won Wimbledon since the 1930s, the rugby union team was regularly annihilated by the All Blacks, and cricket was a disaster. From the mid 1950s, when I started to care, to the mid 1970s, when I gave up hope, England won the Ashes against Australia just once in 10 attempts. Nor did we suffer bad luck, go close or have victory snatched unfairly from our grasp. We just lost.

There were rare moments of glory, mostly provided by Ian Botham, whose heroics brought pride and joy in the early 1980s, or by Graham Gooch and David Gower who grabbed a couple of hard-fought victories a few years later. But by the end of the 1980s, normal service had been resumed. We were thrashed 4–0 in the Ashes in England in 1989 and thumped 3–0 in Australia two years later. And after that England lost every series comfortably (except in 1997, when it lost narrowly), managing to record just seven wins against Australia in 14 years and 32 matches.

So it was not suprising, when the 2005 series rolled around, that most Australians assumed it would be another one-sided contest or even a whitewash. 'I think I was saying 3–0 or 4–0 about 12 months ago', fast bowler Glenn McGrath boasted to reporters (having assumed that it would rain in England as usual), 'but with the weather as it is at the moment, I have to say 5–0.' Jeff Thomson, his predecessor from the 1970s, agreed: 'England will lose the five-Test series 3–0, and the margin will be worse for them if it doesn't rain. If you put the players from Australia and England up against each other it is embarrassing. There is no contest between them on an individual or team basis.'

Another former fast bowler, Terry Alderman, who

destroyed England by taking 42 and 41 Test wickets respectively on the 1981 and 1989 Ashes tours, was equally gloomy about the Poms' prospects: 'If Australia get away to a good start then England have got no chance. They have got to be competitive in that First Test at Lord's, or else it's goodnight.' Since England hadn't beaten Australia at Lord's in 17 attempts since 1934, this did not offer much hope.

Not to be left out of the party, Shane Warne told GQ magazine a month before the off: 'England have never had a real chance in my time, and I can't really see them having one now.'

The Australian went even further, dubbing Ponting's team the 'Untouchables' (in homage to the 1948 champions) and asking sorrowfully: 'Is there anyone out there who can give Australia a decent game of cricket?'

A few months earlier, the New Zealanders had been quite sure they would give the Australians a shake in the three-match Test series that southern summer. According to captain Stephen Fleming and former star all-rounder Chris Cairns, they were fielding their best team ever. However the Kiwis ended up being crushed by the Australian juggernaut, losing two out of three games in their own backyard and being saved by rain in the third. A chastened Fleming admitted afterwards that it was hard to imagine any team capable of beating Australia, adding that the prospect of them getting even better was 'scary'. The most encouragement he could offer was that England would be 'in with a sniff' if it won at Lord's. But as we know, there wasn't much chance of that.

What made the Australians so hard to beat was that they

always put their opponents under so much pressure. They never gave up. They played well, session after session. And if ever they didn't, someone came to the rescue. You could bowl half the Australian side out for 50, and they would still put on 200 for the eighth wicket. Or you could get to 1 for 200 in your own innings and the part-time off spinner would come on and take 4 for 10. It might be a different person from match to match, but someone was always there to step up to the plate. Ricky Ponting's explanation for this resilience was good old Australian mateship: 'It is knowing that when the chips are down and there is a fight to be had, everyone is going just as hard as you are. We will do everything we can to ensure we don't let each other down.'

By contrast, the poor old Poms were wont to scatter at the first whiff of grapeshot. Whether they just weren't good enough or just weren't tough enough was a matter for debate. But one way or another, they had a nasty habit of cracking when the pressure was on – or as soon as Warne came on to bowl. The leg spinner had drawn attention to this in his book *Shane Warne, My Own Story* back in 1997, when he had chided England's players for their lack of killer instinct. They had doubted themselves at key moments, he said, either through lack of confidence or cautious captaincy. Or maybe they just didn't know how to win.

This was a fatal flaw, because sport at the top level is 90 per cent about self-belief and mental toughness. It's what allows you to hole that vital putt, serve that winning ace, take that critical catch or play that match-saving innings. If you don't have that steel-hard nerve, you will never be able to cut it against the best. And sadly, English county cricket did not forge such attitudes. Australian players who came to England for a season went away shaking their heads at how slack and genteel it all was, and at how little anybody seemed to care. When you played in the company of pie-throwers, trundlers and overweight spinners, it was hard to take anything too seriously. For years there had been too many matches, too many poor sides and too many games that meant nothing. There was also too much time sitting in the pavilion, waiting for the rain to stop. None of this was good preparation for facing a pack of snarling Australian fast bowlers or having your parentage called into question by zinc-lipped close-in fielders.

It was no coincidence that the toughest players in England's recent cricketing history – Graham Gooch, Ian Botham, Mike Gatting, Graham Thorpe, Mike Atherton and Alec Stewart – had almost all spent time away from England. They had played in Australia or South Africa as outsiders and had learnt the hard way that they had to be strong to survive.

There was another way in which England often lacked confidence, and that was at the team level, because England's selectors were rarely prepared to stick with a core group of players. They had a habit of picking people before they were ready, ditching them before they had settled and sacking players en masse when things went wrong, as they often did. So a vicious circle developed in which team spirit and confidence were never able to flourish. Famously, in the 1993 Ashes series, England had employed 24 different players in six Test matches, which was enough to make up a First and Second XI, plus a couple of 12th men. This did not encourage players to look after each other, put trust in their mates or feel secure about their own future.

But the good news for England's players and the English public as the much-awaited Ashes series approached was that the worst days were certainly over – which is why there was genuine excitement at the prospect of battle being renewed. After sinking to the bottom of the international ladder in 1999, a watershed had been reached and a whole series of changes made. Most importantly, in 2000, the English Cricket Board had followed Australia's example (10 years late) and introduced central contracts for its squad of core players. Crucially, this allowed Test players to be freed from the county treadmill so they could be properly rested and looked after. They could be given specialist coaching and put through rigorous fitness programs, so they were in physical shape to play the game. The county system had also been given a makeover. Games were now played over four days, which gave time for a result, and the teams had been split into two divisions, which meant that sides were better matched. It also mattered whether you won or lost, because you might go up or down. The ECB also followed another Australian lead (again 10 years late) by setting up its own National Cricket Academy at Loughborough, and appointing former Australian wicket-keeper Rod Marsh as head coach. Finally, the selectors had resolved to play pick-and-stick with their players, which had allowed the Test team to find some consistency, learn to rely on each other and develop team spirit.

One of the men leading this revolution was the new team coach, Duncan Fletcher, who had captained Zimbabwe in the days when cricketing talent was all you needed to get into the team. The other was England's new captain, a phlegmatic Yorkshireman, Michael Vaughan. Both brought an air of calm and professionalism to the job, and a bit more steel and aggression to the way England's top cricketers played the game. Both were well-liked, well-respected and capable, and Vaughan, in particular, seemed to have the killer instinct that had so often been lacking. As a consequence, England's results had improved to the point where their recent record was beginning to look almost Australian. Since losing the last Ashes series Down Under in 2002–3, England had lost only four games out of 30, and only one of its last 18, which had been away from home against South Africa.

In fact, victory in South Africa during the English winter of 2004–5 had made people wonder whether England's plan to regain the Ashes in 2006–7 might be running ahead of schedule. Not only had Vaughan's boys won the series 2–1 but they appeared to have found some fight. On two occasions, they had got themselves into deep strife then managed to dig their way out. In the Second Test in Durban, for example, they had been almost 200 behind on the first innings, but had scored 7 for 570 in the second, and would almost certainly have won the match if bad light had not stopped play. Similarly, in the Fourth Test in Johannesburg, they had started the last day looking like they could only lose or draw. Then Marcus Trescothick had completed a quick-fire 180 and Matthew Hoggard had skittled seven wickets to earn them a famous win. This is what the Australian team had been doing for years, but it now seemed as though England had also found the knack.

This new-look England team was much younger than the Australian side and it had some potential stars. Opening batsman Andrew Strauss had made 650 runs in the South African series at an average of nearly 73, while the colourful Kevin Pietersen had dazzled in the one-day matches, scoring 454 runs at a phenomenal average of 151 and a strike rate of better than one a ball. If he was let loose in a Test match – and could reproduce that form – he could win a game in one session, because he hit the ball so ferociously hard and attacked so savagely. Nor did he suffer from nerves. Playing in front of his native South African crowds (whom he had abandoned in favour of England five years earlier) Pietersen was jeered, booed and heckled, but it just made him play better. Freddie Flintoff, who had so often looked like a pale imitation of Ian Botham, was also finding some consistency at last. He too had the ability to destroy a bowling attack and turn a game, but his bowling was arguably an even stronger suit. Now that he had shed a few kilos, he was fast, hostile, accurate and could reverse-swing the old ball at 90 miles per hour (144 kilometres per hour), which made him another potential match winner. He and seam bowler Matthew Hoggard had split 49 South African wickets between them on tour, easily eclipsing Steve Harmison, the other frontline fast bowler, who at his best in 2004 had taken 7 for 12 against the West Indies and topped the ICC rankings. Indeed, if Simon Jones, England's fourth fast bowler, was fit for the Ashes, Australia would be facing the fastest and most formidable pace attack since the West Indian quicks of the 1980s.

Back in October 2004, before joining Australia's cocky chorus, Warne had told *The Courier-Mail*'s Robert Craddock that he thought the 2005 Ashes series could be close. 'Harmison is as good as anyone in the world. His pace, height and bounce will trouble anyone', he warned. 'If England don't have Harmison and Flintoff . . . it will be a clean sweep for the Aussies. If those two are fit and firing, we will have a real battle on our hands for the first time in 17 years.'

English fans were desperately hoping that this would be so, as were many Australians, and not just because sledging and bad sportsmanship had lost their team so many friends. It was a crashing bore if you always knew the result in advance and if no other team in the world could give you a game. It was like watching Tiger Woods streak the field by 10 shots every time he played. So Australian journalist Matt Price was not alone when he reassured readers of England's *Spectator* that some of his countrymen were praying for an English victory. 'Cricket needs another lopsided Ashes series like Warne requires diuretic pills', Price wrote. 'There's nothing remotely unpatriotic about plumping for England; anyone interested in the longevity of the game above boorish bragging rights craves a genuine contest, not least because the Australians have been ugly victors.'

A number of things might still stop England making a fight of it. Harmison, Flintoff and Jones might not be fit or firing. Pietersen might not get the nod from the selectors. And the Poms might fold under pressure as so many others had done under Australian fire. Last but not least, Shane Warne might run riot again. In almost every series he had played in, he had been the single biggest difference between the two sides, and in 1993, 1994–5 and 2001 he had created havoc. If England was to win this time, its batsmen needed to play the world's best leg spinner far better than they had ever done before. And here, in the nick of time, they had just been handed a secret weapon.

Named after the magician in King Arthur's court at Camelot, Merlyn was an advanced bowling machine that would supposedly teach England's batsmen how to deal with all of Warne's tricks. Born in a barn on the Welsh borders, in the shadow of the Black Mountains, it was the brainchild of an eccentric 71-year-old farmer by the name of Henry Pryor. British history is full of such men, designing clocks to measure longitude, drawing maps of the rocks underneath the surface of the earth, or building hovercrafts from lawnmower engines in the garden shed, and old Mr Pryor was carrying on this great tradition in his effort to rescue English sport. According to his son Matthew, a cricket writer for *The Times*, Henry Pryor had realised his son would never bowl for England and had decided to replace him with a mechanical version. After 15 years of work, he had come up with a prototype that could reproduce the most devastating ball of the day – Waqar Younis's reverse-swinging yorker. But the 'Eureka moment' had come later 'with the discovery of how to spin the ball like Shane Warne'.

Merlyn had begun life as a Heath-Robinson contraption with 12-volt motors, toy car wheels and ball bearings. But the finished version was a big, white machine, around two metres tall and one metre wide, which looked like those mobile floodlights that are wheeled in to illuminate night roadwork. Using a keypad, the operator could program the machine to chuck down just about any ball you could imagine, including off spin, leg spin, seam and reverse swing. It could vary the length and the speed, and do so without telegraphing its intentions to the batsmen (unlike some machines, which have to be tilted up and down). And it was supposed to be clever enough to mimic the loop, drift and dip that Warne himself puts on the ball. It even made the fizzing noise.

Once Pryor had the mechanics right, he invited a few Welsh cricketers up to his barn to try it out, and soon afterwards he installed it in the nets at a nearby comprehensive school. After the bugs had been ironed out, he rang the new National Cricket Academy to offer them a talented fresh recruit. Finding the farm amid the maze of high-hedged country lanes, the academy's assistant coach, John Abrahams, liked what he saw and called Rod Marsh down to look for himself. Before long, Merlyn was being packed into a horse box and taken to the academy's shiny new indoor cricket school for the 2004–5 winter season.

Throughout those cold dark months, while the Test team was in South Africa, word began filtering down the M1 that Merlyn might be able to help neutralise the Warne threat that coming summer. But first reactions from the England team were sceptical, and it was not until one week before the First Test at Lord's in July 2005 that England's captain, Michael Vaughan (who lived near

Loughborough), was asked by team coach Duncan Fletcher to test out its wiles. Days later, the mechanical wizard was packed into its horse box again and driven to Lord's to help England's players prepare to meet their nemesis. In fact, the real Shane Warne was already out in the nets, tuning up his own bowling action with the help of his old mentor, Terry Jenner.

Merlyn's first outing was not a great success. The magic machine had only ever cast its spell indoors, where you could see the red, amber and green traffic light system that announced its intention to deliver another ball. When it was wheeled out onto the grass, into bright sunshine, the signals were invisible, so the batsmen had no idea when to get ready.

But all this is jumping ahead, because there was plenty of cricket to play before this great Ashes series began, and Australia's Untouchables were showing they were not invincible. In the first week after their arrival in early June, they lost to England in a Twenty20 game at Hampshire's new Rose Bowl, where a dismal batting performance saw them bowled out for a miserable 79 runs. Two days later, they were beaten in another one-day match at Taunton, where Somerset's South African and Sri Lankan imports Graeme Smith and Sanath Jayasuriya gave the cream of their bowlers (except Warne) a sound thrashing.

Three days later, on Saturday 18 June, they lined up for their first game in the NatWest one-day series, against Bangladesh. If ever there was a mismatch, this was likely to be it: the world's best-ever team (possibly) playing one of the weakest sides in international cricket, who had lost 96 of their 107 one-day games despite regular encounters

The perfect couple . . .

. . . and the perfect family. Shane has always said he'd give up cricket for his kids.

But, somehow, he is always looking for trouble . . .

. . . and finding it. Shane and Simone split days after the Laura Sayers story was published in London's *Sunday Mirror* in June 2005.

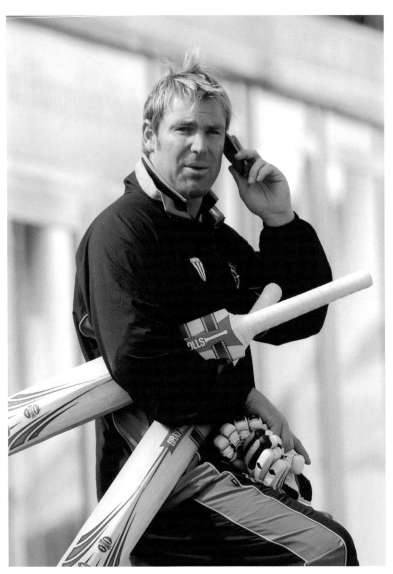

Can I leave a message?

Then came Kerrie ... Rebecca ... Michelle ... and Julia.

The Ashes 2005

'Jimmy Savile' rouses England's Barmy Army.

Tin hat and bugle—all you need for a day at the cricket.

Barmy Queens at Edgbaston.

The Ashes 2005

Umpire Billy Bowden's crooked finger gives Shane his 600th Test wicket, at Old Trafford.

Shane's mentor, Terry Jenner, the one man Warne always listens to, tuned him up before the First Test at Lord's.

England's nemesis: the one man who could deny them the Ashes. Warne took 40 wickets in the series. Australia's other bowlers took 53.

Final Test—The Oval

'Please, God, give me wickets.'
Even umpire Rudi Koertzen thinks
it was close.

Freddie Flintoff gone. Yeess! Surely, Australia will win it now.

'Mate, the Ashes are yours.'
'Thanks, Shane. You dropped 'em.'
Warne (who put down Kevin Pietersen on 15) congratulates him on his 158.

Simone Warne's exclusive interview with *New Idea*, a month after the break-up in 2005, smashed all sales records.

Maybe Shane didn't buy that issue. He was still telling the press he hoped to win her back.

'Not out' after all? These happy-family snaps had Australia's women's magazines a-wondering.

Come in, spinner. Shane invites the cameras round for Christmas 2005, to film him being a dad.

Meanwhile . . . Mmm . . . Hi Pammy.

And guess who's winning the Ashes next time? Shane's statue in London's Piccadilly Circus. (That's Eros in the background.)

with Zimbabwe's Third XI and Kenya, plus one-offs against Scotland and Hong Kong.

It should have been a cakewalk, as Australia's games against Bangladesh always had been in the past. But this was to be the day when everything began to go wrong for Australia, on and off the field, not least because Shane Warne was again making headlines for all the wrong reasons.

22

Bye Bye, Simone

Maybe I need to grow up . . . and maybe I don't. Life is
not a rehearsal, it's about having fun.

From a small office on New Bond Street in London's West
End, PR king Max Clifford runs a virtual monopoly on
kiss-and-tell stories in the United Kingdom. Since the late
1980s, he has placed countless exposés of politicians and
celebrities in the tabloids, and earned six-figure sums for his
talkative clients. His biggest hit in recent years is Rebecca
Loos's story of bonking soccer star David Beckham, which
Clifford sold to the *News of the World* for £300,000, before
earning the England captain's ex-personal assistant another
£400,000 in side deals. Clifford claims to get 100 front-page
stories in the red-tops every year, and these, plus his talent
for self-promotion, have allowed him to corner the market.
He can recommend the best paper, magazine or other
medium to sell to. And he can get top dollar for his clients.

The son of a maid and an electrician, Clifford has used
the gift of the gab to work his way up from the bottom.
He started with a music column in a local London paper,
then moved to EMI as a press officer, just as the Beatles
were coming to fame. He then set up his own PR

consultancy. But it was not till the mid-1980s that he really struck it rich, when he persuaded *The Sun* to run a front-page story about one of his clients. The resulting headline, 'FREDDIE STARR ATE MY HAMSTER', has gone down in history as one of the all-time greats. There is considerable doubt about whether the (then) small-time comedian Freddie Starr ever ate anybody's pet, but the story was enough to put Starr and his PR man on the map.

In his mid-60s, with smooth skin and perfectly coiffed grey hair, Clifford charges his clients £20,000 a month or 20 per cent commission, or possibly both, and tells them that he can either put them in the papers or keep them out. He often boasts that he stops 10 stories for every one that he sells, which he does by promising bigger, better exclusives in exchange, or threatening to put newspapers on his black list. Clifford is a powerful man in Fleet Street and a hard man to say no to. As a tabloid newspaper editor, you would not want to fall out with him.

The point of this preamble is that in April 2005 Clifford was approached by Shane Warne's UK manager, who wanted him to help keep Shane out of the British media. The PR spin king claims he then spent six weeks trying to stem the flood of stories on Warne, women and mobile phones, and managed to spike at least one major exposé. But even Clifford's considerable talents could not turn back the tide of women wanting to cash in on their nights with Shane.

By early summer 2005, Michele Masters was just one of several women negotiating to sell her story – to the *News of the World* in her case, for £50,000 – and one of several who could provide text or voice messages from Shane saying how much he wanted to 'fuck her'. Two young women who worked for a north London real estate agent were also hawking their story of night games with England and Australia's most colourful cricket stars. One of them, a 23-year-old budding glamour model called Gemma Hayley, was the girlfriend of England hero Kevin Pietersen, whom she had met in a fabulously expensive Soho nightclub called Chinawhite. The other, Laura Sayers, was Gemma's 25-year-old workmate and friend, who had made up a foursome with Kevin and Gemma on a big night out and found herself paired with the Australian spinner. They had gone out clubbing in London's West End, before returning to Pietersen's London apartment at two am, where Shane had suggested a foursome. Kevin and Gemma had then disappeared into the bedroom, Laura claimed, after which Shane had taken off all his clothes and begged her for sex.

Like all such women with a story to sell, Laura said she had reluctantly given in to his demands, and claimed she would never have done so had she known he was married.

Gemma and Laura tested their story on three different newspapers – the *Sun*, *Sunday Mirror* and *News of the World* – then apparently went cold on the idea of selling it, changed their mobile phone numbers and tried to get on with their lives. Perhaps the money wasn't good enough, who knows. But the pair then fell out, and the chase resumed, because Laura was definitely interested in talking. For six weeks from early May 2005, the *Sunday Mirror*'s Michael Duffy attempted to convince her she should sell her tale, before one of the other red-tops (who now knew some of the details) spoilt her chance by running it for free. 'I took her and her friends for drinks to explain how the story would run', says Duffy. 'I took her workmates for drinks. I took her ex-boyfriends for drinks. I took friends of her friends for drinks. My receipts for drinks were up to two feet long some nights.' Night after night, Duffy turned up to a dingy pub across the road from Laura's office, armed with a legal contract for her to sign. Night after night he tried to coax her into an agreement, and finally in mid-June he succeeded.

It cost the *Sunday Mirror* more than £10,000 to buy the exclusive rights, plus the price of a holiday in Sardinia for Laura and a friend, so she could be kept out of reach of rival newspapers. Before going to press, Duffy phoned Warne's UK manager, Michael Cohen, to get an official comment. Cohen denied it was true, then called back half an hour later begging the newspaper not to publish.

On Sunday 19 June 2005, the story was plastered across the *Sunday Mirror*'s front page with a large picture of Laura Sayers – buxom and blonde like most of Warne's women – under a huge headline, 'SHANE'S SHAME'. It could hardly have been worse for the cricketer or more embarrassing. The subheading teased: 'Married Aussie cricket legend begged me for sex, but it was OVER in seconds'. And inside were the details:

Shane Warne has been caught out – cheating on his wife with a pretty blonde student.

Laura Sayers, 25, told how the Hampshire captain stripped naked in front of her before begging for sex.

But when Laura gave in to the Aussie dad-of-three's naked demands, she was left stumped in no time.

'It was all over very quickly. I could have been a blow-up doll for all he cared. He just had one thing on his mind', said finance student Laura.

Like others before her, Laura claimed to have been disappointed by Shane's skills in the bedroom, telling the *Sunday Mirror* he was 'not very well-endowed' and just wanted to get laid. She was also less than impressed with his poor post-coital manners. 'As soon as it was over', she said, 'he fell asleep snoring and didn't wake up.' She claimed to the *Sunday Mirror* that she was not the first to blab about it: 'It was supposed to be a private thing', she said, 'but Shane told some of his cricketing friends, and suddenly I had all these people calling me about it. They wanted to know who I'd told and where I live – they told me if his wife found out it would ruin his life. But word got out and it didn't come from me.'

The night before the *Sunday Mirror* hit the streets, Piers Morgan (who had just interviewed Warne for *GQ*) got word that the paper was running the story and phoned the cricketer to ask if it was true. Shane told him bluntly: 'Mate, my marriage is fucked if this comes out. Over.' Morgan then asked him the $64,000 question: 'Is it true?' to which Warne replied: 'Ah, mate. I don't know what was going on, I was out of it.' In the original interview a few days earlier, Morgan had asked Warne how it was that he kept on getting into strife: how could he be so naïve? Warne had fired back:

I'm no dummy mate, that's for sure. But sometimes I suppose I don't think enough about the consequences.

Morgan: Does alcohol play a part in those moments?
Warne: I guess it does, yeah. But I've made some poor choices when I've had too many and I've made some when I've been sober. But I have tried to become a better person in the last two years. The problem is there's still a big kid inside me who likes to have fun. I am passionate about my cricket and I love my family, but I'm also a kid, and maybe I need to grow up.

Then Warne thought for a moment and reconsidered, adding: 'And maybe I don't. Life is not a rehearsal, it's about having fun'.

The First Test at Lord's was still a month away, but the *Sunday Mirror* had managed to time its scoop for maximum impact. Australia was playing its first two games in the one-day series that weekend, and it lost on Saturday to Bangladesh by five wickets. As if that was not dreadful enough, captain Ricky Ponting was also forced to discipline one of his hard-hitting batsmen, Andrew Symonds, who had been hitting the booze instead and turned up drunk for the game. On the Sunday morning, the team bus was late getting to Bristol for the next match against England, so tension was already running high. And it was in this atmosphere that the Aussies discovered their star spinner was again making news. Warne was not due to join them for another four weeks, but already he was screwing things up.

Shane had already refused to comment on the story. And his brother, Jason, now issued a statement to say that the cricketer did not intend to defend himself against every 'publicity-seeking individual' trying 'to gain notoriety' at his expense. Simone, for her part, described it as 'rubbish'. But one week later, the Warnes issued a statement through Jason confirming rumours that their marriage was over. 'It is with regret that we inform you that we have decided to separate', they said. 'We remain the best of friends and will continue to be there for our three beautiful children. Please respect our privacy at this difficult and tough time.'

Three weeks after that, Simone sold her own exclusive interview, for a reported $50,000, to the Australian women's magazine *New Idea*, and told Sue Smethhurst how she had heard the news.

I was still asleep when he came in and woke me up. He sat on the edge of the bed and said: 'Simone, I've got something to tell you'. I knew straight away it wasn't good. His English manager had phoned to tell him that the newspapers were carrying a story that he'd been involved with someone else. I was in shock, I was numb. I said to him: 'How could you be so stupid?' I just couldn't believe he'd done it again.

Simone and the children had given up their lives in Australia to follow Shane to England. They had waved goodbye to their house, their school, their friends and all their support networks, only to find their new life blown apart within days. It was hardly surprising that she was mad at him.

I said: 'Is this the only one? Be honest with me now because I won't ask again.' He said there was two. It was like someone stabbing me in the heart. I was angry, I cried, I broke things, I threw things. I was overwhelmed with disappointment. He had only been gone eight weeks and he couldn't remain faithful for that short space of time. It was devastating. I told him there and then that I was leaving . . . I knew I didn't want to be with this person for one minute longer. He said he was sorry over and over again and he was telling me he didn't want me to go, but it was too late.

Typically, Shane could not even understand what the problem was, and why Simone was walking away from him. 'He just doesn't get it', she told *New Idea*.

He knows I'm hurting, but he doesn't understand that what he is doing is wrong. He actually told me he thought I would never leave him . . . he kept saying 'I don't understand why you have to go, we can get through this.'

Even after Shane's reluctant confession that Laura was not his only side dish, Simone still had no real idea what her husband had been up to. Nor had she any clue that his remorse would be so fleeting. Exactly two days after the *Sunday Mirror* story was published – and after the showdown with Simone in which he begged her to stay – Shane suggested to 20-year-old archaeology student Rebecca Weeden that she should seduce Simone into a threesome with him 'to save his marriage'. It has to be one of the most ridiculous suggestions any man has ever made – and

God forbid Shane is stupid enough to have believed it could work – yet Weeden told the *Daily Mirror* he had planned it precisely:

> He had scripted the whole lot, what he wanted me to say and do. He said he would take his wife for a drink and I was to come over pretending to be a star-struck fan . . . Then I was to say 'Oh, is this your wife?' and start complimenting her and saying how beautiful and attractive she was. He was going to keep buying us all drinks and we would take it from there, he said. I didn't say no. I don't think I said anything, I was just so shocked.

By the time Rebecca Weeden dropped this bombshell in mid-July 2005, telling of her five-week affair with the spinner, two other women had also told the world about their rides on Shane's flipper. One was Michele Masters, whom he had hooked up with in Southampton on arrival, the other was another woman he had met in Southampton, Kerrie Collimore, who claimed they had had sex by the side of the road on the bonnet of Warne's BMW. A 'friend' of Collimore's, who seemed to know all the intimate details of their two-month affair, claimed: 'He couldn't keep his hands off her. He wanted sex every-where – outside, inside, wherever he could.' The same 'friend' had also managed to get hold of 48 explicit messages Shane had left on Kerrie's phone, including one in May 2005, when he had texted her: 'Can't wait to f**k u again' and 'How good was our sex, f***ing very hot . . . How good did it feel?' Another suggested: 'You can be standing there in the rain I can come meet you and then f*** you?' According to the *Daily Mirror*, another message was 'too steamy to print'.

Michele Masters had even more text and voice messages from Shane, for which the *News of the World* had been prepared to offer a great deal of money. One person who read or listened to them in the course of negotiations with the newspaper was horrified at their contents. In his view they were a world away from harmless smutty talk. 'They were disgusting', he says. 'They were frightening. He was almost stalking her. The man is sick.'

Masters had eventually decided not to sell her story – for fear of losing her job, amongst other things – and had managed to calm the media frenzy by offering a sanitised version to her local Southampton paper, the *Daily Echo*. But even this accused Warne of pursuing her relentlessly and texting her 'God knows how many times a day' for weeks. Even while Michele was on holiday in New York Warne had continued chasing her, going round to the flat she shared with her sister and demanding to know where she was. And now, after enduring Shane's pursuit, she was forced to deal with TV crews, photographers and reporters camped on her front lawn, until she managed to give them the slip. 'I waited until it went dark and they gradually went away', she told the *Daily Echo*. 'I jumped in the car and luckily I wasn't followed. I was really upset and frightened. It's not nice to be hounded out of your house.'

Simone and Shane had also fled the media pack. They had taken the children on holiday to Spain, even though they had announced their separation days earlier. 'It was the first real holiday Shane had had with the kids for two years', Simone told *New Idea*. 'The kids had been so looking forward to it, it would have broken their hearts not to go. I thought about not going . . . but Shane couldn't handle them on his own.' It may well have been a wise move, as it happened, because it saved her from having to read new stories about her husband's misdeeds every time she opened a paper.

But just about everyone else in the cricket world was following the saga, Warne's sponsors included. And before long it was not only Simone who was dumping him. In early July, Channel 9 terminated his $300,000-a-year commentary contract, citing his off-field behaviour, although this may just have been a convenient excuse. As one manager explained, 'Shane was paid a lot of money and we didn't get much out of him. In the summer he was playing in Australia, in the winter he was touring or playing for Hampshire, and we couldn't use him anyway because there wasn't any cricket.'

The Australian menswear chain Tarocash also sacked Shane from his $100,000-a-year job as the new face of the company. He had posed for their poster and catalogue shoot at Sydney's Park Hyatt only three months earlier, and everyone had come back saying how much they liked him. Managing Director Steven Liebowitz says he was neither arrogant nor difficult, and a pleasure to work with. 'I was more than happy to have done the deal', he says. 'I liked the guy.'

Liebowitz was amazed at the way his customers reacted. 'We got letters, emails, phone calls. People even came into the stores to complain, saying: "How dare you use this man to promote your company" or "I'm never going to let my husband shop with you again." I was really surprised that the Australian public was so vehemently aggressive about it.' By a stroke of bad luck, Liebowitz had hired a second Australian cricketer to model the Tarocash range, who happened to be Andrew Symonds – the man who had turned up drunk for the match against Bangladesh. This made people even angrier. 'You cannot believe what they were saying', says Liebowitz. 'They accused us of hiring adulterers and drunkards. I had no idea the public could be so judgemental.'

Tarocash had a one-year contract with Warne and an option for another, but there was a 'moral clause' allowing the company to cancel the deal if Warne did anything bad or stupid, and Liebowitz took advantage of it. Before more damage was done to the brand, Warne's posters were ripped down from the shops and the catalogues pulped. His brother, Jason, was told all bets were off. Liebowitz had assumed that his young, male customers would not care that Shane screwed around, but he was mistaken. 'A lot of people really dislike him for what he's done', he says.

Two big questions remained at the end of this sorry saga. One was why on earth did Shane keep on putting everything in his life at risk in this way? The other was would it affect how he played against England?

To everyone's surprise, Shane soon popped up in public to answer the second of these questions. Three weeks after the split with Simone and a week before the First Test at Lord's, he volunteered to talk to the press. As the cameras were setting up, Cricket Australia's media manager told journalists that Warne would not be answering questions about his personal life, only about the Ashes. But this did not stop Shane launching into the subject himself. News from Planet Warne was that things were fine and he would be out there, happy or sad, in the First Test at Lord's giving it his best shot. 'I'm actually doing okay', he told the assembled media, 'and I'm looking forward to the Test. It's always fun to play cricket.'

So how was he coping so well, he was asked? 'Too much practice probably, to be perfectly honest', said Shane in a rare display of insight. 'Whatever happens in your life, you just have to deal with it.' And besides, it wasn't all bad. 'I'm very lucky actually', he continued, 'although we're separated, we're still good friends . . . we speak, you know, every day just about, and I speak to the children just about every day.'

His mates were confident his cricket would not suffer. Michael Slater had found it impossible to play with similar pressures on his personal life, but he knew as soon as the headlines started that Shane would bowl well. He had always answered his critics on the field and always bounced back after injury and scandal. It was almost as if he needed the extra spur to persuade people to love him again. Others expected Warne to 'compartmentalise' it all, or put it to one side when he stepped onto the field. 'Whatever's going on in your private life', says one well-known former Australian Test player, 'you have to be able to go into the dressing-room and leave it all behind. Most top sportsmen can do that, and they wouldn't be there if they couldn't. As soon as you come through the door, you're with the lads, there's a job to do. You focus, lock on. Shane is better than most at doing this, and he has done it again and again over the years.'

Not everyone thought he should be given the chance, though. Some of the shock jocks on talkback radio wanted him sacked, as did *The Sydney Morning Herald*'s Paul Sheehan. 'Shane Warne is a world-class bogan who happens to be a world-class bowler', Sheehan began. 'He is a spinner in every way . . . a proven, serial, reckless, inveterate liar. And . . . as a serial liar he should never again be allowed to debase the Australian colours by wearing them.'

Around the water cooler, at backyard barbecues, and in Australia's newspaper letter columns, there was some sympathy for this view, but there was a louder chorus of disbelief that Warne could have disgraced himself again – and with such an unprepossessing bunch of women. As Sally Morrell asked incredulously in Warne's hometown *Herald Sun*:

> How could he have thrown away his marriage and his family life for a parade of tarty women that look as if they are straight out of the *Big Brother* house? And how could he so publicly humiliate his child-hood sweetheart and the mother of his children, again? It's not as if he fell in love with someone he wants to spend the rest of his life with.

But this was perhaps the point, and perhaps why Shane felt he had done nothing wrong. As he told the *Bulletin*'s Jana Wendt nine months later, 'I've had a few one-night or two-night stands or whatever you want to call it . . . I've never fallen in love with anyone.' His message, presumably, was that none of the affairs had meant anything to him, so in his mind he had never been unfaithful to Simone.

Experts who study sexual behaviour among groups of young males say this is a common mind-set among football players, soldiers and sports teams. According to Michael Flood from Melbourne's La Trobe University, who has researched male sexual attitudes in the Australian Defence Forces, these men typically regard women as sex objects not people, believe their mates are far more important than any woman, and see sexual conquest as a means to achieve status and bond with the group. Flood says they also have double standards about being unfaithful: it is fine for men but not for women.

Put more bluntly, the men see themselves as studs and the women as sluts. According to former federal MP Phil Cleary, this way of thinking is deeply ingrained in the culture of Australian football clubs. And he should know, because he played 250 games for Coburg in the VFL before becoming a premiership-winning coach. Cleary says contempt for women is encouraged by pie and porn nights that the clubs use to raise money. 'If you see these women stripping and getting fucked by some bloke in a footy club, it is pretty ugly. And what lesson do you get from it? Women are fucking whores. And that's why a bloke says, "If I just fucked that woman what does it matter, it's just another fuck." That's the view.'

Some of Warne's schoolmates point out that he grew up in this footy culture and still mixed with the boys from St Kilda. Whether this is relevant or not, he was not the first sportsman to be caught out with his mobile phone. Indeed, his closest mate in the Australian Test team, Damien Martyn, a buddy since their days at the AIS Cricket Academy in 1991, blew his marriage in similar fashion. In June 2003, Martyn's wedding to his long-time fiancée, Helen Appleyard, was called off without explanation. Invitations had been sent out, a reception booked in Melbourne's Crown Casino, and *New Idea* was negotiating to buy the exclusive rights. Two years later, after Simone Warne called time on her marriage to Shane, Appleyard finally revealed that she had dumped Martyn because she had found intimate text messages on his phone from a 21-year-old South African woman. Unlike Simone, Helen did not hang around to give him a second, third and fourth chance. 'I'm surprised Simone Warne tolerated Shane's behaviour for so long', she told *New Idea*. 'For me, the moment I found out Damien was cheating I was out of there. I was heartbroken.'

What put Warne in a different league to most other sportsmen behaving badly was that he continued to do these things again and again, even when he was busted. That's what many people found so hard to figure out. A number of sportsmen I spoke to during the writing of this book admitted to envying Warne's ability to pull women and said they would do the same if they knew they would not get caught. None could work out why he cared so little about exposure. Why was he not more discreet, they asked? Why did he not get rid of his mobile? Why did he keep leaving a trail of evidence for the tabloids to follow? Why was he so stupid?

None of Warne's mates have the answer to these

questions. But most offer the opinion that he is dumb. Some also suggest he believes he is invisible, like he's swallowed a magic pill. He desperately wants to be the boy from Beaumaris, they say, just one of the lads. And he reckons the world should allow him to do that in peace. From there, perhaps, it is a short step to thinking he can do as he likes and no one will notice.

But when you look at the pattern of Warne's behaviour, it seems to be far more pathological, a genuine sickness. One top sports psychologist, who has worked with Australian rugby league's bad boys for many years, says, 'Shane obviously has self-destructive tendencies. In fact he seems to be on a mission to self-destruct, to destroy his marriage, his reputation, everything. He's not a complete dope, he's relatively articulate. He knows what he's doing. So why is he doing it?'

When asked this question by Jana Wendt in her *Bulletin* interview in early 2006, Warne replied: 'A lot of people don't understand. I don't understand . . . Maybe I need to see people about it.'

Simone clearly came to the same conclusion after leaving him, because she said as much to *New Idea* in July 2005: 'I just can't understand why anyone in a normal state of mind would behave like this. I'm not sure if it's a mental or physical problem, but I hope he gets help.'

An Australian team official who talked to Warne shortly after his marriage broke up also reached a similar verdict. 'He has all the right intentions. He loves his kids, he loves his family, he wants to do it right, but he just doesn't know how.'

One leading Australian sex therapist, Dr Janet Hall,

believes that Shane is simply addicted to sex, in that he clearly can't change his behaviour, however much damage he is doing to himself and others. 'He's in deep trouble', she concluded as the scandals became public. 'His marriage is over, his career is in doubt and he is making a public spectacle of himself, but it's like a game to him . . . He does not seem to want to change, and for that reason alone, I think it's unlikely that any sort of therapy will work.'

Luckily, he had another game to fall back on.

23

Simply the Best

I have a message for all you England supporters. Enjoy it while you can.

How would *you* feel at this point if you were Shane Warne? You have blown your marriage apart, your wife and kids have left you, divorce will cost millions and you have lost $400,000 worth of work. Most of all, you have been shamed on the front page of every newspaper in the cricketing world. Even the *Taipei Times* has been tracking your fall. And you are a man who longs to be loved. So would you be defeated, destroyed, in despair? Would you crawl into a hole to escape further public mockery? Would you give up and go home? Or would you carry on as if nothing had happened?

Throughout the 2005 Ashes series, people would ask, 'How does he do it? How can he play so well when he is under such pressure?' So we might as well deal with the question right from the start. And my guess is this: playing cricket is what Shane Warne lives for, what he does better than anything else in his life, and better than anyone else in the world. It is what people love him for, what even his fiercest critics are forced to admire. It is the stage on which he shines, on which he feels secure. So it is also his chance for redemption. Looking back over his career, the highest points have almost always followed his deepest lows, as if he needs to prove again that he can do it, that he is the best, that he deserves our love.

There is a less charitable explanation, which is that deep down he doesn't really care about his home life and his marriage to Simone, and that he is so utterly egotistical that the loss means much less to him than we think. Less than fame, less than cricket, less than the challenge of beating the Poms. Perhaps there is an element of truth in this. Or perhaps you can just call it focus. But at this point Shane seems to have been entirely focused on the job in hand.

He had played in Ashes series before and, like every Australian cricketer, thought them special. What made this the best was that everyone in England believed their team could win. Warne told readers of his *Times* column that he was amazed at how excited people were as the day grew closer. 'I cannot remember a series', he wrote, 'that has been so eagerly anticipated, even in India, where the passion for the game is almost indescribable.' But cricket fans everywhere were relishing the prospect, if only to see Australia get beaten at last. Naturally, Warne was determined he would not let that happen. 'I have never been on a side that has lost the Ashes and I will do everything in my power to keep the record that way.'

It promised to be a hell of a fight, all the same. Australia had struggled in the opening stages of the NatWest one-day series. They had eventually tied the final with England, but had taken a battering along the way, not least from Shane's peroxide pal, Kevin Pietersen, who had rescued England from a seemingly impossible position in the first game in Bristol. With 89 runs needed in 74 balls he had played with such power and aggression that he had knocked off the target with 15 balls to spare. If he was allowed to do the same thing in a Test match, Australia would certainly know it was in a contest.

In his regular *Times* column Warne had been busy telling English fans not to get too cocky about their team's chances, reminding them that Australia had won the World Cup in 1999 and triumphed in the 1997 Ashes series despite worse starts than this. And after Australia's first loss in the Twenty20 game against England, he had ribbed them with this offering:

SORRY, but I spent yesterday morning thinking that I'd missed something. Had England won the Ashes? That's the way it seemed with all the headlines in the papers and the gibes I was getting from cricket fans. I've hardly been able to stop at a traffic light without somebody winding down a window and shouting: '79 all out.' Well, I have a message for all you England supporters. Enjoy it while you can.

England's hard-core fans, the Barmy Army, didn't need reminding that it might all end in tears. Nor did they need any encouragement to have fun. They had earned their Barmy Army monicker by being mad enough to have supported England's cricketers through thick and thin since the early 1990s, and to have enjoyed themselves thoroughly despite constant defeats. The name had been coined by the Australian media back in 1994 as a grudgingly respectful description of a few hundred English supporters who spent that summer Down Under, watching their team get bashed by all and sundry. They were clearly barmy, because they kept on singing and cheering as England lost 3–1 to Australia in the Ashes, then to Zimbabwe and Australia 'A' in the one-day series, and finally to the young lads at the Australian Cricket Academy. And they were obviously an army, because they invaded every match en masse, chanting, waving and having a laugh. I vividly remember them celebrating at the Sydney Cricket Ground in January 1999, on one of many sad days for English cricket, and filling the air with the Barmy Army anthem.

> Everywhere we go-oh
> The people want to know-oh
> Who-ooh-ooh we are,
> And where we come from.
> Shall we tell them
> Whoooooooo we are
> And where we come from?
> We are the England, the mighty, mighty, England,
> We are the Army, the Barmy, Barmy Army!

Their song was followed by a huge roar and 10 minutes of rhythmic chanting, 'Barmy Army, Barmy Army, Barmy Army.' The poor Aussie fans couldn't get a look in. A few tried to hit back with a chorus of 'Aussie, Aussie, Aussie, Oi, Oi, Oi', but they were hopelessly outclassed, just like England's cricketers on the field. At the centre of the Barmy Army action that day was a middle-aged man with white-blond hair, known as Jimmy Savile, after the famous British DJ he was obviously impersonating. You will see him directing traffic at almost every England match, anywhere in the world, decked out in a tall, white top hat with three blue lions, waving a huge St George Cross flag with England written on it, and wearing a shiny red-and-white St George Cross vest.

Not all the soldiers were as daft as their general (real name Vic Flowers), but it helped to be cracked if you were laughing in the face of adversity, as English fans were constantly required to do. From the end of that Ashes tour in January 1995 to the end of 2000, England's cricketers played 29 away matches and won just six times. Yet the Barmy Army kept marching and singing, getting more pissed, more sunburnt and more cheerful as they travelled around the world. And come 2005 they were looking forward, with more hope than conviction, to a famous English victory.

Back in 1995, England's cricketing authorities had done everything in their power to keep the army quiet, warning that their 'repetitive noise and chanting would be unacceptable' at cricket grounds. Stewards at Test matches had confiscated their song sheets and even kidnapped an inflatable Mr Blobby. But now that the army had 32,000 official members it was no surprise the England and Wales Cricket Board had been forced to give in. For the 2005 Ashes series it had even agreed, for the first time, to allow block bookings of 2400 seats at the coming Tests, so they could sit and sing together. And after all the defeats they had seen England suffer, the army's loyal foot soldiers deserved this reward.

Only one ground had refused to agree to this proposal, and that was Lord's, the bastion of the Marylebone Cricket Club and self-styled 'home of cricket'. No doubt the MCC felt that to afford such louts more opportunities to misbehave would be an affront to the traditions of the game. And perhaps it was right. As one writer put it in London's *Daily Telegraph*, 'If there was one place you could escape vexatious people, tie a knotted hanky on your head and lose yourself in Beekeepers' Monthly, it was a cricket ground'. The army had changed all this for ever.

Not everyone loved the army, of course. Several English cricket writers thought them 'excruciatingly boring', 'charmless oiks', or 'some way below primates on the evolutionary scale'. Nor did Australian cricketers find their barracking amusing. Poor Stuart MacGill had been forced to put up with chants of 'Warney, Warney, Warney' every time he came on to bowl at the SCG in 2003 (when Warne was injured) and listen to a bastardised version of the old Liverpool soccer anthem, 'You'll Never Walk Alone' (with new words, 'You'll never play again'). But none had to put up with anything like the abuse that was rained on Shane Warne. And with his personal life spattered over England's tabloids, he was destined to cop more flak in 2005 than ever before. It has to be said Warne took it all with great good humour. 'I have a love-hate relationship with them', he told one talk-show host, 'I love them they hate me'. But he knew the army targeted him because he was so good. 'We respect him 100 per cent', the army's founder, Paul Burnham, explained. 'The real Barmy Army loves the guy to death. Otherwise they wouldn't sing about him so much. The day you stop getting sung about is the day you're not worth anything.'

A former baggage handler with British Airways, before quitting his job to follow England around the world, Burnham had seen Shane humiliate his team so many times that he knew he could sink England single-handed. 'When he comes up to bowl', Burnham said, 'It's "Oh shit, here comes Warney". You're watching a match thinking, "We've survived this Test so far, so not too bad", and then Warne takes his jumper off and gives his hat to the umpire and you're like, "Oh no, here we go"'.

But from where Warne stood on the field it must have been hard to hear this note of respect in the songs they sang. It was certainly not obvious in old favourites such as, 'You fat bastard you ate all the pies', nor in 'Ten men went to bed, went to bed with Shane Warne' (which ended in a chorus of 'Ten men, nine men, eight men, seven men, six men, five men, four men, three men, two men, one man and his sheep went to bed with Shane Warne'). Nor was it crystal clear in another favourite ditty, 'Shane Warne's Villa', which was sung to the tune of Tony Christie's 'Is This the Way to Amarillo?', but with somewhat sharper lyrics:

> Show me the way to Shane Warne's Villa
> He's got his diet pills under his pillow
> A dodgy bookie from Manila
> Nursey's on her mobile phone
>
> La-la lar la-la la-la lar, fat git!
> La-la lar la-la la-la lar, take a bung
> La-la lar la-la la-la lar,
> Warney where's your mobile phone?

The army's latest offering for 2005 was a fresh version of another singalong classic, 'Chirpy, Chirpy, Cheep, Cheep', entitled 'Where's Your Missus Gone?' To which the answer, of course, was 'far, far away'. All in all, given the pressure he was already under, the Barmy Army promised to test Warne's patience to the limit. Not to mention his powers of concentration. But he would have some relief in the First Test at Lord's, where they would be scattered around the ground. He would have time to acclimatise before they really got going.

To win that First Test, England would need to overturn 71 years of history. And it seemed bizarre that the England and Wales Cricket Board had chosen to load its team with such an obvious disadvantage, given its desperate desire to win. But perhaps the ECB had realised that Lord's was not Warne's favourite venue either. Indeed, it was one of the few big grounds in the world where he had never taken five wickets in an innings (and was not on the honours board – a matter that 'disappointed' him). As consolation, the MCC had just hung his picture in the famous Long Room, alongside two other legendary Australian cricketers, Keith Miller and Sir Donald Bradman, and all his team-mates would have to go past it every day as they made their way onto the pitch.

With just a few days to go to the first day's play, set down for Thursday 21 July, Warne was not bowling at his best. Nor were his figures that flash, and the usual band of former players and armchair critics was lining up to write him off, saying he was too old, too predictable and past his use-by date. Terry Jenner, who was in England trying to help the ECB discover new (English) Shane

Warnes, was itching to sort him out, as he had done so many times before. Three days before the game, he went looking for him at a big MCC dinner at Lord's and ran him down within minutes, having a ciggie in smokers' corner. Seeing his old friend, Warne immediately asked: 'What are you doing tomorrow?' to which Jenner replied, 'I was hoping you'd say that'. The next day they met in the nets for one of their longest sessions ever. Warne knew he needed a tune-up and Jenner soon saw what was wrong. 'He was bowling fast, flat, survival stuff', he says. 'He wasn't looping the ball, and he was trying to bowl leg breaks but they weren't spinning.'

The problem, Jenner reckoned, was that Shane had been sending down too many sliders on the damp pitches you find in England early in the season. These are defensive balls: designed to look like leg breaks to the batsman, but squeezed out of the front of the hand so they slide straight through. He was also bowling too much round his body and needed to get his arm higher. But Jenner soon had him sorted, and within a couple of hours he was looping the ball again and spinning it hard.

The England team was also busy sharpening its approach, though not with Merlyn, which was suffering technical failure. Captain Michael Vaughan and coach Duncan Fletcher had warned their charges that England had been bullied by Australia in the past, and that it must not happen again. So they were psyching themselves up for battle, talking about what they would do on the crucial first morning.

It was set to be 'one of the biggest cricketing days for years', Warne told his readers. And he was right. The match had been a sell-out for months, like every other game in the series. Lord's was filled to its 28,000 capacity. There had been a stampede for seats in the Members' Enclosure when the gates opened at 8.30 am. In the pavilion there was barely space to stand.

Under cloudy skies, Australian captain Ricky Ponting won the toss and chose to bat. As the England team filed out of their dressing-room to make their way down to the ground, they had to press through a guard of honour lining the stairs. Then, as they emerged from the Long Room into the Members' Enclosure, a huge roar went up. Even the members – normally so quiet and sedate – were cheering, clapping and shouting good luck. This was no more 'cricket' than the Barmy Army. It was more like a title fight.

After all the months of waiting, even the Lord's crowd was pumped up for battle. But it was nothing compared to the England team and its opening bowler, Steve Harmison, or 'Grievous Bodily Harmison', as *The Sun* now christened him. Steaming in at full speed, arms pumping, he unleashed a flood of pent-up aggression that shook Australia's openers. His first ball landed on a perfect length and flew over off stump. His second – at around 145 kilometres per hour – reared up off the pitch and cracked into Justin Langer just above his elbow. Australian physio Errol Alcott ran onto the field to inspect the damage, and play was held up for five minutes. Soon the TV cameras were homing in on an ugly golf-ball-sized lump. Yet there was no sign of Harmison saying sorry. The mild-mannered fast bowler later admitted he was trying to rough up his opponents, to set the tone for the series. 'One way to do that was to get them out; another was to scare them; and a third was to hit them', he said. As it turned out, he hit all of Australia's top three batsmen, hard. 'It was like Wild West cricket out there. There were bodies everywhere', he told Peter Hayter in the team's account of the series, *Ashes Victory*.

Matthew Hayden was next to take a hit, smacked on the helmet as he missed a pull shot. Then it was captain Ponting's turn, struck hard on the helmet's metal grille, which was crushed into his cheek by the force of the impact. There was blood everywhere. Again, a break in play was needed while the physio stitched him up. And again, not one of the English fielders came up to see if he was okay. Justin Langer, a decent, honest, straight-talking bloke, went over to his Middlesex team-mate Andrew Strauss to see what was going on. 'This really is war out here', said the Australian. 'You're not even going up and seeing if he is all right.' No one contradicted him, and no one moved. For now, this was how the battle was going to be fought.

Moments later, Harmison had Ponting caught at slip with a peach of a ball that leant away from off stump. And then the fruit came falling. By the time tea drew near, he had collected 5 for 43 and Australia was all out for 190. It was game on. The crowd couldn't believe it.

But coming into this series Glenn McGrath had been telling his team-mates he was bowling better than ever. And on this ground that was a frightening prospect. On his debut at Lord's in 1997 he had scythed through England's batting, taking a career-best 8 for 38. Four years later, he had followed it with eight wickets in the match. Now he conjured up another wicked spell. 'He was bowling like God', said Marcus Trescothick, who was his first victim, caught at slip, first ball after tea. Four balls later, his opening partner, Andrew Strauss, was trudging back to the pavilion, closely followed by England's captain, Michael Vaughan, new boy Ian Bell, and the out-of-form Freddie Flintoff. In the space of five devastatingly accurate overs, McGrath took five wickets for just two runs. In under an hour, half the England side, and almost its entire top order, was surgically removed for just 21 runs. It was a calamity, but a familiar one. By close of play England had collapsed to 7 for 92, and it was no consolation that 1997 had been worse. On that occasion, McGrath's eight-wicket massacre had knocked over the England team for 77 runs, their worst score at Lord's in more than 100 years.

Kevin Pietersen and Steve Harmison counterattacked briefly the next morning to get within 35 runs of the Australian total, but England was soon being whipped again. Australia batted sensibly and solidly, with a tremendous 91 from new boy Michael Clarke. And after missing half-a-dozen chances to get back in the match, England's batting again collapsed. The rain came down for most of Sunday – with more forecast for the final day – but even the weather wasn't enough to save them. England threw away their last four wickets in the hour of play squeezed between showers, and slid to a 239-run defeat. It was a good old-fashioned English capitulation, like so many others in Ashes history.

Glenn McGrath's 9 for 82 earned him man of the match and silenced those English critics who had dared to suggest that he was over the hill. Nor was anyone now accusing Warne of being fat, old and past it. He had taken six wickets and bowled beautifully, and according to Brett Lee, there was no one to touch him: 'Warne is the world's best. His persona and presence out there are fabulous. I definitely believe he is the best he has ever been: he gets better with age.' His only regret was that he still had not got his name on that honours board. But seeing his picture alongside the greats had been a thrill.

If England could dredge anything positive from this disaster – apart from their fast bowlers' hostility on that first morning – it was Kevin Pietersen's defiance. At the end of the first innings he had mounted a brutal assault on Warne's and McGrath's bowling, smashing 21 runs off just nine balls. One cross-batted swat for four to an excellent ball from McGrath was so audacious that even the bowler laughed. K. P. or 'the skunk' as he was now being called because of his black-and-white hair, had crashed another four and a huge straight six in the same over, before tonking Warne back over his head for a massive six into the second tier of the grandstand. He had winked at his Hampshire team-mate after doing that, and had received a pat on the back plus a 'Well batted' from Warne in return. But next ball, the crafty leg spinner had invited him to cash in again and had exacted revenge, having him caught brilliantly on the boundary, just short of the rope. 'You're always learning', Pietersen had commented afterwards with a smile, before going back to make 64 in his second dig, to add to the 57 made in the first.

That apart, there was really no cause for comfort. After

all the hope, hype and hot air, England had been blown away with the minimum of fuss. Their chances of winning the Ashes now looked slim. The last time they had come from behind to do so was in 1981, when Botham and Willis had stolen the match at Headingley. And those were surely once-in-a-lifetime heroics.

Not surprisingly, the Australians were cock-a-hoop. 'I wouldn't say we've destroyed their confidence with our performance at Lord's, but we've gone some way to doing that', Ponting told reporters, adding, 'We've got a very good chance of winning 5–0.' McGrath also predicted 5–0 and told the world, 'It doesn't matter what they [England] do. If we play our game well we'll win.' He even shed a tear for how one-sided the series had become. 'I think the most disappointing aspect of England's performance was their lack of resilience', he said sadly. 'The way the match finished when we picked up those wickets cheaply on the fourth day was a bit too easy, like the fight had gone.'

Only Warne was publicly cautious, telling his *Times* readers that it was now the Australians' turn not to get cocky. There was a lot more cricket to be played and England could only get better. Parroting his message to English supporters before the series began, he should perhaps have said to Australian fans: 'Enjoy it while you can.'

But after this defeat, how on earth could you think the result was in doubt? If England lost at Edgbaston, it would be all over bar the shouting. And the bookies were confident this would happen. You could get 4 to 1 against England winning the game and 10 to 1 against them regaining the Ashes, which Ponting reckoned was fair, because the difference between the two sides at Lord's was 'vast'.

Personally, I thought this offer too good to miss. In a two-horse race you only need one to fall. And, strangely enough, that was just about to happen. My only regret is that I didn't put the house on it.

24

Freddie, Freddie, Freddie

Well batted Freddie, well played, mate.

It may not have been the Ball of the Century, but it was arguably the ball of the series. Just one hour before the Second Test was due to start at Edgbaston, Australian fast bowler Glenn McGrath trod on a cricket ball that had been left on the playing field and twisted his ankle. He knew instantly he had done it some serious damage. 'It felt like the sole of my foot was pointing to the sky when I went down', he said afterwards. 'I realised before I hit the ground I was out of this Test match.'

It all happened so quickly. One moment he was turning to catch a football that was being thrown to him, the next he was on the grass writhing in pain. It was a freak accident, an extraordinary piece of bad luck and a terrible blow for Australia. But it was also a huge boost to England, because it levelled the contest in dramatic fashion. Not only had McGrath taken half England's wickets at Lord's, but he was easily Australia's most dangerous strike bowler. The last time he had missed an Ashes Test, at the SCG in 2003, Australia had crashed to a big defeat, and there was now every chance they would do so again. Brett Lee, Jason Gillespie and Michael Kasprowicz certainly held no horrors by comparison. As Geoff Boycott bluntly observed from the safety of the commentary box, the first lacked control, the second was a shadow of his former self, and the third was simply pedestrian. In his view, England had nothing to fear.

When news of McGrath's mishap reached the England dressing-room, there was no disguising the players' relief. Marcus Trescothick's instant reaction was, 'Crikey, this is going to make things a bit easier.' But in case the injury wasn't enough to tip the balance in England's favour, Ricky Ponting jumped onto the scales himself. Edgbaston was a flat track, so the captain who won the toss normally batted first, as Australia had done for years: bat first, build a big score, then let Warne loose on a wearing pitch. But Ponting had studied the stats, which revealed that the side batting first had won only one of the last 13 Tests here. So he told England to put their pads on. Back in the dressing-room, getting their second lucky break of the morning, the Poms were open-mouthed. 'If someone had offered us first use we would have bitten their arm off', said Trescothick.

Almost immediately, Ponting realised he would pay for his mistake, because it was clear there was no pace or venom in the pitch. The fourth ball of Lee's first over even bounced twice before reaching the keeper. Moments later, Trescothick made it clear how high the cost might be, thumping three fours off the same bowler with his favourite cover drive. Within an hour, he and Strauss had pushed the score past 60 and hit Australia's opening bowlers out of the attack. And when Warne came on he received even harsher punishment, getting hammered for 21 runs in his first three overs. Strauss was the first to take to him, dancing down the pitch and lofting the ball back over his head for four, a shot he had practised the previous day in the nets against Merlyn. Then Trescothick joined the party, hitting the leg spinner for six straight down the ground. By lunch, England had galloped to 132 for the loss of one wicket, with Trescothick taking 18 off Lee's last over.

In the Eric Hollies stand where the Barmy Army had its block booking, the fans must have been pinching themselves. This is what Australia normally did to England, rather than the other way around. Even though the match was just two hours old, the noise was already rising, the beer was flowing and 'Barmy Army' chants were echoing round the ground. As Trescothick and his captain, Michael Vaughan, led the way off the field, the sell-out crowd stood and applauded.

Could it last, though? Four years earlier against Australia on this same ground, England had gone from 1 for 106, just before lunch, to 9 for 191 by mid-afternoon and all out by tea. And soon after the break it seemed to be heading this way again, as the score collapsed from 1 for 164 to a sick-looking 4 for 187. It was now up to Pietersen to mount a rearguard action, with the help of Freddie Flintoff, who had managed just three runs in his two knocks at Lord's.

This partnership, too, was nearly over in a flash. Sizing up his fourth ball from Warne, Flintoff couldn't decide whether to go for it, and ended up chipping the ball weakly towards mid-off, where Kasprowicz was waiting. As the ball lobbed inches out of reach of the fielder's outstretched arm, Freddie kicked himself awake. After all the pep talks from his captain about taking the game to the Aussies, being aggressive and leaving nothing in the locker, his in-decision had nearly cost him his wicket. 'I decided from that point I wasn't going to die wondering', he said later. 'I had to be positive.' And with that, he launched into the sort of full-on attack for which he was renowned. A four off Warne to mid wicket was followed by a towering six over long on, which ended in the stands. He motored to his 50 in just 44 balls, and the 100 partnership with Pietersen arrived in just over an hour. It was short and violent, like a summer storm, and by the time the onslaught was over, the advantage was firmly back with England.

At tea, the score had nudged past 290 with just four wickets down. And when Flintoff was out shortly after-wards, Pietersen took up the cudgels, cracking Lee for three fours in his first over, then pulling him for six off the front foot, leaving the bowler open-mouthed. Every one of these shots was greeted with a roar from the crowd and an aerial leap from nine members of the Barmy Army, wearing white badger stripes in their hair and T-shirts bearing one letter apiece, which read P – I – E – T – E – R – S – E – N.

Even when he holed out in the deep after a whirlwind 78, the runs kept coming apace. By the close of play, England had amassed a score of 407 at more than five runs an over. It was an amazing total in such a short time, the best in a day from England for 60 years, but the Australians were relieved it had not been worse. With a bit more application and a little less haste, England might well have piled on 550 runs and batted Australia out of the game. As it was, Ponting's men came off the field looking shell-shocked, but knowing they had every chance of catching their opponents if they batted well.

Next morning, Australia also set off at breakneck speed, with Ponting crashing 61 off his first 67 balls. But just as the doomsayers in Channel 4's commentary team were predicting a huge Australian total, England's answer to Shane Warne surprised everyone by taking a wicket. Coming into this match, Ashley Giles had been ridiculed as a waste of space by two former Test cricketers. Ex-Zimbabwe captain Dave Houghton had said it was like having 10 men against 11 with him in the side, while ex-Australian fast bowler Terry Alderman had suggested that anyone who got out to Giles should go home and hang himself. So it was fitting that he should make the break-through, getting Ponting caught off a top edge as he tried to sweep.

Giles was certainly not in Shane Warne's class, but he was the first to admit it. You could see from the super slo-mo shots that he barely spun the ball as it flew through the air, and he didn't frighten batsmen the way Warne did. Nor were his figures remotely as good: he had taken one-quarter of the wickets at half the strike rate and roughly twice the cost. But on this day, on his home ground, it all came right. Having removed Ponting, he also got rid of Michael Clarke, who was looking dangerous. And finally, he bowled the great leg spinner himself, who jigged down the pitch to slog him for six and missed.

The other Australian batsmen fell slowly but steadily to some magnificent reverse swing from Flintoff and Jones, and (in Damien Martyn's case) a superb piece of fielding by Michael Vaughan. By late on the second day, they were all out, leaving England 99 runs ahead.

With just 35 minutes left to stumps, Trescothick and Strauss now got stuck into the fast bowlers for the second time in 36 hours and seemed to be cruising. Then Warne bobbed up for the last over of the day and wove a little piece of his magic. He too was on 99, one short of his 100th Test wicket in England, and bowling to Strauss, whom he had already fooled in the first innings with a huge-spinning leg break that the opener had tried to cut. He spent an age with Ponting discussing the field placings, to ramp up the tension, then crowded the batsman with a ring of close fielders – two slips, a silly point, a leg gully and a short fine leg – to further play on his nerves. Finally he ran in to bowl and produced the exact same ball that had flummoxed the left-hander the day before, fizzing out of the bowlers' footmarks, wide outside stump. This time, Strauss opted to play safe and block it with his pads, but once again the spin deceived him. It was another one of those can't-believe-it balls, spinning two feet across his body to demolish leg stump. All he could do was stand there and stare at the mess, just as Mike Gatting had done more than a decade earlier, wondering what on earth had gone wrong.

Warne had been taunting the England opener on and off the field by calling him Daryll, after his famous bunny, Daryll Cullinan. And now, as he walked back to the pavilion, Strauss wondered if Shane might be right. He was also trying to figure out why his long sessions with Merlyn hadn't protected him better. Strauss had clocked up more hours than anyone with the mechanical wizard, but had assumed Warne would bowl over the wicket, rather than round, so he had got his angles wrong. Shane, however, believed he was just wasting his time, because the machine could never match him. 'I reckon I've found a new buddy', he bragged to his *Times* readers. 'Good on you, Merlyn – judging by some of the results, you're on my side.'

Next morning was Saturday, fancy dress day for the Barmy Army, and they did themselves proud. There were a dozen Queens, complete with crowns, rubber faces, false bosoms and brightly coloured dresses. There were also convicts, Frenchmen in black berets, several clones of English cricket icon W. G. Grace, and a colony of rabbits in blue bunny suits, not to mention a bevy of surgeons in full operating-theatre garb. But the wackiest and weirdest prize went to a dozen policemen and prison guards from Wolverhampton who came dressed from head-to-toe in pink shiny stuff, masquerading as Whoopee Cushions. God knows what relevance it had to cricket or anything else, especially since they lacked the sound effects that would have made sense of it all. But they won the prize all the same.

With England effectively 1 for 124, the loyal fans were confident their team would crack on to a big lead, even if Warne was at his best. But Brett Lee was soon knocking the stuffing out of their costumes. In his second over he had Trescothick caught behind, slashing outside the off stump, to make it 2 for 27. Three balls later he bowled

Vaughan with a scorcher that beat him all ends up, to make it 3 for 29. And seven balls after that he put paid to nightwatchman Hoggard, to make it 4 for 31. In came Pietersen again, hero of Lord's, with yet another rescue needed. His first ball from Lee got the faintest touch on his glove, which was pouched by Gilchrist down the leg side. The Australians erupted – huge shouts, arms in the air, celebrations at the ready – only to find that umpire Billy Bowden either hadn't heard the noise or believed the ball had hit his arm. It could have been 5 for 31, but it was not.

Soon Pietersen was taking advantage of this let-off by wreaking havoc again. He hoisted his second ball from Warne over mid wicket for six with an extraordinary scooping shot that suggested a talent for the Spanish ball game pelota. Three balls later he took a big step forward and hoiked one from outside off stump for a more orthodox six over long on. Shortly after, his Hampshire team-mate, Warne, took revenge. Fencing at a ball outside his leg stump, Pietersen was caught by Gilchrist, one-handed low to the ground, and given out. This time, the replays suggested the ball had hit his thigh, chest and elbow, rather than his bat or glove, but it was payback for his earlier reprieve. Two minutes later, Bell got the faintest of touches to a ball that spun past his forward defensive shot, and England was six wickets down with a lead of just 174. Now it was up to Flintoff to do something to keep the match and the series alive. As he had done so often before, Warne was threatening to tear England's innings apart.

And there was more drama to come. England's

would-be saviour had been in 10 minutes when he tried to force the leg spinner through the covers and sank to the ground clutching his left shoulder, obviously in pain. The England team physio, Kirk Russell, rushed onto the pitch to see how bad it was, and an agonising wait followed while he manipulated the arm to see if the shoulder had popped out of its socket. From the stands, it looked bad for Flintoff and worse for England. If he could not continue, the fans might as well pack up and go home. The Aussies could start on their lap of honour. And even if he struggled on, the chances of him working a miracle now seemed slim indeed. But struggle on he did. For the next hour he prodded and steered the ball for a few singles, sometimes with only one hand on the bat. At lunch he was still there, by which time England had limped to 6 for 95.

With another 50 runs they might well be in with a shout, but could they get them? In the first over after lunch, Lee removed Geraint Jones, last of the recognised batsmen, with a brutal delivery that reared up, caught the splice and flew to second slip, to make it 7 for 101. Then Ashley Giles hung around for 45 vital minutes while the score ticked on to 7 for 131. But at this point, Warne made a double strike, bowling a beauty to Giles that he nicked to Hayden at slip, and trapping Harmison next ball for a golden duck. He was now on the way to a hat-trick – which would be only the second in his life – and surely thinking of the first time he had achieved it. Eleven years earlier, at the MCG, he had skittled three Poms in a row, with England's number 11 his third victim. But this time it was not to be: the hat-trick ball was so wide that

Simon Jones was able to watch it through to the keeper. Next ball he creamed Warne through the covers for four. And then the jolly giant roused himself into action.

Flintoff had popped a few painkillers in the lunch break and been told his shoulder was okay, and he now decided it was time to have a thrash. He swung wildly at the first ball of the next over from Kasprowicz, missing it completely. The next he carted for six over mid wicket, and two balls later he did it again with an even bigger hit. Then a single gave the strike to Jones, who drove the fast bowler for four. Poor Kasper was so unsettled by this onslaught that he prolonged the agony by bowling three no-balls and eventually conceded 20 runs off the over. Lee then replaced him and fared no better. With all nine fielders hugging the boundary rope, Flintoff simply thumped it over their heads. His first six cleared the crowd, sailed over the pavilion roof at long on and came to rest on the gantry holding the TV cameras. He followed this with a savage cut for four, which the diving Clarke could not stop, and another big six that just cleared the long-on rope. Inevitably, it was Warne who brought this madness to an end, bowling him as he tried to slog another six over the mid-wicket boundary. But by this time, Flintoff had long passed Botham's record of six sixes in an Ashes match and put England firmly back in charge. He and Jones had scored 51 runs off 49 balls since the last wicket had fallen, of which Flintoff had accounted for 39. As he headed back to the pavilion to a riotous reception from the crowd, Shane shouted after him several times, 'Well batted Freddie, well played mate', finally getting his message heard above the din.

But if Flintoff had saved England from almost certain defeat, Warne had given Australia a sporting chance of victory. He had bowled unchanged throughout the last two sessions and taken six English wickets at the cost of only two runs an over. Bowling from round the wicket into the rough, he had even stopped Freddie attacking. Indeed, until that last flurry against the fast bowlers, he had looked like stealing the match for Australia.

It was now teatime on the third day, and one thing was obvious: this game was not going to end in a draw. There were two whole days left for Australia to make 282 runs – which would be easily the highest-ever successful run chase on this ground – or for England to get 10 wickets, and there was not a drop of rain in sight. So, once again, battle resumed, and once again the openers got off to a good start, with Langer and Hayden coasting along to 47 for no wicket at four runs an over, without looking troubled. Harmison and Hoggard did not look like getting a wicket. Nor did Giles. Only Flintoff and Jones had not yet been tried.

It was only an hour since Freddie's heroics with the bat had ended and perhaps three hours since he had clutched his shoulder in pain. So there were obviously some doubts about whether he would be up to bowling at speed. These were instantly dispelled. On a hat-trick from the first innings, after trapping Gillespie and Kasprowicz with two vicious inswinging yorkers, he steamed in at full tilt to Justin Langer and bowled him second ball. It was a beauty, angled in to the batsman from round the wicket on a perfect length, though lucky to cannon off his elbow onto the stumps. Flintoff leapt into the air and the crowd erupted. Suddenly, everyone was on their feet, waving flags, clapping, cheering, chanting, 'Freddie, Freddie, Freddie.' The Barmy Army bugler struck up the *Flintstones* theme. The game had sprung to life.

Ricky Ponting was next man in, looking for a big score. His first ball from Flintoff was a corker. Fast and bang on a length, it jagged back sharply from outside off stump and hit him on the pads, plumb in front. Again, there was a huge roar from the crowd and a loud appeal from Flintoff, but it was 'Not out': just too high. Watching from their dressing-room the Australians must have shifted uncomfortably. Ponting had barely had time to see the ball, let alone get his bat on it. And now, as Flintoff steamed in again, the crowd got behind him, with a roar that built to a crescendo as he released another 145 kilometre-per-hour rocket that Ponting managed to parry. A grin on his face, Flintoff walked back to his mark and charged in again, with an even bigger roar from the crowd as he struck Ponting on the pad for a second time. Another huge shout from Flintoff, again 'Not out', and a huge sigh from the crowd. Only one more ball to survive. Again the charge, again the roar and now Flintoff drew Ponting forward into a defensive prod which just clipped the ball as it nipped away this time and flew high to the keeper, Geraint Jones, who was smiling even before he took the easy catch. It was a magnificent ball and a magnificent over. But what made it so memorable was the context and the atmosphere. Planting his feet a metre apart, Flintoff threw his arms wide, tilted his head back and hollered to the sky, as a bunch of England players launched themselves onto his massive frame.

There were moments in the next two hours when Australia looked comfortable again, particularly when Damien Martyn was batting, but wickets continued to fall steadily. And when Flintoff trapped Gillespie l.b.w. for the second time in the match, it was 7 for 137 and Australia appeared to be on the verge of defeat. With 145 runs still to go to victory, England needed just three wickets to wrap it up. Now it really was a formality, or so it appeared. So Vaughan asked the umpires for an extra half hour's play to finish it off.

But it's never over till it's over, as England would learn repeatedly in this series. And Shane Warne loves a crisis, as he would show so many times. Arriving at the crease to join Australia's last specialist batsman, Michael Clarke, he advised the 24-year-old to have some fun and enjoy himself, which is always a good motto in these situations. The pair of them then set about doing exactly that. Warne, in particular, looked in ominous form, sweeping Giles for two sixes over square leg and moving across his wicket to glance Harmison's yorker down to fine leg for four. Clarke was also looking dangerous, and he undoubtedly had the talent to steer Australia to victory. He had burst onto the Test scene 10 months earlier, with 151 on his debut against India, and followed that with 141 in his first Test on Australian soil. He had also scored three centuries for Hampshire in 2004. And for once, he was playing sensibly and not taking too many risks.

As close of play drew near, he and Shane had narrowed the gap by almost 40 runs, to leave Australia only 107 short of a famous win. But Harmison summoned up the rage he had shown at Lord's for the final over of the day. His first ball had Clarke playing and missing; his second reared up at the batsman's face, caught the shoulder of the bat and dropped just short of gully; his fourth also climbed steeply and cracked the Australian on the hand. Finally, having softened him up, Harmison fooled the batsman with a perfect slower ball, at two-thirds normal pace, which Clarke played all around as it crashed into his stumps. It was a brilliant piece of bowling and a surprise to all, because Harmison was not known for his subtlety.

Next morning was Sunday and there was another full house, even though it was expected to be all over very quickly. Touts outside the ground were getting £100 a ticket, so desperate were England's fans to see their team win at last. Inside, there was a carnival atmosphere again, with another parade of outlandish costumes. There were cowboys and Indians, masked superheroes, and a bus-load of pretend Portuguese cricketers with false black moustaches. Lady Godiva was also there for the finale, with three heavily padded imitators of the ample English umpire David Shepherd. Not to be outdone, Australia's travelling supporters, the Fanatics, were also out in force, warming up with a chorus of, 'One hundred and seven to go, one hundred and seven to go, hi-ho the dairy-oh, one hundred and seven to go'. It promised to be a wonderful morning. And at this stage it was simply fun: the Australians didn't expect to win, the English were sure of victory. It was not even tense.

TV and radio commentators have to make it seem like a contest, though, so we were all reminded that Warne had scored two centuries for Hampshire this season, one of them off only 78 balls. And Lee, we were told, could also bat. But with only two wickets to fall and 107 to get, it was surely academic. Except that, once again, no one seemed to have explained this to Warne and Lee, who started swinging and scoring as if they meant to win the match. Maybe all Shane's mates at Mentone had been right to judge him a better batsman than bowler, because he looked in no trouble at all. True, England was not bowling well, but he was cutting the short ones (of which there were plenty) and moving across to the full-length balls to paddle them down to fine leg. After nine overs he and Lee had knocked 38 runs off the target and England supporters were beginning to think it was time to stop. Then, having looked like he might steal the match all over again, Warne stepped back and across to another Flintoff yorker, lost his balance and trod on his off stump. He departed, head down, to the relief of England fans and a rousing chorus of 'Where's your missus gone?' He deserved much better.

Yet if the game was almost certainly now lost, even Australian fans could console themselves with the thought that an English victory would keep the series alive. And they could also thank providence that it was Michael Kasprowicz, not Glenn McGrath, one of the world's worst batsmen, who was walking out to the wicket.

So once again, the crowd sat down to wait for the end – one wicket to get and 62 runs needed – and still it didn't happen, despite some extremely hostile bowling from Flintoff. In one over from the paceman, Lee was struck hard on the tip of his elbow, then caught behind off his thigh pad. Moments later, there was a huge shout for l.b.w. against Kasprowicz, which looked out. But the

Australians survived the storm and hit back, taking 13
runs off an over from Giles, with Lee hitting two sumptu-
ous lofted fours down the ground and Kasprowicz adding
another almost as good. Now England began to look
ragged and the runs started flowing again. The fast
bowlers had been bowling too short all morning; now
they also bowled wide, with Harmison giving away four
byes down leg side to reduce the target to 20.

Then came a moment when England should have won
the match. Kaprowicz played a deliberate upper cut
over the slips, and the ball hung in the air as it went to
Simon Jones at third man. This was more than a chance.
This was all England needed. Surely he was going to catch
it? But the fielder hesitated, misjudged it, dived too late
and failed to hold on. Several England players thought
what the crowd was thinking: their team-mate had just
dropped the match, not to mention the Ashes and
England's cricket revival. Next ball, Flintoff sprayed one
wide and full down the leg side for four byes, and three
more off the over knocked the target down to six, which
was being counted down in huge numbers on the big
electronic screen.

English fans were now sitting with their heads in their
hands or between their knees. The Fanatics were on
their feet, clapping and singing. You could see who
was winning just by looking at the crowd. Around the
ground, the terrible truth was dawning on England
supporters that their team had blown it. How could they
lose after having the match sewn up like that? But how
typical, all the same. You could almost hear the sound of
wrists being slit. England's players looked tired and

beaten, knowing a loss would never be forgiven, that the press would crucify them. It was too awful to contemplate.

Two tight overs followed from Harmison and Flintoff, yielding only one run apiece. Then Harmison ran in again, with just four runs needed to win. One shot would do the trick, and a wide full toss to Lee offered the perfect opportunity, but he could only steer it to cover for a single. Now it was Kasprowicz who had a chance to make a name for himself, one nick through the slips or one glance down to fine leg. And sadly he did, but not as he planned. It was a brute of a ball from Harmison that reared up off a length towards his rib cage. Kasprowicz ducked his head and twisted his body out of the way, but left his bat and gloves behind. The ball hit a glove and looped in the air to Jones the wicket-keeper, who was already moving fast to his left, and now dived, rolled and came up, grasping a catch he would never forget. By the time Billy Bowden had his finger up, the England players had converged to bury keeper and bowler in a jumping, bouncing embrace.

Away from the main scrum, Michael Vaughan was running in a wide circle, like a kid playing aeroplanes, arms out, head back, banking into the turn as he made for Freddie Flintoff, the man whose brilliance had undoubtedly won the match. The big Lancashire lad grabbed his captain by the legs and hoisted him into the air, while Vaughan held him by the ears, wondering whether to give him a kiss.

Back on the pitch, Kasprowicz and Lee both sank to their knees, alone in their misery, shattered at having come so close. Lee's innings in particular had been brave and brilliant. He had stood up to everything that England's fast bowlers could throw at him and taken some fearful punishment, not least from Flintoff, who now ran over to comfort and commiserate. Soon afterwards, several other England players were lining up to shake his hand and praise him for his efforts. It was a wonderful end to a wonderful match, perhaps the best ever – unless you were Australian – and played in the best spirit. None could remember a game that had swung so dramatically or been played at such a pace.

In the stands, the crowd was now on its feet, cheering, dancing, chanting, delirious that England had got out of jail. Only the Fanatics in their block of green and gold now looked glum. Who could blame them? Moments earlier, the match had been theirs. And replays suggested it should have stayed that way, because Kasprowicz's hand had not been touching the bat when the ball had hit. But all that was ancient history. It was far too late to rewind. Thank God it was – for the sake of cricket fans and TV networks everywhere – because the contest was now alive again. Everything was still to play for.

As the crowds departed, Shane Warne led a few of the Aussie players across to the England dressing-room to congratulate the victors and sink a few beers, and eventually both teams ended up there, chewing the fat, proud to have been a part of an incredible game, one they would never forget.

25

Shane, Shane, Shane

There is no such thing as a lost cause for us . . . we are not going to admit defeat until the last wicket falls or the last run is scored.

Old Trafford was where Warne's amazing career took off with THAT BALL to Gatting in 1993. And all the hype in advance was that he would destroy England again. He was also certain to pass another important milestone.

Shane's 10 scalps at Edgbaston had left him on 599 Test wickets, and it did not take him long on the first day to get his 600th: Trescothick caught by Gilchrist as he tried to sweep. The 21,000-strong capacity crowd gave him a standing ovation as he stood there, a happy smile on his face, holding the ball aloft and spinning through 360 degrees to salute the fans. As a section of the Barmy Army launched into a chorus of 'We wish you were English', he pointed to a small white band on his wrist and kissed it for the cameras. 'It is pretty emotional for me', he said afterwards.

When Simone and the children went home, Brooke gave me the wristband and said, 'You've got to be strong, Daddy.' It just says 'Strength' on it . . . I spoke to all of the three kids this morning and Brooke said, 'I like your white wristband, Daddy', and I said, 'Well if it happens today, it's for you, Jackson and Summer.'

England had won the toss and elected to bat, not wanting to face Warne on the last day on a wearing pitch. But Old Trafford did not prove to be its usual spinner's paradise. Nor did Warne loom as Shane the Destroyer. And again it was the Australians who were under the gun as England posted another big score of 444. The key to this was a wonderful 166 from their captain, Michael Vaughan – the first century from anyone in this series – and a cluster of dropped catches.

Australia's fielding was like England at its worst. And seeing the batsmen then punish the opposing team by thrashing the bowlers all round the ground was also horribly familiar to English fans. But for once it was the Australians paying for their mistakes. By the time Trescothick fell to Warne for 63, an hour after lunch, England had sailed merrily along to 1 for 163. And two hours later, when Vaughan was the next to go, another 127 had been added and the game was almost out of Australia's reach. A couple of dismissals late in the day helped even things up. Then Flintoff and Jones pushed on next morning to take the score to 6 for 433 before Warne removed England's new 'Mr Incredible', and the rest went quietly.

The big surprise of the English innings was that

McGrath took no wickets – since he was the other man England feared – but it was an even bigger shock that he was playing at all. He had torn two ligaments in his fall at Edgbaston, and feared the injury might keep him out of the series. Yet he came through a fitness test on the morning of the match, to his team-mates' obvious relief. Whether he was really 100 per cent was doubtful, because he was not as sharp as usual. But Lee and Warne both bowled well and picked up four wickets apiece.

So, once again, the Australians found themselves chasing a big total and struggling to stay in the match. And despite a good start, it soon went pear-shaped, as Giles again made the crucial breakthrough. First, he had Justin Langer caught at short leg, trying to muscle him through the leg side; then he had Matthew Hayden l.b.w. to one that trapped him on the crease. Finally, he got Damien Martyn with an absolute beauty – one of the best balls he'll ever bowl – which spun so much even Shane would have been proud of it.

When Warne came out to bat at 5 for 129, there was the real possibility that Australia would be forced to follow on for the first time in almost two decades. Yet he set about the bowling as if he were playing village cricket or with his mates down at the beach – slashing, hooking and cutting the ball for a succession of boundaries. And he was still there enjoying himself when play ended for the day, with Australia in serious strife on 7 for 214. Watching back in Melbourne, his Mentone mates would have been proud of him.

The next morning, the rain came, as it does in Manchester, where even in summer you need a raincoat one day in three, so play started at 4.10 pm. And even though Australia still needed 31 to avoid batting again, Warne was again in slog mode, and he was lucky not to be out twice: first, to an easy stumping off Giles, then to an even easier catch off the same bowler, which keeper Geraint Jones put down. Yet he kept on belting the ball regardless and saved the follow-on. He was finally out on Sunday morning for a swashbuckling 90 (including 11 fours and a six), chancing his arm once too often, and Australia's innings finished soon afterwards on 302.

England now had a sizeable lead of 142, but with less than two days to play, it was doubtful there was time to force a victory. Losing most of Saturday had given Australia a chance of survival, or even of victory. But for once, things went smoothly, with England cruising to 6 for 280 declared, thanks to a fine century from Strauss, who thumped Warne for six to get into the 90s, then cracked McGrath for four to bring up his 100. Warne went over to shake his hand and congratulate him, which was the least he could do after all his taunting. But a few days later, the leg spinner was still boasting to *Times* readers that Strauss was his new bunny.

No advance tickets had been sold for the last day of the match, presumably on the basis that the game might be over, so there was a mad rush to get into the ground next morning. Hundreds queued on the pavement overnight, and by dawn thousands more had joined them, hoping to see another English victory. But by 8.40 am, all the seats were sold and the gates had to be closed. According to police, some 20,000 people were turned away or stopped at tram stops and bus stations in the city before they could start their journey. Cricket in England had never seen anything like it.

No one had ever chased more than 418 runs to win a Test match, so if Australia succeeded in getting the 423 they needed, it would be a new world record. A more realistic task was to bat out the day for a draw. And even this began to look difficult when Justin Langer departed to the very first ball of the day, which he nicked to the keeper as it shimmied away off a perfect length. At lunch it was 2 for 121, with all results still possible, and then it began to unravel. First, Martyn was sent packing with a poor l.b.w. decision, then the left-handers, Katich and Gilchrist, were again mesmerised by Flintoff, to bring the score to 5 for 182, with 50 overs still to survive. So far it was all going well for England, who seemed set for their second successive victory.

This left England with a sizable lead of 142, but the good news for Australia was that Ponting was looking rock solid and capable of anything – pulling, hooking and driving towards a captain's century. And Michael Clarke was also in form. Together, they rattled the score along to 5 for 263 before England made a dramatic double strike. First, Jones bowled Clarke with a magnificent inswinger that had him shouldering arms as his stumps were demolished; then Hoggard trapped Gillespie l.b.w., for the fifth time in the series. This left Australia in dire straits at 7 for 264, with 31 overs still to go. So once again, Warne came out to the crease to help save Australia from defeat. This time, he was more careful than usual, but again he needed some luck. With 17 overs left, he was dropped by Pietersen at short mid wicket, which should have made it

SPUN OUT

8 for 313 and England's match. Instead, he stood firm for
another seven vital overs before he was finally dismissed by
Flintoff with another catch that nearly went down. This
time Strauss cupped his hands to receive the ball, missed
completely, and watched as it ricocheted off his leg past
Geraint Jones, who jackknifed brilliantly to grab it at full
stretch.

Now it was 'game on' again: two wickets to fall, 10
overs to go, with only the tail to keep the Poms at bay. In
the stands, the Barmy Army were trying to cheer and
chant their team to victory, but the minutes ticked by,
Brett Lee rode his luck and the bowlers could do nothing.
Then, with the game almost saved, the Australian captain
swished at a Harmison bouncer (in an apparent attempt
to keep the strike) and feathered a catch down the leg
side to Jones. As the England players celebrated, he stayed
rooted to the spot, staring at the ground – angry,
despondent, appalled. After an amazing rearguard action
in which he had batted almost seven hours for a chance-
less 156, Ponting had thrown it all to the wind, or as he
later described it, 'cocked it up'. It was now 9 for 354,
with four overs still to go, and the crowd was going wild.
Maybe, maybe, maybe, they would see another last-ditch
victory. Like Edgbaston, it was going right down to the
wire.

The man now walking to the wicket to save Australia,
Glenn McGrath, had once been advised by Steve Waugh
to consider batting left-handed to improve his form.
During his 12 years in the team, he had made the number
11 spot his own, clocked up more ducks than anyone in
Test history apart from Courtney Walsh, and averaged

just seven runs per innings. Yet what he lacked in batting skill he made up for in self-belief and determination. As he marched out to possible execution, he was probably more confident than he was entitled to be. Especially since there were nine men clustered around the bat. But it was Lee to face first, with five slips, two gullies, a short leg and a short cover, waiting for a tickle. All Glenn had to do was watch as three perfect leg cutters from Flintoff whistled past his team-mate's bat at 145 kilometres per hour, without quite catching the edge. One loud appeal was rightly turned down. The other close shaves just produced oohs and aahs from the crowd.

Then it was McGrath's turn to repel the enemy, jabbing his bat down on a succession of attempted yorkers from Harmison, and watching the short ones as they rocketed through to the keeper.

Games at this level (and at this juncture) are about nerve and guts as much as technique, but they're also about luck and fine margins. Now, after beating Lee with three outswingers, Flintoff produced a ball that angled back into his stumps and smacked him on the pad. There was no doubt it would have made a mess of his wicket, but the l.b.w. law says the batsman is not out (if he's playing a shot) unless the ball hits the pad inside the line of the stumps. And this may (or may not) have been a few millimetres outside. In any case, umpire Billy Bowden decided not to send Lee on his way, so Australia survived. And that was pretty much it. Glenn justified his self-confidence by surviving a few more balls from Harmison, then pinched a single and let Lee take the glory. As the latter raised his arm in triumph, the Australian team members leapt from their seats on the dressing-room balcony, as if they had just won the World Cup final.

It was now England's turn to look glum and defeated. This was the best they had played so far, and undoubtedly a moral victory. But the score was still 1–1. And they were left with the fear that this Australian side was impossible to kill. There was also the danger that their chance might be gone; that Australia would play much better and coast to victory. This is what McGrath and his mates were soon shouting from the rooftops, and also what the bookies believed. Even after this performance, you could still back England at 4 to 1 to win the Ashes – odds that I found too good to resist.

However, Warne now seemed less sure that Australia would triumph. Instead of predicting England would lose because they weren't good enough, he was now telling his *Times* readers the Poms would struggle to get the victory needed to bring the Ashes home. 'The pressure is on England, not us', he assured them.

> Somewhere, they have to beat us . . . they could not bowl us out on the final day at Old Trafford and only just managed to get over the line at Edgbaston. They know, and we know, that we can do better. We have also shown that we will fight from whatever position. There is no such thing as a lost cause for us . . . we are not going to admit defeat until the last wicket falls or the last run is scored.

Watching from back home, it was clear to most people that Warne himself was the main obstacle to an England win, unless the rest of the Australian team suddenly sharpened up its act. And this was hard for some to swallow. Six weeks earlier, they had consigned Shane to the dust heap of history – or the sin-bin in the sky – for being a serial adulterer and an incorrigible idiot. Now he was carrying the hopes of a nation, so a process of rehabilitation and forgiveness began. He might be a chump, it was argued, but you had to admit he was also a genius. So perhaps all that off-field stuff didn't really matter? Writing in *The Australian*, cricket correspondent Peter Lalor summed up the confusion: 'He could be canonised, or fired from one. Both acts would be similarly legitimate.' But this was progress. Six weeks earlier, there had been no question of sainthood. Shane was simply a sinner.

In England, cricket had now knocked football off the front pages, even though the Premier League had kicked off again. And the Fourth Test at Trent Bridge ensured that it stayed there. Once again, Australia lost Glenn McGrath to injury – this time to his elbow – and once again, Ricky Ponting lost the toss, so England opted to bat.

Watching it back on the highlights, you have to wonder whether you're looking at the right DVD, because Ponting keeps calling 'Heads', the coin keeps coming down tails and Vaughan says exactly the same thing every time it happens: 'We're going to bat . . . put some runs on the board . . . put pressure on the Australians.' And sure enough, that's what ensues.

Once again, Trescothick and Strauss made it look easy, cruising to a 100 partnership at five an over, before rain forced England off the field at 1 for 129 with Vaughan and Trescothick in full flow. When play resumed after the break it was all a bit harder. For a brief moment on the second morning, with the score at 5 for 241, it even looked like Australia might peg England back. Then a commanding century from Flintoff and a 177-run stand with Geraint Jones put paid to that hope. By teatime on the second day, England had racked up 477 runs for its biggest total so far.

Trent Bridge is on the river and the damp atmosphere helps swing bowlers, while there's shine on the ball. And Australia was soon in deep trouble, with three wickets in quick succession, all l.b.w., to late-swinging balls. Hayden and Martyn fell to Hoggard, and Ponting to Simon Jones, to make it 3 for 22. By the end of the day, England was in total control, with Australia reeling at 5 for 99, still 378 runs behind. The next day, the tailenders managed to push the score on to 218, thanks to another fantastic knock from Brett Lee, who scored 47 in 44 balls. But it was not enough the avert the follow-on. For the first time in 17 years and 191 Test matches, Australia was forced to trudge out to the middle and start batting again.

Then came a tremendous fight-back, in which Langer, Clarke and Katich all scored 50s, Ponting and Warne got close, and everyone except debutant Shaun Tait got into double figures. Once again, Shane played a vital role in getting Australia back into the match. He arrived with six wickets down and his team only 18 runs ahead of England, to smash 45 runs off 42 balls in another dazzling display, dancing down the pitch to hit Giles for two sixes and a four, and cutting, driving and pulling the fast bowlers for boundaries. And once again, he fell to Giles, trying once too often to cart him into the stands. But by then, Australia was well on its way to a fighting 387, which left England just 129 to win.

Given that it had made nearly 500 in its first innings and that Australia had reached close to 400 in its second, this was not a demanding target. And at 0 for 32, with Warne yet to bowl, it seemed a simple task. But if there was one man in this series who could turn a game on its head, it was Shane Keith Warne, saint and sinner, genius and fool. His first ball trapped Trescothick, caught at silly mid-off. Next over he removed England's captain with a ball that was as good as any he has bowled, drifting into the legs, spitting across the body and catching the edge of Vaughan's bat on its way to the slips. Twenty minutes later, he removed Strauss with almost an identical ball, which the left-hander nicked to short leg as it spun across him. And England was suddenly 3 for 57.

Warne seemed to be bent on winning the Ashes single-handed. He was appealing as if his life were at stake. Loudly, urgently, aggressively, desperately, determined to get the answer he wanted. When he wasn't bowling, he was standing at first slip, talking, moving, willing the ball to fly to him, apparently convinced it was just about to happen and the match was about to turn. And perhaps it was, because England's batsmen were so shaken by his three quick strikes that they began to lose the plot. First, Bell threw his wicket away to make it 4 for 57, hooking violently at a head-high bouncer from Lee. Then Pietersen did his best to get himself out heaving at Warne, before he and Flintoff briefly restored sanity and took the score past

100. Whereupon, things got interesting again. First, Pietersen launched a full-blooded drive at a missile from Lee that even God wouldn't hit for four. Then Lee bowled Flintoff with one that God couldn't have kept out – which jagged back half a metre to take out off stump. It was now 6 for 111, and England had all but self-destructed.

It was time for deep breaths and common sense. Even a little bit of caution. Instead, there was another rush of blood. With 13 runs needed, Geraint Jones jigged down the pitch to hoist Warne for six and was stumped, to make it 7 for 116. Once again, it was to be an incredible nail-biting finish. Only this time England's batsmen were entirely to blame.

But cometh the hour, cometh the man, and two England tailenders now did what Warne, Lee, Kasprowicz and McGrath had done several times with the bat for Australia. Poor Ashley Giles had been hiding in the pavilion all afternoon, unable to watch, unable to talk, hoping his moment would not come. Matthew Hoggard had also been praying his presence would not be needed. But they held their nerve admirably to drag England over the line. Now it was England's turn to behave like World Cup winners.

It was almost too much. Hoggard was in tears. Even Warne was misty eyed. Three games in a row had ended like this. What the hell was going on?

It was certainly not cricket as most people knew it. Once upon a time you could pack your lunch and head off to a match for a quiet day of contemplation and prayer. You could even have a quick nap and not miss a thing. On one famous occasion in the 1930s, a county captain was reputed to have got married on Saturday morning in the middle of his side's innings and come back three hours later to find the same pair batting, with only a few more runs on the board. This was a different game, almost a different universe. It was entertaining, exciting, nerve-racking and thoroughly bad for one's health. But as Martin Johnson pointed out in the UK *Telegraph*, you had to get used to it:

> The survival kit for the Test match spectator has undergone a sweeping change in recent years, from sandwich tin and coffee flask, to incontinence pants and blood pressure pills. You leave your seat for a call of nature at your peril, for fear of coming back to find someone's stumps splattered, a search party attempting to locate the ball from the pavilion roof, or two players standing eyeball to eyeball proffering what is euphemistically known as a frank exchange of views.

And there was one more match to go, which might yet turn out to be the best of all.

26

It's Not Over Till
It's Over

I would like him to be in my side for as long as
he can walk.

Warne had declared that the Fifth Test would be his last on English soil, and he expected it to be one of the toughest. He had vowed not to be part of an Australian team that surrendered the Ashes after 16 years, but he knew it would take all their experience and character to secure the win needed to draw the series and retain the urn. Since that first victory at Lord's, Australia had been playing catch-up and its star players had been struggling. Shane told the world he was sure they would come good, but he could hardly say anything else. And already, he was thinking about what he might do if Australia failed to perform. Travelling in a cab across London, he told Keith Blackmore, sports editor of *The Times*, that he would give up cricket if Australia lost the Ashes, and concentrate on winning back his kids, because he missed them so much. When Blackmore suggested he could never do that, because he loved the game and was still the best bowler in the world, Warne replied he was worn out.

He had bowled a lot of overs in this series, and at 36 years old it was taking him longer and longer to recover after each game. 'I must admit my body feels pretty sore', he admitted in his *Times* column shortly after the Trent Bridge defeat. 'After breakfast on Monday morning, the day after the Test, I went back to bed and slept through to the afternoon.' But it was not just bowling that was tiring him out. If England's tabloids were to be believed, he was burning the candle at both ends, chasing blondes, and playing as hard by night as he was by day.

Most of his team-mates saw little of him during off-field hours. He rarely socialised with them when they weren't playing cricket and seemed to be keeping out of their way on this tour. Adam Gilchrist and Matthew Hayden both had their wives and families with them, and most of the rest had partners or girlfriends, and they assumed he was steering clear because he was embarrassed. Journalists saw room-service trays outside his hotel-room door and figured he was on the straight and narrow for a change. But a blonde promotions model called Julia Reynolds knew otherwise. 'Stunning Julia Reynolds', as *The Sun* and *Daily Mirror* insisted on calling her, had hooked up with Shane at a function in Birmingham during the Second Test, and they had been trying for a rematch ever since. They had finally got together on the second day of the Trent Bridge Test and engaged in what *The Sun* described as a 'marathon sex session', which had supposedly 'sapped his strength' and 'helped England win'. According to *The Sun*, the couple's 'FIVE-HOUR lustathon in Room 811 of the city's Park Plaza Hotel . . . left Warne admitting he was completely "s****** out"'.

The excitement in all of this for the English papers was that Warne had been out for a golden duck in Australia's first innings the following morning. As the stunning Ms Reynolds told the *Daily Mirror*, 'I wasn't that surprised he was out for nought because when he left me he looked pretty exhausted. I guess you could say I've done my bit for England.' Shane's moll had text messages to back up her claims and had obviously visited his room, but whether she had bonked him senseless and sabotaged his batting was another matter. Even if she had – which seemed unlikely – at least he had an excuse for playing badly, unlike most of his team-mates, whom he had rescued so often.

The showdown at London's famous Oval cricket ground, starting on 8 September, was now set to be the biggest sporting event in England since the World Cup Final at Wembley in 1966. And there was about as much chance of getting a ticket, because the match had been a sell-out for months. On the opening day, queues started forming at the turnstiles by eight o'clock in the morning, and thousands of ticket holders were still waiting patiently outside the ground as play got under way. One penthouse across the road from the Vauxhall End of the ground had been rented out for $55,000 for the five days of the match, and touts were running a secondary market at $1400 a seat. People were perched on rooftops, clustered at windows, crowded onto balconies. Building workers in a tower block overlooking the pitch had downed tools and were sitting on the scaffolding. Everyone else was watching on TV, listening on radio or following it on their laptops around the world. Back in Australia, where the match was due to start at 7.30 pm, two million people were glued to their television sets, hoping to see their team come good at last.

Naturally, the Barmy Army was out in force, thousands strong, ready to sing its boys to victory. And all started well. Once again, Ponting lost the toss – the third time in a row – and Vaughan chose to bat on a hard, flat pitch that looked full of runs. Once again, England's captain said they would try to 'put some runs on the board and put Australia under pressure'. And soon it was business as usual, with Trescothick and Strauss smacking the Aussie fast bowlers to all parts of the ground. With barely an hour gone, they were cruising towards another century stand, scoring five runs an over and threatening to take control of the match. The English cricket anthem, 'Jerusalem', was already ringing round the ground.

Despite England's wins at Trent Bridge and Edgbaston and its near miss at Old Trafford, Australia had come into this match as hot favourites, with millions of dollars wagered on them to win. But as the score rattled along, their odds blew out rapidly to 4 to 1 against. After 16 years of being whipped by the Old Enemy, England looked set to take revenge. On a pitch like this, who could bowl them out?

The answer, of course, was Shane Warne, who came into the attack and started to weave his magic. Suddenly, the whole mood changed. Suddenly, the England openers were groping for the ball. Suddenly, anything seemed possible again.

It took him 15 balls to strike – though there were some oohs and aahs from the crowd before that – and Trescothick was the victim. Failing to spot the slider – a ball that looks like a leg break but goes straight on – he played for the turn, and edged low down to Hayden at slip, who followed the ball with both hands and snatched it off his boot for a fantastic catch.

Next in was England's captain, Michael Vaughan, who was soon settling everyone's nerves with a couple of elegant, well-struck fours that made it look easy. Then he tried to repeat the trick with one that bounced higher than expected and pulled the ball tamely to Clarke at short mid wicket. It was now 2 for 102.

Right on cue, around 100 Australian Fanatics, dressed in green and gold, jumped to their feet and started singing, 'Michael Vaughan is shit', to the tune of 'Kumbaya'. Sitting in front of the Barmy Army, they were outnumbered by 20 to one, but they had fuelled themselves up by drinking lager from plastic medical bags that would normally hold saline solution or intravenous drip. The Barmy Army, who were also well into the beer by this stage, instantly fired back with a chorus of, 'You all live in a convict colony', to the tune of 'Yellow Submarine'. As these songs competed for supremacy, 23-year-old Ian Bell walked to the wicket to see if he could do better. He had struggled in the series and was lucky to be still in the side, but two 50s at Old Trafford and the selectors' new pick-and-stick policy had saved him. This was his chance to repay their faith. His first ball from Warne struck him on the pad. His next, after a brief interval facing McGrath, did the same. Only this time it was another slider and he was plumb in front of his stumps. Up went Billy Bowden's crooked finger – out – and click went the scoreboard to 3 for 104.

The Barmy Army had gone quiet. They had stopped

singing about Warne and his pies, Warne and his missus, and Australia's convict past. They could sense a successful summer slipping away. But next on the block was Kevin Pietersen, with his badger-stripe hair, who had dazzled at Lord's and Edgbaston and put Australia to the sword in the one-day series. Surely he could be relied on to avert the massacre? He thumped his first ball from fast bowler Shaun Tait, for four, and dispatched his fifth for another boundary. Ten runs off the first over, time for lunch: regroup and settle the nerves.

However, facing Warne after the break, Pietersen looked almost as much at sea as his mates. He defended a few, then had an almighty swipe and missed completely. Then, after prodding a few more, he tried to whip a straight one out to the mid-wicket boundary, missed again and looked round in amazement to see his stumps in disarray. It was 4 for 131. In 15 minutes either side of lunch, Warne had turned the game.

So once again, it was Flintoff to the rescue. As he walked to the middle, the Barmy Army bugler struck up the *Flintstones* theme, and chants of 'Super Freddie' rang round the ground. Some even bowed down in homage. A few were wearing helmets in anticipation of the sixes he and Pietersen were expected to hit, which seemed a bit optimistic under the circumstances. But he at least would not be rushed into throwing his wicket away. And with Strauss also playing solidly, or rather better than that, the pair of them set about rebuilding. The left-hander had already cut, driven and pulled his way past 50, without looking troubled, and he now set his sights on another 100. He was particularly good against the fast bowlers, but he also had the measure of Warne, who had ridiculed him so often in this series. Merlyn had finally done the trick. Super Freddie played the leg spinner even better. He reached his 50 off Warne with two crashing fours to square leg (the second almost a six), and thumped his next ball straight down the ground for another boundary. Soon afterwards, he hoisted one into the stands at long on for a massive six. Thus was peace restored. For the next two-and-a-half hours, in which 140 runs were added, England looked like it might even pass 400 again and set Australia an impossible task. But eventually, Flintoff was caught in the slips off McGrath for 72 (by Warne, of course) and England wobbled once more.

By the end of the day, the advantage was back with Australia, thanks entirely to the boy from Black Rock. He had dismissed England's top five batsmen – including Strauss for 129 – and had had a hand in getting rid of the sixth. What is more, he had done it on a pitch that gave him no help, and on which no other spinner in this match would take a wicket. Few of his deliveries were unplayable – and the one that got Vaughan was plain ordinary – but he had a knack of making fools of batsmen. Even when the ball was doing nothing, he could bluff them into thinking it was. And that was almost as dangerous. Without him, England would have been breaking open the bubbly. As it was, 7 for 319 was a long way short of a decent score.

The next day, England stuttered to 373 all out and Australia cantered to 0 for 112 without looking threatened. Simon Jones (who had taken 18 wickets in three-and-a-half matches) was injured, Harmison was not firing and Giles was finding nothing in the pitch. Yet when the umpires gave Hayden and Langer the chance to come off for bad light, the batsmen had no hesitation in heading to the dressing-room. Perhaps they could be forgiven for not wanting to face Flintoff's 145 kilometres-per-hour missiles in the dark. And perhaps they knew rain was on the way. But it seemed so un-Australian to turn tail like this when time was of the essence and only a win would do. Steve Waugh and Allan Border would surely never have allowed it. For some observers, this was the moment Australia surrendered its crown, because Hayden and Langer now sat in the pavilion for 80 minutes when they could have been making runs.

Eventually, the rain did come to wash out the rest of the second day. It was still falling the next morning when play was due to restart. The third day was spent dodging showers, as Australia crawled its way to 2 for 275, anchored (in more senses than one) by Matthew Hayden, who was desperate to post a decent score and hang on to his place in the team.

Come Sunday morning, the powerful Queenslander revealed that Australia's plan was to 'bat, bat and bat some more . . . then we'll see if we can bat some more and take it to them on the last day'. By that time, if things went right, the Poms would be 200 behind, fighting to save the game, and facing Warne on a wearing pitch, for which they would need all their nerve and luck to survive. But with the light gloomy and rain still in the air, time was already getting short. And Australia had reckoned without Freddie Flintoff, who now put in another Mr Incredible performance to blast through the top order. He had removed Ponting late on Saturday with corker to make it 2 for 264, and in his first full over he got Martyn with one that also reared off a length and came through faster than expected, causing him to balloon a catch to mid wicket. An hour later, with fielders and batsmen all finding it hard to see the ball and catches going down, he produced two perfect inswingers to Hayden and Katich to trap them both l.b.w. Finally, his pace and bounce did Warne for a duck, as he tried to hook and skied the ball straight to Vaughan, who juggled an easy catch and just held on.

But the biggest roar of the day was reserved for Hoggard, who produced another beautiful inswinger to send Gilchrist packing l.b.w. For only the second time in the series, the Australian wicket-keeper had been looking dangerous, taking 23 off just 20 balls, and threatening to restore Australia's advantage. Soon afterwards, the Yorkshireman had Clarke l.b.w. with the exact same ball, and almost immediately he followed this up by disposing of McGrath and Lee. In just under two-and-a-half hours, England had taken eight Australian wickets for just 90 runs. It was easy to see how it had happened: magnificent bowling from Flintoff, who had bowled unchanged; bad light and swing to make it difficult for the batsmen; and some rash shots from the Australians, who were paying for their lack of urgency on the previous two days.

Against all the odds, Australia had been dismissed six runs short of England's total. And with the advantage surrendered, their task soon got even harder, because the light closed in after only five overs, and Michael Vaughan did not need to be asked twice if he wanted a break. Normally, the sight of batsmen scurrying back to the pavilion when there is no rain falling is enough to draw catcalls from the crowd, but Vaughan and Trescothick walked in to cheers and a standing ovation from the England fans. With their team needing only a draw to win back the Ashes, they were happy to sit it out. Even if they had paid upwards of £60 ($150) a ticket, it was better to watch the grass grow than wickets fall, which seemed to be the alternative. Warne had just dismissed Strauss with his fourth ball of the innings and was looking more dangerous than ever.

As the crowd waited for the umpires to return, the Barmy Army put up umbrellas to encourage the skies to open and the bugler began 'Singing in the Rain'. Not to be outdone, the Fanatics stripped off their shirts to pretend the sun was shining. One wag even held up a standard lamp and a paper sun. Before long, the drizzle did come down, but briefly, and the teams soon came back on, with every Australian player wearing sunglasses.

Then the light darkened again and (eventually) drizzle set in for the day. With two hours left, play was abandoned, with England on 1 for 34. Almost 50 overs had been lost to the weather, which had greatly increased England's chance of saving the match. It was sad that the laws of cricket allowed it, given that Ponting had agreed to bowl spinners from both ends. But the umpires believed it would be 'unfair' to play on.

So, after seven-and-a-half weeks of nail-biting suspense, 8656 balls, 5467 runs and 173 wickets, the fate of this incredible series came down to the last day of the last Test. And this time the forecast was good. Watery sun was poking through the clouds, but the rain had gone, so

England would either have to bat all day or get so far ahead that Australia could not catch them. With a lead of 40 runs and only one wicket down, it should not be hard, because the pitch was playing no tricks. But as Ashley Giles told TV viewers before play began, England never seemed to be able to make these tasks easy.

For a time, it did all go smoothly. Vaughan hit McGrath for a string of fours and England cruised into the 60s without cause for alarm. Then McGrath bowled his trademark ball, which jinks away off a perfect length, and Vaughan was caught in spectacular style by Adam Gilchrist, who reached one-handed far to his right to pluck the ball out of the air. Ian Bell was out next ball, first ball, to make it 3 for 67. McGrath was poised on a hat-trick in his last match in England. Now it was the turn of the Aussies in the crowd to jump up and down and whoop with joy.

In the Channel 4 commentary box, everyone was suddenly reaching for the heart pills again. 'Surely, surely, surely, we can't have another finish like the ones we've had before', gasped England's one-time captain Tony Greig.

'You'd better believe it, Tony. That's exactly where we're heading', former Australian opener Michael Slater replied.

Almost immediately, it seemed the prediction had come true. McGrath's first ball to Kevin Pietersen was a wicked bouncer which homed in on his face and nearly knocked his head off as he tried to get out of the way. There was a noise, a shout, and all the fielders went up. Surely it was out, first ball, caught at slip, a brute of a delivery. This was a disaster for England. But umpire Billy Bowden shook his head firmly and everyone breathed again. Remarkably, the replays showed it was the right decision, because the ball had shaved past his glove and cannoned off his upper arm. Once again, it was a matter of millimetres between possible victory and certain defeat.

Five balls later, still on nought, Pietersen had another life. Down the other end facing Warne, he got an edge to a ball that spun away and flew quickly to Gilchrist. The wicket-keeper snatched at the catch and missed, but deflected it off the back of his glove, wrong-footing Hayden, who scrabbled for the ball at slip as it bounced off his leg and fell to the turf. Soon afterwards, with 15 runs on the board, the pied South African had his biggest let-off of all, edging a half-volley from Lee straight to Warne, who cupped both hands to his chest and dropped the easiest of chances. He was normally so reliable. He never spilled catches like this one. And he had certainly never before missed one that would cost his team so dear.

Some batsmen get nervous when they're dropped. Others take heart. Pietersen decided to go for his shots. In the next over he hit his Hampshire team-mate for a huge six over long on, breaking his bat in the process. Encouraged by this, four balls later he repeated the shot from outside leg stump. It was magnificent stuff, if bad for the nerves. At the end of the over, Trescothick went down the pitch to say, 'Well played.' Pietersen smiled and replied: 'Yeah, I've had enough of blocking. I'm gonna smash it.'

By now, the score was looking almost respectable at

3 for 109, but Warne struck again, getting Trescothick l.b.w. with a ball that turned square from outside off stump. And twenty minutes later, after several near misses, he fooled Flintoff into giving him a return catch. He spread his hands wide, threw his head back and bellowed 'Yeeees', holding the note a full five seconds. With England now 5 for 126 the Australians had their tails up, and Lee came roaring in for the next over faster than ever. His first ball kicked up off the pitch and cracked into Pietersen's ribs, obviously hurting him, then popped into the air just short of leg slip. England's physio ran out to apply the magic spray and Lee ran in again, this time to smack Pietersen under the armpit. But the next was the best of all. Speeding towards him at 150 kilometres per hour, the ball went straight at the batsman's head, thumped into his glove and flew high over the slips as Pietersen fell in a heap on the ground. Thus did the teams go to lunch, with England's score still looking sick, but with its saviour still alive.

In many matches there comes a moment when the game is won or lost, and if Pietersen had fallen to Lee in that over, nothing would have stood in the way of an Australian victory. But the way he savaged Lee's bowling immediately after lunch was arguably what won it for England. 'It was him or me', Pietersen said later. Watching it back on the highlights, it is hard to imagine anyone batting better or with more aggression. Perhaps Viv Richards in his pomp could have matched it, but it was breathtaking to watch. He cracked the first and second balls for two apiece, then hooked the fourth for six over the fielder at square leg. The next over, he hooked another bouncer for six over square leg, and followed it with two majestic fours, one from a ball timed at 155 kilometres per hour. Warne in the slips watched open-mouthed in amazement; Lee shook his head in disbelief. Ponting looked glum. What could you do in the face of an onslaught like this? It took incredible skill and nerve for Pietersen to do it, and even more to bring it off. The adrenaline must have been flowing like a river. In Lee's next over, he faced just two balls, because Collingwood was on strike, but he smacked both for four, one so amazing that you could only laugh out loud. It was flat-batted off a perfect length straight back past the bowler with frightening power. In 14 balls he had hit Lee for 35 runs. England and Australia's entire summer was in the balance, yet he was blazing away like it was a Twenty20 thrash.

Even Geoff Boycott was giggling. After the first innings, he had chided Pietersen for being too big for his boots and told him to bat more responsibly. 'Pietersen's hubris seems to be getting the better of him', Boycott told his UK *Telegraph* readers. 'He wants to be the superstar, he wants the acclaim and the adulation, but he has not yet put in the performances to back up that attitude.' Well, now he had started to. But he was still not playing like Geoff. And thank God for that.

Almost eight million people in England were now watching this game on TV, which was more than the final episode of *Big Brother* and a record for Channel 4. The gardens and supermarkets of the nation were empty. Another two million or more were watching in Australia where it was 11.30 at night. And the BBC's Test-Match-Special chatroom was getting emails from all over the world – the Congo, Canada, Iraq, Romania, Bolivia, Russia, Japan, Germany, Togo, Spain, the USA, Korea, Holland, Hungary, Singapore – where cricket was not even played. Most were from English and Australian expats, listening to the webcast or following the ball-by-ball commentary on their computers. For millions, this match had brought their lives to a halt.

Even now, after all these fireworks, England was nowhere near safe. But there were no alarms for a while, as the score ticked over and both batsmen went quiet. With Warne bowling round the wicket into the rough, even Pietersen was blocking the ball with his pads instead of taking him on. And Collingwood was happy to defend the other end. Then, one hour after lunch, Warne struck for the 10th time in the match, having Collingwood snapped up by Ponting, off bat and glove, just inches from his crease. It was now 6 for 186, with nearly four hours to go and a lead of under 200. Five overs later, another one bit the dust, as Geraint Jones had his off stump skittled by an inswinger from Tait. It was 7 for 199, with only the tail to keep Pietersen company. But just as the match appeared to be in Australia's hands, England took its turn to prove that it's never over till it's over. Giles hung in doggedly, and they took tea with a lead of 227 runs, which might almost be enough.

By this time, Kevin Pietersen had belted two fours off Tait to reach his hundred, which he celebrated with an aerial leap and his arms held high. Off came the hat to reveal the badger stripe. Up jumped the crowd. The army cheered, the bugler played, the chants rang out. Even the Australians joined in the applause. It had been a magnificent innings, the only thing that had stood in their way. And if they did have to give back the Ashes it was fitting to do so to a performance such as this. If you had to lose the crown, it was good to do it to someone who dared to be king.

But it wasn't yet lost or won. England still needed to survive another 10 or 15 overs to take the match beyond reach. By then, Australia would simply not have time to get the runs.

Even now, Pietersen could not resist going out in style. After another 15 minutes of blocking he got a bouncer from Lee that had six written all over it and smashed it into the stands. Then he was off again, with a huge six over long off and a smash through square leg to take 12 runs off Warne's next over. Minutes later, he hoisted the leg spinner for another towering six into the stands, his seventh in the innings, which he followed with four more to take him to 150. Now it *was* all over. The man who had nearly not been selected in the beginning had saved England from certain defeat and become the highest scorer in the series. It was five pm when he finally fell, clean-bowled by McGrath, but by then his work was done. He walked off the ground to clapping, cheering, waving flags and a forest of hands, held high above heads by everyone in the crowd, like thousands of pointed hats. As he took off his helmet and waved his bat to 23,000 delirious English fans, his friend Shane Warne ran 30 metres to congratulate him: a great sporting gesture from one of the world's great sportsmen.

When the last wicket fell 45 minutes later, with England 350 runs ahead, the contest was long since over. The two old warriors, Shane Warne and Glenn McGrath, who had put fear into so many teams over the years, walked off the field to yet another standing ovation, with their arms around each other's shoulders, McGrath looking happy, Warne looking drained. Warne might well be back, however forcefully he denied it, but this was definitely the last the English crowds would see of McGrath. He would not be charging in at the age of 40.

Sadly it all ended in a whimper. One bouncer was enough to have the umpires looking at their light meters again, and inviting Hayden and Langer to bolt for the pavilion. Twenty minutes later, play was abandoned. There was a strange mood in the Australian dressing-room as they waited for sentence to be passed. The disappointment was palpable. 'We patted each other on the back and shook hands', Warne said later. 'Ricky Ponting said a few words and I just went around everybody to say: "Well tried, we'll get them next time." '

There was no doubt that Kevin Pietersen was man of the match, despite Shane's efforts. Nor could there be any debate about who were the stars of the series: Freddie for England and Shane for Australia. Warne had nearly won it for his team at Edgbaston, staved off defeat at Old Trafford, nearly stolen a victory at Trent Bridge, and frightened the life out of England's batsmen with 12 wickets at The Oval. His 40 wickets in the series were almost as many as the other Australian bowlers had managed between them. Six times in 10 innings he had taken the first wicket, and only once had he been given the chance to bowl on the sort of wearing pitch that most spinners need to weave their spells. 'He's had an amazing series and he doesn't give up or stop trying,' said Adam Gilchrist. 'He's one of the greatest players ever to play. To be associated with him and keep wicket to him is a huge thrill.'

His captain, Ricky Ponting, echoed these sentiments, telling the BBC, 'I would like him to be in my side for as long as he can walk.'

Accepting his award to applause from The Oval crowd, Warne was generous, as ever. 'It was an amazing series. England were just too good for us', he said. And as the roar died down, he had a word for the fans as well. 'The crowds in all the Tests have been sensational', he said. 'It's just a pleasure to play here.'

The scenes that followed were like nothing cricket has ever witnessed, with a blizzard of red-and-white confetti filling the air, magnums of champagne sprayed everywhere and English hymns filling the ground. Throughout the series, the fans had played a huge part in willing on their team, and rarely had they gone too far. As Australia's hopes had dwindled that afternoon, some of the Barmy Army had teased the champion leg spinner by singing, 'Warney dropped the Ashes', which was a taunt he did not deserve. Thankfully, they repaired some of this damage by serenading him later with a rousing chorus of, 'We wish you were English', which he acknowledged, to the astonishment of his colleagues, with a wave of his hat.

After the presentations, the speeches and the inevitable press conference, Warne and his team-mates joined the England team in their dressing-room. Warne and Pietersen sat relaxing in one corner, Hayden, Langer and Flintoff chatted earnestly in another. 'If there had been a fly on the wall it wouldn't have been able to distinguish between losers and winners that night', Hayden said later. 'Everyone was just relieved that the extraordinary roller-coaster ride had come to an end.'

Needless to say, England partied long and hard that night, with Flintoff, Pietersen and Vaughan leading the charge. The next day, 200,000 people turned out on the streets of London to wave St George Cross flags as the team's open-topped bus made its way to a packed Trafalgar Square for a victory rally. Rashly, the arrangements for this celebration had been made in advance, in anticipation of the victory. Cancellation had at times been close.

But the real winner in this amazing series was cricket, Warne told his *Times* readers, apologising for the tired old cliché: 'Anybody who cares for the game should rejoice.' And it was true. Not only had it been the most exciting Test series ever, but Australia now had someone to play against and there was already a return match to look forward to. Best of all, it had been played in the right spirit for once. Instead of snarling and aggro, there had been sportsmanship and respect. Warne and Flintoff had set an example of how it should be done. It had not made them or their teams any less competitive, because all had tried till the last. It had made it a joy to watch.

Whether we will ever see the like of it again, who knows. In the meantime, said Warne, 'It was a privilege to be part of an occasion that kids in the grounds will be telling their grandchildren about in 50 years.' It was also a privilege to watch him at his best.

27

D–I–V–O–R–C–E

I can't bring myself to even speak to him.
I just want to hide under a palm tree with my kids.

A the end of September 2005 Shane flew into Melbourne from London, called a news conference at the airport and vowed to rescue his marriage. God knows why he thought this was possible, after the way in which he had humiliated Simone. Having just performed miracles on the cricket field, perhaps he thought he could do the same in his personal life. 'We're still friends', he told the army of reporters sent to greet him. 'We still speak all the time, so we've just got to work out what we both want and which way we're going to go and which road we go down.'

Unfortunately, he had not told Simone about his re-conciliation plans, and she claimed to know nothing about them. 'I'm not really familiar with what Shane said', she told a journalist who asked for her reaction the next day. 'I've been in Sydney for the TV show.'

While her husband had been busy taking English wickets and bowling maidens over, Simone had signed up with Channel 7 to appear in a new quiz show called *Celebrity*

Spelling Bee, which was a brave choice for someone who had left school at 15 to become a hairdresser. (Rumours soon started flying around that she had been asked to spell 'phlegm' and offered 'F – L – E – M'). She was keen to chat about this new TV career. 'I don't know if it's a fresh start . . . but it's new to me and I'm enjoying it. I haven't really been able to do this in the past because we've got three young children.' More to the point, no one had asked her.

There were other projects in the pipeline, such as appearing at the Melbourne Cup as a 'celebrity', and joining the cast of *Dancing with the Stars*, so perhaps she did have a future in television. But it seemed to escape her that she was only in demand because she was married to someone famous and that TV's love affair with her was likely to be short-lived. As one male TV executive observed unkindly, it was not as though the commercial stations were short of attractive blonde women with big tits and no special talent.

But after all those years of being in Shane's shadow, it was obviously refreshing to be the centre of attention and to be noticed for herself (even if interviewers still wanted her to talk about him). In July, she had signed a 'World Exclusive' deal with *New Idea* (Channel 7's stablemate) to tell all about their split, and had managed to do so frankly and with dignity. From a commercial point of view she had been a huge success, because the issue broke all sales records. She had been interviewed in her Brighton home, two weeks after the break-up, unpacking the boxes that had been on their way to England. She seemed to be doing fine. But having put Shane on a final warning in 2004, she must have known it might end this way (unless she was in la-la land), so she'd had time to prepare herself. Now she was just relieved to have made the break. 'Sad as it is, I knew I had to do this to protect my kids and maintain some sense of pride . . . I feel comfortable now that I can move on and be happy.'

It was a bit early to be so thoroughly over the pain, perhaps, but this is the style of such confessions, and it's surely what readers want: a woman who is strong, empowered and unharmed, despite the appalling way she has been treated by her husband.

She and the children had not seen much of him anyway, because he was so rarely at home. 'I've basically been a single parent since Brooke was born eight years ago', Simone admitted. 'They would get a few days with him here or there, maybe a week or a month, but fatherhood has never been a full-time job for Shane.' He had missed the births of two of their children because he was on tour. And even during his 12-month drug ban, he had spent months away from the family, working for Channel 9 and travelling.

Nor was she destitute, as the magazine's photo spread made clear. She had been snapped in nine or ten different locations around her luxurious Brighton home – the pool, the sunroom, the lounge, the kitchen, the family room and the garden – wearing eight different outfits from a Melbourne designer (no doubt provided for the shoot), and a stack of jewellery. Strangely enough, she was also still sporting her big diamond wedding ring. So perhaps she hadn't written him off entirely, whatever she said.

And indeed, she did try to save the relationship. One

month after her *New Idea* exclusive, she was reading an article in Melbourne's *Sunday Life* magazine about sportsmen behaving badly. Her attention was grabbed by the words of a so-called professional mentor, Damien Foster, who counsels some of the bad boys of football. Foster was saying that, 'anyone who looks at the Shane Warne story and thinks it's about sexual appetite is missing the point'. Simone thought this made sense. According to Foster, it was more likely to be about insecurity, low self-esteem and a need to be loved – all of which Shane had in spades. She picked up the phone and rang him immediately, even though it was Sunday morning. At first, Foster thought it was a friend taking the mickey, but when she told him to ring her back at home, he was intrigued. He agreed to meet her, talked to her for three hours and came away impressed. What he liked about her was that she did not badmouth her husband, despite all the hurt he had caused, and seemed genuinely concerned about his welfare. So he agreed to talk to Shane and see what happened.

Nothing eventually came of this rescue mission because Warne and Foster did not hit it off, and Shane was not thrilled at the prospect of being counselled. But when the cricket star flew in to Melbourne in September, it was all still on the agenda, which was perhaps what encouraged Shane to think Simone might have him back. She had also told him he could stay in the guest room at their Brighton home, so he would be close to the kids, and this, too, may have sent the wrong message.

To outsiders, it seemed bizarre that Simone was still so forgiving. It certainly added fuel to rumours that they were getting back together again. It was also enough to send the women's magazines into a frenzy, with a rush to get pictures of the pair out with their children, and run stories about them looking 'more like a couple in love than a couple on the brink of divorce'. *New Idea*, which had been given the inside running by Simone only two months earlier, was bold enough to run the headline 'SHANE NOT OUT!' and to venture, 'Things look good for the shamed cricket star'.

Such stories sell magazines, of course, and plenty of them in Shane and Simone's case. And the next few months would see life breathed constantly into the tale, with teasers such as 'SIMONE BACK IN SHANE'S ARMS' or the shameless 'WE'RE STILL IN LOVE'. It was hardly surprising if journalists were confused, though. He was still in the house at Christmas time, when Channel 9's cameras filmed him giving presents to his kids. And the Australian cricket team came over for its annual barbecue before the Boxing Day Test match, for which Simone arranged the catering. Even his team-mates weren't sure what was happening. But the truth was that even Simone wasn't going to let him humiliate her all over again.

Shane tried to put a brave face on it all by telling some of his mates that he welcomed the split and was glad to be out of a loveless marriage. According to his version of events, he had not wanted to hurt Simone by dumping her, and had made a fool of himself with all these women so she could escape with dignity. But if you believed that, you would believe anything. He told others that Simone had been tough on him and locked him out of the house. And at various times he was either staying at Crown Casino or with friends. His team-mates reckoned he had not expected her to walk out on him and could not believe it when she did. Only when he had been back in Australia for a couple of months did the truth hit home, or so they said.

With Shane you never knew what to believe, though. I saw him at Brisbane airport in November 2005, the morning after Australia had romped to victory in the First Test against the West Indies at the Gabba. He was extraordinarily well turned out for a 9.30 am plane trip back to Melbourne, in a sharp, shiny black suit and a crisp white shirt. And for some reason he was wearing dark wraparound sunglasses inside the terminal. Whether this was to hide the effects of a big night or to give himself protection from fans it was hard to know. But even from the back, in this garb, his hair was instantly recognisable, with its straw-like crown around a growing bald patch in the middle. I didn't stop to say hello, but I couldn't help noticing what he was reading. Headed 'I SHAGGED SHANE', it was Kerrie Collimore's first-person account of their summer affair in England, served up for the lads' magazine *FHM*. One person who did stop to say g'day reported that Shane was complaining he would never be able to get a root again. 'How am I ever going to get another woman', he asked plaintively, 'when all they want to do is bonk you for money?'

With others he put a different spin on it, bragging that he now had three times as many women after him. That's the message he had for an old team-mate who asked him how things were going. 'It's terrific', Shane replied. 'Now I'm free I can do anything I like all the time.' To which the friend replied, 'What the hell are you talking about? You've always rooted everything that moved.'

After the initial noises about putting his marriage back together again, Shane was soon acknowledging it was over. In November, he confided off-camera to a female journalist from Channel 9 that he was going to get a divorce, which one assumes was not just a come on. Soon afterwards, Simone said they had agreed a settlement and would not be fighting in court. 'Neither of us wanted it to turn nasty', she told New Idea, to whom everything was now confided. 'We have spent so much time together and we have many happy memories, and because of that I don't want to turn against him.' The magazine told its readers that divorce would cost Shane $10 million; although where they got this figure from was anybody's guess. Simone 'refused to comment', and Shane's brother and manager, Jason, denied it.

At this stage, the couple was proposing to live in the family home together until Shane gave up cricket. 'It sounds strange . . . but the house is big enough to cope', said Simone, 'and it's good for the kids to have him around. It's almost like we're flat-mates.' He was only in Australia about three months of every year, she said, and in Melbourne for half of that, so it would not involve much contact. But by April 2006, the plan had changed: she had bought another house just round the corner, which she was going to knock down and rebuild. And she couldn't wait to move in.

By this time, Simone's TV career was blossoming. She was a huge success on Dancing with the Stars, despite (or perhaps because of) the fact that she was a hopeless dancer. She had tried, cried and won the hearts of thousands. A few complained that she wasn't really a star and was only married to one. But she was emboldened by the whole experience, telling *New Idea* (as ever): 'The TV work has given me confidence and helped me grow. I've always been happy to be a stay-at-home mum, but now I've been given the chance to do some things for myself and I'm really enjoying it.'

Shane was also doing well, because the Ashes triumph had put him back on the sponsors' radar. Before the series, the best he could boast was a deal with Advanced Hair Studio, which was giving him free laser therapy and serum treatment to help his own hair grow back, and paying him a decent whack for spruiking its products. Shane was the ideal person for this market, because he sent bald blokes the message that even they could get laid. His other deal was with Messages on Hold, a company that played recorded messages to people waiting in phone queues, where his prowess was legendary. But no one else had shown much interest. Even if beer-swilling, pizza-eating, sports-loving Aussie blokes still loved him, most women thought him appalling. So there was a limit to what he could usefully promote.

However, his feats on the field in England now put him back in favour. The new man in charge at Channel 9 was his old Melbourne mate Eddie McGuire, and there was talk of him being welcomed back into the fold. He also landed a major sports-equipment deal – his first since losing Nike in 2001. It was notable that this was in England not Australia, and with Mitre, a company that has no great presence in cricket, but it was a comeback, nevertheless. And it was an arrangement that was ideal for both parties, because Shane would give spin clinics to budding young English bowlers. This was the perfect role for him as he was great with kids, possibly because he was still one himself. It might also grow into something that would keep him occupied, wanted and loved in years to come. He liked to think there were plenty of young cricketers who wanted to grow up to be like him. And no doubt there still were. Aged 11 and under, they were not yet old enough to realise their hero had feet of clay.

As Shane explained the finer points of leg spin to a group of young Indian kids at the first of these clinics in the East End of London in May 2006, the news hoardings were advertising yet another sex scandal. This time, it was worse than ever, because there were pictures and a video to go with the story. Rupert Murdoch's *News of the World* had caught Shane on hidden camera with two well-stacked blondes and a 3-foot inflatable penis. And it was not a pretty sight. They were both topless, clad only in G-strings, and he was in an unflattering pair of Playboy underpants of the budgie-smuggling variety.

One of the women was an MTV presenter, the other a TV gardener (who does her planting in a skimpy bikini). It was not immediately clear whether they had set him up at the paper's suggestion or done it off their own bat, then sold the story. But however it had happened, Shane had fallen for it. He had driven up to London straight after a game against Middlesex and walked straight into the honey trap. And all the sordid details were captured on tape and in print.

First he whooped and cheered as Emma – who appeared as Kylie Minogue's double in the film *Street*

Fighter – did a striptease. Then he watched pal Coralie
get her kit off. Soon all three were kissing, fondling
and playing with the giant inflatable.

The newspaper claimed to have video and stills of him
having sex with both women on a fold-down bed in
what looked like a seedy hotel room. But the
bowdlerised version that appeared in newspapers
around the world and on the internet was more than
enough. It was a tragic scene, like something out of a
bad porn movie, and sad that he had been entrapped in
this way. He no longer had a wife to cheat on and there
was no suggestion that he was harassing the two women
– but England's tabloids still considered him fair
game. Perhaps he would now stop complaining that
the media in Australia was so much meaner than
in the UK.

To add insult to injury, there were text messages to go
with the story. In one, Shane boasted that Simone was fed
up with his sexual demands: 'That's why I got divorced.
She said that I was killing her.' We will skip the rest for
taste reasons, but it had Shane admitting graphically that
his appetite was 'out of control'. When one of the women
texted him back to say she wrote a sex addiction column
in a lads' magazine, Shane replied: 'How horny . . . I am
like a dog on heat.'

This was the last straw for his long-suffering wife, who
now told *New Idea* she would like to cut him off for good.
She would go back to using her maiden name when the
divorce came through and was no longer answering his
calls. 'I can't bring myself to even speak to him', she said.

'I just want to hide under a palm tree with my kids.' When asked what advice she'd give her husband, Simone said: 'Grow up and take some responsibility for your actions.'

Simone would have to speak to him eventually, of course, but she had given up trying to help. He had hurt her too often. 'He needs . . . to take a long hard look at himself', she told *New Idea*.

> He says he is desperately sorry he has hurt me again, so why does he keep on doing it? I wish I knew . . . If this was the behaviour of an immature teenager, you could try to explain it away, but not a grown man with three children who love him more than anything and miss him like crazy.

As yet, the kids were too young to know what their dad had been up to. But sooner or later they would have to deal with the jibes at school, and it would not be fun. Shane often said his kids meant the world to him, and complained about the media harassing them, yet he clearly never considered what his own behaviour might be doing. 'I'm trying to bring up our children to behave responsibly and show respect for others', Simone said angrily. 'How am I supposed to explain this to them?'

Explaining it to Channel 9 might also be a problem. It might even put paid to the new $300,000 contract Shane was negotiating. But as the former host of the AFL *Footy Show*, Eddie McGuire was unlikely to regard Shane's latest escapade as a hanging offence, especially since he had once described women who slept with AFL players as 'predators'.

In the meantime, bonking the blondes had clearly not harmed Shane's bowling. He had driven back to Southampton the next morning and taken 7 for 99 against Middlesex, to record his best figures of the season. And scandal or no scandal, he would always be welcome at the club. Hampshire's chairman, Rod Bransgrove, told me in early 2006 that Warne's off-field antics didn't bother him, and that their new captain was more than they had ever hoped for and everything they had possibly dreamed of. A multi-millionaire businessman who owns the rights to *Basil Brush* and *Postman Pat*, Bransgrove believes Warne has 'Australianised' the team and taught them that no match is ever lost.

How has he done this? 'Fantastic commitment', says Bransgrove, 'and tremendous natural charisma; people find it very hard not to like him.' And as for the headlines? 'Yeah, he's made mistakes, but he's not the pariah they'd like to make him out to be.' Warne's Hampshire team-mates also love him. 'We have won some games we had no right to', says Shane's fellow spinner Shaun Udal, adding, 'He has been brilliant for me, instilling enormous self-belief and confidence and making me really enjoy my cricket again . . . The guy is a genius.'

Since the Ashes ended in September 2005, Warne has been bowling better than ever. He skittled South Africa on the last day of the Durban Test in March 2006 on a wicket that gave him no help, and took the man of the match award despite Ricky Ponting's century in each innings. And he was in great form before that against the West Indies. I saw him at the First Test in Brisbane in November 2005, winning the match with 5 for 48 in the first innings, which put him back to number one in the ICC rankings for the first time since 1995, and he was busting to tell the world he was back to his best.

To get to the press conference, I descended into the belly of the Gabba, underneath the new concrete stands, past the empty indoor cricket nets, and into a cubbyhole close to the players' dressing-rooms. Warne chatted with reporters as soon as he arrived, played with the microphone and fooled around. And when the first question was asked he came alive, as if someone had switched him on. He was bowling better than ever, he told us, because he was fit at last. 'Between 1998 and 2001, I had four injuries', he explained. 'Two shoulder operations, an operation on my finger and an operation on my knee. So for three years, I was never really comfortable with what I was doing and I was sort of just surviving.'

Since then, four injury-free years had given his body time to heal. He now has his fearsome flipper working again, even though the crucial spinning finger is bent and crooked. He has also mastered the wrong 'un again, with a different action, because his shoulder no longer works the same way. And he is getting wickets faster than ever, because batsmen are going after him. 'They used to just sit on me and wear me down . . . Now they are taking me on.' In 2005 he took a staggering 96 Test wickets, which is 24 more than his previous best in 1993. Not surprisingly, he is talking about playing for another three years. Maybe even going back to England for the Ashes in 2009, by which time his tally could be close to 1000.

But however long Shane chooses to keep playing, there will inevitably come a day when he has to hang up his boots, when he stops breaking records, winning matches and putting the fear of God into batsmen. And what will he do without it? Cricket is his life, his security blanket, his escape from the traumatic world beyond the boundary. Will his life unravel, as some suggest?

It's a question that all top sportsmen have to face sooner or later, and one that several superstars have been unable to answer. Indeed, the more brilliant, the more charismatic, the more famous you are, the more likely it seems that retirement can bring you down. Think Gary Ablett, George Best, Paul Gascoigne, Diego Maradona and boxer Frank Bruno, to name but a few.

Some cope better than others with the loss of fame and adulation. It helps not to have taken it all too seriously and not to believe the hype. It helps, too, to have family and friends to fall back on. But Shane scores poorly on all of these measures. He loves being loved, adores the spotlight and craves attention wherever he goes. And his stupidity has cut him off from his wife and children. He also has few if any close friends among his mates in the Australian cricket team. 'I certainly can't think of any', says one former player who knows him well. I suggest a couple of names and he shakes his head. 'No, I mean people you'd keep on seeing after your career is over. I don't think there is anyone like that.' Another who knows him intimately has reached the same conclusion. 'I don't think he has a true friend: someone he can talk to or someone he listens to and relies on. Good people have given up on him because he won't listen to them and won't take their advice.'

So it will be a lot harder for Shane than most. He has

spent his life being pampered, praised, acclaimed and adored, and he has grown used to being treated like a god. Suddenly, he will have to return to reality. The cameras won't seek him out, the press won't chase him, the attention will be gone. So too will the camaraderie, the adrenaline, the rush of competition, in fact just about everything he has lived for since he was a teenager. And having devoted all his energies to being the best and staying at the top, what will he have to fill his time? He may feel like the oxygen has been sucked out of his life.

Shane is a strong character and a cheerful fellow. Unlike so many sportsmen who go off the rails, he does not have a problem with drink or drugs. So with luck, his resilience and love of the game will save him. He genuinely wants to give something back to cricket, to share his knowledge and teach his tricks to others. And cricket will want his talents. Maybe it will be as a coach or a teacher, as an inspiration to a new generation of spinners. Maybe it will be as a commentator, so he can keep on giving pleasure to cricket fans everywhere. And maybe it will be exciting enough to fill the void of retirement.

Here's hoping he's not as fragile or as flaky as some of the superstars who have gone before. Here's hoping his mental toughness and sense of mischief will pull him through. And here's hoping he will be remembered in the way he wants: 'As an entertainer. Someone who never gave up, never ever. Who busted his gut and had lots of fun doing it.'

Let's not be morbid, anyway. It's not over yet. Shane is already plotting Australia's Ashes revenge. And it's going to be another magical ride.

References

Chapter 1—Suck on This

20   Warne, Shane & Ray, Mark, 1997, *Shane Warne, My Own Story*, Swan Publishing, Perth.

21   Overton, Peter, 20 February 2005, 'Getting of Wisdom', *60 Minutes,* Channel 9, Sydney.

22–3 Overton, Peter, 20 February 2005, 'Getting of Wisdom', *60 Minutes,* Channel 9, Sydney.

Chapter 2—Look at Me, Look at Me

36   Martin, Ray, 25 February 2003, *A Current Affair*, Channel 9, Sydney.

37   Hobson, Richard, 2002, *Shane Warne, My Autobiography*, Hodder & Stoughton, London.

Chapter 3—Kick in the Guts

40   *The Mentonian*, Mentone Grammar School, 1987.

46   *The Mentonian*, Mentone Grammar School, 1987.

51–2 Piesse, Ken, 1995, *Warne: Sultan of spin*, Modern

Publishing Group, Baxter, Victoria.

53   Grant, Trevor, 2 January 1993, 'A new star is Warne', *Herald Sun*, Melbourne.

54   Grant, Trevor, 2 January 1993, 'A new star is Warne', *Herald Sun*, Melbourne.

57   Piesse, Ken, 2005, *Down at the Junction: St Kilda Cricket Club, the first 150 years*, St Kilda Cricket Club, Melbourne.

Chapter 4—Boys Will Be Boys

65   Piesse, Ken, 1995, *Warne: Sultan of spin*, Modern Publishing Group, Baxter, Victoria.

67   Jenner, Terry (with Piesse, Ken), 1999, *T.J. Over the Top: Cricket, prison and Warnie*, Information Australia, Melbourne.

68   Jenner, Terry, 2005, unpublished DVD.

74   Hobson, Richard, 2002, *Shane Warne, My Autobiography*, Hodder & Stoughton, London.

74   Piesse, Ken, 2000, *The Complete Shane Warne*, Viking, Sydney.

Chapter 5—A Star is Warne

88   Visual Entertainment Group (under licence from the Australian Cricket Board), 2000, *Shane Warne: The world's greatest ever spin bowler*, Melbourne.

90–1 Ray, Mark, 27 October 1991, 'Warne looks for a break', *The Sunday Age*, Melbourne.

92   Visual Entertainment Group, (under licence from the Australian Cricket Board), 2000, *Shane Warne:*

The world's greatest ever spin bowler, Melbourne.

93   Warne, Shane & Ray, Mark, 1997, *Shane Warne, My Own Story*, Swan Publishing, Perth.

95   31 December 1991, *Herald Sun*, Melbourne.

95   Grant, Trevor, 2 January 1993, 'A new star is Warne', *Herald Sun*, Melbourne.

97   Benaud, Richie, 4 January 1992, 'Warne does it right', *Herald Sun*, Melbourne.

97   O'Reilly, Bill, 5 January 1992, 'Warne passes all the tests', *The Sun-Herald*, Sydney.

98   1 January 1992, 'In Warne ear . . .', *Herald Sun*, Melbourne.

Chapter 6—Fame at Last

101   Marsh, Rod, 4 January 1992, 'Come back to academy, Shane', *Herald Sun*, Melbourne.

102   Jenner, Terry (with Piesse, Ken), 1999, *T.J. Over the Top: Cricket, prison and Warnie*, Information Australia, Melbourne.

106   Piesse, Ken, 2000, *The Complete Shane Warne*, Viking, Sydney.

107   Warne, Shane & Ray, Mark, 1997, *Shane Warne, My Own Story*, Swan Publishing, Perth.

108   Warne, Shane & Ray, Mark, 1997, *Shane Warne, My Own Story*, Swan Publishing, Perth.

109   Smithers, Patrick, 24 August 1992, 'Warne triumphs on day for spin brotherhood', *The Age*, Melbourne.

110   Piesse, Ken, 2000, *The Complete Shane Warne*, Viking, Sydney.

111   Reed, Ron, 20 December 1992, 'Time to pay',
       Herald Sun, Melbourne.

111   Wilkins, Peter, 30 December 1991, 'Test call has
       Warne in a spin', *The Sydney Morning Herald*.

114   Grant, Trevor, 2 January 1993, 'A new star is
       Warne', *Herald Sun*, Melbourne.

Chapter 7—Ball of the Century

116   BBC TV, 4 June 1993, re-played in *Shane Warne:
       The world's greatest ever spin bowler*, Visual
       Entertainment Group (under licence from the
       Australian Cricket Board), 2000, Melbourne.

117   BBC TV, 4 June 1993, re-played in *Shane Warne:
       The world's greatest ever spin bowler*, Visual
       Entertainment Group (under licence from the
       Australian Cricket Board), 2000, Melbourne.

118   30 August 1882, *Sporting Times*, London.

119   Johnson, Martin, 3 November 1993, 'Wanted:
       dextrous thinker with a rhino's hide', *The
       Independent*, London.

119–20 Bennett, Marjory, 1 January 1995, 'The Sultan
       of spin', *The Sun-Herald*, Sydney.

122   Reuters, 30 December 1994.

122   Reuters, 30 December 1994.

123   7 October 2001, 'Unspun Hero', Sport Monthly,
       The Observer, London.

124   Warne, Shane & Ray, Mark, 1997, *Shane Warne,
       My Own Story*, Swan Publishing, Perth.

125   Healy, Ian & Craddock, Robert, 1996, *The Ian
       Healy Story: Playing for keeps*, Swan Publishing,
       Perth.

REFERENCES

Chapter 8— 'Sex Test Flop'

131   20 June 1993, 'I hit ace for six', *Daily Mirror*,
      London.
131   Craddock, Robert, 25 June 2005, 'A simple but
      complicated man', *The Courier-Mail,* Brisbane.
133   25 June 1993, 'Lisa hits back at bimbo taunts',
      Accrington Observer.
134   Lander, Chris, 8 June 1993, 'Shane on you
      England, you have been Warne-d', *Daily Mirror*,
      London.
139   Fraser, Alan, 29 March 1997, 'The turning point',
      Daily Telegraph, Sydney (reprinted from *Daily
      Mail*, London).
139   Hayes, Liz & Taylor, Stephen, 8 November 1998,
      'Come in spinner', *60 Minutes*, Channel 9, Sydney.

Chapter 9—Fuck off, Fuck off

142   Slater, Michael, 14 March 2005, *Enough Rope,
      with Andrew Denton*, ABC TV, Sydney.
143   Price, Matt, 23 July 2005, 'Why Aussies are
      rooting for the Poms', *The Spectator*, London.
144–5 Bryson, Bill, 2000, *Down Under*, Doubleday,
      Sydney.
147   Visual Entertainment Group (under licence from
      the Australian Cricket Board), 2000, *Shane Warne:
      The world's greatest ever spin bowler*, Melbourne.
150   Waugh, Steve, 1994, *Steve Waugh's South African
      Tour Diary*, Pan Macmillan, Chippendale, NSW.
151   Mcfarline, Peter, 8 March 1994, 'A boorish Warne

sours the sweet taste of unity', *The Age*,
Melbourne.

151 9 March 1994, 'Let there be no more Warneings',
The Sydney Morning Herald, Sydney.

153 Hughes, Merv (with Keane, Patrick), 1997, *Merv:
The full story*, HarperCollins, Pymble, New South
Wales.

153 Ray, Mark, 13 March 1994, 'Is sportsmanship
dead? Cricket – when going gets tough, Australians
cut rough', *The Age*, Melbourne.

154 Keane, Patrick, 6 March 1994, 'Please give me
another chance, Warne asks', *The Age*, Melbourne.

154 April 1994, *Cricketer*, Melbourne.

155 Visual Entertainment Group (under licence from
the Australian Cricket Board), 2000, *Shane Warne:
The world's greatest ever spin bowler*, Melbourne.

155 Smith, Patrick, 18 March 1997, *The Age*, Melbourne.

155 April 1994, *Cricketer*, Melbourne.

156 Hobson, Richard, 2002, *Shane Warne, My
Autobiography*, Hodder & Stoughton, London.

156 Stoll, Sharon & Rudd, Andy, 2004, 'What type of
character do athletes possess?' *The Sport Journal*,
Vol. 7.

Chapter 10—Playing Away

159 Healy, Ian & Craddock, Robert, 1996, *The Ian
Healy Story: Playing for keeps*, Swan Publishing,
Perth.

160 Smethurst, Sue, 30 July 2005, 'Shane tore our
family apart', *New Idea*, Sydney.

164 Bennett, Marjory, 1 January 1995, 'The sultan of spin', *The Sun-Herald*, Sydney.

164 Boon, David, 1996, *Under the Southern Cross: The autobiography of David Boon*, HarperCollins, Pymble, New South Wales.

166 Waugh, Steve, 2005, *Out of My Comfort Zone: The autobiography*, Viking, Camberwell, Victoria.

167 Weidler, Danny, 24 January 2005, 'Back from the dark side', *Inside Cricket*, Sydney.

170 Fishman, Roland, 1991, *Calypso Cricket: The inside story of the 1991 Windies tour*, Margaret Gee Publishing, Sydney.

171 Craddock, Robert, 16 August 2003, 'Sportsmen behaving badly', *Herald Sun*, Melbourne.

174 Smith, Amanda, 25 October 2002, 'Married to the game', *The Sports Factor*, ABC Radio National, Sydney.

175 Pringle, Derek, 9 May 2003, 'Don't marry a cricketer', *Daily Telegraph*, London.

175 Overton, Peter, 24 March 2002, 'Men of Waugh', *60 Minutes,* Channel 9, Sydney.

Chapter 11—Comeback Kid

181 Craddock, Robert, 4 December 1996, 'Wizard Warne back with bite', *The Courier-Mail*, Brisbane.

182 Warne, Shane & Ray, Mark, 1997, *Shane Warne, My Own Story*, Swan Publishing, Perth.

182 Fraser, Alan, 29 March 1997, 'The turning point', *Daily Telegraph*, Sydney (reprinted from *Daily Mail*, London).

185 Blake, Martin, 29 December 1997, *The Age*, Melbourne.

186 Knox, Malcolm, 6 January 1998, 'Warne reigns supreme', *The Sydney Morning Herald*, Sydney.

186 Craddock, Robert, 6 January 1998, '300 not out: Shane joins cricket's true greats', *Daily Telegraph*, Sydney.

186 Hadfield, Warwick, 7 January 1998, 'Warne can take 600 – Benaud', *The Australian*.

186 6 January 1998, 'Warne joins 300 club', *Illawarra Mercury*, Wollongong, New South Wales.

187 Coward, Mike, 6 January 1998, 'Hail Lillee's kindred soul, warts and all', *The Australian*.

190 Boon, David, 1996, *Under the Southern Cross: The autobiography of David Boon*, HarperCollins, Pymble, New South Wales.

191 Piesse, Ken, 2000, *The Complete Shane Warne*, Viking, Sydney.

192–3 16 April 1998, 'Warne to put up with pain', Reuters.

193 Deeley, Peter, 8 May 1998, 'Year out now for Warne', *Electronic Telegraph*, London.

193 Hobson, Richard, 2002, *Shane Warne, My Autobiography*, Hodder & Stoughton, London.

193 Reed, Ron, 29 July 1998, 'I may never play again', *Herald Sun*, Melbourne.

194 Chappell, Ian, 18 October 1998, 'Warne: ready, willing and almost able', *Electronic Telegraph*, London.

195 Smith, Robert, 30 December 1998, 'Warne relishes return against England for Test finale', AFP.

Chapter 12—Money for Nothing

197   Conn, Malcolm, 9 December 1998, 'Cricket's
betting scandal: Test stars were paid by bookie',
The Australian.

198   Conn, Malcolm, 9 December 1998, 'Cricket's
betting scandal: Test stars were paid by bookie',
The Australian.

200   O'Regan AM, QC, Rob, February 1999, *Report of
ACB Player Conduct Inquiry*, Melbourne.

201   Hobson, Richard, 2002, *Shane Warne, My
Autobiography*, Hodder & Stoughton, London.

203   Knight, James, 2002, *Mark Waugh: the biography*,
HarperCollins, Pymble, New South Wales.

207   Condon, Paul, May 2001, *Report on Corruption in
Cricket*, International Cricket Council, Dubai.

207   O'Regan AM, QC, Rob, February 1999, *Report of
ACB Player Conduct Inquiry*, Melbourne.

208   O'Regan AM, QC, Rob, February 1999, *Report of
ACB Player Conduct Inquiry*, Melbourne.

209   O'Regan AM, QC, Rob, February 1999, *Report of
ACB Player Conduct Inquiry*, Melbourne.

210   Cross, John, 9 February 1999, *Daily Mirror*,
London.

211   11 December 1998, Voice of Mirror Sport, *Daily
Mirror*, London.

213   Border, Allan & Craddock, Robert, 29 November
1996, 'Shane is tailor-made for captain', *Daily
Telegraph*, Sydney.

214   Warne, Shane & Ray, Mark, 1997, *Shane Warne,
My Own Story*, Swan Publishing, Perth.

215   Horan, Mike, 7 January 1999, 'A man destined to one day captain his country', *Herald Sun*, Melbourne.

215   Horan, Mike, 8 January 1999, *Herald Sun*, Melbourne.

216   Horan, Mike, 29 January 1999, *Herald Sun*, Melbourne.

216   Conn, Malcolm, 3 February 1999, *The Australian*.

Chapter 13—Zero to Hero

222   Knox, Malcolm, 3 April 1999, *The Sydney Morning Herald*.

223   Subscriber email, crikey.com.au.

225   Anderson, Ian, 6 April 1999, *Waikato Times*, New Zealand.

227   Voteline 1998, 18 November 1998, *Herald Sun*, Melbourne.

229–30 Walters, Mike, 8 May 1999, 'Warne plans to drive them all barmy with another World Cup war dance', *Daily Mirror*, London.

231   22 May 1999, Reuters.

231   Blake, Martin, 23 May 1999, *The Sun-Herald*, Sydney.

231   Hobson, Richard, 2002, *Shane Warne, My Autobiography*, Hodder & Stoughton, London.

231   Waugh, Steve, *Out of My Comfort Zone: The autobiography*, Viking, Camberwell, Victoria, 2005.

232–3 Hitchen, Alexander, 30 May 1999, 'Cricket ace Warne's wicket games with maiden', *News of the*

World, London.

234 Chappell, Ian, 13 June 1999, 'Warne facing moment of truth', *Daily Telegraph*, London.

234 Waugh, Steve, 1999, *No Regrets*, Harper Sports, Pymble, New South Wales.

235 Australia v South Africa, 13 June 1999, ball-by-ball commentary, Cricinfo.

236 Henderson, Michael, 18 June 1999, *Daily Telegraph*, London.

237 Chappell, Ian, 18 June 1999, 'Irrepressible Warne triumphant', *Daily Telegraph*, London.

237–8 Deeley, Peter, 21 June 1999, 'Warne the winner considers his future', *Electronic Telegraph*.

Chapter 14—Fame Therapy

243 Slater, Michael, 14 March 2005, *Enough Rope with Andrew Denton*, ABC TV, Sydney.

243 Walters, Mike, 8 May 1999, 'Warne plans to drive them all barmy with another World Cup war dance', *Daily Mirror*, London.

245 November 1998, *The Panel*, Channel 10, Melbourne.

245 Morgan, Piers, September 2005, 'The Piers Morgan interview: Shane Warne', *GQ*, London.

246 Wendt, Jana, 14 March 2006, 'Shane Warne, behind the shades', *The Bulletin*, Sydney.

246 17 December 1997, Channel 9 News.

247 Munro, Mike, 6 January 1998, *A Current Affair*, Channel 9, Sydney.

250 Munro, Mike, 1 December 1999, *A Current Affair*,

Channel 9, Sydney.

253   20 February 2000, *Sunday Mail*, Auckland.

253   27 February 2000, AAP.

253–4 20 February 2000, *The Sun-Herald*, Sydney.

254   18 February 2000, NZPA, Wellington.

254   Hobson, Richard, 2002, *Shane Warne, My
       Autobiography*, Hodder & Stoughton, London.

255   Gibson, Mike, 23 February 2000, *Daily Telegraph*,
       Sydney.

257   15 March 2000, 'Lillee applauds Warne for record-
       breaking feat', www.baggygreen.com.au.

258   Baum, Greg, April 2000, 'Five cricketers of the
       century: Shane Warne', *Wisden Cricketers'
       Almanac*.

Chapter 15—Oh Donna

261   Rock, Lucy, 10 June 2000, 'Shame Warne', *Daily
       Mirror*, London.

267   Munro, Mike, 15 June 2000, *A Current Affair*,
       Channel 9, Sydney.

269   Munro, Mike, 16 June 2000, *A Current Affair*,
       Channel 9, Sydney.

273–4 Bond, Jeff, February 2006, *The Pedestal
       Syndrome*, unpublished paper.

Chapter 16—Life in the Old Dog

277   Hobson, Richard, 2002, *Shane Warne, My
       Autobiography*, Hodder & Stoughton,
       London.

277   Munro, Mike, 16 June 2000, *A Current Affair*, Channel 9, Sydney.

278–9 Hobson, Richard, 2002, *Shane Warne, My Autobiography*, Hodder & Stoughton, London.

280   Hobson, Richard, 2002, *Shane Warne, My Autobiography*, Hodder & Stoughton, London.

281   Hobson, Richard, 2002, *Shane Warne, My Autobiography*, Hodder & Stoughton, London.

282   Knox, Malcolm, 19 March 2000, 'Trapped between puberty and mid life crisis', *The Sydney Morning Herald*.

283   March 2001, 'The 2000 love 'em or leave 'em readers' poll', *Inside Sport*, Sydney.

284   Stevens, Mark, 28 October 2000, 'Bionic man in need of repairs', *Daily Telegraph*, Sydney.

285   Conn, Malcolm, 17 March 2001, 'Worried Warne's watershed', *The Australian*.

287   Conn, Malcolm, 24 March 2001, 'Age is catching up with the current crop', *The Australian*.

287   Etheridge, John, 22 March 2001, 'On the row dividing Aussie cricket', *The Sun*, London.

287   Wilde, Simon, 8 April 2001, 'Warne out', *Sunday Times*, London.

288   Dobell, George, 16 April 2001, 'Jenner: selectors were right to stick with Warne', Cricinfo.

290–1 Flokis, Patricia, August 2002, 'Shane's battle of the bulge', *Australian Women's Weekly*, Sydney.

291   McClure, Geoff, 14 October 2002, 'Vintage stuff, Shane!' *The Age*, Melbourne.

292   Buckle Greg, 22 October 2002, 'Warne turns over a new leaf', Reuters.

Chapter 17—Dumb and Dumber

298   12 February 2003, *Daily Telegraph*, Sydney.

298   Le Grand, Chip, 14 February 2003, 'Party girl mum who just wanted Warne to look good on telly', *The Australian*.

300   Craddock, Robert, 13 February 2003, 'Ponting chooses Warne's own words', *Daily Telegraph*, Sydney.

300   16 February 2003, 'Warne knew the risks: McGrath', AAP.

301   Martin, Ray, 20 February 2003, *A Current Affair*, Channel 9, Sydney.

303   Horan, Matthew, 23 February 2003, 'I'm a victim of doping hysteria: Warne's reaction', *Sunday Telegraph*, Sydney.

305   Warne, Shane, 24 February 2003, 'My torment', *Daily Telegraph*, Sydney.

305   Martin, Ray, 25 February 2003, *A Current Affair*, Channel 9, Sydney.

307   Williams, Mr Justice, 26 February 2003, 'Reasons for judgement', ACB anti-doping committee hearing of charges against Shane Keith Warne, Melbourne.

307   Reed, Ron, 27 February 2003, 'Goodwill is on the turn', *Herald Sun*, Melbourne.

308   Craddock, Robert, 27 February 2003, 'Wise up Warnie', *Herald Sun*, Melbourne.

308   Pierik, John, 27 February 2003, 'Only one guy knows what the truth is', *Herald Sun*, Melbourne.

Chapter 18—As Bad as it Gets

311   Schmidt, Michael, 10 August 2003, 'Shane wanted me to keep quiet', *Sunday Times*, Johannesburg.

313   Radio 3AW, Melbourne.

313   Martin, Ray, 12 August 2003, *A Current Affair*, Channel 9, Sydney.

315–16 Martin, Ray, 14 August 2003, *A Current Affair*, Channel 9, Sydney.

318   Curro, Tracey, February 2004, 'Why I stayed with Shane', *Australian Women's Weekly*, Sydney.

319   Channel 7 News, Melbourne.

319   Overton, Peter, 20 February 2005, 'Getting of Wisdom', *60 Minutes,* Channel 9, Sydney.

319   Press statement from Simone Warne, 23 August 2003.

320   30 August 2003, 'My wild nights with Shane', *New Idea*, Sydney.

322   Wenn, Rohan, 25 August 2003, *Today Tonight*, Channel 7.

322   Wenn, Rohan, 26 August 2003, *Today Tonight*, Channel 7.

323   Curro, Tracey, February 2004, 'Why I stayed with Shane', *Australian Women's Weekly*, Sydney.

Chapter 19—On Top of the World

327   Atherton, Michael, 21 January 2004, 'Warne: has time passed him by?', *Daily Telegraph*, London.

332   Hopps, David, 13 March 2004, 'Warne wins the 500 in fairytale style', *The Guardian*, London.

332 Warne, Shane, 15 March 2004, 'Exile ends with rush of joy at the capture of my 500th Test wicket', *The Times*, London.

332 Craddock, Robert, 13 March 2004, 'Mum's the word for players', *Daily Telegraph*, Sydney.

333 20 March 2004, 'I don't think I could have bowled much better', Cricinfo.

337 Williamson, Martin, 10 May 2004, 'Muted, hollow, underwhelming', The Paper Round, Cricinfo.

339 Ryan, Christian, 17 May 2004, 'PM throws spanner in works—again', Cricinfo.

340 Dorries, Ben, 14 July 2004, 'I will struggle', *Herald Sun*, Melbourne.

341 Lalor, Peter, 16 October 2004, 'King of spin steps on to the throne', *The Australian*.

341 Coward, Mike, 16 October 2004, 'Showman at odds with art', *The Australian*.

342 Roebuck, Peter, 16 October 2004, 'Arise, Warnie, the greatest slow on Earth', *The Sydney Morning Herald*.

Chapter 20—Good Boy at Last?

346 Overton, Peter, 20 February 2005, 'Getting of Wisdom', *60 Minutes,* Channel 9, Sydney.

350 14 March 2005, 'Warne now calls England home', Cricinfo.

352 28 June 2005, 'I didn't wreck Shane's marriage', *Daily Echo*, Southampton.

353 Morgan, Piers, September 2005, 'The Piers Morgan interview: Shane Warne', *GQ*, London.

Chapter 21—The Old Enemy

358 8 September 2004, 'Ashes warning from McGrath', BBC Sport online.

358 19 July 2005, 'Australia will sweep Ashes: McGrath', ABC News online.

358 12 April 2005, 'Thomson predicts Ashes mismatch', BBC Sport online.

359 Fitzsimons, Peter, 7 January 2006, 'That's the spirit this country was built on!', *The Sydney Morning Herald*.

359 Morgan, Piers, September 2005, 'The Piers Morgan interview: Shane Warne', *GQ*, London.

359 24 December 2004, 'Memories ensure merciless approach', news.com.au.

360 Warne, Shane & Ray, Mark, 1997, *Shane Warne, My Own Story*, Swan Publishing, Perth.

365 Craddock, Robert, 4 October 2004, 'Shane Warne on facing both his and the Australian team's final frontier', *Herald Sun*, Melbourne.

365 Price, Matt, 23 July 2005, 'Why Aussies are rooting for the Poms', *The Spectator*, London.

Chapter 22—Bye Bye, Simone

374 Duffy, Mike, 19 June 1995, 'Shane Warne sex shame', *Sunday Mirror*, London.

375 Morgan, Piers, September 2005, 'The Piers Morgan interview: Shane Warne', *GQ*, London.

377 Smethurst, Sue, 30 July 2005, 'Shane tore our family apart', *New Idea*, Sydney.

378   Smethurst, Sue, 30 July 2005, 'Shane tore our family apart', *New Idea*, Sydney.

379   Allen, Vanessa & Parry, Tom, 21 July 2005, 'Shame Warne: the fifth woman. Will you seduce my wife?' *Daily Mirror*, London.

380   28 June 2005, 'I didn't wreck Shane's marriage', *Daily Echo*, Southampton.

383   Caldwell, Alison, 14 July 2005, 'Shane Warne says break up won't affect his game', *AM*, ABC Radio, Sydney.

384   Sheehan, Paul, 4 July 2005, 'Time to dethrone the king of the bogans', *The Sydney Morning Herald*.

384   Morrell, Sally, 18 July 2005, 'Warnie caught out once too often', *Herald Sun*, Melbourne.

384   Wendt, Jana, 14 March 2006, 'Shane Warne, behind the shades', *The Bulletin*, Sydney.

386   8 August 2005, *New Idea*, Sydney, quoted 7 August 2005, AAP, Sydney.

387   Wendt, Jana, 14 March 2006, 'Shane Warne, behind the shades', *The Bulletin*, Sydney.

387   Smethurst, Sue, 30 July 2005, 'Shane tore our family apart', *New Idea*, Sydney.

387   9 July 2005, 'Shane's wicket ways', *New Idea*, Sydney.

Chapter 23—Simply the Best

390   Warne, Shane, 15 June 2005, 'Enjoy the moment, England', *The Times*, London.

394   Francis, Tony, 21 July 2005, 'Barmy brigade still proud to be loud', *Daily Telegraph*, London.

394   29 September 2005, *The Frank Skinner Show*,
      ITV 1, London.

399   England Cricket Team & Hayter, Peter, 2005,
      Ashes Victory, Orion, London.

400   England Cricket Team & Hayter, Peter, 2005,
      Ashes Victory, Orion, London.

401   23 July 2005, 'Warne wants fitting Lord's finale',
      BBC Sport online.

402   Miller, Andrew, 24 July 2005, 'Vaughan under
      pressure as Aussies scent blood', Cricinfo.

402   Townsend, Nick, 28 August 2005, 'The Ashes
      2005: Vaughan variety show pulls curtain down on
      Australia', *Independent on Sunday*, London.

Chapter 24—Freddie, Freddie, Freddie

406   England Cricket Team & Hayter, Peter, 2005,
      Ashes Victory, Orion, London.

408   Hughes, Simon, 16 September 2005, 'England hero
      Flintoff is a man for all seasons', *Daily Telegraph*,
      London.

411   Warne, Shane, 9 August 2005, 'We went out just to
      have some fun and nearly won', *The Times*, London.

Chapter 25—Shane, Shane, Shane

423   Coupar, Paul, 11 August 2005, 'Vaughan and
      Warne play to type', Cricinfo.

430   Warne, Shane, 25 August 2005, 'England beware,
      things are about to get tougher', *The Times*,
      London.

431   Lalor, Peter, 17 August 2005, 'When going got tough, so did Warne', *The Australian*.

435   Johnson, Martin, 10 August 2005, 'Who needs one-day cricket?', *The Age*, Melbourne (reprinted from *Daily Telegraph*, London).

Chapter 26—It's Not Over Till It's Over

438   Warne, Shane, 31 August 2005, 'Australia in no mood to surrender main prize', *The Times*, London.

438   Parker, Andrew, 22 September 2005, 'Shane got Ashes duck after a 5-hour sex romp', *The Sun*, London.

439   Chaytor, Rod, 22 September 2005, 'Shane tried his googlies on Julia the night before a Test . . . and was out for a duck the next day', *Daily Mirror*, London.

444   2005, *Fifth Test, The Ashes, the greatest series*, a Sunset + Vine production for DD Home Entertainment, London.

447   2005, *Fifth Test, The Ashes*, the greatest series, a Sunset + Vine production for DD Home Entertainment, London.

448–9 Telegraph Group Ltd, 2005, *England's Ashes: The story of the greatest Test series of all time*, Harper Sport, London.

450   Boycott, Geoffrey, 9 September 2005, 'Careless approach allows opportunity to go begging', *Daily Telegraph*, London.

453   Warne, Shane, 14 September 2005, 'Add courage

to brilliance: the recipe for a star like Pietersen', *The Times*, London.

454 12 September 2005, 'Aussies admit best team won Ashes', BBC Sport online.

454 12 September 2005, quoted in 'Ashes log: Fifth Test—Monday', BBC Sport online.

454 Telegraph Group Ltd, 2005, *'England's Ashes, The story of the greatest Test series of all time'*, Harper Sport, London.

455 Warne, Shane, 14 September 2005, 'Add courage to brilliance: the recipe for a star like Pietersen', *The Times*, London.

Chapter 27—D-I-V-O-R-C-E

457 29 September 2005, 'Warne vows to save marriage', AAP.

458 Ansari, Khalid, 4 October 2005, 'Warne's sure but Simone doubtful', Mid-Day.com, Bombay.

458 Smethurst, Sue, 30 July 2005, 'Shane tore our family apart', *New Idea*, Sydney.

462 November 2005, *FHM*, Sydney.

463 Smethurst, Sue, 7 January 2006, 'Flying Solo', *New Idea*, Sydney.

464 Smethurst, Sue, 7 January 2006, 'Flying Solo', *New Idea*, Sydney.

465 Weatherup, James, 7 May 2005, 'Wicket ace Warne's leg over with 2 maidens (and a 4ft inflatable googly), Shane on you', *News of the World*, London.

466 Fidgeon, Patrice, 15 May 2006, 'Simone's fury: call me Callahan', *New Idea*, Sydney.

467 Fidgeon, Patrice, 15 May 2006, 'Simone's fury: call me Callahan', *New Idea*, Sydney.

Photo and Text Acknowledgements

Acknowledgements are due to the following photographers, authors, publishers and agents for permission to include photographs and extracts from newspaper and magazine articles, books and television transcripts.

Picture Section 1

Page 1   Newspix

Page 2   Library, Mentone Grammar

Page 3   *Lancashire Evening Telegraph*

Page 4   Ray Kennedy/Fairfaxphotos.com (top)
                Herald & Weekly Times Photographic
                Collection (bottom)

Page 5   Empics/Snapper Media (top)
                Getty Images (bottom)

Page 6   Newspix

Page 7   Empics/Snapper Media (top)
                APL/John &Lorraine Carnemolla (bottom)

Page 8   Empics/Snapper Media (top)
                Getty Images (centre)
                Empics (bottom)

Page 9   Getty Images (top)
                Newspix/Matt Turner (bottom)

PHOTO AND TEXT ACKNOWLEDGEMENTS

Page 15   Empics/Snapper Media
Page 16   Getty Images

Extracts
Anderson, Ian, 6 April 1999, *Waikato Times*, New
    Zealand.
Craddock, Robert, 25 June 2005, 'A simple but
    complicated man', *Courier-Mail*, Brisbane.
All material quoted from *New Idea* reprinted with
    permission of the publisher.

Every effort has been made to identify copyright holders
of photographs and extracts in this book. The publishers
would be pleased to hear from any copyright holders who
have not been acknowledged.

Index

INDEX

INDEX

GERRARD
My Autobiography

Steven Gerrard is a hero to millions, not only as the
inspirational captain of Liverpool FC, but as a key
member of the England team. Here, for the first time,
he tells the story of his lifelong obsession with football,
in an honest and revealing book which captures the
extraordinary camaraderie, the teeth-grinding tension
and the high-octane thrills of the modern game
as never before.

A relatively private figure, Steven has rarely spoken
out in public. Now, his legions of fans are allowed an
intimate glimpse of what makes their hero tick.
He describes for the first time the torturous will-he-won't-he
Chelsea rumours – and his undying passion for Liverpool.
We experience first-hand the highs of winning in Istanbul
and elsewhere, as well as the lows of being parted from
his much-loved family and friends. And, or course,
the book contains a full blow-by-blow account of
England's World Cup campaign in Germany 2006
and Liverpool's 2006–07 season.

Steven Gerrard's book is the definitive football
autobiography. Like its subject, it's honest, passionate
and exhilarating. If Steven Gerrard isn't your hero yet,
by the time you've read this he will be . . .

'FOOTBALL BOOK OF THE YEAR'
News of the World

9780553817331

BANTAM BOOKS

THE PLAYER
Boris Becker

Boris Becker shot to fame in 1985 when at seventeen years old he became the youngest player ever to win the men's final at Wimbledon. He went on to win two more Wimbledon titles, and a total of forty-nine singles and fifteen doubles crowns, making him one of the greatest players of the twentieth century. But his life off the court has always attracted as much attention as his triumphs on it.

Now, in this remarkably candid and thought-provoking autobiography, Boris Becker tells the real story behind the headlines. He speaks of the seconds before the serve that made him the youngest Wimbledon winner of all time, and of the minutes after being sentenced as a tax evader. He talks about his marriage, his illegitimate daughter, and his painful divorce. He reveals his emotions at the end of his tennis career, and his battles with pills and alcohol. He also shares his memories of the good times, the championship wins, the make-or-break matches, and the highs and lows of life on the international circuit.

Boris Becker has written this autobiography not just for his fans but also for his children, that they may one day read the true account of their father's remarkable and often controversial, life.

9780553817164

BANTAM BOOKS